small arms survey
2014

---

women and guns

THE GRADUATE INSTITUTE | GENEVA
INSTITUT DE HAUTES ÉTUDES
INTERNATIONALES ET DU DÉVELOPPEMENT
GRADUATE INSTITUTE OF INTERNATIONAL
AND DEVELOPMENT STUDIES

small
arms
survey

CAMBRIDGE
UNIVERSITY PRESS

University Printing House, Cambridge CB2 8BS, United Kingdom

One Liberty Plaza, 20th Floor, New York, NY 10006, USA

477 Williamstown Road, Port Melbourne, VIC 3207, Australia

314-321, 3rd Floor, Plot 3, Splendor Forum, Jasola District Centre, New Delhi - 110025, India

79 Anson Road, #06-04/06, Singapore 079906

Cambridge University Press is part of the University of Cambridge.

It furthers the University's mission by disseminating knowledge in the pursuit of
education, learning and research at the highest international levels of excellence.

www.cambridge.org
Information on this title: www.cambridge.org/9781107661776

First published 2014

A catalogue record for this publication is available from the British Library

ISBN 978-1-107-04197-4 Hardback
ISBN 978-1-107-66177-6 Paperback

Cambridge University Press has no responsibility for the persistence or
accuracy of URLs for external or third-party internet websites referred to in
this publication, and does not guarantee that any content on such websites is,
or will remain, accurate or appropriate.

FOREWORD

Last year was highly significant for conventional arms control because of the adoption of the historic Arms Trade Treaty (ATT). It is the first-ever global, legally binding regulation of the conventional arms trade negotiated within the United Nations.

The ATT sets robust standards against which arms transfer decisions must be assessed. Well over half of UN member states have already signed the ATT, but we should not rest until all states have done so.

One of the most impressive outcomes of the ATT negotiations was the successful inclusion of small arms under its scope, and the fact that the treaty also covers the trade in ammunition. It clearly prohibits exports of arms and ammunition that would violate Security Council arms embargoes or that could be used against civilians and in the commission of serious violations of international law.

Moreover, the ATT requires states to regulate arms brokering, to take measures to prevent diversion of weaponry, and to assess the risk that exports of arms and ammunition would be used in the commission of grave violations of international humanitarian law or human rights law. All these provisions are particularly relevant for the issue of small arms.

Another 'first' with respect to the development of global norms was last year's Security Council Resolution 2117 on the issue of small arms. Its adoption reflects the widespread conviction that effectively dealing with conflict and post-conflict settings requires a specific focus on improving small arms control measures.

The theme of this year's *Survey* is aptly chosen. UN arms control processes are increasingly converging with the women, peace, and security agenda established by UN Security Council Resolution 1325 and related instruments. Language on gender-based violence and on women's participation in the promotion of peace and security can be found in the ATT, the outcome document of the UN Programme of Action's Second Review Conference (2012), and the above-mentioned Security Council resolution.

Moreover, the two resolutions adopted by the Security Council on women, peace, and security in 2013 mention the provisions of the ATT that exporting states parties take into account the risk of conventional arms or items being used to commit or facilitate serious acts of gender-based violence or serious acts of violence against women and children. One of these resolutions urges member states and United Nations entities to ensure women's full and meaningful participation in efforts to combat and eradicate the illicit transfer and misuse of small arms and light weapons.

Such convergence between previously compartmentalized topics is important because, for too long, women and girls were pictured solely as victims of armed conflict and domestic violence, not as the key actors for change that they are. It will be critical, as the 2014 *Survey* also points out, that this 'enabling' language actually assist women in becoming full and meaningful participants in the international peace and security agenda.

In words and images, the *Small Arms Survey 2014*, with its usual analytical rigour, helps us understand the latest developments—and future possibilities—in arms control, peace, and security. I have no hesitation recommending it to all those interested in these vital topics.

—Angela Kane
United Nations High Representative for Disarmament Affairs

CONTENTS

Chapter 1. In War and Peace: Violence against Women and Girls

Chapter 2. Converging Agendas: Women, Peace, Security, and Small Arms

Special Feature. Women behind the Gun: Aiming for Equality and Recognition

Chapter 3. Breaking New Ground?: The Arms Trade Treaty

Chapter 4. Trade Update: Transfers, Retransfers, and the ATT

Chapter 5. Countdown to Catastrophe: The Mpila Ammunition Depot Explosions

Chapter 6. Across Conflict Zones: Ammunition Profiling

Chapter 7. Signs of Supply: Weapons Tracing in Sudan and South Sudan

Chapter 8. On the Record: Illicit Weapons in the United States

Index

ABOUT THE SMALL ARMS SURVEY

The Small Arms Survey is an independent research project located at the Graduate Institute of International and Development Studies in Geneva, Switzerland. Established in 1999, the project is supported by the Swiss Federal Department of Foreign Affairs and current or recent contributions from the Governments of Australia, Belgium, Denmark, Finland, Germany, the Netherlands, New Zealand, Norway, the United Kingdom, and the United States, as well as from the European Union. The Survey is grateful for past support received from the Governments of Canada, France, Spain, and Sweden. The Survey also wishes to acknowledge the financial assistance it has received over the years from foundations and many bodies within the UN system.

The objectives of the Small Arms Survey are: to be the principal source of public information on all aspects of small arms and armed violence; to serve as a resource centre for governments, policy-makers, researchers, and activists; to monitor national and international initiatives (governmental and non-governmental) on small arms; to support efforts to address the effects of small arms proliferation and misuse; and to act as a clearinghouse for the sharing of information and the dissemination of best practices. The Survey also sponsors field research and information-gathering efforts, especially in affected states and regions. The project has an international staff with expertise in security studies, political science, law, economics, development studies, sociology, and criminology, and collaborates with a network of researchers, partner institutions, non-governmental organizations, and governments in more than 50 countries.

NOTES TO READERS

Abbreviations: Lists of abbreviations can be found at the end of each chapter.

Chapter cross-referencing: Chapter cross-references are fully capitalized in brackets throughout the book. One example appears in Chapter 6: 'In fact, the many ammunition samples that bear no correspondence with authorized trade data underline the lack of such a correlation, emphasizing the need for in-depth research to determine the origins of ammunition found in conflict environments (WEAPONS TRACING).'

Exchange rates: All monetary values are expressed in current US dollars (USD). When other currencies are also cited, unless otherwise indicated, they are converted to USD using the 365-day average exchange rate for the period 1 September 2012 to 31 August 2013.

Small Arms Survey: The plain text—Small Arms Survey—is used to indicate the overall project and its activities, while the italicized version—*Small Arms Survey*—refers to the publication. The *Survey,* appearing italicized, relates generally to past and future editions.

Small Arms Survey

Graduate Institute of International and Development Studies

47 Avenue Blanc

1202 Geneva, Switzerland

t +41 22 908 5777 **f** +41 22 732 2738

e sas@smallarmssurvey.org **w** www.smallarmssurvey.org

ACKNOWLEDGEMENTS

This is the 14th edition of the *Small Arms Survey*. Like previous editions, it is a collective product of the staff of the Small Arms Survey project, based at the Graduate Institute of International and Development Studies in Geneva, Switzerland, with support from partners. Numerous researchers in Geneva and around the world have contributed to this volume, and it has benefited from the input and advice of government officials, advocates, experts, and colleagues from the small arms research community and beyond.

The principal chapter authors were assisted by in-house and external contributors, who are acknowledged in the relevant chapters. In addition, chapter reviews were provided by: Naeemah Abrahams, Holger Anders, Flora Bertizzolo, James Bevan, Richard Boulter, Stuart Casey-Maslen, Neil Corney, Alex Diehl, Vanessa Farr, Charles Frisby, Dell Higgie, Philippe Houliat, Roy Isbister, Nic Jenzen-Jones, William Kull, Rahel Kunz, Mike Lewis, Chris Loughran, Sarah Masters, Cédric Poitevin, Madhumita Sarkar, Jeffrey Stirling, Rachel Stohl, Sarah Taylor, Jon Vernick, Karl Wagner, and Adrian Wilkinson.

Anna Alvazzi del Frate, Eric G. Berman, Keith Krause, Emile LeBrun, and Glenn McDonald were responsible for the overall planning and organization of this edition. Alessandra Allen and Estelle Jobson managed the production of the *Survey*. Tania Inowlocki copy-edited the book; Jillian Luff produced the maps;

Small Arms Survey 2014

Editors	Glenn McDonald, Emile LeBrun, Anna Alvazzi del Frate, Eric G. Berman, and Keith Krause
Coordinator	Glenn McDonald
Publication Managers	Alessandra Allen and Estelle Jobson
Designer	Rick Jones, StudioExile
Cartographer	Jillian Luff, MAP*grafix*
Copy-editor	Tania Inowlocki
Proofreader	Donald Strachan

Principal chapter authors

Introduction	Anna Alvazzi del Frate and Glenn McDonald
Chapter 1	Dariusz Dziewanski, Emile LeBrun, and Mihaela Racovita
Chapter 2	Megan Bastick and Kristin Valasek, Geneva Centre for the Democratic Control of Armed Forces (DCAF)
Special feature	Tania Inowlocki
Chapter 3	Sarah Parker
Chapter 4	Paul Holtom, Irene Pavesi, and Christelle Rigual
Chapter 5	Pierre Gobinet
Chapter 6	Nicolas Florquin and Jonah Leff
Chapter 7	Emile LeBrun and Jonah Leff
Chapter 8	Matt Schroeder

Rick Jones provided the design and the layout; Donald Strachan proofread the Survey; and Margaret Binns compiled the index. Daly Design created the illustrations in Chapter 7. John Haslam and Carrie Parkinson of Cambridge University Press provided support throughout the production of the *Survey*. Imène Ajala, Hasnaa El Jamali, David Gertiser, Sarah Hoban, Elli Kytömäki, and Emilia Richard fact-checked the chapters. Olivia Denonville managed photo research, with input from Martin Field. Cédric Blattner and Elise Lebret Agneray provided administrative support under the direction of Carole Touraine, who is responsible for the *Survey's* financial oversight.

The project also benefited from the support of the Graduate Institute of International and Development Studies.

We are extremely grateful to the Swiss government—especially the Department for Foreign Affairs and the Swiss Development Cooperation—for its generous financial and overall support of the Small Arms Survey project, in particular Tiziano Balmelli, Erwin Bollinger, Prasenjit Chaudhuri, Vincent Choffat, Sabrina Dallafior Matter, Alexandre Fasel, Thomas Greminger, Jasna Lazarevic, Urs Schmid, Paul Seger, Frédéric Tissot-Daguette, Tobias Vestner, and Claude Wild. The Survey has also benefited from financial support in recent years from the Governments of Australia, Belgium, Denmark, Finland, Germany, the Netherlands, New Zealand, Norway, the United Kingdom, and the United States.

The project further benefits from the support of international agencies, including the International Committee of the Red Cross, the Bureau for Crisis Prevention and Recovery of the UN Development Programme, the UN High Commissioner for Refugees, the UN Mine Action Service, the UN Office for the Coordination of Humanitarian Affairs, the UN Office for Disarmament Affairs, UN-Habitat, the UN Institute for Disarmament Research, the UN Office on Drugs and Crime, and the World Health Organization.

In Geneva, the project has benefited from the expertise of Anthony Andanje, Michael Biontino, Silvia Cattaneo, Silvia Mercogliano, Elsa Mouelhi-Rondeau, Namdi Payne, Kristine Pelz, Jarmo Sareva, and Makoto Tanabe.

Beyond Geneva, we also receive support from a number of colleagues. In addition to those mentioned above and in specific chapters, we would like to thank Philip Alpers, Wolfgang Bindseil, David Lokulutu Bongwele, Maria Brandstetter, C.J. Chivers, Andrew Cooper, Steve Costner, Mathew Geertsen, Thomas Goebel, Gillian Goh, Claudio Gramizzi, Natalie Jaynes, Aaron Karp, Adèle Kirsten, Aurélie Lamazière, Myriam Marcuello, Sonal Marwah, Hideki Matsuno, Frank Meeussen, Sho Morimoto, Daniël Prins, Adam Ravnkilde, Jorge Restrepo, Damien Spleeters, Zahir Tanin, and Savannah de Tessières.

Our sincere thanks go out to many other individuals (who remain unnamed) for their continuing support of the project. Our apologies to anyone we have failed to mention.

—**Keith Krause**, Programme Director
Eric G. Berman, Managing Director
Anna Alvazzi del Frate, Research Director

A soldier from an all-female unit of Indian UN peacekeepers patrols a street in Monrovia, Liberia, April 2007.
© Aubrey Wade/Panos Pictures

Introduction

Sustained research and analysis have confirmed that the problem of small arms violence cannot be separated from other aspects of human society and culture. Investigations into gun violence that neglect the social relations between men and women, for example, are now seen as incomplete. Gender-conscious programme design and implementation, long features of the development agenda, are increasingly reflected in efforts to promote security. As our understanding of the small arms problem expands, so too does the potential for new, more effective solutions.

The *Small Arms Survey 2014* contributes to this evolution by seeking to unpack, in its first section, the complex, shifting relationship between women and guns. The second section presents new information and analysis under the broad rubric of 'weapons and markets'. The chapter summaries below present some of the findings emerging from this research.

WOMEN AND GUNS

The first section of this volume examines the relationship between women and guns in a wide range of settings. While women (and girls) bear a substantial part of the overall burden of firearm violence, this is only part of the story. Women are also firearm owners and users, police officers, and combatants. They are increasingly involved in peace and disarmament processes, and in the design and implementation of national gun control policies.

Both chapters in this first section, but especially Chapter 1, highlight the multiple features and consequences of armed violence for women and girls in conflict, post-conflict, and non-conflict settings. They describe that sexual violence, in particular rape, is often used as a weapon of war. Yet violence against women and girls (VAWG) is also pervasive in non-conflict settings, where it is often deeply rooted in the cultural frameworks of otherwise peaceful societies.

Firearms feature in gender-based violence as they do in most other types of violence. VAWG is common within the household; domestic disputes often escalate if a gun is at hand. Every year, approximately one-third of the 66,000 female victims of homicide die from firearm injuries. Rates of femicide—the killing of a woman because of her gender— are particularly high in countries where other forms of violence are widespread, firearms are widely available, and the investigation and prosecution of gender-based violence is weak (Alvazzi del Frate, 2011). Among the different types of firearms used to kill women in the United States, handguns are the most widely used, accounting for about 70 per cent of the victims in 2011 (FBI, n.d.).

Survivors of gun violence—an average of three for every gun fatality (Alvazzi del Frate, 2012, p. 94)—include not only those who survive firearm injuries, but also relatives of those who die or are permanently affected by gunshots. Female survivors therefore include the widows and orphans of victims, as well as the mothers, wives, and daughters of those who suffer long-term disabilities as a consequence of gun violence.

Women are also owners and users of firearms, although firearm owners worldwide are overwhelmingly male. Among gun owners in European Union countries, for example, there are eight men for every woman (EC, 2013, p. 8). The ratio is similar in the United States, where women hold significantly fewer guns than men and appear to prefer handguns to rifles and shotguns (Hepburn et al., 2007, p. 18). Surveys consistently show a much lower percentage of female firearm ownership in the United States and a decline in ownership rates of around 20 per cent for both sexes since the late 1970s (NORC, 2013).

Most of the available sex-disaggregated data on gun ownership comes from the United States and reflects its unique gun culture. Gun advertising has been targeting women since the 1980s, when many producers began to promote firearms designed for women (Winddance Twine, 2013, p. 8). Among these were guns in appealing colours and shapes, as well as ones small enough to carry in a purse.

In the United States and elsewhere, women's ownership and use of firearms tend to be rooted in strong cultural and social values. To some extent, social norms are shifting—as reflected, for example, in the steady increase in the number of all-female events and competitors in Olympic shooting sports since 1984 (ISSF, n.d.). Notwithstanding its social basis, female gun ownership can also derive from individual preferences and circumstances. While some women argue that owning a gun is 'key to female empowerment, freedom and personal security' (Cordani, 2010, p. 94), others become owners because they inherit firearms that are meant to stay in the family. Some women decide to acquire a gun for self-protection, while others practice shooting as a form of sport.

Some women join the police, now a desirable career for women in many cultures (Horne, 2006; SPECIAL FEATURE). Policing has changed over time, with women police officers increasingly carrying and using firearms as part of routine work in the same way as their male counterparts. Yet the literature also shows that female officers are significantly less likely to use 'excessive' force than men, are less frequently involved in police brutality and misconduct, and—across all types of policing work—use weapons less often than their male colleagues (Lonsway et al., 2002).

The proportion of women in national armed forces is still rather small, varying between 0.4 per cent in Bolivia and 14–15 per cent in countries such as the Czech Republic, Slovenia, and Uruguay (Donadio et al., 2010, p. 56; Schjølset, 2013, pp. 578–79). Nevertheless, the proportion of female military recruits is increasing in NATO countries (Schjølset, 2013). NATO member Norway recently became the first to make military service compulsory for both women and men (Reuters, 2013). In 2013, the US military lifted a 20-year-old ban on women in combat roles (Bowen, 2013). By the end of 2013, some US servicewomen had successfully completed specialized military training as part of broader research designed to help the Marine Corps and other branches of the US armed forces determine how to integrate female soldiers into front line work (Cox and Hoffman, 2013). Whatever the specific outcomes of this initiative, the increased participation of women in the armed and security forces of many countries is one of the most visible signs of a shift towards greater gender equality.

Although there are calls to increase the participation of women in peacekeeping missions (WOMEN, PEACE, AND SECURITY), the female presence in peacekeeping, especially the military component, remains low. As of September 2013, women made up only 5 per cent of military experts and 3 per cent of troops (UN, 2013). Approximately 10 per cent of police peacekeepers were women, a proportion that has remained stable over the past few years (UN, 2013).

Very few of the women and girls who use guns use them to commit crime. The overall proportion of female offenders is quite small, and female perpetration of firearm crime is rare. In the United States, only about 4 per cent of all identified perpetrators of firearm homicide from 2000 to 2010 were female, with this figure varying only slightly from year to year. A few of these homicides were deemed 'justifiable' as they resulted from the use of a firearm in self-defence. In fact, the proportion of 'justifiable' homicides, as a share of total firearm homicides committed by women, doubled between 2000 and 2010 (from 2.3 to 5 per cent) (FBI, n.d.).

The lone, gun-toting criminal is a rarity among women. More often, female 'outlaws' carry and use firearms as members of gangs and non-state armed groups (NSAGs). All-female or mixed male–female gangs are relatively common in many parts of the world, although female gang members tend to use weapons, especially firearms, less often and 'with lesser intensity' than male gang members (Moestue and Lazarevic, 2010, p. 185). There are exceptions, however. In Guatemala, women gang members are increasingly involved in serious crime, reflected in the sharp increase in the number of women arrested in the country and in the size of its female prison population (Rossi, 2012; Tatone, 2013).

Women and girls sometimes furnish much of the 'manpower' of NSAGs: nearly one-third of Sandinista troops in Nicaragua, around 30–40 per cent of the FARC in Colombia, and at least one-third of Tamil Tiger combatants in Sri Lanka (Goldstein, 2003, pp. 81–83). While many women join NSAGs freely, others are either forced to join or to fulfil roles at odds with their cultural values, including the use of armed violence. They frequently perform relatively unimportant, even humiliating tasks and may face scepticism, ridicule, outright opposition, or even violence from male combatants. Many women combatants also face greater difficulty reintegrating into society following the end of armed conflict. While experiences vary from group to group, those of women in NSAGs are often very similar to those of women serving in national armed forces (SPECIAL FEATURE).

As acknowledged in UN Security Council Resolution 1325—which fuses the women and security agendas—women also have a role to play in the development and implementation of post-conflict peace processes, and in the promotion of peace generally. Until recently, the Resolution 1325 process was relatively distinct from the UN small arms process, yet the UN Programme of Action's 2012 Review Conference and the Arms Trade Treaty of 2013 (ATT) have introduced some measure of convergence (WOMEN, PEACE, AND SECURITY).

WEAPONS AND MARKETS

The second section of the *Small Arms Survey 2014* comprises six chapters that involve hardware questions (weapons and ammunition) or examine small arms markets, both legal and illicit. The first chapter in this section, Chapter 3, reviews the main provisions of the ATT and considers its likely future impact. Chapters 4 (Trade update) and 7 (Weapons tracing) in this section—as well as Chapter 2 (Women, peace, and security)—also consider the ATT in relation to issues such as trade transparency, the potential convergence of national arms export decisions, and the evolution of the women, peace, and security agenda.

As noted in Chapter 3, the Treaty's influence will depend on the extent to which ATT states parties translate their commitments into concrete action. This is equally true of established control instruments, such as the UN Programme of Action and the International Tracing Instrument. Chapters 6 and 7 demonstrate how basic tracing methods—for both weapons and ammunition—can assist in mapping sources of illicit supply to NSAGs in conflict and post-conflict countries.

In considering the potential of new instruments and applications, the existing toolkit should not be overlooked. That includes international standards for the management of ammunition stockpiles, the neglect of which can prove devastating—both to the people living next to ammunition depots and to entire countries, as discussed in Chapter 5. It is equally important to make full use of available information, including police data, which, as Chapter 8 demonstrates, can dispel popular myths about crime guns in the United States and help point policy-makers in new directions.

Definitions

The Small Arms Survey uses the term 'small arms and light weapons' to cover both military-style small arms and light weapons, as well as commercial firearms (handguns and long guns). Except where noted otherwise, it follows the definition used in the report of the UN Panel of Governmental Experts on Small Arms (UNGA, 1997):

Small arms: revolvers and self-loading pistols, rifles and carbines, sub-machine guns, assault rifles, and light machine guns.

Light weapons: heavy machine guns, grenade launchers, portable anti-tank and anti-aircraft guns, recoilless rifles, portable anti-tank missile and rocket launchers, portable anti-aircraft missile launchers, and mortars of less than 100 mm calibre.

The term 'small arms' is used in this volume to refer to small arms, light weapons, and their ammunition (as in 'the small arms industry') unless the context indicates otherwise, whereas the terms 'light weapons' and 'ammunition' refer specifically to those items.

'Armed violence' is defined as 'the use or threatened use of weapons to inflict injury, death or psychosocial harm' (OECD, 2011, p. ii).

CHAPTER HIGHLIGHTS

Women and guns

Chapter 1 (Violence against women and girls): Violence against women and girls is a global concern, although its prevalence varies across regions and countries. This chapter examines sexual and domestic violence—two pervasive forms of VAWG—both internationally and through the experiences of two countries emerging from conflict: Liberia and Nepal. It reviews gendered perceptions of guns and pays special attention to the role of social norms as risk factors. By condoning violent behaviour, such as wife beating or rape within intimate relationships, social norms can perpetuate a cycle of violence. Alongside legislative and policy measures, both Liberia and Nepal have launched initiatives to change social attitudes towards VAWG. There and elsewhere, however, more concerted action is needed.

Chapter 2 (Women, peace, and security): A strong international normative framework addressing the impacts of armed conflict on women, and women's participation in peacemaking and post-conflict reform and development, has evolved since the adoption of United Nations Security Council Resolution 1325 in 2000. This chapter explores how this framework has addressed small arms control and traces the recent convergence of the two agendas. In some countries, the different perceptions and impacts of small arms on women and men are reflected in gun control policy, but rarely in concrete action. Women's networks have played an essential role in identifying the linkages between gender and small arms, and in advocating for appropriate policy and legal responses.

Special feature: The women and girls presented in this collection of illustrated original interviews and group portraits have something in common: at some point in their lives, whether as adults or as children, legally or illicitly, they all became intimately familiar with small arms. The section provides first-hand testimony and impressions from women soldiers who served in Afghanistan and Iraq; rebel fighters from Colombia, Iran, and Syria; a South African prison guard; a Kenyan policewoman; UN peacekeepers in Côte d'Ivoire and Liberia; former child soldiers of the Lord's Resistance Army in Uganda; and an Irish bodyguard. They speak to issues ranging from sexism and the pursuit of gender equality to the practical application of UN Resolution 1325 and slow shifts in the dynamic between men and women.

Weapons and markets

Chapter 3 (Arms Trade Treaty): Negotiation of the Arms Trade Treaty was a complex and ambitious undertaking. The text of the treaty, adopted by UN member states on 2 April 2013, reflects the compromises necessary to achieve agreement, but the broad support the UN membership has demonstrated for the ATT suggests that many states see it as a game changer. As the excitement following its adoption subsides, the question becomes: what does the ATT do and what will it change? This chapter reviews the ATT's provisions, situates the treaty within the existing arms transfer control framework, and assesses its potential impact on existing state practice—in particular, its promises of greater scrutiny of arms transfer decisions and of more responsible decision-making.

Chapter 4 (Trade update): This chapter presents updated information on the authorized small arms trade, with sections that identify main actors (top and major exporters and importers), new developments in transparency (the Small Arms Trade Transparency Barometer 2014), and global trends from 2001 to 2011 (including the near doubling in the value of the trade). The chapter also considers some of the possibilities—and opportunities—the ATT presents in two specific areas: unauthorized retransfer and trade transparency. Unauthorized retransfer is something of a blind spot for the ATT, although other instruments and good practice guidelines offer useful guidance in addressing it. While the ATT may prove more effective in increasing global trade transparency, this will depend on the extent to which ATT reporting draws on other transparency instruments.

Chapter 5 (Mpila explosions): On 4 March 2012, a series of explosions destroyed several military barracks in the Mpila area of Brazzaville, in the Republic of the Congo (RoC), affecting two densely populated districts of the city. The explosions claimed at least 300 lives, injured more than 2,500, and displaced more than 120,000 people. The broader economic impacts of the blasts were important, long-lasting, and country-wide. The tragedy was preventable yet, two years on, the root cause of the explosions—poor ammunition stockpile management—has not been properly addressed, nor have their broad socio-economic consequences been fully remedied. This chapter unpacks the direct and indirect consequences of the blasts and probes the long-term ammunition procurement and stockpiling practices that led to the Mpila tragedy.

Chapter 6 (Ammunition profiling): This chapter examines the characteristics of small-calibre ammunition circulating in seven countries and territories affected by conflict or post-conflict instability in Africa and the Middle East. It highlights the role that stockpiles of ammunition produced during the cold war continue to play in fuelling armed conflict, underlining the importance of efforts to reduce surpluses. The chapter also reveals the presence of newly produced cartridges in most of the countries and territories under review. While ammunition produced in China and the former Eastern Bloc remains dominant overall, the prevalence of cartridges of Sudanese and Iranian manufacture is noteworthy. The chapter also highlights the circulation in these areas of unmarked cartridges, whose origin is often unknown, raising new hurdles for arms monitors.

Chapter 7 (Weapons tracing): What arms and ammunition do rebel groups and tribal militias in Sudan and South Sudan have, and how have they obtained them? Following more than two years of investigation, the Small Arms Survey finds that Khartoum government stockpiles are the primary source of weapons to non-state armed groups of all allegiances in Sudan and South Sudan, primarily through deliberate arming, but also through battlefield capture. Among the newer weapons documented, Chinese- and Iranian-manufactured small arms and ammunition are prominent, as is Sudanese-made ammunition. Information supplied by exporting government agencies, weapons manufacturers, and other private companies have assisted in these investigations, whose results show the potential of independent, expert-led, and donor-supported conflict tracing.

Chapter 8 (Illicit small arms): US cities are changing. Crime and poverty persist in some areas, but the vibrancy and prosperity of previous eras has returned to others. Despite these changes, decades-old images of street gangs conducting urban warfare with automatic rifles and machine pistols continue to shape public perceptions of urban violence and criminal guns. This chapter assesses the accuracy of these and other assumptions about illicit weapons in the United States. It analyses records of more than 140,000 small arms and light weapons taken into custody by police in eight US cities and towns, presenting important new information on the weapons acquired by US criminals, in particular felons, drug dealers, and gang members.

CONCLUSION

Full implementation of the women, peace, and security agenda is still some way off, especially where small arms are concerned. In many parts of the world, women (and girls) continue to be killed, maimed, and injured for social and cultural reasons. At the same time, their complete and equal involvement in security promotion often seems more of an aspiration than a reality.

Meanwhile, the effect of the ATT remains to be determined. The treaty's very existence—something many thought unlikely, even impossible, a few years ago—represents an important achievement. But, if it is to have any real impact on arms transfer practices, the ATT will have to jump over the same hurdle that has prevented many established small arms instruments from having full effect—namely, the translation of commitments on paper into concrete action. While the effective implementation of small arms control standards may have significant costs and require sustained political attention, the neglect of such standards can impose human and financial costs that are many times greater—as the Mpila ammunition depot explosions illustrate.

This edition of the *Small Arms Survey* has also demonstrated the value of available, but untapped information, including police data and weapons and ammunition markings in conflict-ridden areas. In aggregate, this data serves to map the types of firearms used by criminals in the United States, as well as insurgent arms supply in Africa and the Middle East.

In short, the 2014 *Survey* casts a light on specific, often persistent threats to the security of women, girls, men, and boys around the world—presenting several tools, methods, and information sources, both old and new, that can improve our understanding of these threats and help us overcome them. ◾

—Anna Alvazzi del Frate and Glenn McDonald

LIST OF ABBREVIATIONS

ATT	Arms Trade Treaty
FARC	Fuerzas Armadas Revolucionarias de Colombia
NSAG	Non-state armed group
VAWG	Violence against women and girls

BIBLIOGRAPHY

Alvazzi del Frate, Anna. 2011. 'When the Victim Is a Woman.' In Geneva Declaration Secretariat. *Global Burden of Armed Violence 2011: Lethal Encounters*. Cambridge: Cambridge University Press.

—. 2012. 'A Matter of Survival: Non-lethal Armed Violence.' In Small Arms Survey. *Small Arms Survey 2012: Moving Targets*. Cambridge: Cambridge University Press, pp. 79–105.

Bowen, Robert. 2013. 'Pentagon Lifts Ban on Women in Combat; Some Men Can't Handle It.' *Examiner.com* (United States). 24 January.
<http://www.examiner.com/article/pentagon-lifts-ban-on-women-combat-some-men-can-t-handle-it>

Cordani, Andreina. 2010. 'Girls with Guns.' *Marie Claire*. July, pp. 94–100.

Cox, Matthew and Michael Hoffman. 2013. 'Female Marines Make History at Infantry Training.' Military.com (United States). 21 November.
<http://www.military.com/daily-news/2013/11/21/female-marines-make-history-at-infantry-training.html>

Donadio, Marcela, et al. 2010. *Women in the Armed and Police Forces: Resolution 1325 and Peace Operations in Latin America*. Buenos Aires: RESDAL.
<http://www.resdal.org/genero-y-paz/women-in-the-armed-and-police-forces.pdf>

EC (European Commission). 2013. *Firearms in the European Union*. Flash Eurobarometer 383. Brussels: European Commission.
<http://ec.europa.eu/public_opinion/flash/fl_383_en.pdf>

FBI (Federal Bureau of Investigation). n.d. *Supplementary Homicide Report: File Listings for 2000–2011*. Correspondence from the Criminal Justice Information Services Division, 3 December 2013.

Goldstein, Joshua. 2003. *War and Gender: How Gender Shapes the War System and Vice Versa*. Cambridge: Cambridge University Press.

Hepburn, Lisa, et al. 2007. 'The US Gun Stock: Results from the 2004 National Firearms Survey.' *Injury Prevention*, Vol. 13, No. 1, pp. 15–19.
<http://injuryprevention.bmj.com/content/13/1/15.abstract>

Horne, Peter. 2006. 'Policewomen: Their First Century and the New Era.' *Police Chief*, Vol. 73, No. 9. September.
<http://www.policechiefmagazine.org/magazine/index.cfm?fuseaction=display&article_id=1000>

ISSF (International Shooting Sport Federation) n.d. 'The Shooting Sports at the Olympic Games.'
<https://www.issf-sports.org/theissf/championships/olympic_games.ashx>

Lonsway, Kim, et al. 2002. *Men, Women, and Police Excessive Force: A Tale of Two Genders—A Content Analysis of Civil Liability Cases, Sustained Allegations, and Citizen Complaints*. Arlington, VA: National Center for Women and Policing.
<http://www.womenandpolicing.org/PDF/2002_Excessive_Force.pdf>

Moestue, Helen and Jasna Lazarevic. 2010. 'The Other Half: Girls in Gangs.' In Small Arms Survey. *Small Arms Survey 2010: Gangs, Groups, and Guns*. Cambridge: Cambridge University Press, pp. 185–207.

NORC (United States National Opinion Research Center). 2013. 'GSS (General Social Survey): Data Analysis Using SDA.' Accessed 24 October 2013.
<http://www3.norc.org/gss+website/>

OECD (Organisation for Economic Co-operation and Development). 2011. 'Breaking Cycles of Violence: Key Issues in Armed Violence Reduction.' Paris: OECD. <http://www.oecd.org/dac/incaf/48913388.pdf>

Reuters. 2013. 'Norway Becomes First NATO Country to Draft Women Into Military.' 14 June.
<http://www.reuters.com/article/2013/06/14/us-norway-women-conscription-idUSBRE95D0NB20130614>

Rossi, Victoria. 2012. 'The Role of Women in Guatemalan Extortion Gangs.' *InSight Crime*. 18 October.
<http://www.insightcrime.org/news-briefs/women-role-guatemala-extortion>

Schjølset, Anita. 2013. 'Data on Women's Participation in NATO Forces and Operations.' *International Interactions*, Vol. 39, No. 4. September–October, pp. 757–87. <http://www.tandfonline.com/doi/pdf/10.1080/03050629.2013.805326>

Tatone, Michael. 2013. 'Women in Guatemala Jails Doubled in 8 Years.' *InSight Crime*. 19 March.
<http://www.insightcrime.org/news-briefs/number-of-women-in-guatemalan-jails-has-doubled-in-8-years>

UN (United Nations). 2013. 'United Nations Peacekeeping: Gender Statistics.'
<http://www.un.org/en/peacekeeping/resources/statistics/gender.shtml>

UNGA (United Nations General Assembly). 1997. *Report of the Panel of Governmental Experts on Small Arms*. A/52/298 of 27 August (annexe).
<http://www.un.org/depts/ddar/Firstcom/SGreport52/a52298.html>

Winddance Twine, France. 2013. *Girls with Guns: Firearms, Feminism, and Militarism*. New York: Routledge.

A relative shows the photo of a woman who was shot and killed by an unidentified man
on her way to work at an assembly plant in San Salvador, July 2013.
© Ulises Rodriguez/Reuters

In War and Peace

VIOLENCE AGAINST WOMEN AND GIRLS

1

INTRODUCTION

While the use of violence against women and girls (VAWG) as a 'weapon of war' has received widespread international attention, researchers have only recently begun to assess its prevalence in peacetime and transitioning societies. The World Health Organization (WHO) finds that 36 per cent of women aged 15–69 worldwide have experienced either non-partner sexual violence or physical or sexual violence by an intimate partner, or both (WHO, 2013, p. 20). Analysts have also increasingly documented the role of guns in the context of intimate partner violence against women.[1]

VAWG is a global phenomenon, but its prevalence varies depending on a range of individual, family, community, and social factors whose interaction is not well understood. Among the broadest set of influences on VAWG are social norms that inform how men and women regard and interact with one another. Widely held attitudes about the roles of women in the home and community, the acceptability of punishing women who deviate from expected behaviour, and norms surrounding the use of guns and violence as a means of resolving conflict are among the many factors that influence VAWG.

After a brief global survey, this chapter reviews available VAWG rates (including gun-related VAWG), relevant social norms, and programming responses in Liberia and Nepal, two countries emerging from the long shadow of conflict. The devastating civil war in Liberia killed an estimated 250,000 people; the collective activism of women was an important element in its ultimate resolution (Foster et al., 2009, pp. 3, 19). The Maoist insurgency in Nepal (1996–2006), in which women were prominent participants, left some 13,000 dead (INSEC, n.d.). This chapter presents the following findings:

- In Liberia, women are twice as likely as men to find that a husband is sometimes justified in beating his wife, suggesting that many women have been socialized to accept domestic violence.
- Research suggests that guns are present in only a small proportion of VAWG incidents in Liberia, although surveys tend to underestimate the full role of guns in VAWG.
- In Nepal, the caste system, ethnic and economic cleavages, and the profile of the victim appear to influence the type and prevalence of VAWG. For example, women from marginalized groups are at a notably elevated risk of experiencing some type of victimization in their lifetimes.
- Lingering pre-conflict and conflict-era dynamics surrounding VAWG influence the prevalence and types of VAWG in post-conflict environments.
- At the global level, development sector practitioners seek to change social norms that influence VAWG; these efforts are seen as an indispensable step towards improving the security of women and girls over the long term.
- More research is needed to shed light on how guns are used in VAWG and what norms surround them, including in post-conflict and low-income environments, where research has been limited to date.

This chapter begins with a brief review of the key aspects of VAWG at the global level, paying particular attention to the influence of social norms. It then describes findings from recent research in Liberia and Nepal, presenting data on the prevalence of VAWG and relevant norms. The following discussion touches on some of the challenges in responding to VAWG and reshaping underlying social norms in post-conflict environments. The chapter concludes with a recap of the main arguments and findings.

VAWG IN GLOBAL PERSPECTIVE

Key terms and concepts

The UN Declaration on the Elimination of Violence against Women defines *violence against women and girls* as:

> *any act of gender-based violence[2] that results in, or is likely to result in, physical, sexual, or psychological harm or suffering to women, including threats of such acts, coercion or arbitrary deprivation of liberty, whether occurring in public or in private life* (UNGA, 1993, art. 1).

This definition encompasses physical, sexual, and psychological violence that occurs in the family or community or is perpetrated or condoned by the state.

VAWG has emerged as a focus area for research and policy-making in recognition that gender-based victimization of women is widespread, follows some identifiable patterns, and is deeply rooted—in the sense that it may be condoned or acceptable according to prevailing social norms. These gendered and normative considerations are built into the term *violence against women and girls*.

The photo of a victim of a double homicide, targeting her and a second woman, is displayed at the reception of her former workplace.
© Tannis Toohey/Toronto Star/Getty Images

This study focuses on two prevalent types of VAWG. For the purposes of this chapter, *domestic violence* is violence committed against a woman by her current or former intimate male partner, with whom she need not be cohabiting; it includes acts of physical, sexual, and emotional abuse, as well as controlling behaviour that constrains her mobility or her access to friends or relatives (WHO, 2005, p. 13). *Sexual violence* is:

> *any sexual act, attempt to obtain a sexual act, unwanted sexual comments or advances, or acts to traffic, or otherwise directed, against a person's sexuality using coercion, by any person regardless of their relationship to the victim, in any setting, including but not limited to home and work* (WHO, 2007, p. 5).

A third type of VAWG, *femicide*—the murder of women and girls because of their gender[3]—is also considered. While much of the research on VAWG has focused on intimate partner violence (domestic and sexual), the full spectrum of VAWG is much broader. Among many other forms, it includes violence committed as a result of dowry disputes and under the banner of 'honour', as well as female infanticide, genital mutilation, and selective foeticide.

A global phenomenon

Although violence against women is a global phenomenon, official data shows sizable national and regional variations and often suffers from under-reporting. Because significant social stigma and fear of retaliation are associated with the reporting of domestic and sexual violence in many countries, anonymous surveys often provide a better indication than data derived from health responders and police records (Krug et al., 2002, p. 150). In a compilation of national surveys from around the world, UN WOMEN reveals that 60 per cent of women in the Pacific island state of Kiribati reported experiencing domestic violence in their lifetimes, and 41 per cent of Costa Rican women reported having experienced sexual violence in their lifetimes, the highest rates in each category (UN WOMEN, 2011).

Violence against women often suffers from under-reporting.

While a valuable starting point for examining the national prevalence of VAWG, compilations such as these suffer from the fact that definitions and survey methodologies vary from country to country, undermining cross-national comparisons (Ellsberg and Heise, 2005, p. 27). A more recent WHO report on representative, population-based studies with estimates for intimate partner violence in a selection of states finds that 36 per cent of women aged 15–69 world-wide have experienced some form of physical and/or sexual violence (WHO, 2013; see Figure 1.1). The findings challenge the notion that only developing countries have high rates of violence against women. Indeed, a higher percentage of women reported having experienced physical and/or sexual violence in the high-income countries under review than in low- and middle-income countries in Europe and the Western Pacific.

International studies that apply common methodologies across countries provide a firmer basis for comparisons of VAWG. WHO's *Multi-country Study on Women's Health and Domestic Violence against Women* (2005) compares interviews conducted with 24,000 women in 15 sites in 10 (non-conflict) countries around the world.[4] The report finds that domestic and sexual violence against women is common around the world. In every research site except one—Japan—'more than a quarter of women in the study had been physically or sexually assaulted at least once since the age of fifteen' (WHO, 2005, p. 83). At least half of all women in the rural communities of Bangladesh, Ethiopia, and Peru said that they had been physically or sexually assaulted by an intimate partner since turning 15 (p. 28; see Figure 1.2).

Similarly, the International Violence against Women Survey, which covers 11 countries and territories,[5] finds that 35–60 per cent of respondents said they had experienced violence at the hands of a man during their lifetime, and that fewer than one-third of them reported their experience to the police. The survey also shows that women victims were more likely to report to the authorities violence committed by strangers than intimate partner violence (Johnson,

Figure 1.1 **Percentage of 15–69-year-old women who report having experienced intimate partner violence and/or non-partner sexual violence, worldwide and by WHO income region, 2010**

■ Global   ■ High-income countries   ■ Low- and middle-income countries

PERCENTAGE OF WOMEN WHO EXPERIENCED VIOLENCE

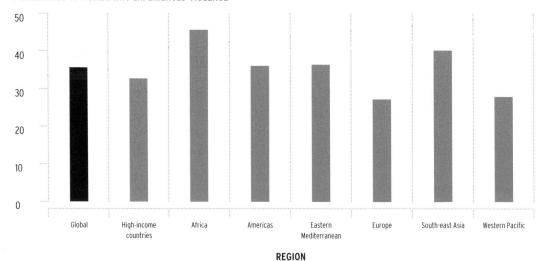

Source: WHO (2013, p. 20)

Figure 1.2 **Percentage of ever-partnered women who report having experienced physical violence or sexual violence by an intimate partner, by location**

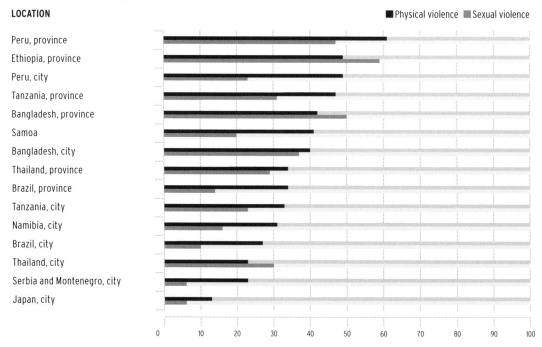

Source: WHO (2005, p. 29)

Ollus, and Nevala, 2007, pp. 34–9, 137–9). The survey does not ask about guns, and the relationship between weapons and different forms of VAWG remains an emerging area of study (see Box 1.1).

The role of social norms

As is the case with other complex social phenomena, the risk and protective factors underlying VAWG remain difficult to understand. The ecological—or social-ecological—model identifies multiple levels of influence on violent behaviour. At the *individual* level, perpetrators may suffer from biological or psychological factors, such as depression, which influence their use of violence. *Relationship*-level factors may include a history of violence within the family or intimate relationships. The *community* level encompasses influences from within the neighbourhood, workplace, and social networks. Finally, at the *societal* level, norms—embodied in and emerging from historical, social, political, and economic dynamics, as well as laws—influence behaviour (Krug et al., 2002, pp. 12–13).[6] The ecological model has proven useful in generating typologies of risk and protection factors, yet the relative importance of each 'level' and the interaction among levels remain poorly understood.

Social norms have been described as 'expectations about action—one's own action, that of others, or both—which express what

---

Box 1.1 Guns and VAWG

Data on gun use is limited for most forms of VAWG other than femicide. Victimization surveys may ask about the use of weapons, for example, but the reported frequency of gun use is typically low, and most surveys do not document the specific types of weapon. Instead, analyses that focus on guns used in VAWG tend to rely on health data on firearm injuries. This approach undoubtedly underestimates the role of guns in VAWG more broadly, as the available health data on female victimization is likely to suffer from systematic underreporting. In countries where the collection of health data is not prioritized, including in many post-conflict environments, these data problems are likely to be compounded.

Recent work on femicide worldwide has generated some general observations on the connections between lethal violence and VAWG. It is now understood, for example, that national homicide levels are correlated with higher national rates of lethal violence against women, and in countries with the highest levels of lethal violence, women are at higher risk of being attacked in the public sphere, including by gangs and organized criminal groups (Alvazzi del Frate, 2011, pp. 114, 130). Moreover, countries with high femicide rates show high percentages of femicides committed with firearms (p. 131).

Guns are almost certainly used in only a small fraction of non-fatal incidents of VAWG globally, but their high lethality makes them a special focus of concern, especially in countries where guns proliferate. One important question that researchers have tried to answer is: Are women at a higher risk of gun-related killings where rates of civilian firearm ownership are higher? Two studies suggest that in 25 high-income countries, women are indeed at a higher risk. In one of these 25 countries, the United States–where civilian gun ownership is high–women were 12 times more likely to be killed with a gun than in the other 24 countries taken as a whole: 1.2 vs. 0.1 per 100,000 (Richardson and Hemenway, 2011). A previous cross-national survey shows similar results (Hemenway, Shinoda-Tagawa, and Miller, 2002).

In lower-income countries and post-conflict contexts, gender-disaggregated data is scarce on both violence and civilian ownership of firearms. Further research is thus required to determine whether similar correlations exist between gun availability and women's victimization. Indeed, researchers and advocates have pointed to a 'pressing need' for gun-related data collection on VAWG (Small Arms Survey, 2013, p. 39; ACUNS VLO, 2013, p. 101).

---

action is right or wrong' within a particular social group (Coleman, 1987, p. 135). Norms are accompanied by social rewards, such as approval and prestige, or social sanctions, such as disapproval or exclusion. In the context of VAWG, social norms determine whether domestic or sexual violence may be regarded as normal—or justifiable—in certain situations. Social norms also define the ways in which violent behaviour may be incentivized through social approval or deterred through stigmatization. Based on international case studies, Box 1.2 identifies norms that influence the likelihood of VAWG. Many examples of such norms relate to notions of masculinity that project violence as the prerogative of men.

Box 1.2 Examples of social norms

Social norms that influence the likelihood of VAWG

Domestic violence

- A man is socially superior and it is his right to assert power over a woman.
- A man has the right to restrict a woman's freedom.
- Divorce is shameful, and a woman is responsible for keeping a marriage together.
- A man has the right to 'correct' or punish female behaviour that he feels deviates from social norms.
- Physical violence is a justifiable way for men to resolve conflicts in an intimate relationship.
- Domestic violence is taboo and reporting it is disrespectful.
- A man's honour is linked to a woman's sexual behaviour; transgressions of sexual norms disgrace the entire family, which can justify honour killings.

Sexual violence

- Sex is a man's right within a marriage.
- Sexual violence is an acceptable way of punishing women or putting them in their place.
- Women are responsible for controlling a man's sexual urges.
- Sexual activity–including rape–is an indication of masculinity.
- Sex and sexuality are taboo subjects.

Social norms that support militarized masculinities

- Owning and using guns are rites of passage for manhood.
- Men are the protectors of their partners and families, and this role automatically gives them the right to control them.
- Guns are markers of courage and warrior status.
- Guns are a source of security.
- Guns are status symbols for other men, women, and the community more broadly.
- Men should be tough, strong, and brave.

Sources: Myrttinen (2003, pp. 1–2); RWAMREC (2010, p. 50); Small Arms Survey (2003, p. 179; 2005, p. 205); Theidon (2009, p. 21); Wepundi et al. (2012, p. 42); WHO (2009, p. 5)

The interpretation of guns as signifiers of masculinity is common to many societies, from the United States to Kosovo and from Brazil to Kenya and Yemen.[7] The presence of conflict can trigger what some scholars have termed 'hyper-masculinities' revolving around physical strength, control, and aggressiveness, often tied to participation in military or paramilitary activities (Ní Aoláin, Cahn, and Haynes, 2012, pp. 234–35). These forms of violent, militarized masculinities associate manhood with guns and do not disappear with the end of conflict (Theidon, 2009, p. 17; Eriksson Baaz and Stern, 2009, p. 4). A qualitative study on Colombian paramilitaries argues that the line between the 'combat zone' and the 'home' has become progressively blurred, which can translate into increased rates of domestic violence in the post-conflict period (Theidon, 2009, pp. 17, 21).

The average rate of domestic violence in countries where it is highly accepted—that is, where it is normative—is more than double the average of countries where its acceptance is low (OECD, 2013a, p. 7). This correlation remains strong, even when controlling for country income levels or for the presence and quality of legislation that prohibits domestic violence. These findings signal that economic development and changes to laws alone will not reduce VAWG without parallel changes to social norms.

Where domestic or sexual violence is not considered transgressive, armed or non-armed VAWG has become 'normalized' (Moser, 2004, p. 6). A 2013 survey of six Asia–Pacific countries shows a widespread acceptance—including by women—of social norms legitimizing domestic or sexual violence within and outside the home (Fulu et al., 2013, p. 98). A recent cross-national study finds that around half of all women believe that domestic violence is justified in at least one of the following situations: if a wife goes out without telling her husband, if she neglects the children, if she argues with her husband, if she refuses sex, or if she burns the food (OECD, 2013a, p. 7).[8] The same study shows that women's attitudes vary across geographical regions.

At the national level, men and women's attitudes are broadly predictive of domestic violence, yet the extent to which they are predictive can vary, as revealed by a 2008 review of ten Demographic and Health Surveys (Hindin, Kishor, and Ansara, 2008, p. 56). Even within countries, the acceptability of domestic violence may vary significantly in terms of both the perceived gravity of the transgression and the appropriateness of the abuse or punishment. As one analyst notes: 'Violence that is viewed as "without just cause" or is perceived as excessive is more likely to be condemned by women themselves and by others' (Heise, 2011, p. 13).

LIBERIA

Background

Sexual violence was a key feature of Liberia's civil conflict, during which rape was widely used as a 'weapon of war' (Omanyondo, 2005, p. 11). As a result, the conflict is often presented as the starting point of VAWG in Liberia. Yet VAWG was already routine prior to the outbreak of hostilities and, while many women and girls acted as soldiers during the war or provided support in other ways, the conflict only served to entrench pre-existing patriarchal structures and patterns of violence (Dziewanski, 2012, p. 1). Indeed, pre-war gender inequalities and the marginalization of women, together with the wartime militarization of masculinities, have led to widespread VAWG in contemporary Liberia.

> Marital rape and domestic violence were common in the pre-war era in Liberia.

Prior to the war, gender inequality in Liberia already permeated all aspects of social and economic life, with boys being taught hunting and security provision, while girls' upbringing focused on their domestic and family roles. A rural woman was often treated as her husband's property; in the event of the husband's death, the next male relative would inherit her. Even within the marriage, the wife's status was determined largely by the number of sons she bore (Liberia, 2011b, p. 24). Focus group discussions with women in Margibi County provide anecdotal evidence that pre-conflict VAWG was pervasive, although largely confined to domestic settings and occurring within intimate relationships. According to the focus groups, marital power relations were skewed in favour of men, with women often having very little control over their lives or bodies. As a result, marital rape and domestic violence were common, though often hidden within households (Dziewanski, 2011, pp. 3–4).

During the civil war period, the use of sexual violence spread beyond the domestic realm, gaining ground as a method of terrorizing and dehumanizing women and their communities (Specht, 2006, p. 32). As men were the primary fighters and holders of guns, they were also in a position to oppress and abuse women. Meanwhile, moral and legal standards faded during the conflict—especially with respect to the treatment of girls—and an upsurge in the use of rape ensued (p. 45). In instances of rape, the perpetrator may no longer be shamed by the community, which further exacerbates the vulnerability of women and girls (Sarkar, Syed, and Nzau, 2009, p. 5). The norms acquired during the conflict, along with pre-war gender inequalities, continue to influence post-conflict social norms about rape in Liberia (Liberia, 2008a, p. 54; Dziewanski, 2011, pp. 3–4).

The prevalence of VAWG

The Liberia National Police is the agency responsible for monitoring crime and violence in Liberia. Police arrest data shows that rape and sexual assault rank among the most common forms of violence reported nationwide (Liberia, 2012, pp. 17–18). The agency reported 405 and 324 incidents of rape[9] and sexual assault in 2011 and 2012, respectively (p. 18). Police capacities to respond to and investigate crime and violence are still low, which contributes to under-reporting. For example, a lack of mobility due in large part to a shortage of vehicles and fuel means that survivors often have to pay for the police to come and investigate incidents (de Carvalho and Nagelhus Schia, 2009, p. 3). These expenses are beyond the means of many Liberians. Police also often lack both investigative resources and the

A poster reading 'rape is a crime' forms part
of a campaign to combat human rights abuses,
Monrovia, July 2006. © Betty Press/Panos Pictures

capacity to provide adequate security for survivors. This can further contribute to under-reporting, as survivors may hesitate to come forward if their security cannot be assured.

Liberia's Ministry of Gender and Development also tracks data on cases that are reported to the police, the courts, health care and psychosocial services, safe houses, and legal aid providers. It produces monthly and annual reports on the incidence and character-istics of different types of domestic and sexual violence. As a UN fact sheet underscores:

> In 2012, the Ministry of Gender and Development reported a total of 2,493 sexual and gender-based violence crimes across Liberia, up from 2,029 cases in 2010. A majority of these (58 per cent) were rape cases, of which 92 per cent or 1,348 involved rapes of children between the ages of three months to 17 years. In the first six months of 2013, four referral hospitals in Monrovia alone treated 814 rape cases, 95 per cent of which were children. In 2012, a total of five child deaths were recorded as a result of rape. So far this year [prior to mid-2013], ten children have died as a direct result of being raped (UNMIL, n.d.).

As noted above, VAWG surveys are generally less susceptible to under-reporting than national monitoring (Krug et al., 2002, p. 150). Two representative surveys that recently measured VAWG in Liberia are the Small Arms Survey's Liberia Armed Violence Assessment—conducted in 2010 and published in 2012—and the Liberia Demographic and Health Survey (LDHS) of 2007. Although there have been considerable advances over the past decade in measuring VAWG through survey research, differences in methodologies make comparisons challenging, as evidenced by the divergent findings from the two studies reviewed here.

The study conducted by the Small Arms Survey finds that 13.5 per cent of all surveyed households (n=2,894) reported at least one incident of crime or violence, with women and men experiencing similar levels of victimization across all types of crime and violence. When asked specifically about sexual and domestic violence committed against women, 0.7 per cent of households reported an incident in the year preceding the survey—0.5 per cent reported an incident of sexual violence and 0.2 per cent reported an incident of domestic violence in which women were targeted (Small Arms Survey, 2010).

While the Small Arms Survey measures VAWG as a broad category in the context of other types of crime and violence, the LDHS devotes an entire section to measuring VAWG. The LDHS probes the issue using questions about the occurrence of specific types of violence—such as pushing, slapping, and burning. It finds that approximately 33 per cent (n=4,897) of women aged 15–49 who were ever married experienced physical violence at the hands of a husband or partner at some point in the year before the survey, and that 35 per cent experienced domestic violence at some point in their lives (Liberia, 2007, pp. 226–34). Moreover, it reveals that 17.6 per cent of Liberian women aged 15–49 have experienced sexual violence in their lifetimes.[10] Despite its detailed investigation of VAWG, the LDHS warns that 'the possibility of some underreporting of violence cannot be entirely ruled out in any survey' (p. 227).

Unlike the LDHS, the Small Arms Survey household survey also measures weapon use in VAWG. It reveals that in approximately one-third (32.5 per cent) of all incidents of reported VAWG, some form of weapon was used. In only two of these instances was a firearm reportedly used; other weapons included homemade weapons, bladed weapons, and blunt objects. Overall, the survey finds that weapons use is less common in sexual and domestic violence than in other types of violent crime. In measuring perceptions of firearms among Liberian women and men (n=2,461), it shows that both groups overwhelmingly referred to guns as a threat to safety (85.5 per cent of women and 79.4 per cent of men) rather than as a source of security (12.0 per cent of women and 16.0 per cent of men) or normal to own (2.5 per cent of women and 4.7 per cent of men) (Small Arms Survey, 2010).

Many Liberian women say a husband is sometimes justified in beating his wife.

Social norms

The LDHS gathered information on men's and women's attitudes towards domestic violence. Almost six out of ten Liberian women said that a husband was justified in beating his wife under certain circumstances. Only about half as many men concurred (Liberia, 2007, pp. 213–15).[11] It appears that Liberian women, largely confined to performing household chores and childrearing duties from an early age, have been highly socialized into an acceptance of domestic abuse as a normal state of affairs (Lamere, 2012, p. 1). It is not unusual for women to be socialized and intimidated into accepting, tolerating, and rationalizing domestic violence (UNICEF, n.d.). It is not uncommon for women to respond to domestic violence with feelings of guilt and self-blame (Krug et al., 2002, p. 109). Such reactions may reflect patriarchal social attitudes that hold women—rather than men—responsible for abuse.

Survey data also suggests that Liberians will condone rape in certain situations, such as within intimate relationships. A 2008 study (n=1,000) conducted by the UN Mission in Liberia finds that 44 per cent of persons surveyed expressed the view that there was no such thing as 'rape' in marriage or other intimate relationships. The report notes that 'those who believed that rape could not be committed within marriage based their opinion largely on traditional and religious understandings of marriage and dating relationships', in which a woman is required to submit to her male partner (UNMIL, 2008, pp. 7–8).

The persistence of VAWG is often explained by a lack of capacity in the formal criminal justice system. In Liberia, harsh sentences under the rape law send the important message that rape is unacceptable in Liberian society. But this and other relevant laws are not effectively enforced, and many cases are settled out of court because police and courts often lack the capacity to respond to cases appropriately (Dziewanski, 2011, pp. 20–23). As a result, survivors may be reluctant to bring cases forward, opting instead for informal mechanisms of dispute resolution.

Even if the formal criminal justice system were able to deliver effective access to justice, it would not be the forum of choice for many rural Liberians. Especially in rural areas, the traditional (informal) justice system is perceived as better able to repair damaged social relations and produce reconciliation among the parties involved. Far from resolving the underlying dispute, the formal criminal justice system in Liberia may be perceived as aggravating adversarial relations—if the case reaches court at all (Isser, Lubkemann, and N'Tow, 2009, pp. 3–4). According to a survey conducted by the Centre for the Study of African Economies, of a total of 3,181 civil cases, only 3 per cent were taken to court. By comparison, 38 per cent were heard in an informal forum and 59 per cent in no forum at all. Of 1,877 criminal cases, only 2 per cent were taken to a formal court, 45 per cent to an informal forum, and 53 per cent to no forum at all (p. 4).

Despite its prohibition, the practice of forced marriage persists in Liberia. In exploring differences between urban and rural VAWG, the LDHS shows that 47 per cent of 15–49-year-old women living in urban areas reported that they had experienced domestic violence at some point in their lives, compared to 41.7 per cent for the same age group in rural areas (Liberia, 2007, pp. 228–30). These figures may reflect differences in attitudes towards domestic violence between women living in urban and rural areas. The percentage of all women aged 15–49 who agreed that a husband was justified in hitting or beating his wife for at least one specified reason was 52.3 per cent among urban respondents, compared to 64.5 per cent among respondents from rural areas (p. 214). Slightly more rural women reported ever experiencing sexual violence—17.9 per cent compared to 17.1 per cent in urban areas (p. 230).

The practice of forced—or early—marriages persists in Liberia, despite being formally prohibited. While the official marriage age is 18 years for women, data from the LDHS shows that 8.7 per cent of girls 15–19 years of age were married, divorced, or widowed (Liberia, 2007, p. 77). Analysis of cases of gender-based violence reported to the Ministry of Gender and Development between January 2009 and May 2011 (n=309) indicates that the majority of victims of sexual violence were 15–19-year-old girls (Dziewanski, 2012, p. 8).

Forced or early marriage can have long-term ramifications as girls tend to take on childrearing and domestic duties at the expense of educational pursuits and, consequently, of opportunities to secure employment and attain independence (Liberia, 2011b, p. 58). Within a marriage, young girls may be subordinated to their older partners in family decisions, such as when to have children and how many children to have (Monekosso, 2001). Further, women who are married according to Liberian customary practices are considered men's property and, as a result, have a limited capacity to contribute to decision-making within the household and are bound to bearing and bringing up children and serving their husbands (CEDAW, 2008, p. 77). Those who break with the social norms dictated by customary authorities may experience violence intended to make them conform (Liberia, 2008a, p. 164).

Programming

The National Plan of Action for the Prevention and Management of Gender Based Violence in Liberia calls for approximately USD 15 million to be allocated to programmes aimed at reducing and preventing gender-based violence in Liberia (Liberia, 2006, p. 8). While funded interventions target both sexes, women comprise the vast majority of victims of gender-based violence in Liberia. The plan calls for the funds to support psychosocial and economic empowerment; the provision of health, protection, security, and legal services; and coordination activities. The second phase of the Plan of Action (2011–15) increases the budget requirement for programming in these areas to more than USD 34 million (Liberia, 2011a, 6).

In response, significant international aid has been dedicated to programming aimed at preventing and responding to VAWG in Liberia. In a 2010 mapping of armed violence reduction and prevention programming, the Organisation for Economic Co-operation and Development (OECD) estimates that some USD 16 million has been allocated annually on programmes in Liberia that have some self-identified sexual or domestic violence prevention component (OECD, 2010). International funds are designated for the enhancement of national capacities to prevent and respond to sexual and domestic violence in Liberia, through direct support to government ministries, departments, and agencies, as well as international and national non-governmental organizations working in the area of prevention and response.

One such project was entitled Men and Women in Partnership–Liberia. A four-month initiative funded by Irish Aid and implemented by the International Rescue Committee, it was designed to examine Liberian men's knowledge, attitudes, and beliefs about gender relations and VAWG and to encourage participants to practice gender-equitable behaviour in their homes and communities. The project urged participants to take concrete steps to equalize the balance of power between themselves and the women in their lives. Change was effected through a curriculum of workshops and training sessions aimed at altering social norms around VAWG (IRC, 2011, pp. 2–4, 13).

A community radio station in Sinoe County broadcasts programmes on key social issues, including those related to health, women, and children's rights, Liberia, April 2012. © Shehzad Noorani/Associated Press

A recent evaluation of the International Rescue Committee project registered positive changes in terms of the knowledge, attitudes, and behaviour of participants as well as of their spouses and partners. It found that, by the end of the programme, gender sensitivity had increased among men and that progress had been made towards improving attitudes about gender roles. Men were more likely to agree that couples should make joint household decisions, that women should participate in political discussions, that men should help with household work, that domestic violence was unacceptable in all situations, and that there was such a thing as rape in marriage (IRC, 2013, pp. iv, 2, 16–18). Spouses and partners of participants reported that the men in their lives were violent less often across all types of violence,[12] implying the general success of the programme in promoting gender-equitable social norms as a protective factor against VAWG. Measures of violence indicated a 10–80 per cent change between baseline and endline measures (p. 35).

Further anecdotal evidence suggests that the project has had a positive impact at the community level. Some programme participants reportedly served as advocates for gender-sensitive behaviour, raising awareness about gender issues among men and rebuking instances of domestic violence and sexual harassment in their communities (IRC, 2013, pp. iv, 12).

The International Rescue Committee project was found to increase gender sensitivity among Liberian men.

Despite the general success of the project, a small minority of participants maintained strong opinions against equal gender roles and some men continued to act violently. During follow-up interviews, 10–15 per cent of spouses and partners of the men who participated in the project reported that they had experienced at least one of four types of abuse in the previous month: burning, pushing or shaking, slapping, or punching (IRC, 2013, p. 25). The continued presence of these types of VAWG is an indication of the challenges projects face in changing social attitudes and norms.

The Norwegian Refugee Council's Women's Rights through Information, Sensitization and Education (WISE) project is another example of a prevention-focused intervention that focused on empowering women and men to counter VAWG in their communities. As part of this project, the Norwegian Refugee Council partnered with 28 community-based groups of men, women, and youths across Bong, Margibi, Montserrado, and Nimba counties to carry out activities aimed at preventing gender-based violence in their communities. Many of the participants were already active as leaders of civil society or religious organizations. As WISE Women and WISE Men, the participants were trained to identify risk factors and the effects of gender-based violence and to design and implement advocacy campaigns on these issues. They met on a monthly basis with other community members to conduct discussions about the causes and consequences of gender-based violence, encouraging and empowering others to develop their own strategies for community awareness, prevention, and reduction campaigns (NRC, n.d.).

NEPAL

Background

Though limited information is available on the situation of women in Nepal prior to 1990, it is clear that the civil codes of 1853 and 1963–64 undergirded a patriarchal society in which women's rights were secondary to those of the 'father' as the head of the family (Lohani-Chase, 2008, pp. 39–40; Sangroula, n.d., p. 1). The Panchayat system and 'nationalization' of Nepal, which began in 1962, homogenized class and gender relations to the detriment of more egalitarian indigenous subcultures. Although the democratic movement of the 1990s saw increased activism for the rights of women, VAWG re-emerged and escalated with the eruption of the civil war in 1996 (Lohani-Chase, 2008, pp. 41–44, 46–50, 97–99).

Nepalese activists perform a street drama during a protest against increasing violence against women, Kathmandu, January 2013. © Prakesh Mathema/AFP Photo

Sexual violence was widely used as a weapon of war by all sides during the ten-year civil conflict. In 2004 alone, the media reported on 367 cases of conflict-related rape. That same year, between 1,040 and 1,200 women were reportedly murdered, injured, raped, or abducted (UNFPA, 2007, p. 5). Sexual violence during the conflict was severely under-reported, due to fears of repercussions, repeat victimization, and social and cultural taboos (TRIAL and HimRights, 2013, pp. 5–6).

Besides direct victimization, the conflict also aggravated existing vulnerabilities of Nepali women. This period saw a rise in the number of war widows, single mothers, women heads of household, and 'conflict wives' (who married soldiers and were subsequently abandoned when garrisons relocated) (Arino, 2008, p. 7). The war also amplified trafficking of women and girls, particularly for prostitution in neighbouring countries (Hamal, 2007, p. 240). Women were also the primary victims of war-induced internal displacement. In 2007, women and children accounted for about 80 per cent of the estimated 100,000–200,000 internally displaced people in Nepal (UNFPA, 2007, p. 5).

The decade-long conflict also provided a degree of liberation for women. Of the 19,602 People's Liberation Army combatants demobilized by the United Nations Mission in Nepal, 3,846 were women—almost 20 per cent of the forces. Their inclusion in armed combat challenged reigning stereotypes of women as objects of protection, while also providing an avenue for them to escape their unfavourable social and economic conditions (Arino, 2008, p. 8). The 'emancipation' of women was part of Maoist ideology during the war and in subsequent peace negotiations, as evidenced by Maoist-led campaigns against alcohol and domestic violence, and by the inclusion of articles on women's equality in the peace negotiations agenda and Maoist programmes (ICG, 2005, pp. 15–6). Despite these advancements, scholars have pointed to the exploitation of this pro-women stance to boost recruitment during the war or to secure post-conflict votes; they also call attention to the persistence of discrimination in the post-conflict period (Tamang, 2009, p. 66; Arino, 2008, p. 9).

Girls and young women also actively participated in the conflict as combatants. According to some studies, the majority of female combatants from rural areas were 14–20 years old, suggesting that age played a large role in the selection of fighters (Arino, 2008, p. 9). By one account, nearly one-third of the 3,000 former child soldiers discharged by the Maoist forces in February 2010 were girls (IRIN, 2010). Once discharged, many female combatants (women and girls) faced new economic hardships, discrimination, and even violence for challenging widely accepted social norms (Colekessian, 2009).

Since 2009, Nepal has made efforts to remove legal discrimination against women, particularly through amendments to the country's civil code on marriage, parental authority, domestic violence, and inheritance rights (OECD, 2013b, p. 21). Even though the social changes brought on by the war and the post-conflict legislative reforms have provided for a degree of emancipation and higher awareness of women's rights, they have not succeeded in uprooting established social norms that legitimize VAWG and the subordination of women.

VAWG remains prevalent in the post-conflict era in Nepal.

The prevalence of VAWG

Although persistent under-reporting precludes a reliable quantification of VAWG in Nepal, studies suggest that it remains prevalent in the post-conflict era. For instance, WOREC Nepal reports a total of 1,473 cases of VAWG in 2012. This total comprises 768 domestic abuse cases and 215 rapes, the two most commonly reported categories of violence (WOREC Nepal, 2012, p. 14). Another surveillance mechanism registered 464 cases of rape and sexual abuse in 2011. Of these, 328 cases were rape and 136 were sexual abuse (INSEC, 2012a, p. 22). Official crime records of the Nepal Police indicate that 557 cases of rape were officially reported between August 2011 and July 2012 (Racovita, Murray, and Sharma, 2013, p. 46).

The 2011 Demographic and Health Survey reports that 21.5 per cent of women respondents aged 15–49 have experienced physical violence at least once since turning 15, and that 9.3 per cent experienced such violence within the 12 months prior to the survey. Moreover, 12.3 per cent of women in the same age category reported that they had experienced sexual violence at least once in their lifetime (Nepal, 2012, pp. 236–38). Another survey on the topic of VAWG demonstrates that more than one-third of Nepalese women interviewed experienced some form of VAWG in their homes (Paudel, 2007, p. 210). The study defines VAWG broadly, considering not only domestic violence and sexual violence, but also psychological and economic violence. Of the women who reported experiencing VAWG, 45.4 per cent said they had experienced domestic violence and 17.6 reported experiencing sexual violence at some point in their lives (p. 214).

Besides direct victimization, women and girls also report perceptions of insecurity. Although men are the primary victims of armed violence worldwide, respondents of a 2011 victimization survey stated that Nepali women were equally likely to fall victim to violence as Nepali men (Racovita, Murray, and Sharma, 2013, p. 42). Female respondents to the same survey reported feeling more insecure walking outside their home at night or in remote areas than did male respondents (IDA and Small Arms Survey, 2012).

Beyond these findings, activists and scholars have highlighted how the caste system, economic status, and personal characteristics can affect the type and magnitude of violence to which women and girls are subjected in Nepal. Women from marginalized groups—such as Muslims, the lower-caste Dalits, and the indigenous Janajati—experienced higher levels of spousal victimization in their lifetimes (Tuladhar et al., 2013, p. 24). According to a 2007 study, more than half (54 per cent) of the Dalit women had experienced VAWG in the home, a higher proportion than in any other group interviewed. In contrast, one-quarter (28 per cent) of Brahmin and Chhetri women and girls had experienced some form of VAWG (Paudel, 2007, p. 213).

Other characteristics, such as place of residence, number of living children, and education level also affect the distribution of VAWG. According to the Demographic and Health Survey conducted in Nepal in 2011, more women aged 15–49 in rural areas reported experiencing physical violence than the same age group in urban areas: 22.3 per cent vs. 19.3 per cent, respectively. In addition, a somewhat greater percentage of women living in rural settings reported experiencing sexual violence at some point in their lives after age 15 than did those living in urban areas (12.9 per cent vs. 10.7 per cent, respectively) (Nepal, 2012, pp. 236–38).

Women from marginalized groups experienced higher levels of spousal victimization in their lifetimes.

The same survey finds that the rate of victimization increases with the number of children born. Indeed, 39 per cent of women who had more than five living children reported experiencing some form of violence, compared to 25 per cent who had one or two living children. Violence appears to be inversely correlated with the level of education, with 36 per cent of women with no education and 24 per cent of those with just a primary education reporting victimization (Nepal, 2012, p. 244).

Data on sexual violence suggests that girls aged 10–14 are the primary victims of rape (INSEC, 2012a, p. 22). Girls are also at risk of other types of violence in Nepal, such as forced child marriage (CREHPA, 2007, p. 1; ICRW, 2013, p. 7).

Guns and gendered attitudes towards firearms

Much of the armed violence in Nepal tends to involve unsophisticated instruments, such as crude or bladed weapons (Racovita, Murray, and Sharma, 2013, p. 54). Nevertheless, gun violence targeting women and girls is also present and sometimes results in injury or death, although it generally takes the form of threats or intimidation within the family, which is seldom reported (Alvazzi del Frate, 2011, pp. 131, 133).[13] The INSEC Small Armed Violence Surveillance System shows that in 2012 more than 100 cases of domestic violence involved the use of weapons (such as sticks, blunt objects, knives, and firearms). These incidents claimed 26 lives and injured 75 people (INSEC, 2012b, p. 13).

Gun ownership is closely tied to power and social status in Nepal. According to a 2011 study, firearms were perceived by some Nepalese as being the prerogative of powerful men, rather than of the 'common people' (IDA and Saferworld, 2011, p. 28). This perception is borne out by the low rate of civilian firearm ownership, which was reported at less than 2 per cent in 2011 (Racovita, Murray, and Sharma, 2013, p. 57).

Asked why they did not own firearms, Nepali women were marginally more likely than men to say they 'do not like guns' or that 'guns represent a danger for the family'. Conversely, more women than men offered social or historical reasons for household firearm ownership: 'weapons are part of tradition' or 'they were left over from the war'. Male respondents opted to stress the protective capacity of firearm ownership and cited 'fear of the future' as another rationale (IDA and Small Arms Survey, 2012).

Women's attitudes towards weapons also shape the general discourse on guns, either by legitimizing their use, or by limiting it. In Nepal, women are generally perceived as opposing the use of firearms. According to a 2012 household survey, more than 90 per cent of respondents (n=3,048) agreed that women were 'not at all tolerant of firearm use or ownership' in their community; in contrast, only about 73 per cent of respondents claimed the same was true of the general population (IDA and Small Arms Survey, 2012). This suggests a generally negative view of firearms in society, particularly among women.

Social norms

In 2012, Nepal ranked 36th out of 86 countries in the OECD's Social Institutions and Gender Index, which evaluates discriminatory social institutions—such as early marriage, unfair inheritance practices, and VAWG—in more than 100 countries (OECD, n.d.). This ranking suggests a degree of institutionalization of discriminatory norms in Nepal. A 2011 survey of 1,000 Nepali men finds that close to half of the respondents agreed that violence against a woman was justifiable in some cases (see Table 1.1). Similarly, more than half of the respondents claimed that a wife should tolerate violence in order to keep the family together (Nanda, Gautam, and Verma, 2012, p. 27).

At the family level, an imbalanced power relation within a couple and the perception of violence as an acceptable corrective also serve to fuel VAWG. For instance, more than 77 per cent of male survey respondents agreed that the husband or partner had the right to discipline his wife or female partner if she did something he deemed wrong (Nanda, Gautam, and Verma, 2012, p. 27). Even among the police, lawyers, and public health providers, violence against one's wife is considered acceptable in some situations, as revealed by an attitude survey conducted in 2007 (see Table 1.2). Almost 40 per cent of the survey respondents agreed that wife beating was justified if the woman was rude to the in-laws. Spousal disobedience was also considered as justification for violence by 40 per cent of police respondents, 33 per cent of family planning providers, and 22 per cent of government health service providers (Paudel, 2007, p. 221).

Notions of chastity, honour, and purity shape what is perceived as acceptable behaviour for women and girls; such social codes also prescribe punishment for certain transgressions. Premarital sex is still taboo for many in Nepal, as

Table 1.1 Men's attitudes towards VAWG in 2011, in selected districts, by type of VAWG (n=1,000)

Type of VAWG	Attitudes that directly or indirectly support VAWG in Nepal	% of respondents who agree*
Domestic violence	There are times when a woman deserves to be beaten.	43.6
	If a woman does something wrong, her husband or partner has the right to punish her.	77.3
	A woman should tolerate violence in order to keep her family together.	50.8
Sexual violence	A woman cannot refuse to have sex with her husband.	52.1
	When a woman is raped, she is usually to blame for putting herself in that situation.	20.6
	If a woman does not physically fight back, it is not rape.	58.0
Son preference	Not having a son reflects bad karma and a lack of moral virtue.	9.5
	A woman's most important role is to produce a son for her husband's family.	21.6
	Fathering a male child shows you are a real man.	31.4

Note: * Out of 100 per cent; the remaining percentage disagreed with the statements. The survey interviewed men aged 18-49. The sample included 400 households from urban areas and 600 from rural ones in three districts in Nepal: Saptari, Gorkha, and Dang.

Source: Nanda, Gautam, and Verma (2012, pp. 27, 44)

Table 1.2 **Attitudes of health workers, lawyers, and police to wife beating in Nepal (n=331)**						
Wife beating is justified if:	State health service providers (n=74)	Family Planning Association of Nepal (FPAN) (n=27)	FPAN community counsellors (n=144)	Police (n=38)	Government lawyers (n=23)	Nepal Bar Association (n=25)
Wife refuses sex	12%	7%	15%	11%	11%	10%
Wife disobeys her husband	22%	33%	20%	40%	28%	20%
Wife fails to do her domestic duties	12%	7%	16%	26%	11%	13%
Husband suspects his wife is unfaithful	19%	18%	25%	34%	22%	40%
Wife is unfaithful	32%	44%	33%	55%	44%	43%
Wife is rude to in-laws	27%	44%	32%	45%	50%	40%

Source: Paudel (2007, p. 221)

it is seen to contravene norms of chastity. In this vein, premarital sex is often thought to bring shame on the whole family (Adhikari and Tamang, 2009, p. 241; Samuels and Ghimire, 2013, p. 6). *Chhaupadi*, the now outlawed practice of segregating women during menstruation, draws on a belief that menstruating women are impure and that only isolation will prevent them from contaminating or bringing misfortune on the household (IRIN, 2011; Samuels and Ghimire, 2013, p. 7; Pradhan et al., 2011, p. 59). The behaviour of the wife or daughter is often tied to the honour of the head of household, or the family as a whole.

Social norms that establish the man as the titular head of household can also inscribe a relationship of domination, with marriage granting a husband sexual rights over his wife. Indeed, more than 50 per cent of survey respondents in three Nepali districts said that a woman may not refuse to have sexual relations with her husband (Nanda, Gautam, and Verma, 2012, p. 27). Respondents to a smaller study went so far as to declare that violence was justified if the wife refused sex (Paudel, 2007, p. 221). According to one interviewee, even 'if a [married] woman does not feel like having sex, she has to do it anyhow if [her husband] feels like it' (Waszak, Thapa, and Davey, 2003, p. 83). A recent study reports that about three in five women have experienced some type of sexual coercion by their husband (Adhikari and Tamang, 2010, p. 1). The Nepali government reformulated the definition of rape to include forced sexual acts within marriage, thus criminalizing the practice. However, scholars and activists argue that awareness and enforcement of this law remains limited (Nanda, Gautam, and Verma, 2012, p. 59).

Throughout Nepal, a social preference for boys still finds expression in sex-selective abortions. Some researchers argue that close to 20 per cent of all abortions are sex-selective, although precise information is difficult to obtain due to the criminalization of the practice (Bhandari and Mishra, 2012, p. 47). A 2007 household survey on the perceived value of sons reveals that respondents (n=2,474) almost unanimously agreed that sons were necessary in a family to support the parents in old age, to secure family lineage, and to provide financial support (CREHPA, 2007, p. 12). The same study suggests that women who do not produce sons are often subjected to social opprobrium.

Girls in Nepal remain at risk of being married off as children, as many families continue to view them as an economic liability because of the informal requirement of a dowry provision, and because they leave their home upon

A lawyer counsels two women at a shelter for victims of domestic violence in Chitwan province, Nepal, January 2013. © Traci White

marriage and thus cannot provide for their parents in old age (Nanda, Gautam, and Verma, 2012, p. 7). Though the practice has reportedly decreased, according to Nepal's 2011 Demographic and Health Survey nearly 41 per cent of Nepalese women aged 20 to 24 were married before they turned 18 (Nepal, 2012, p. 68).

Programming

Public authorities and non-governmental organizations (NGOs) alike have campaigned for an end to VAWG in Nepal. Only a small number have taken targeted approaches by focusing on particular risk or aggravating factors, such as gun ownership or social norms that condone VAWG. The Government of Nepal declared 2010 the 'Year to End Gender-Based Violence' and formulated a national strategy for the prevention of gender-based violence with a special focus on VAWG (Nepal, 2009, p. 1). In 2011, Nepal was among the first countries to develop a five-year national action plan on the implementation of United Nations Security Council Resolutions 1325 and 1820 (Nepal MHP, New ERA, and ICF International, 2011, p. iv).

A mapping of 36 Kathmandu-based NGOs involved in VAWG prevention and reduction identified awareness and advocacy, prevention, and support services as key areas of work (Asia Foundation, 2010, pp. 8–11). The mapping found that, among other factors, the failure to target perpetrators of VAWG and to address social and cultural taboos that perpetuate VAWG in Nepal was limiting the effectiveness of the agenda. Targeting the different facets of VAWG and their links to social norms holds promising potential for programming in Nepal.

CHANGING NORMS

The previous sections highlight survey findings on VAWG in Liberia and Nepal and on norms that appear to influence the types and prevalence of VAWG in the two countries. While the recent conflicts have influenced patterns of violence in post-conflict Liberia and Nepal—whether by aggravating women's socioeconomic vulnerabilities or by amplifying trafficking or sexual violence—norms that affect the use of VAWG pre-date the conflicts and continue to evolve. This section discusses general approaches and challenges to changing the social norms that underpin VAWG.

Promoting new attitudes

The importance of changing norms concerning the use of VAWG has become a recurring theme in discussions of femicide and other types of violence against women (ACUNS VLO, 2013, p. 181). At the global level, interventions are challenging the social norms that support VAWG (WHO, 2009, pp. 6–11); these can be integrated into other approaches, such as improved data collection, legal reform, economic empowerment, and increased provision of VAWG response services. Such interventions are indicative of a growing awareness that the reduction and prevention of VAWG depends on changing discriminatory social norms at both the individual and social levels (Population Council, 2008, p. 36).

At the global level, interventions are challenging the social norms that support VAWG.

Efforts to alter norms have been categorized based on their target groups: universal, selective, or indicated. Universal prevention campaigns focus on large-scale awareness-raising and sensitization, while selective and indicated campaigns are both targeted. The selective approach focuses on members of a particular group within a population—such as those who are considered at risk of engaging in violent behaviour—while the indicated approach is directed at individuals who already have a problem (Berkowitz, 2010). The two most common of these strategies are universal prevention through awareness-raising campaigns and selective prevention through small group workshops (Heise, 2011, pp. 14–16).

Awareness-raising and advocacy campaigns, such as South Africa's One in Nine Campaign,[14] often take the form of decentralized coalitions of individuals and organizations that distribute materials and technical resources (Bennett, 2008, pp. 6–9). Universal awareness-raising campaigns have been employed to address a wide range of health issues, such as nutrition, exercise, smoking, safe sex, alcohol consumption, and drunk driving (WHO, 2009, p. 9).

While awareness-raising initiatives can change behaviour, the effects are often modest. One meta-analysis, which examined results from more than 400 health campaigns, found an average behavioural change of about 5 percentage points in the intervention communities (Snyder, 2007, p. S33). Nevertheless, small changes can have a substantial effect across the entire affected population through a multiplication effect, as when men who change their attitudes influence other men (Evans, 2006, pp. 1207–10).

For group-focused interventions, such the International Rescue Committee's Men and Women in Partnership–Liberia and the Norwegian Refugee Council's WISE project, the mode of delivery, the populations targeted, and the length of engagement vary greatly. At their best, such initiatives are based on evidence, informed by theory, and embedded in a broader programme of sustained intervention and engagement. The example of focus group-based interventions from Liberia provides evidence that interventions directed at particular groups can have a positive impact on changing discriminatory social norms. As shown in Liberia and Nepal, differences in attitudes and behaviour—for example, between urban and rural and among different ethnic and religious groups—often exist within the same country. Interventions provide the opportunity for normative messaging to be tailored to specific groups and presented in extended and interactive formats, unlike broader awareness-raising campaigns (Berkowitz, 2010). Yet if workshops are one-off events, follow-up or support is limited, and peer educators or staff are poorly trained, the impact on deeply embedded social norms will be minimal (Heise, 2011, p. 16).

Reaching men and their guns

Like conflict-era attitudes, guns remain present after the end of a conflict, and some of them are used in acts of VAWG. The surveys in Liberia and Nepal offer only the tip of the iceberg in terms of data on the roles of guns in VAWG; further research on the connections is needed at the local, national, and global levels. It is clear, however, that highly militarized societies present particular risks for victimization to both men and women.

Thanks primarily to the advocacy of women's groups, the international normative frameworks on small arms control and women, peace, and security have become linked (WOMEN, PEACE, AND SECURITY). This development has gone hand in hand with an increase in awareness among donors, multilateral agencies, policy-makers, and researchers that a gendered perspective to gun violence is necessary. This perspective must recognize 'the different situations, needs, and resources of men and women, boys, and girls' (Geneva Declaration, 2006, p. 2). At the advocacy level, the VAWG component is becoming more prominent in arms control campaigns that try to achieve greater security for both men and women (WHO, 2005, p. 3).

There is also growing awareness of the need for interventions that target men and address notions of men's use of violence and guns as manly or heroic. In a range of countries, research and campaigns have sprung up to address the masculinities component of VAWG. Men are also needed as spokespersons to speak out to other men about the unacceptability of violence (WHO, 2005, p. 93). In addition to countering notions that it is socially acceptable for men to condone violence, these kinds of efforts provide alternative role models of masculine behaviour.

To be most effective, initiatives aimed at changing social norms around the use of violence need to be accompanied by broader development efforts. In Liberia, for instance, despite progress made since the end of the civil war, gender still plays a decisive role in determining access to economic opportunities, intensifying what the government calls the 'feminization of poverty' (Liberia, 2008a, p. 163). In Liberia and elsewhere, women who are economically vulnerable can be forced into work situations where they are likely to fall victim to sexual or physical violence. Further, women continue to have limited access to education, health care, and legal and judicial services, which further inhibits their equal participation in society.

CONCLUSION

The prevention of VAWG depends in part on altering social norms that influence men and women's attitudes to sexual and physical violence inside and outside marriage, as well as socially constructed notions of masculinity and femininity. A 'gendered' perspective to VAWG and its prevention is fundamental.

Societies emerging from conflict face particular challenges with respect to VAWG. The society may continue to be militarized in the post-war period and, where fighters used sexual violence as a tool of war, the effects are likely to be felt for some time. Guns may be more prevalent in the post-conflict environment as well and thus readily available for use in gender-based violence.

Research in Liberia some ten years after the official cessation of hostilities documents a society in which women, even more than men, accept physical abuse in some circumstances as normal within a marriage. In both Liberia and Nepal, young girls are the most vulnerable to sexual violence. In both countries, a wide range of norms persist that condone such behaviour. While such attitudes were reinforced during the wars, widespread VAWG also pre-dates the conflicts.

Efforts to alter attitudes that support VAWG take time. They are at their initial stages in both of the countries reviewed, although programmes such as the Men's Dialogue Groups and the WISE project in Liberia represent perhaps the leading edge of this type of work. VAWG interventions are likely to be most effective when they are part of a wider multi-dimensional approach that includes legal reform—such as the criminalization of marital rape—and accountability for perpetrators.

The surveys in Liberia and Nepal also highlight some of the challenges of collecting accurate data on VAWG in post-conflict environments and of obtaining better information about the roles that guns may play. Under-reporting remains a key problem, with rates of national prevalence of VAWG varying with—and showing sensitivity to—the methodology used. The further evolution and dissemination of good practices for collecting data and conducting surveys on VAWG in challenging environments could improve not only the quality of data but its comparability across regions. The success of interventions to prevent VAWG ultimately depends in part on the soundness and accuracy of the underlying evidence base. ■

ABBREVIATIONS

FPAN	Family Planning Association of Nepal
LDHS	Liberia Demographic and Health Survey
NGO	Non-governmental organization
OECD	Organisation for Economic Co-operation and Development
VAWG	Violence against women and girls
WHO	World Health Organization
WISE	Women's Rights through Information, Sensitization and Education

ENDNOTES

1   Small Arms Survey (2013, ch. 1) provides a survey of the literature on gun-related intimate partner violence.

2   In reference to women, the term *gender-based violence* is often used interchangeably with *violence against women*. Both reflect the normative component of violence, that is, the influence of social expectations about gender roles.

3   For statistical purposes, this definition is often expanded to the killing of all women, regardless of motivation.

4   The study countries included Bangladesh, Brazil, Ethiopia, Japan, Namibia, Peru, Samoa, Serbia and Montenegro, Tanzania, and Thailand (WHO, 2005).

5   The International Violence against Women Survey was an international comparative project with a focus on criminal justice aspects of violence against women. It was carried out in Australia, Costa Rica, the Czech Republic, Denmark, Greece, Hong Kong, Italy, Mozambique, the Philippines, Poland, and Switzerland (Johnson, Ollus, and Nevala, 2007).

6   A distinction is made between 'formal' norms, as embodied in laws and statutes, for example, and 'informal' norms, which are unlegislated (Helmke and Levitsky, 2004, p. 727). The former are often the focus of international development assistance on the assumption that legal changes are the first step to changing deeper attitudes and beliefs. Nevertheless, violence against women remains widespread in many places where formal laws may prohibit it, pointing not only to implementation challenges, but also to the difficulty of modifying underlying informal norms.

7   Small Arms Survey (2003, p. 179; 2005, p. 211; 2006, p. 302); Wepundi et al. (2012, p. 42).

8   The study includes more data for women than men; sex-disaggregated data on attitudes would provide a more complete picture (OECD, 2013b, p. 7).

9   Rape includes rape, gang rape, and statutory rape.

10   The LDHS does not estimate rates of sexual violence for the year preceding the survey.

11   A higher proportion of Liberian women than men stated that a husband was justified in beating his wife when she: burns the food (14 per cent of women vs. 5.1 per cent of men), argues with him (42.7 per cent vs. 20.0 per cent), goes out without telling him (41.9 per cent vs. 16.2 per cent), neglects the children (44.6 per cent vs. 16.9 per cent), or refuses to have sex with him (21.7 per cent vs. 5.8 per cent) (Liberia, 2007, pp. 214–15). The percentage of women who agreed with at least one specified reason was 59.3 per cent, as compared to 30.2 per cent of men.

12   Each respondent was asked whether, in the month preceding the survey, her husband: physically forced her to have sex with him (39.4 per cent decrease); threatened or attacked her with a weapon (81.7 per cent decrease); burned her on purpose (20.1 per cent decrease); punched her with his fist (55.3 per cent decrease); slapped her (53.5 per cent decrease); pushed her or shook her (29.4 per cent decrease); insulted her or made her feel bad about herself (37.7 per cent decrease); or became angry with her (9.9 per cent decrease) (IRC, 2013, p. 35).

13   In Nepal, firearms comprise pistols, revolvers, rifles, and shotguns, including the craft rifle commonly referred to as *katuwa* (Racovita, Murray and Sharma, 2013, pp. 55–56).

14   South Africa's One in Nine Campaign uses a variety of strategies to 'harness the power of print and electronic media to educate and inform key institutions and the public about legal and social dimensions of sexual violence' (Bennett, 2008, p. 6). The campaign's name references a study conducted on sexual violence whose findings show that only one in nine rape survivors reports the attack to the police. Since 2006, the One in Nine Campaign has engaged in ongoing public and media activism (Bennett, 2008, p. 6). Though the campaign serves as a prominent example of awareness raising in the area of VAWG, its activities have yet to be evaluated. The lack of evaluation of these types of programmes is a common problem.

BIBLIOGRAPHY

ACUNS VLO (Academic Council on the United Nations System Vienna Liaison Office). 2013. *Femicide: A Global Issue that Demands Action.* Vienna: ACUNS.
    <http://www.genevadeclaration.org/fileadmin/docs/Co-publications/Femicide_A%20Gobal%20Issue%20that%20demands%20Action.pdf>

Adhikari, Ramesh and Jyotsna Tamang. 2009. 'Premarital Sexual Behavior among Male College Students of Kathmandu, Nepal.' *BMC Public Health*, Vol. 9. <http://www.biomedcentral.com/1471-2458/9/241>

—. 2010. 'Sexual Coercion of Married Women in Nepal.' *BMC Public Health*, Vol. 10. <http://www.biomedcentral.com/content/pdf/1472-6874-10-31.pdf>

Alvazzi del Frate, Anna. 2011. 'When the Victim Is a Woman.' In Geneva Declaration Secretariat. *Global Burden of Armed Violence: Lethal Encounters.*
    Cambridge: Cambridge University Press, pp. 113–44.
    <http://www.genevadeclaration.org/measurability/global-burden-of-armed-violence/global-burden-of-armed-violence-2011.html>

Arino, Maria Villellas. 2008. 'Nepal: A Gender View of the Armed Conflict and the Peace Process.' Peacebuilding Papers (Quaderns de Construcció de Pau)
    No. 4. Barcelona: Escola de Cultura de Pau. <http://escolapau.uab.cat/img/qcp/nepal_conflict_peace.pdf>

Asia Foundation. 2010. 'Nepal: Preliminary Mapping of Gender Based Violence.' Kathmandu: Asia Foundation.
    <http://asiafoundation.org/resources/pdfs/GBVMappingNepal.pdf>

Bennett, Jane. 2008. *Challenges Were Many: The One in Nine Campaign, South Africa.* Toronto, Mexico City, and Cape Town: Association for Women's
    Rights in Development.

Berkowitz, Alan. 2010. 'Fostering Healthy Norms to Prevent Violence and Abuse: The Social Norms Approach.' Keith Kaufman, ed. *The Prevention of
    Sexual Violence: A Practitioner's Sourcebook.* Holyoke, MA: NEARI Press, pp. 147–71.

Bhandari, Parasmani and Shiva Raj Mishra. 2012. 'Female Feticide: A Mass Murder.' *Health Prospect*, Vol. 11, pp. 47–49.
    <http://nepjol.info/index.php/HPROSPECT/article/download/7434/6029>

CEDAW (Committee on the Elimination of Discrimination against Women). 2008. *Consideration of Reports Submitted by States Parties under Article 18
    of the Convention on the Elimination of All Forms of Discrimination against Women Combined Initial, Second, Third, Fourth, Fifth, and Sixth
    Periodic Reports of States Parties Liberia.* CEDAW/C/LBR/6 of 13 October. New York: CEDAW.
    <http://reliefweb.int/sites/reliefweb.int/files/resources/936997CAE8D9CB4749257605000A0AE8-Full_Report.pdf>

Colekessian, Ani. 2009. *Reintegrating Gender: A Gendered Analysis of the Nepali Rehabilitation Process.* Santo Domingo, Dominican Republic: United
    Nations International Research and Training Institute for the Advancement of Women.
    <http://reliefweb.int/sites/reliefweb.int/files/resources/4DF98D25D63E5852852577CA00683717-Full_Report.pdf>

Coleman, James. 1987. 'Norms as Social Capital.' In Gerard Radnitzky and Peter Bernholz, eds. *Economic Imperialism: The Economic Method Applied
    Outside the Field of Economics.* New York: Paragon, pp. 133–56. <ftp://soc.cornell.edu/vgn1/norms-as-social-capital.pdf>

CREHPA (Center for Research on Environment Health and Population Activities). 2007. 'Sex Selection: Pervasiveness and Preparedness in Nepal.' Kathmandu:
    CREHPA. September. <http://www.unfpa.org/gender/docs/studies/nepal.pdf>

de Carvalho, Benjamin and Niels Nagelhus Schia. 2009. 'The Protection of Women and Children in Liberia.' Policy Brief. Oslo: Norwegian Institute of
    International Affairs.

Dziewanski, Dariusz. 2011. *Assessment of Gender-based Violence (GBV) Data in Liberia*. Oslo: Norwegian Refugee Council.

—. 2012. *Peace without Security: Violence against Women in Liberia*. Liberia Armed Violence Assessment Issue Brief No. 3. Geneva: Small Arms Survey.

Ellsberg, Mary and Lori Heise. 2005. 'Researching Violence against Women: A Practical Guide for Researchers and Activists.' Washington, DC: World Health Organization and Program for Appropriate Technology in Health (PATH). <http://whqlibdoc.who.int/publications/2005/9241546476_eng.pdf>

Eriksson Baaz, Maria and Maria Stern. 2009. 'Why Do Soldiers Rape? Masculinity, Violence, and Sexuality in the Armed Forces in the Congo (DRC).' *International Studies Quarterly*, Vol. 53, Iss. 2, pp. 495–518.

Evans, W. Douglas. 2006. 'How Social Marketing Works in Health Care.' *British Medical Journal*, Vol. 332, No. 7551, pp. 1207–10. <http://www.ncbi.nlm.nih.gov/pmc/articles/PMC1463924/>

Foster, Dulce, et al. 2009. *A House with Two Rooms: Final Report of the Truth and Reconciliation Commission of Liberia Diaspora Project*. St. Paul, MN: Dispute Resolution Institute Press. <http://www.theadvocatesforhumanrights.org/uploads/A+House+with+Two+Rooms.pdf>

Fulu, Emma, et al. 2013. *Why Do Some Men Use Violence against Women and How Can We Prevent It? Quantitative Findings from the United Nations Multi-country Study on Men and Violence in Asia and the Pacific*. Bangkok: United Nations Development Programme et al. <http://unwomen-asiapacific.org/docs/WhyDoSomeMenUseViolenceAgainstWomen_P4P_Report.pdf>

Geneva Declaration (Geneva Declaration on Armed Violence and Development). 2006. Geneva, 7 June. <http://www.genevadeclaration.org/fileadmin/docs/GD-Declaration-091020-EN.pdf>

Hamal, Babita. 2007. 'Impacts of Armed Conflicts on Women in Nepal.' *Gender Technology and Development*, Vol. 11, No. 2, pp. 235–42.

Heise, Lori. 2011. *What Works to Prevent Partner Violence? An Evidence Overview*. London: STRIVE, London School of Hygiene and Tropical Medicine. <http://r4d.dfid.gov.uk/PDF/Outputs/Gender/60887-PartnerViolenceEvidenceOverview.pdf>

Helmke, Gretchen and Steven Levitsky. 2004. 'Informal Institutions and Comparative Politics: A Research Agenda.' *Perspectives on Politics,* Vol. 2, Iss. 4, pp. 725–40.

Hemenway, David, Tomoko Shinoda-Tagawa, and Matthew Miller. 2002. 'Firearm Availability and Female Homicide Victimization Rates among 25 Populous High-Income Countries.' *Journal of the American Medical Women's Association*, Vol. 57, No. 2, pp. 100–04.

Hindin, Michelle, Sunita Kishor, and Donna Ansara. 2008. *Intimate Partner Violence among Couples in 10 DHS Countries: Predictors and Health Outcomes*. DHS Analytical Studies No. 18. Calverton, MD: Macro International, Inc. December. <http://www.measuredhs.com/pubs/pdf/AS18/AS18.pdf>

ICG (International Crisis Group). 2005. *Nepal's Maoists: Their Aims, Structure and Strategy*. Asia Report No. 104. Kathmandu and Brussels: ICG. 27 October.

ICRW (International Center for Research on Women). 2013. 'Asia Child Marriage Initiative: Summary of Research in Bangladesh, India and Nepal.' New Delhi: ICRW.

IDA (Interdisciplinary Analysts) and Saferworld. 2011. *A Safer Future? Tracking Security Improvements in an Uncertain Context*. Kathmandu: IDA and Saferworld. September.

— and Small Arms Survey. 2012. 'Armed Violence Assessment in Nepal.' Database. Geneva: Small Arms Survey.

INSEC (Informal Sector Service Centre). 2012a. *A Study on Violence Due to Witchcraft Allegation and Sexual Violence*. Kathmandu: INSEC. <http://www.whrin.org/wp-content/uploads/2013/07/Witchcraft-report-INSEC.pdf>

—. 2012b. *Report on Small Arms Violence: January–December 2012*. Kathmandu: INSEC.

—. n.d. 'No. of Victims Killed by State and Maoist in Connection with the "People's War.": 13 Feb. 1996–31 Dec. 2006.' Kathmandu: INSEC.

IRC (International Rescue Committee). 2011. 'Men and Women in Partnership: Guidance Note.' Project document. Monrovia: IRC Liberia.

—. 2013. *International Rescue Committee: Liberia Men's Dialogue Groups Endline Study*. Project document. Monrovia: IRC Liberia.

IRIN (Integrated Regional Information Networks). 2010. 'NEPAL: Reintegration Challenges for Maoist Female Ex-combatants.' 14 April. <http://www.irinnews.org/report/88806/nepal-reintegration-challenges-for-maoist-female-ex-combatants>

—. 2011. 'Nepal: Emerging from Menstrual Quarantine.' 3 August. <http://www.refworld.org/docid/4e3f7ae82.html>

Isser, Deborah, Stephen Lubkemann, and Saah N'Tow. 2009. *Looking for Justice: Liberian Experiences with and Perceptions of Local Justice Options*. November. Washington, DC: United States Institute of Peace. <http://www.usip.org/sites/default/files/PW63-Looking for Justice-Liberian Experiences with and Perceptions of Local Justice Options.pdf>

Johnson, Holly, Natalia Ollus, and Sami Nevala. 2007. *Violence against Women: An International Perspective*. New York: Springer.

Krug, Etienne G., et al., eds. 2002. *World Report on Violence and Health*. Geneva: World Health Organization. <http://whqlibdoc.who.int/publications/2002/9241545615_eng.pdf>

Lamere, Carolyn. 2012. 'Taking On Domestic Violence in Post-Conflict Liberia.' NewSecurityBeat. 16 August. <http://www.newsecuritybeat.org/2012/08/taking-on-domestic-violence-in-post-conflict-liberia/#.UTobdI5Ly2x>

Liberia. 2006. National Plan of Action for the Prevention and Management of Gender Based Violence in Liberia. Monrovia: Republic of Liberia. November.

—. 2007. *Liberia Demographic and Health Survey 2007*. Monrovia: Republic of Liberia. <http://www.measuredhs.com/pubs/pdf/FR201/FR201.pdf>

—. 2008a. Poverty Reduction Strategy. Monrovia: Republic of Liberia. <http://www.imf.org/external/pubs/ft/scr/2012/cr1245.pdf>

—. 2008b. Government and United Nations Joint Programme to Prevent and Respond to Sexual Gender Based Violence. Monrovia: Republic of Liberia.

—. 2011a. National Action Plan for the Prevention and Management of Gender-Based Violence in Liberia (2nd Phase) 2011–2015. Monrovia: Ministry of Gender and Development.

—. 2011b. 'In-depth Study on Reasons for High Incidence of Sexual and Gender Based Violence in Liberia—Recommendations on Prevention and Response.' Monrovia: Government of Liberia.

—. 2012. Liberia National Police Annual Report 2012. Monrovia: Republic of Liberia.

Lohani-Chase, Rama. 2008. 'Women and Gender in the Maoist People's War in Nepal: Militarism and Dislocation.' Dissertation. New Brunswick, NJ: Rutgers, The State University of New Jersey.

Monekosso, Ticky. 2001. 'Africa's Forced Marriages.' BBC. 8 March. <http://news.bbc.co.uk/2/hi/africa/1209099.stm>

Moser, Caroline. 2004. 'Urban Violence and Insecurity: An Introductory Roadmap.' Environment & Urbanization, Vol. 16, No. 2, pp. 3–16.

Myrttinen, Henri. 2003. 'Disarming Masculinities.' Disarmament Forum, Vol. 5, No. 4. Geneva: United Nations Institute for Disarmament Research, pp. 37–46.

Nanda, Priya, Abhishek Gautam, and Ravi Verma. 2012. Study on Gender, Masculinity, and Son Preference in Nepal and Vietnam. New Delhi: International Center for Research on Women.

Nepal. 2009. National Plan of Action for 'Year Against Gender Based Violence, 2010.' Kathmandu: Office of the Prime Minister and Council of Ministers. 25 November.
<http://www.engagingmen.net/files/resources/2010/lbelbase/National_Plan_of_Action_for_Year_Against_Gender_Based_Violence_2010.pdf>

—. 2012. Nepal Demographic and Health Survey 2011. Kathmandu: Ministry of Health and Population.
<http://www.measuredhs.com/pubs/pdf/FR257/FR257%5B13April2012%5D.pdf>

Nepal MHP (Ministry of Health and Population), New ERA, and ICF International. 2011. Nepal Demographic and Health Survey 2011: Preliminary Report. Kathmandu: US Agency for International Development.

Ní Aoláin, Fionnuala, Naomi Cahn, and Dina Francesca Haynes. 2012. 'Masculinities and Child Soldiers in Post-Conflict Societies.' In Frank Cooper and Ann McGinley, eds. Masculinities and the Law: A Multidimensional Approach. New York: New York University Press, pp. 231–51.

NRC (Norwegian Refugee Council). n.d. 'Project Factsheet: Women's Rights through Information Sensitization and Education (WISE).'
<http://www.nrc.no/arch/_img/9474672.pdf>

OECD (Organisation for Economic Co-operation and Development). 2010. Mapping Armed Violence Reduction and Prevention Programming in Liberia. Paris: OECD.

—. 2013a. 'Transforming Social Institutions to Prevent Violence against Women and Girls and Improve Development Outcomes.' March.
<http://www.oecd.org/social/poverty/OECD_DEV_Policy%20Brief_March%202013.pdf>

—. 2013b. 2012 SIGI Social Institutions and Gender Index: Understanding the Drivers of Social Inequality. Paris: OECD.
<http://www.oecd.org/dev/50288699.pdf>

—. n.d. 'SIGI: Social Institutions and Gender Index.' Accessed December 2013. <genderindex.org>

Omanyondo, MarieClaire. 2005. Sexual Gender-Based Violence and Health Facility Needs Assessment: (Lofa, Nimba, Grand Gedeh and Grand Bassa Counties) Liberia. Monrovia: World Health Organization. <http://www.who.int/hac/crises/lbr/Liberia_RESULTS_AND_DISCUSSION13.pdf>

Paudel, Ghiridhari Sharma. 2007. 'Domestic Violence against Women in Nepal.' Gender Technology and Development, Vol. 11, No. 2, pp. 199–233.

Population Council. 2008. Sexual and Gender Based Violence in Africa: Literature Review. Nairobi: Population Council.
<http://www.popcouncil.org/pdfs/AfricaSGBV_LitReview.pdf>

Pradhan, Ajit, et al. 2011. 'A Review of the Evidence: Suicide among Women in Nepal.' London: Options Consultancy Services Ltd.
<http://www.nhssp.org.np/gesi/Suicide%20among%20women%20in%20Nepal%20Final.pdf>

Racovita, Mihaela, Ryan Murray, and Sudhindra Sharma. 2013. In Search of Lasting Security: An Assessment of Armed Violence in Nepal. Geneva: Small Arms Survey. May.

Richardson, Erin and David Hemenway. 2011. 'Homicide, Suicide, and Unintentional Firearm Fatality: Comparing the United States with Other High-Income Countries, 2003.' Journal of Trauma, Vol. 70, pp. 238–43.

RWAMREC (Rwanda Men's Resource Centre). 2010. Masculinity and Gender Based Violence in Rwanda: Experiences and Perceptions of Men and Women. Kigali: RWAMREC and Rwanda MenEngage Network.

Sarkar, Madhumita, Sadiq Syed, and Musili Nzau. 2009. Strategic Inquiry on Prevention and Response to Gender Based Violence (GBV) in Liberia. Monrovia: Government of Liberia and United Nations GBV Joint Programme.

Samuels, Fiona and Anita Ghimire. 2013. 'Social Norms for Adolescent Girls in Nepal: Slow but Positive Progress.' ODI Country Briefing. London: Overseas Development Institute.

Sangroula, Yubaraj. n.d. 'Violence against Women: Nepal's Situation.' <http://www.academia.edu/196352/Violence_Against_Women_Nepals_Situation>

Small Arms Survey. 2003. Small Arms Survey: Development Denied. Oxford: Oxford University Press.

—. 2005. Small Arms Survey: Weapons at War. Oxford: Oxford University Press.

—. 2006. Small Arms Survey: Unfinished Business. Oxford: Oxford University Press.

—. 2010. 'Perceptions of Security and Patterns of Victimization in Liberia: Consolidated Data Collection.' Unpublished data.

—. 2013. *Small Arms Survey 2013: Everyday Dangers*. Cambridge: Cambridge University Press.

Snyder, Leslie. 2007. 'Health Communication Campaigns and Their Impact on Behavior.' *Journal of Nutrition Education and Behavior*, Vol. 39, pp. S32–S40.

Specht, Irma. 2006. *Red Shoes: Experiences of Girl-combatants in Liberia*. Geneva: Programme on Crisis Response and Reconstruction, International Labour Office. <http://www.ilo.org/wcmsp5/groups/public/@ed_emp/@emp_ent/@ifp_crisis/documents/publication/wcms_116435.pdf>

Tamang, Seira. 2009. 'The Politics of Conflict and Difference or the Difference of Conflict in Politics: The Women's Movement in Nepal.' *Feminist Review*, Vol. 91, No. 1, pp. 61–80.

Theidon, Kimberly. 2009. 'Reconstructing Masculinities: The Disarmament, Demobilization, and Reintegration of Former Combatants in Colombia.' *Human Rights Quarterly*, Vol. 31, No. 1, pp. 1–34.

TRIAL and HimRights (Swiss Association against Impunity and Himalayan Human Rights Monitor). 2013. 'Executive Summary of the Written Information for the Follow-up to the Concluding Observations of the Committee on the Elimination of Discrimination against Women with Regard to Nepal's Combined Fourth and Fifth Periodic Reports.' August.
<http://www.trial-ch.org/fileadmin/user_upload/documents/CAJ/Nepal/TRIAL_CEDAW_Nepal_Exec._Summ_9.08.13.pdf>

Tuladhar, Sabita, et al. 2013. 'Women's Empowerment and Spousal Violence in Relation to Health Outcomes in Nepal: Further Analysis of the 2011 Nepal Demographic and Health Survey.' Calverton, MD: Nepal Ministry of Health and Population, New ERA, and ICF International.
<http://www.measuredhs.com/pubs/pdf/FA77/FA77.pdf>

UNFPA (United Nations Population Fund). 2007. *Priority Areas for Addressing Sexual and Gender Based Violence in Nepal*. Kathmandu: UNFPA Nepal.

UNGA (United Nations General Assembly). 1993. Declaration on the Elimination of Violence against Women. A/RES/48/104 of 20 December.
<http://www.un.org/documents/ga/res/48/a48r104.htm>

UNICEF (United Nations Children's Fund). n.d. 'Sexual and Gender Based Violence (SGBV).'
<http://www.unicef.org/wcaro/english/wcaro_liberia_fact_CP_SGBV.pdf>

UNMIL (United Nations Mission in Liberia). 2008. 'Research on Prevalence and Attitudes to Rape in Liberia, September to October 2008.' Monrovia: UNMIL.
<http://www.stoprapenow.org/uploads/advocacyresources/1282163297.pdf>

—. n.d. 'Facts about Rape in Liberia.' Fact sheet. <http://unmil.unmissions.org/Portals/unmil/RapeFactSheet_FOLD_No_Bleed.pdf>

UN WOMEN (United Nations Entity for Gender Equality and the Empowerment of Women). 2011. 'Violence against Women Prevalence Data: Surveys by Country.' <http://www.unifem.org/attachments/gender_issues/violence_against_women/vaw-prevalence-matrix-2011.pdf>

Waszak, Cynthia, Shyam Thapa, and Jessica Davey. 2003. 'The Influence of Gender Norms on the Reproductive Health of Adolescents in Nepal–Perspectives of Youth.' In Sarah Bott et al, eds. *Towards Adulthood: Exploring the Sexual and Reproductive Health of Adolescents in South Asia*. Geneva: World Health Organization, pp. 81–85.

Wepundi, Mannaseh, et al. 2012. 'Availability of Small Arms and Perceptions of Security in Kenya: An Assessment'. Special Report. Geneva: Small Arms Survey.
<http://www.smallarmssurvey.org/fileadmin/docs/C-Special-reports/SAS-SR16-Kenya.pdf>

WHO (World Health Organization). 2005. *Multi-country Study on Women's Health and Domestic Violence against Women*. Geneva: WHO.

—. 2007. *Ethical and Safety Recommendations for Researching, Documenting and Monitoring Sexual Violence in Emergencies*. Geneva: WHO.

—. 2009. *Changing Cultural and Social Norms that Support Violence*. Briefing on Violence Prevention: The Evidence. Geneva: WHO.
<http://whqlibdoc.who.int/publications/2009/9789241598330_eng.pdf>

—. 2013. *Global and Regional Estimates of Violence against Women: Prevalence and Health Effects of Intimate Partner Violence and Non-Partner Sexual Violence*. Geneva: WHO. <http://apps.who.int/iris/bitstream/10665/85239/1/9789241564625_eng.pdf>

WOREC Nepal (Women's Rehabilitation Centre Nepal). 2012. *Annual Report 2012*. Balkumari, Lalitpur: WOREC Nepal.

ACKNOWLEDGEMENTS

Principal authors

Dariusz Dziewanski, Emile LeBrun, and Mihaela Racovita

Students demonstrate with toy rifles to demand that the Filipino government support the Arms Trade Treaty, Manila, March 2012. © Pat Roque/AP Photo

Converging Agendas
WOMEN, PEACE, SECURITY, AND SMALL ARMS

2

INTRODUCTION

In April 2013, cautious celebrations greeted the news that the United Nations General Assembly had finally adopted the Arms Trade Treaty (ATT). The ATT has been hailed as a victory for women in that it will require states parties to take into account the risk of small arms being used to commit or facilitate serious acts of gender-based violence, such as domestic and sexual violence, before authorizing their transfer abroad. For women's civil society organizations (CSOs) and disarmament CSOs, which have often joined forces, this marks an important achievement in the long struggle to prevent the misuse of small arms.

The years 2012–13 saw multiple causes for celebration, as the international women, peace, and security and small arms agendas have finally converged within international policy. The outcome of the 2012 Review Conference of the UN Programme of Action (PoA), the ATT, and the September 2013 United Nations Security Council Resolution (UNSCR) on small arms control each include specific language on gender-based violence or women's participation. In parallel, the two 2013 resolutions on women, peace, and security both reaffirm the provisions in the ATT; the second of these, UNSCR 2122 of October 2013, contains a groundbreaking operative paragraph urging women's full participation in controlling illicit small arms.

Such policy coherence was not always the case. Earlier international law and policies, such as the 1979 Convention on the Elimination of All Forms of Discrimination against Women (CEDAW) and the 1995 Beijing Declaration and Platform for Action (PfA), set the stage for addressing the differing ways in which small arms affect and involve men, women, girls, and boys. Nonetheless, the first five UNSCRs on women, peace, and security, beginning with UNSCR 1325, made no mention of 'small arms', the 'arms trade', or 'weapons'. Despite this crucial omission, the International Action Network on Small Arms (IANSA) states that 'Resolution 1325 has also proven to be a decisive mandate for the field of small arms policy and practice' (IANSA, 2008, p. 1). Actors ranging from the UN Secretary-General to disarmament non-governmental organizations (NGOs) have drawn policy, research, and advocacy linkages between the UN Security Council's women, peace, and security agenda and small arms. In addition, a number of national-level action plans on women, peace, and security and on small arms refer to aspects of the 'other agenda'; for example, a national action plan on small arms may refer to the importance of women's participation in community education to prevent the misuse of firearms.

This chapter describes the increasing convergence of the international women, peace, and security agenda and the small arms control agenda, highlighting the crucial role that women and women's organizations have played in the process. It finds that:

- CEDAW and the Beijing Declaration and PfA provide a strong normative basis for connecting the women, peace, and security and the small arms agendas.

- Until 2013, the UNSCRs on women, peace, and security, aside from references to disarmament, demobilization, and reintegration (DDR), were silent on the topics of small arms and disarmament.

- Key actors have linked four mandates in the UNSCRs on women, peace, and security to small arms, namely the protection of civilians, including from sexual violence; women's participation; supporting local women's peace and conflict resolution; and DDR.

- Recent UN monitoring frameworks on UNSCR 1325 include specific indicators and targets pertaining to small arms and disarmament.

- While one quarter of existing national action plans for the implementation of UNSCR 1325 (1325 NAPs) refer to small arms, they rarely operationalize this policy linkage by requiring concrete actions. Likewise, while national action plans on small arms occasionally mention women, they do not translate this into required actions.

- The ATT and the UNSCRs on women, peace, and security and on small arms adopted in 2013 finally firmly connect these two international policy agendas. National action plans on UNSCR 1325 and on small arms have the potential to be stronger and more effective by giving concrete expression to this policy convergence.

This chapter is divided into four main sections. The first section provides an overview of women, peace, and security issues, including the origins of the UNSCRs on women, peace, and security and a summary of women's roles in relation to small arms in the context of armed conflict. The second section analyses how the international policy framework on women, peace, and security has—and has not—addressed small arms, including through the seven UNSCRs on women, peace, and security, CEDAW, and the Beijing Declaration and PfA. The third section considers how small arms feature in 1325 NAPs, 43 of which have been adopted to date; it examines the implementation of relevant parts of the 1325 NAPs of the Philippines and Senegal, whose provisions on small arms are the most detailed. It also explores how women, peace, and security issues have—and have not—been addressed in a number of national action plans on small arms. The final section then reviews how the women, peace, and security agenda has been embodied in recent developments in small arms law and policy, through the PoA, the ATT, and the UNSCR on small arms.

WOMEN, PEACE, AND SECURITY OVERVIEW

Origins of the UNSCRs on women, peace, and security

The 15 UN Security Council members unanimously adopted UNSCR 1325 on women, peace, and security on 31 October 2000 (UNSC, 2000). The words 'groundbreaking' and 'landmark' are often used to describe UNSCR 1325, with reference to both the topic and the process of developing the resolution. For the first time since its inception in 1945, the UN Security Council directly addressed the impact of armed conflict on women and their roles in establishing peace and security. In previous resolutions, only a few passing references had been made to women as either victims or members of 'vulnerable groups' (Cohn, 2007, p. 2). Today the resolution is being used not only to mainstream gender in the UN architecture on peace and security, but also by CSOs around the world to advocate everything from increased representation of women in government to support for psychosocial care for victims of sexual violence. Since UNSCR 1325, six more UNSCRs on women, peace, and security have been adopted.

The idea of raising the topic of women, peace, and security in the UN Security Council was first aired in discussions among NGOs in the Women and Armed Conflict Caucus during the 1998 UN Commission on the Status of Women

(CSW) (Cohn, 2007, p. 4). Two years later, six international NGOs created the NGO Working Group on Women, Peace and Security for the specific purpose of advocating the passage of a UNSCR on this topic. These were: Amnesty International, the Hague Appeal for Peace, International Alert, the Women's Caucus for Gender Justice, the Women's Commission for Refugee Women and Children, and the Women's League for International Peace and Freedom. UNSCR 1325 is noteworthy in that it is one of the few if not the only resolution whose initial driving force was comprised of NGOs, which produced background research, engaged in lobbying, and drafted the text.

All six of the founding members were directly working on issues related to women and armed conflict, but only two explicitly focused on women and disarmament. Within the NGO Working Group, the Women's League for International Peace and Freedom and the Hague Appeal for Peace, both of which have a long history of disarmament work, pushed for the initial draft of UNSCR 1325 to include references to the international arms trade and the importance of disarmament. However, these topics were rejected by other Working Group members as 'too political' (Cohn, 2007, p. 12). Self-censorship among the NGOs thus partially accounted for the end result of a resolution with no mention of 'small arms', the 'arms trade', or 'weapons'. Box 2.1 discusses 'men, peace, and security', another set of issues arguably missing from the text.

Malaysian women peacekeepers of the UN Interim Force in Lebanon (UNIFIL) at a medal ceremony in Kawkaba, Lebanon, January 2012. © Pasqual Gorriz/UN Photo

Box 2.1 What about men, peace, and security?

There have been many valid conceptual critiques of the UNSCRs on women, peace, and security. In particular, their focus on women rather than gender has been both lauded and lambasted. In total, UNSCR 1325 contains 33 references to 'women', 13 to 'girls', 11 to 'gender', 3 to 'children', and 2 to 'civilians'; it only uses the term 'male' once and makes no reference to 'men' or 'boys'. Defenders claim that the focus on women redresses the past invisibility of women as both victims and actors and reflects the needs and priorities identified by grassroots women's organizations in conflict and post-conflict contexts. It is also viewed as a pragmatic approach to ensure that women are not 'lost' in the efforts to mainstream gender, including when it comes to funding allocation.

On the other hand, this approach has been criticized for essential- izing women as either victims or peacemakers and brushing over the importance of context-based, complex gender relations that shape both women's and men's roles and needs during and after conflict. As the gender roles of men and women are constructed in opposition to each other, simply focusing on women's roles may actually per- petuate the insecurity women experience by failing to look at the gendered root causes of violent behaviour, and overlooking how understanding and bringing about changes in male gender roles– that is, masculinities–can be an effective tool for violence prevention.

In addition, by making men invisible in the peace and security con- text, the resolutions fail to acknowledge the diversity of roles men play, not just as perpetrators of violence but as activists for peace and as victims of war. For example, in Liberia a survey found that 33 per cent of male combatants and 7 per cent of male non-combatants had expe- rienced sexual violence, and around the world men are a vast majority of victims of small arms violence, constituting 90 per cent of firearms casualties (Feuerschütz, 2012, p. 13; WHO, 2001, p. 3). CSOs have drawn attention to the importance of engaging with men on peace and secu- rity issues, in particular in the field of small arms, and the topic of 'men, peace, and security' has recently started to gain traction (USIP, 2013).

Nevertheless, the NGO Working Group, in consultation with women's organizations from conflict and post-conflict contexts and in partnership with the UN Development Fund for Women (UNIFEM), saw the resolu- tion as a way to mandate the UN peace and security structure to address the horrifying impact war was having on women and the barriers they faced in taking a seat around the peace negotiation table (Cohn, 2007, p. 11). These concerns are clearly reflected in the final language of UNSCR 1325 and have shaped the discourse surrounding the resolu- tion. The subsequent six UNSCRs on women, peace, and security each have their own ori- gin story, some linked to CSO advocacy and others driven by UN member state priorities.

Women, war, and small arms

The UNSCRs on women, peace, and secu- rity seek to address the realities faced by women and girls in armed conflict and post- conflict contexts. In reality, they cover a lim- ited range of women's actual roles, needs, and priorities. Armed conflict creates an environment of extreme vulnerability to many different forms of violence and deprivation. Yet, armed conflict also creates space to tran- scend traditional gender roles, as men, women, girls, and boys may take on new roles as combatants, heads of house- hold, community leaders, and peace activists. When it comes to small arms, women have, among other roles, taken up arms as combatants, smuggled weapons across borders, and organized local and national disarmament initiatives.

Beyond the issue of access to DDR, women as perpetrators of armed violence have garnered relatively little attention on the international women, peace, and security agenda in comparison to other roles, such as victims of armed violence or peacemakers. Often sensationalized in the popular media, female combatants and women or girls associated with fighting forces are the norm in armed conflicts throughout the world. From Colombia, El Salvador, Eritrea, and Liberia to Nepal, Sri Lanka, and Syria, women and girls have taken up weapons and served as combatants, including as perpetrators of human rights violations. In Nepal, for instance, women composed 20 per cent of Maoist army personnel; in Colombia, women constituted 30–35 per cent of the Revolutionary Armed Forces of Colombia; and 33 per cent of the Eritrean People's Liberation Front were women, including 13 per cent of frontline fighters (UNMIN, 2008; Drost, 2011; Freedom House, 2011). Women and girls have also taken on essential support functions such as cooks, spies, paramedics, teachers, couriers, mechanics, drivers, and porters.

Just as with men and boys, in some contexts women and girls have largely joined voluntarily, as in Colombia and Sri Lanka, while in other contexts girls were often forcibly recruited, as in Liberia. Forcibly recruited girl combatants face the prevalent threat of sexual violence, including rape and so-called 'AK-47 marriages', which are the equivalent of sexual slavery (Schroeder, Farr, and Schnabel, 2005, p. 17). Women and girls can thus end up in a position of being simultaneously a perpetrator and a victim of armed human rights violations.

'Civilian' women also act in support of armed combatants—whether by providing moral support, encouraging community mobilization, offering food, funds, safehouses, or medical attention, producing arms, or smuggling weapons and ammunition. In Nigeria the militant organization Boko Haram has recruited women as arms couriers to smuggle AK-47s and improvized explosive devices under their traditional religious clothing; the women carry these loads as though they were babies on their backs (Onuoha, 2013). In Syria, women have also been involved in smuggling arms from one region to another in support of the Free Syrian Army (Cheikhomar and Austin, 2013).

During and following conflict, women, men, boys, and girls face multiple forms of violence and deprivation as direct and indirect consequences of small arms prevalence and misuse. Research in Cambodia, for example, has

A woman poses with her husband's assault rifle in the weapons workshop that he runs from their home, Misrata, Libya, June 2011.
© George Henton/Flickr Vision/Getty Images

demonstrated that, if small arms are not removed following the cessation of conflict, they may be directed towards the civilian population or may be used in interpersonal violence (ICRC, 1999, pp. 9–11). Sex-disaggregated data that allows a rigorous assessment of differential impacts of armed violence in conflict on men, women, boys, and girls is scarce due to the general difficulties of data collection in such contexts, as well as the under-reporting of gender-based violence due to social taboos and stigmatization.

Women can be key players in the prevention of armed violence.

Nonetheless, examples of direct small arms violence faced by women during and after war include domestic and sexual violence, injury, and murder. Rates of domestic violence are high during armed conflict and increase in its aftermath, with women suffering the brunt of this form of violence (Farr, 2006, p. 46). Multiple research studies confirm that the increased availability of guns during the conflict in Northern Ireland meant more dangerous forms of violence in the home (McWilliams, 1998, p. 131). The International Rescue Committee observed a similar trend in 2011 in Côte d'Ivoire, where during the armed conflict rates of reported domestic violence rose by 43 per cent (IRC, 2012, p. 7). Numerous studies have also documented the link between small arms and sexual violence (Farr, Myrttinen, and Schnabel, 2009; AI, 2012b). In a 2013 report on Syria, interviewed refugees cited rape as the main reason their families fled the conflict, and women and girls who had been attacked noted that it was primarily committed by armed men (IRC, 2013, pp. 2, 6). In the countries with the highest rates of femicide (the killing of a woman), which include Colombia, El Salvador, and Guatemala, more than 60 per cent of femicides perpetrated in 2004–09 involved the use of a firearm (Geneva Declaration Secretariat, 2011, p. 131). In addition, women are robbed, traumatized, trafficked, displaced, and forced into marriage or prostitution at gunpoint (Kalitowski, 2006; FEIM et al., 2011). Indirect consequences of armed violence on women include taking on the role of head of household when a partner is killed, taking care of injured family members, and the inability to access work, education, and health care due to the threat of armed violence.

Women are not only perpetrators and victims of small arms violence, but also have proven to be key players in preventing it. From lobbying at the UN to initiating local youth programmes, women have been at the forefront of many international and national initiatives to remove small arms from their communities, at times evoking UNSCR 1325 and making the link to broader peace and security concerns. For example, in Mali in the early 1990s, women talked their male family members into giving up their weapons, and at times brought weapons hidden by men to collection sites (Farr, Myrttinen, and Schnabel, 2009, pp. 343–44). In the late 1990s, women in Albania were a strong force in sensitizing their communities to the dangers of weapons and mobilizing community members to hand in guns (pp. 336–37). Women also play a crucial role in local policy-making and small arms monitoring activities. In 2010, 100 pastoralist women from the frontier Indigenous Network in Kenya submitted a petition and a regional plan on firearms control to the government, listing local arms markets, smuggling routes, and arms traffickers (Masters, 2010).

INTERNATIONAL POLICY FRAMEWORK ON WOMEN, PEACE, AND SECURITY AND SMALL ARMS
UNSCRs on women, peace, and security

Together, the seven UNSCRs on women, peace, and security constitute an international policy framework and an important platform for action and advocacy for civil society. Table 2.1 contains a brief outline of the contents of each UNSCR on women, peace, and security. Regardless of whether they are legally binding for states,[1] as a CEDAW Committee member has emphasized, they are:

important political frameworks for advancing advocacy on women, peace and security, especially as they con-
sistently remind Member States of their legally binding obligations under international law (Patten, 2012, p. 5).

This international agenda has three main focus areas: the protection of women's and girls' human rights in armed conflict and post-conflict settings, in particular the protection from sexual violence; the full and equal participation of women in peace and security; and gender mainstreaming in UN peacekeeping and peacebuilding. To this end, the resolutions include specific mandates directed at different actors, including UN member states, the UN Secretary-General, all parties to armed conflict, all actors involved in peace agreements, civil society, and regional bodies.

Though none of the five first UNSCRs on women, peace, and security specifically mention 'small arms', the 'arms trade', or 'weapons', they do include four mandates that actors ranging from the UN Secretary-General to arms control advocates have linked to small arms, namely the protection of civilians from human rights abuses, including sexual

Table 2.1 Overview of UNSCRs on women, peace, and security

Resolution number	Date	Overview of contents
1325	October 2000	Calls for increased representation of women in conflict prevention and management, including as peacekeepers. Mandates incorporating a gender perspective in peacekeeping operations, including DDR and peace agreements. Calls for the protection of women and girls from gender-based violence.
1820	June 2008	Demands an end to all acts of sexual violence against civilians during armed conflict. Urges preventive and responsive actions, including training programmes, enforcing military discipline, vetting armed and security forces, consultation with women's organizations, equal access to justice, and prosecution of perpetrators.
1888	September 2009	Also focuses on prevention and response to sexual violence in armed conflict. Requests the establishment of a Special Representative of the UN Secretary-General on sexual violence in conflict and UN women's protection advisers in peacekeeping missions. Urges legal and judicial reform at the national level and support to victims.
1889	October 2009	Urges women's participation in all stages of peace processes, including political and economic decision-making. Requests the UN Secretary-General to increase the number of gender advisers as well as female UN Special Representatives and envoys. Calls for gender mainstreaming in all post-conflict peacebuilding and recovery.
1960	December 2010	Also focuses on prevention and the response to sexual violence in armed conflict. Requests the UN Secretary-General to establish monitoring, analysis, and reporting on conflict-related sexual violence.
2106	June 2013	Also focuses on prevention and the response to sexual violence in armed conflict. Emphasizes the important role women and women's organizations play in addressing sexual violence and links sexual violence to HIV/AIDS.
2122	October 2013	Focuses on implementation of the women, peace, and security agenda across the Security Council's work, with an emphasis on women's leadership and participation in conflict resolution and peacebuilding. Calls for a high-level review of UNSCR 1325 implementation in 2015.

violence; women's participation in peace and security decision-making; supporting local women's peace and conflict resolution initiatives; and DDR.

Since 2013, policy-makers and advocates no longer need to read between the lines of UNSCR texts to make the linkage between women, peace, and security and small arms. UNSCRs 2106 and 2122 both make overt references to small arms, citing the ATT and, for the first time, including an operative paragraph encouraging women's participation in small arms action.

Protection from human rights abuses, including sexual violence

Although they include clear language on the protection of civilians, the first five UNSCRs on women, peace, and security lack any direct wording linking small arms with human rights abuses. However, the reports of the UN Secretary-General on women, peace, and security do recognize this linkage, in particular as concerns the perpetration of sexual violence. Prevention of and the response to sexual violence in conflict has been given particular prominence within the international women, peace, and security agenda, with both the United States and the United Kingdom championing the issue in the UN Security Council. To date, the Security Council has adopted four resolutions specifically focused on sexual violence: UNSCRs 1820, 1888, 1960, and 2106, and in response the UN Secretary-General appointed a Special Representative on Sexual Violence in 2010. The Special Representative chairs the UN Action against Sexual Violence in Conflict (UN Action), a coordinating mechanism for the activities of 13 UN entities.

The UN Secretary-General's 2011 report on women, peace, and security clearly states that '[g]ender-based violence is more prevalent and more severe when guns are readily available' (UNSC, 2011a, p. 15). In his October 2012 report, the UN Secretary-General goes even further: 'The availability and limited control of small arms and light weapons continue to facilitate gender-based crimes, such as rape and other forms of sexual abuse and violence' (UNSC, 2012, para. 35). Likewise, in his March 2013 annual report on sexual violence in conflict, he notes the exacerbating influence of the proliferation of small arms in relation to sexual violence in Côte d'Ivoire and Darfur (UNSC, 2013a, paras. 34, 72). The UN Secretary-General also encourages member states, donors, and regional organizations to improve data collection and analysis on the linkages between the widespread availability of illicit small arms and conflict-related sexual violence, and to put in place effective arms control measures (para. 130(e)).

This call to action does not appear to have been translated into UN practice. For instance, UN Action's field activities to address sexual violence in the Democratic Republic of the Congo (DRC), Liberia, and Darfur do not seem to have included a focus on small arms.[2] The UN Mission in DRC's *Comprehensive Strategy on Combating Sexual Violence*, developed in 2008–09, is intended to address sexual violence in a holistic manner. It highlights ensuring equal access by women and men to disarmament programmes and including procedures to assist survivors of sexual violence going through disarmament. However, the strategy does not acknowledge that disarmament is a factor in preventing sexual violence, nor does it include broader measures to remove small arms from communities (UN Action, n.d.b).

The most recent UNSCR on sexual violence in conflict, UNSCR 2106 of June 2013, is thus significant in that it makes note of the ATT (discussed below) in its preamble:

> *the provision in the Arms Trade Treaty that exporting States Parties shall take into account the risk of covered conventional arms or items being used to commit or facilitate serious acts of gender-based violence or serious acts of violence against women and children* (UNSC, 2013b).

This is the first UNSCR on women, peace, and security to explicitly mention arms. UNSCR 2106 does not, however, request any specific actions by UN agencies or states to address small arms in relation to combating human rights abuses, including sexual violence.

Women's participation and supporting local women's peace initiatives

NGOs working on small arms have taken UNSCR 1325's call for UN member states to increase the representation of women in decision-making with regard to conflict prevention and resolution as a mandate to increase women's participation in small arms policy-making processes (Dube, 2010, p. 4). This interpretation was strengthened by the 2010 and 2012 UN General Assembly Resolutions on 'women, disarmament, non-proliferation and arms control'. The controversial 2012 resolution urges member states, subregional and regional organizations, and the UN to promote the representation of women in all decision-making processes related to disarmament, non-proliferation, and arms control, particularly with respect to the prevention and reduction of armed violence and armed conflict (UNGA, 2012b).

As a follow-up to this resolution, in 2013 the UN Secretary-General sought the views of member states on its implementation. The replies submitted by Argentina, Australia, the European Union, Lithuania, the Netherlands, Portugal, and Switzerland specifically mention their national and regional plans to implement UNSCR 1325 as helping to increase the number of women in decision-making positions within the field of disarmament. Additional activities mentioned in the report include supporting women's participation in regional and international negotiations on the ATT and PoA and lobbying for the inclusion of references to gender perspectives and UNSCR 1325 in these policies (UNGA, 2013b).

Another linkage between the UNSCRs on women, peace, and security and small arms has been made in response to Article 8(b) of UNSCR 1325, which urges all actors involved in negotiating and implementing peace agreements to support local women's peace initiatives and indigenous processes for conflict resolution. The UN Secretary-General, in his 2002 study on women, peace, and security, makes this connection, noting that formal peace processes generally include 'global disarmament'; that women are key actors in informal peace processes that include disarmament; and that 'women around the world have continued to pursue the goal of disarmament, including [. . .] strengthening controls over the production and sale of conventional arms' (UN, 2002, pp. 53–54).

> UNSCR 2122 explicitly acknowledged for the first time the importance of women's participation in disarmament.

With the passing of UNSCR 2122 in October 2013, the importance of women's participation in disarmament was explicitly acknowledged for the first time within the UNSCRs on women, peace, and security. This resolution includes an operative paragraph urging 'Member States and United Nations entities, to ensure women's full and meaningful participation in efforts to combat and eradicate the illicit transfer and misuse of small arms and light weapons' (UNSC, 2013d, para. 14). Though this mandate narrowly focuses on illicit transfer and misuse, the specific wording on small arms included in a UNSCR on women, peace, and security is a significant achievement and bodes well for increasing acceptance of the relevance of small arms control efforts to the international women, peace, and security agenda.

Disarmament, demobilization, and reintegration

Perhaps the most overt linkage between the first five UNSCRs on women, peace, and security and small arms are the DDR-related mandates that call for the different needs of female and male ex-combatants to be taken into account. Not only does the process of disarming, demobilizing, and reintegrating ex-combatants involve collecting and disposing of small arms, but this wording has also been broadly interpreted by the 2002 UN Secretary-General study on women, peace, and security to encompass other weapons-collection activities. Discussions around gender and DDR have largely focused on making DDR processes accessible and suited for female ex-combatants and women and girls associated with fighting forces. To this end, the UN has appointed gender advisers, implemented programmes targeting female ex-combatants, provided gender training to DDR personnel, and developed policy guidance on gender and DDR, such as the UN Integrated DDR Standards and UNIFEM Standard Operating Procedures on Gender and DDR (UN, 2006; UNIFEM, 2004).

The UN Secretary-General's 2002 study sets the precedent for a wider interpretation of UNSCR mandates on DDR that is directly related to small arms, namely community-level weapons collections programmes. The study clearly states that community disarmament initiatives are 'of great importance to women because of heightened threats to their personal security with the proliferation of weapons in post-conflict situations' and lauds women and girls for their active participation in weapons collection programmes (UN, 2002, p. 129). The study also specifically acknowledges that consultation with community-level women's groups and women can provide important information regarding attitudes towards the weapons within the community, traditional mechanisms to respond to the problem of high numbers of weapons, and, potentially, the identification of weapons caches and trans-border weapons trade (p. 131). Finally, the study includes a concrete recommendation for action, to recognize and utilize the contributions of women and girls in weapons collection programmes and ensure that they benefit from these programme incentives (p. 138).

Indicators offer a global monitoring framework that can link UNSCR 1325 and small arms.

The fact that the 2002 UN Secretary-General's study on women, peace, and security—which was mandated in UNSCR 1325—recognizes that small arms proliferation poses a security risk to women and highlights their active role in disarmament has been crucial in solidifying the linkage between the women, peace, and security agenda and small arms. It opened the door to the inclusion of activities on small arms and gender in UN reporting on women, peace, and security. For instance, the UN Secretary-General's 2006 report on the implementation of the UNSCRs on women, peace, and security notes that the UN Department for Disarmament Affairs provided training to parliamentarians in Latin America and the Caribbean on mainstreaming a gender perspective into national firearms legislation (UNSC, 2006, p. 7). With the two latest UNSCRs on women, peace, and security including specific wording related to small arms, this linkage may be more strongly reflected in future UN action and reporting on implementation.

Monitoring, evaluation, and indicators

A common critique of the UNSCRs on women, peace, and security is that they lack accountability mechanisms to incentivize and monitor states' implementation. UNSCR 1325 does not include any mechanisms aside from reporting by the UN Secretary-General (Bastick and de Torres, 2010, p. 3). UNSCR 1889 goes a step further by requesting the UN Secretary-General to develop a set of global indicators to track the implementation of UNSCR 1325, which could serve as a common basis for reporting by United Nations entities, other international and regional organizations, and member states (UNSC, 2009, para. 17).

In his 2010 report, the UN Secretary-General presents the indicators developed by the Technical Working Group on Global Indicators for Resolution 1325. In total, 26 indicators were developed and arranged under the headings of prevention, participation, protection, and relief and recovery. Under the category of protection, indicator 17 clearly demonstrates that, even though it continues to be a heatedly debated topic, it is now increasingly possible to address small arms in the context of the international women, peace, and security agenda. The indicator—the existence of national mechanisms for the control of small arms and light weapons—seeks to track the presence and gender sensitivity of mechanisms and structures to regulate small arms. The indicator can be measured using data on the existence of a national coordination agency on small arms and the number and type of small arms available per 10,000 population (UNSC, 2010, p. 8).

As of late November 2013, these indicators had not yet been reported upon. However, they have the potential to provide a global monitoring framework that clearly links UNSCR 1325 and small arms. A civil society initiative to develop and monitor indicators on women, peace, and security has not included a specific indicator on small arms, despite mentioning women, small arms, and the ATT in the section linking UNSCR 1325 to key policy debates (GNWP, 2012).

Finally, at the institutional level, the *UN Strategic Results Framework on Women, Peace, and Security: 2011–2020* includes outputs and targets designed to assess implementation in 2015 and 2020 (UN, 2011). Out of 22 outputs listed, two specifically mention small arms or disarmament. Output 3.2.1 is for the UN to provide support and capacity to strengthen gender-responsive mechanisms for the control of small arms. The target for 2014 is that 75 per cent of UN-sponsored and -led disarmament and arms control programmes mainstream gender throughout programme design and delivery (for 2020, the target is 100 per cent). Output 1.1.3 is that UN-supported disarmament, non-proliferation arms control, and armed violence prevention and reduction activities include consultation and active involvement of women's leaders and groups. The targets for 2014 and 2020 are inclusive and effective consultation and involvement of women leaders and groups in 50 per cent and 75 per cent, respectively, of UN-supported disarmament activities. If implemented, these targets would link up small arms with the women, peace, and security agenda at the levels of state and UN implementation.

CEDAW and the Beijing Declaration and Platform for Action

The 1979 Convention on the Elimination of All Forms of Discrimination against Women and the 1995 Beijing Declaration and PfA form the backbone of the international policy agenda on women, peace, and security. They established the conceptual basis for this agenda, with both policies and their reporting processes addressing women, peace, and security, including making the link to small arms. Furthermore, CEDAW and the Beijing Declaration and PfA both have regular and comprehensive reporting mechanisms. It is curious that, considering their relevance to women, peace, and security, these policies are often sidelined in discussions on this agenda.

The CEDAW Committee underscored the gender dimensions of the arms trade during the ATT negotiations.

As of 1 November 2013, 187 states were parties to CEDAW, a legally binding instrument that requires states to adopt appropriate legislation and other measures to prohibit discrimination against women and to establish legal protection for the equal rights of women. States parties to CEDAW are required to report regularly on the progress of their implementation to the UN CEDAW Committee. During the course of the negotiations on the ATT, the CEDAW Committee actively underscored the gender dimensions of the arms trade—and its links to conflict-related sexual violence, domestic violence, and violence against protestors or actors in resistance movements (CEDAW Committee, 2012). Committee members have pointed out that small arms must be regulated if states are to prevent forms of violence such as domestic violence and sexual violence, as required under Article 2, and to ensure women's participation in public life, as required under Article 7 (Patten, 2012, pp. 4–5).

Accordingly, in some of its recent concluding observations on state reports, the CEDAW Committee has urged governments to better regulate small arms. For example, in its March 2013 concluding observations to the Government of Pakistan, the Committee expressed deep concern over the widespread illicit trade and sale of small arms and their use against women in the context of internal armed conflicts. It analysed this as a 'failure of the State party to comply with its due diligence obligation, under article 2 of the Convention, to prevent, investigate, prosecute and punish such acts of gender-based violence' and urged Pakistan to '[e]nact legislation strictly regulating the trade, sale and possession of small arms, and sanction violations thereof severely' (CEDAW Committee, 2013a, paras. 13, 14(d)). In its subsequent session, the CEDAW Committee voiced similar concerns about the impact of small arms on the security of women in the DRC, urging the government not only to regulate the arms trade effectively and control the circulation of illicit small arms, but also to consider ratifying the ATT (CEDAW Committee, 2013b, paras. 9(i), 10(h)).

In its October 2013 general recommendation on women in conflict prevention, conflict, and post-conflict situations, the CEDAW Committee states that arms control is necessary to prevent gender-based violence and calls for the ratification and implementation of the ATT (CEDAW Committee, 2013c, paras. 29, 33(e)). The CEDAW Committee's engagement with small arms regulation in this manner clearly demonstrates the applicability of international law obligations on discrimination and prevention of violence against women to small arms control.

The Beijing Declaration and PfA built upon the initial mandates of CEDAW and broadened the focus from non-discrimination to promoting the equal rights of women by establishing an agenda for women's empowerment. It was the outcome document of the UN-convened Fourth World Conference on Women, held in Beijing in 1995. It focuses on 12 critical areas, including armed conflict, and lists hundreds of actions to be taken by governments, financial and development institutions, and NGOs, including women's groups. Although it is not legally binding, UN member states report on their implementation of the Beijing Declaration and PfA every five years and NGOs often submit shadow reports. The CSW reviews the reports and issues official recommendations.

It was not a coincidence that initial discussions linking women, peace, and security to the UN Security Council took place in the Women and Armed Conflict Caucus of the CSW. The aim of this Caucus was to review the implementation of the Beijing PfA's chapter on women and armed conflict. The chapter contains specific wording linking women and disarmament, acknowledging that women's NGOs have called for a reduction in the international trade, trafficking, and proliferation of weapons. It also highlights that women living in poverty, particularly rural women, suffer because of the use of arms and that 'the negative impact on development of excessive military expenditures, the arms trade, and investment for arms production and acquisition must be addressed' (UN, 1995, art. 138). This description is followed up with strategic objective E.2: 'Reduce excessive military expenditures and control the availability of armaments.' In order to meet this objective, governments are tasked with appropriately reducing excessive military expenditure, including trade in arms, as well as combating illicit arms trafficking (art. 143). At a more general level, the critical area on women and armed conflict also highlights women's under-representation in peace and security decision-making and calls for their full involvement in all efforts for the prevention and resolution of conflicts (art. 134).

> International law obligations on the prevention of violence against women are applicable to small arms control.

Unlike the text of the first six UNSCRs on women, peace, and security, the Beijing Declaration and PfA explicitly link the arms trade to armed violence and outline how women are both victims of armed violence and actors for arms control and disarmament. The UNSCRs on women, peace, and security have clearly drawn both content and language from CEDAW and the Beijing Declaration and PfA, but in many ways they have depoliticized the message. Critical engagement on the issues of poverty, terrorism, occupation, and disarmament are essential parts of the discussion on women and armed conflict in the Beijing Declaration and PfA but remain largely absent from the UNSCRs on women, peace, and security. The international agenda on women, peace, and security will need to reclaim CEDAW and the Beijing Declaration and PfA to address women and small arms comprehensively.

NATIONAL IMPLEMENTATION OF THE INTERNATIONAL POLICY FRAMEWORK ON WOMEN, PEACE, AND SECURITY AND SMALL ARMS

Control of small arms, while guided by international and regional norms, actually occurs at the national and sub-national level through domestic legislation, regulations, and practice. Accordingly, many of the policy objectives and obligations embodied in the UNSCRs on women, peace, and security require national-level action to be realized. This section outlines, first, how states have implemented the international women, peace, and security agenda through national and regional action plans. It then examines the manner in which small arms have been addressed in 1325 NAPs, with short case studies on the Philippines and Senegal. The section then offers a more limited examination of how women, peace, and security issues are addressed in national action plans on small arms, highlighting some of the shortcomings in the plans reviewed.

1325 national action plans

As previously mentioned, UNSCR 1325 and the following women, peace, and security resolutions primarily address the UN system. They do nonetheless urge UN member states to take action in a number of areas. In 2002, both the UN Secretary-General and the Security Council encouraged member states to develop action plans with goals and timetables to implement certain aspects of UNSCR 1325 (UNSC, 2002a, action 15; 2002b). By 2005, this had crystallized into a call for all UN member states to develop a national action plan (1325 NAP) or other national-level strategies to ensure implementation of UNSCR 1325 (UNSC, 2005). Since 2006, the CEDAW Committee has also consistently referred to UNSCR 1325 in its concluding observations on states' reports, and has at times urged states to develop a 1325 NAP.[3]

Although the uptake was initially slow, as of November 2013 43 of 193 states had adopted a 1325 NAP (PeaceWomen, n.d.; see Table 2.2). In some cases these plans also address subsequent resolutions, for example UNSCR 1820 on sexual violence in conflict. The first 1325 NAPs were adopted by European donor states and aimed to guide development assistance in addressing the needs and promoting the participation of women in conflict-affected states. Since 2007, a number of conflict-affected states have also adopted 1325 NAPs. While most of the states with 1325 NAPs are in Europe, North America, and Africa, the group comprises a mix of donor/developed, post-conflict, developing, and transitional states. Nepal and the Philippines are the only Asian countries with 1325 NAPs, and Chile is the only South American country.

A number of regional and sub-regional organizations have also developed policies to facilitate the implementation of UNSCR 1325 at the regional and national levels. These include the regional action plan of the Economic Community of West African States (ECOWAS), strategies and indicators of the European Union, regional action plans for the Great Lakes and the Pacific, and the regional strategy on women and peace and security of the League of Arab States.

Table 2.2 States with 1325 NAPs*

Year adopted	Country (year revised)
2005	Denmark (2008)
2006	Norway (2011)
	Sweden (2009)
	United Kingdom (2010, 2012)
2007	Austria (2012)
	Côte d'Ivoire
	Netherlands (2011)
	Spain
	Switzerland (2010)
2008	Finland (2012)
	Iceland (2013)
	Uganda
2009	Belgium
	Chile
	Guinea
	Liberia
	Portugal
2010	Bosnia and Herzegovina
	Canada
	DRC
	Estonia
	France
	Italy
	Philippines
	Rwanda
	Serbia
	Sierra Leone
2011	Burundi
	Croatia
	Georgia
	Guinea-Bissau
	Ireland
	Lithuania
	Nepal
	Senegal
	Slovenia
	United States
2012	Australia
	Germany
	Ghana
2013	Kyrgyzstan
	Macedonia
	Nigeria

Note: * As of January 2014.
Source: Global Gender Program (n.d.)

Not only can 1325 NAPs be a useful tool for translating the specific obligations of UNSCR 1325 into coherent policy and strategic responses, but they can also help civil society to hold their governments accountable. A 1325 NAP aims to build awareness and ownership of women, peace, and security commitments among different national actors, and to strengthen coordination, accountability, and monitoring and evaluation of a government's activities regarding women, peace, and security. While they generally address the prevention of gender-based violence and the need for an increased representation of women in decision-making, the NAPs vary as to whether and how they address such issues as the inclusion of local women in peace processes, DDR, security sector reform, and small arms (Gumru and Fritz, 2009, p. 218).

States have engaged with UNSCR 1325 as emblematic of a range of aspirations and commitments related to gender, women's empowerment, and security, often going beyond the specific UN member state obligations set out in the UNSCRs in their 1325 NAP. In almost all countries with a 1325 NAP, there has been active civil society participation in its development and monitoring.

As with other gender policies, in many countries 1325 NAP implementation is weak. This is often due to a combination of a lack of institutional buy-in, a lack of accountability mechanisms and monitoring and evaluation frameworks, and inadequate budgetary allocation (GNWP, 2013a, pp. 2–4). As of October 2012, only seven countries had published dedicated budgets to meet their women, peace, and security commitments (UNSC, 2012, para. 6).

The 1325 NAPs recognize the link between women or gender and small arms issues.

Nonetheless, in a number of countries, adopting a 1325 NAP has led to concrete, positive outcomes. In Nepal, for instance, the 1325 NAP has facilitated the allocation of specific budgetary resources for women, peace, and security activities; partnership between government, civil society, and other development partners; an increased emphasis by the police and military on implementation of obligations under UNSCR 1325; and the setting of quotas for women's participation (GNWP, 2013b). In the Philippines, the 1325 NAP has helped women to gain access to peace processes (GNWP, 2013a, p. 2).

1325 NAPs and small arms

Despite the absence of direct reference to small arms in UNSCR 1325, one-quarter of the 1325 NAPs recognize the link between women or gender and small arms issues (see Table 2.3). Issues highlighted include the likelihood that women and girls are affected by small arms violence, and the importance of involving women in the control of small arms. With the exception of Liberia, the Philippines, Senegal, and Uganda, however, current 1325 NAPs do not actually commit to any action to enact or support small arms regulation, or they do so in a vague way that is difficult to measure. Nor do any of the 1325 NAPs refer to the need for arms regulation itself to be gender-responsive, for instance through provisions to prevent the threat or use of small arms in domestic violence (see Box 2.2). Based on a review of the 43 1325 NAPs, Table 2.3 cites references to small arms issues, aside from those related to DDR.[4]

Has the mention of small arms in 1325 NAPs made a difference in lawmaking, community education mechanisms, or disarmament programming? Since many of the 1325 NAPs have only recently been adopted and because their implementation has been poorly monitored, it is not possible to draw any generalizable conclusions. Instead, implementation of the small arms commitments in the 1325 NAPs of the Philippines and Senegal are examined below. These countries are chosen because: 1) their 1325 NAPs contain detailed provisions on small arms; and 2) since adopting their NAPs, these countries have developed gun control laws. This allows for an examination of what impact the linking of the women, peace, and security and the small arms agendas in national policy has had.

Table 2.3 1325 NAPs that refer to 'arms control', 'firearms', 'small arms', or 'weapons'

Country	Year adopted	Relevant text
Australia	2012	Australia also supports [. . .] international work on matters that link closely with the Women, Peace and Security agenda. This includes work on [. . .] small arms control (Australia, 2012, p. 10). Through its engagement in multilateral disarmament conventions, Australia raises the profile of gender issues and works for the inclusion of women in relevant processes around conventional weapons control. For example, Australia highlights the importance of involving women in the control of small arms and light weapons due to their specific impact on women and girls in conflict situations (p. 40).
Belgium	2009	Belgium pays attention to the specific position of women and children in the context of illicit trade in small arms and light weapons, since women and children frequently are the first victims of violence committed with these weapons. Belgium supports the 2001 UN Action plan on the fight against the illicit trade in small arms and light weapons and promotes the proposal of an international treaty on the arms trade. Such a treaty should contain proper criteria for the export of arms, avoiding that arms could be exported to countries marked by conflicts, internal instability or the non-respect of human rights (Belgium, 2009, p. 13).
Denmark	2008	Denmark will, through the Ministry of Foreign Affairs strive to: [. . .] Support the role of female leaders in community training and education on weapons, demobilisation and responsibility (Denmark, 2008, p. 26).
Germany	2012	The Federal Government is working toward integrating a gender perspective into international efforts to curb the proliferation of small arms. Following the end of a conflict, small arms often remain available and affordable and increase the risk of both domestic and sexual violence. The Federal Government makes sure that its project work to combat illegal small arms also takes in consideration gender-specific issues, and in particular secures the involvement of women in the control of small arms. Germany heads the 'Group of Interested States in Practical Disarmament Measures' (GIS). This group provides a forum for exchange through project work and political measures, with the aim of supporting implementation of the United Nations' Programme of Action on Small Arms and Light Weapons, which regularly deals with gender-specific issues. The Federal Government examines projects dealing with the control of small arms with regard to their gender-based relevance, thereby underlining the significance of this aspect (Germany, 2012, p. 14).
Ireland	2011	Ireland is involved in a range of [. . .] small arms and light weapons (SALW) risk education [. . .] initiatives (Ireland, 2011, p. 12).
Liberia	2009	*Strategic Issues:* Government promotes women's full participation in all conflict prevention, peace building and post-conflict recovery processes at community, county, national and sub-regional levels. [. . .] *Outputs:* [. . .] Trained women living close to border areas better able to identify and address [. . .] small arms issues. *Indicator:* [. . .] Reduced reporting of [. . .] small arms incidents (Liberia, 2009, pp. 31-32, 35).
Norway	2006	Where Norway is involved in security sector reform and arms control measures, the difference between women and men in terms of vulnerability must be taken into consideration (Norway, 2006, p. 15).
	2011	Norway will also seek to ensure that the gender perspective is taken into account in humanitarian disarmament and efforts against armed violence, for example in connection with the clearance of unexploded ordnance and support to victims. We will also support efforts that highlight how the living conditions of women and girls are affected by easy access to weapons and widespread armed violence. This will entail strengthening the implementation of SCR 1325 and women's participation in processes relating to disarmament and control of conventional weapons.

▶

Country	Year adopted	Relevant text
		Priority area 3 Post-conflict situations and peacebuilding Norway will seek to increase the participation of women in peacebuilding and post-conflict situations, and to strengthen the gender perspective in reconstruction processes. *Goals:* Local women participate in decision-making processes in post-conflict situations and peacebuilding efforts *Activities:* [. . .] Help to strengthen the integration of SCR 1325 into processes relating to disarmament and control of conventional weapons, including clearance of unexploded ordnance and assistance to victims *Timeframe:* 2011-13 *Ministry:* MFA (Norway, 2011, pp. 14-16).
Philippines	2010	*Action point:* Develop, enact and implement policies that ensure protection and security for women affected by armed conflict, especially IP [indigenous] and Moro women; *Result statement:* The enactment of policies (including legislation) that protect the security of women in conflict situations, especially IP and Moro women; *Indicators:* [. . .] Adoption of mechanisms to regulate the transfer and use of the tools of violence in armed conflict, particularly small arms and light weapons; *Target period of completion:* 2011 (Philippines, 2010, pp. 5-6).
Portugal	2009	Portugal interprets resolution 1325 in a comprehensive manner, which includes [. . .] internal promotion of the coherence and implementation of national policies of disarmament and control of light weapons, of public safety, and of the fight against gender-based violence in defence of human rights, including those of women, young women, and girls (Portugal, 2009, p. 5; DCAF translation from the Portuguese).
Senegal	2011	*Objective 12:* Implementation of operational structures and mechanisms to strengthen the physical security and the protection of women and girls. *Actions:* Analyse the phenomenon of small arms and light weapons trafficking. Strengthen the mechanisms to control the flow of small arms and light weapons. The type and quantity of small arms and light weapons. *Indicators:* National mechanisms for the control of small arms and light weapons. The national mechanisms for the control of small arms and light weapons will be evaluated on the basis of the following elements: the presence of a national coordination structure for the control of small arms; [and] the number and type of small arms per 10,000 inhabitants. [. . .] *Actors:* Ministry of the Armed Forces; Mouvement contre les Armes Légères en Afrique de l'Ouest/Senegal (MALAO); National coordination cell of the Armed Forces on the control of small arms and light weapons; the Committee to Combat Violence Against Women, etc. (Senegal, 2011, pp. 36-37; DCAF translation from the French).
Serbia	2010	Systematic measures are not yet in place that would help eradicate violence against women, overcome gender stereotypes, limit the use of firearms and solve other problems posing a threat to peace and security (Serbia, 2010, p. 54).
Uganda	2008	[T]he situation in the Great Lakes Region (GLR) is very complex and greatly exacerbated by the proliferation of small arms and light weapons (Uganda, 2008, p. 9). The conflicts in Uganda have among other factors been caused by: [. . .] The misuse of the gun, which has caused insecurity, impunity of armed forces, human rights abuse, criminalisation, proliferation of small arms (pp. 14-15). [. . .] Uganda is also signatory to: [. . .] the Bamako Declaration on an African Common Position on Illicit Proliferation, Circulation and Trafficking on Small Arms and Light Weapons (2000); the Nairobi Protocol for the Prevention, Control and Reduction of Small Arms and Light Weapons (pp. 19-20). *Strategic Objective:* Build community and institutional capacity to ensure the elimination of [gender-based violence] in society [. . .] *Result Indicator:* [. . .] Regional mechanisms in place to combat the problem of arms trafficking and illegal acquisition of arms (pp. 65, 70).

Women hold signs that refer to Sepur Zarco, a military base where sexual slavery took place during the country's conflict, during a demonstration for the International Day for the Elimination of Violence Against Women, Guatemala City, November 2012. © Johan Ordonez/AFP Photo

Box 2.2 Targeting domestic violence in small arms regulation

Domestic violence prevention and response is part of the women, peace, and security discourse, even if not explicitly mentioned in the UNSCRs. A number of 1325 NAPs include activities directed at domestic violence.

Women have for many years underscored the use of legal and illegal guns in domestic violence—be it in intimidation, injury, or murder. In 2009, IANSA launched a global campaign entitled 'Disarm Domestic Violence' to lobby for laws to prevent perpetrators of domestic violence from accessing guns. Firearm laws can take account of domestic violence in a variety of ways, such as by:

- prohibiting an individual subject to a domestic violence restraining order or with a domestic violence conviction from purchasing or possessing a firearm;
- empowering police to remove firearms from the home when responding to a domestic violence incident;
- empowering courts to require perpetrators of domestic violence to surrender their firearms;
- requiring current and former spouses to be questioned and/or notified before a gun licence is issued;
- requiring background checks to be conducted before any gun sale; and
- requiring safe storage and separation of guns and ammunition (Frattaroli, 2009, p. 9; BCPR, 2008, p. 27).

Where such reforms have been adopted, for example in Australia, Canada, some of the United States, and South Africa, gun homicide rates for women have dropped dramatically (AI, IANSA, and Oxfam International, 2005, p. 14; Abrahams et al., 2012, p. 3).

Implementation of 1325 NAP small arms commitments in the Philippines

Amnesty International Philippines finds that almost 60 per cent of documented human rights violations over the past decade involved the use of small arms and light weapons, with the Philippines ranked tenth in the number of deaths caused by gun homicides in the world (AI, 2012a). The Small Arms Survey has estimated privately owned firearms holdings in the country at 5.3 million (Small Arms Survey, 2002, p. 99).

A number of women's CSOs lobbied vigorously for their government to support the ATT and argued for small arms issues to be included in the 1325 NAP (Galace, 2010). CSO consultations with communities underscored the importance of reducing small arms proliferation to protect women from sexual, domestic, and other gender-based violence. On this basis, civil society proposed a separate action point in the 1325 NAP for the creation and enforcement of laws regulating the possession of small arms, with the following indicators:

- research on women victims of gun violence is undertaken and publicized;
- training on women's human rights is added as a requirement before a licence or renewal of licence is issued to gun owners, manufacturers, or distributors;
- guns surrendered by rebel returnees are destroyed and not recirculated; and
- the firearms registration system is improved.

The government agency responsible for implementing the 1325 NAP argued that the language on small arms was not germane to a 1325 NAP and proposed its deletion. The compromise reached was that small arms regulation is not a separate action point, but an indicator—'Adoption of mechanisms to regulate the transfer and use of the tools of violence in armed conflict, particularly small arms and light weapons'—under a more general action point, namely 'Develop, enact and implement policies that ensure protection and security for women affected by armed conflict, especially IP [indigenous] and Moro women' (Philippines, 2010, pp. 5–6). While the indicator is not as gender-responsive as had been hoped, women's civil society did achieve a concrete commitment by the government to adopt mechanisms to regulate the transfer and use of small arms.

In May 2013, the Comprehensive Firearms and Ammunition Regulation Act was signed into law. Firearms licences may only be granted to applicants who have not been convicted of any crime involving 'moral turpitude'; have passed a psychiatric test; and have not been convicted and are not accused in a pending criminal case for a crime punishable with a penalty of more than two years (Calica, 2013). While these requirements might help deny a licence to a person with a conviction for domestic violence, there are no explicit provisions in this regard in the Act. Representatives of women's CSOs have regretted that civil society was not consulted in developing the law, commenting that 'those who developed the legislation were not aware that it was mandated under the 1325 NAP' and that the 1325 NAP did not help women to gain access to the process.[5]

The 1325 NAP did not help Filipino women to gain access to the firearms legislation process.

In August 2013, police invited three civil society representatives, along with gun owners' associations, to participate in a stakeholders hearing and consultation meeting on the Act's implementing rules and regulations. This was an opportunity for women to make comments and suggestions regarding the standards of individuals who conduct the neuro-psychiatric and drug tests to meet the licensing requirements; the number of sectors and occupations exempted from needing a permit to carry a gun; and the lack of criteria provided for who can be given a licence to possess multiple firearms. Women civil society representatives also suggested that an applicant's prior history of domestic violence, including incident reports and protection orders, be considered when issuing a licence to further protect women from violence involving firearms at the hand of their partners (WE Act 1325, 2013). As of September 2013, these implementing rules and regulations were reportedly ready to be submitted to the chief of the Philippine National Police for approval (Suerte Felipe, 2013); however, the CSO representatives had not received any response to their proposed amendments. Women's CSOs envision lobbying for amendment of the law; they continue to use the 1325 NAP to lobby for a voice in small arms policy.[6]

Implementation of 1325 NAP small arms commitments in Senegal

The Small Arms Survey estimates that there are some 230,000 civilian-held firearms in Senegal (Small Arms Survey, 2007, ch. 2, annexe 4). Senegalese CSOs have for many years drawn on the normative strength of UNSCR 1325 to engage women in arms control. Le Mouvement contre les Armes Légères en Afrique de l'Ouest (MALAO), for example, has led awareness-raising programmes for women in communities in the conflicted Casamance region of Senegal, helping them to develop strategies and identify incentives to convince people to hand over their weapons, and training them on weapons safety and collection. Likewise, Senegalese women's CSOs have lobbied for ratification of the ECOWAS Convention on small arms and the ATT (Panapress, 2008).

Gun control CSOs participated in the process of developing Senegal's 1325 NAP, which was adopted in 2011. The 1325 NAP makes clear commitments to address small arms, calling for analysis of the phenomenon of arms trafficking and strengthening the mechanisms to control arms flows. In December 2011 the National Commission against the Proliferation and Illicit Circulation of Small Arms and Light Weapons (which includes CSOs as members) adopted a national action plan on small arms and light weapons. State authorities have validated the small arms NAP and the

Ministry of the Armed Forces is charged with mobilizing the resources for its implementation (Bathily, Keita, and Labou, 2012, p. 15). Unfortunately, the plan has not been publicly distributed so it is not possible to assess whether the 1325 NAP is reflected in the contents. Senegal also signed the ATT in April 2013.

Addressing the need for analysis identified in the 1325 NAP, MALAO published a study on arms trafficking in Senegal in December 2012. The study underlines the related human costs, including rape and domestic violence, and identifies inadequate enforcement of existing laws and their lack of harmonization with the ECOWAS Convention as key problems. Relevant authorities are also collaborating with CSOs to construct a database of information on violence and firearms from police, hospitals, and the judicial system.

With regard to control mechanisms, the National Commission has been undertaking a review of the legal framework on firearm ownership, and new legislation is expected by the end of 2013. This includes at least two provisions that address concerns about firearms being used in domestic violence. First, an investigation that includes seeking the opinion of the applicant's partner (man or woman), if applicable, must be carried out before an applicant may be granted a firearms permit. Second, no person who has been accused of or prosecuted for acts of domestic violence may be granted a permit. These provisions were introduced into the law upon the insistence of CSOs, including women's groups.[7] Although some CSOs are frustrated by the slow pace of implementation of the 1325 NAP commitments, it does appear that in Senegal recognition of small arms issues in the 1325 NAP has helped to drive action to address gender issues in firearm regulation.

> **New Senegalese legislation is to include provisions that address the use of firearms in domestic violence.**

Small arms NAPs and gender

National plans of action on small arms are not the focus of this chapter, and a comprehensive review of all existing plans has not been undertaken. However, it is notable that some small arms NAPs have made specific reference to the use of arms in violence against women, the differing perspectives of men and women on arms, and the potential for women to be actors in small arms policy.

In Kenya, CSOs working on women's issues were consulted in the development of the small arms NAP. The plan suggests that awareness raising programmes should take into account the different perceptions of men and women. In Uganda, the Ministry of Gender was involved in developing the small arms NAP. The preparatory population surveys in Kenya and Uganda, both of which attempted to be representative in terms of gender and other characteristics, collected sex-disaggregated data (Kenya, 2006; Uganda, 2007). Kosovo's 2010–12 small arms NAP includes as one of its nine key objectives: 'Promote participation of women (civil society and other groups) in development and implementing of [small arms and light weapons] control policies, violence prevention and disarmament strategies' (Kosovo, 2009, p. 9). In all three cases, however, neither involving women nor collecting sex-disaggregated data is included in the actual programme of activities and associated indicators that constitute the action plan.

The DRC's small arms NAP for 2012–16 acknowledges that small arms are misused in rape, attempted rape, and domestic violence. Its recommendations call for civilian disarmament programmes that take into account the differing perceptions of men and women and their varying levels of trust in institutions; they also urge community women to be engaged in educating the public about the NAP (DRC, 2011, pp. 31, 49, 51). However, again, none of these gender-responsive recommendations is included in the actual log frame of activities and indicators to implement the NAP. A representative of a women's CSO stated in 2011 that 'there is no gender perspective' in DRC's National Commission to fight small arms and light weapons (WILPF, 2011, p. 9).

Experience has shown that, when gender commitments such as those above are not made measureable through the use of indicators, are not monitored, and are not anyone's specific responsibility, they are rarely implemented. In the context of a small arms NAP, moreover, it may be of particular concern that few of the officials responsible for its monitoring and implementation are likely to be gender experts or adept at using indicators in a gender-responsive manner. Box 2.3 suggests ways in which a small arms NAP could ensure that commitments embedded within the international women, peace, and security agenda are concretely incorporated.

THE INTERNATIONAL POLICY FRAMEWORK ON SMALL ARMS: MAKING THE LINKS

In 2012–13, the UN Security Council and UN member states finally recognized that binding commitments are needed to ensure that

> **Box 2.3 Ways to address women, peace, and security issues in a small arms NAP**
>
> - Involve women's CSOs, survivors of armed violence, experts on gender and small arms, and the government ministry responsible for women and/or gender in the process of developing the small arms NAP.
> - Explicitly acknowledge international commitments under the UNSCRs on women, peace, and security, CEDAW, and the Beijing Declaration and PfA, as well as national legislation and policy related to gender and women.
> - Require that all research and data collection in relation to small arms and the implementation of the small arms NAP be sex- and age-disaggregated.
> - Identify concrete activities to reduce the use of arms in domestic and sexual violence against women, girls, men, and boys. Include indicators such as: 1) the percentage of domestic homicides and injuries involving arms; and 2) the level of armed violence against women, girls, men, and boys.
> - Specify that community education initiatives must address women, girls, men, and boys and target their different perceptions of small arms.
> - Identify women's CSOs, female elders, and community women (as appropriate) as potential partners for disarmament and education activities.
> - Commit to developing and implementing a process to assess the risk that any arms exports might be used to commit or facilitate serious acts of gender-based violence or serious acts of violence against men, women, girls, or boys (see the section on the ATT).

small arms controls address the particular needs and roles of women. This recognition took hold largely because of the energy and commitment of networks of national and international women's organizations in lobbying for the PoA and the ATT to address gender-based violence. Their work also influenced the CEDAW Committee, discussed above, the UN Secretary-General, and the Security Council. The Security Council adopted the first UNSCR on small arms that refers to women in September 2013.

The UN Programme of Action

The PoA, adopted by UN member states in 2001, acknowledges the negative impact of the illicit trade in small arms on children, women, and the elderly (UN, 2001, preambular para. 6). Perhaps to counter the portrayal of women as 'hapless victims, rather than as key resources in combating armed violence' (Dehesa and Masters, 2010, p. 4), for the first PoA Review Conference in 2006, the UN Coordinating Action on Small Arms issued 'guidelines for gender mainstreaming for the effective implementation of the PoA' that drew upon the experiences of CSOs in the Caribbean, Latin America, South Asia, and elsewhere. These guidelines were updated for the PoA's 4th Biennial Meeting of States in 2010 with the support of IANSA, producing a comprehensive document that clearly links implementation of the PoA with the women, peace, and security agenda in relation to arms trafficking, DDR, national and regional structures, and the involvement of civil society (UNODA and IANSA, 2010). But the template for states to report on their implementation of the PoA, issued around the same time, does not facilitate reporting on how these linkages are made in national legislation.

An elderly woman crosses paths with a member of the Special Police
Operations Battalion during a search for firearms and drugs in the
favela of Cantagalo, Rio de Janeiro, December 2009.
© Spencer Platt/Getty Images

IANSA and other NGOs continued to lobby for the small arms and women, peace, and security agendas to be better integrated, including at the 2012 PoA Review Conference. Progress was finally achieved in the Review Conference's Declaration, which underscores the need to involve women in efforts to combat illicit trade in small arms, and the 2012–18 implementation plan for the PoA, in which states undertake to:

> facilitate the participation and representation of women in small arms policymaking [. . .] and to explore means to eliminate the negative impact of the illicit trade in small arms and light weapons on women (UNGA, 2012a, para. II.2.i).[8]

The Arms Trade Treaty and gender

On 2 April 2013, the General Assembly adopted the text of the ATT. During the preceding decade, a range of CSOs had campaigned together as 'Control Arms' for a robust and effective ATT. Women's groups and organizations were an important part of this campaign, notably as part of the IANSA Women's Network, and lobbied for the ATT to include binding measures to prevent gender-based violence, and to ensure women's participation in the implementation of the treaty.[9] Masters describes as a key moment for NGOs, UN diplomats, and delegates alike the concurrence of the CSW and the first meeting of the Open-Ended Working Group on an ATT, in March 2009. IANSA women organized a joint event with the UN Office for Disarmament Affairs that linked the themes of both meetings, helping to put women on the ATT's agenda.[10] Yet, despite sustained advocacy from women's groups throughout the ATT negotiations, inclusion of the term 'gender-based violence' proved controversial to the end. Several states took issue with the terms 'gender' and 'gender-based violence', arguing that they had no agreed legal definition.

The final text was cautiously welcomed by NGOs as the first treaty that recognizes the link between gender-based violence and the international arms trade. The ATT's preamble notes that civilians, 'particularly women and children',[11] account for the vast majority of those adversely affected by armed conflict and armed violence. The operative provisions require exporting states to assess the risk that the weapons being transferred could be used 'to commit or facilitate serious acts of gender-based violence or serious acts of violence against women and children' (UNGA, 2013a, art. 7(4)). States are to deny an arms export if there is an 'overriding risk of any of the negative consequences' listed in Article 7(1), including serious violations of international humanitarian and human rights law (UNGA, 2013a, art 7; ARMS TRADE TREATY). As many acts of gender-based violence constitute serious violations of international humanitarian law or human rights law, or undermine peace and security, they should be captured by this requirement to deny an export (Green et al., 2013, p. 553).

Generally, for the ATT to make a difference for women, states parties will need to develop robust processes by which to assess the risk that weapons could be used to commit or facilitate serious acts of gender-based violence or violence against women—and then act to deny arms export authorizations if such risks arise. Many questions remain as to how this risk assessment will be undertaken, who will do so, and how women and women's organizations will

An Iraqi man mourns the death of his wife who was killed following an attack, claimed by Al-Qaeda, on the Syrian Catholic Church, Baghdad, November 2010. © Ahmad Al-Rubaye/AFP Photo

be consulted (Dharmapuri, 2013). The development of guidelines for ATT implementation will thus need to involve experts on the treatment of gender-based violence in international law (Green et al., 2013, p. 559). While the ATT gathers the 50 ratifications it needs to enter into force, women's organizations and others have an opportunity to work on such issues in order to translate the ATT's important—yet still vague—protections against gender-based violence into tangible reality.

The UNSCR on small arms

Intense civil society lobbying for a gender-responsive ATT may have led the UN Secretary-General to emphasize women's experiences of armed conflict in his 2011 report to the Security Council on small arms (UNSC, 2011b). The Secretary-General's subsequent August 2013 report on small arms contains a section dedicated to sexual violence in conflict, reconfirming that 'an abundance of uncontrolled weapons and a context of lawlessness lead to increases in gender-based violence, which includes rape, abduction into sexual slavery and trafficking' (UNSC, 2013c, para. 20). The report encourages the Security Council's informal expert group on the protection of civilians to consider these linkages (paras. 19–23).

In September 2013 the Security Council adopted its first thematic resolution exclusively dedicated to small arms and light weapons.[12] The NGO Working Group on Women, Peace and Security (of which IANSA is now a member) lobbied to ensure that connections with women and gender were made and a number of the issues they raised were incorporated into UNSCR 2117 (NGOWG, 2013). The preamble of that resolution notes the disproportionate impact of small arms on violence perpetrated against women and girls, and that the presence of small arms exacerbates sexual and gender-based violence. The operative text urges states, UN entities, and (sub)regional organizations to do more to facilitate 'women's full and meaningful participation in all policymaking, planning, and implementation processes to combat and eradicate the illicit transfer, destabilizing accumulation and misuse' of small arms (UNSC, 2013e, para. 12). It repeats calls found in the UNSCRs on women, peace, and security for DDR to take into account the particular needs of women and children associated with armed forces and armed groups, to provide for such women's full access to DDR programmes, and for those planning DDR to consult with women's CSOs (para. 12).

However, the Security Council missed the opportunity, highlighted by the NGO Working Group on Women, Peace and Security, to specify that UN sanctions regimes and monitoring criteria should take account of gender considerations. Nonetheless, the recognition of the crucial contributions of women to small arms control is important and will be a further tool for women to leverage access to national and international processes.

CONCLUSION

This chapter introduces the international women, peace, and security agenda, grounded in UNSCR 1325, and maps its synergies with small arms control. Examination of women's experiences in conflict and post-conflict contexts reinforces the critical need for international policies and, more importantly, national-level initiatives to take into account the multiplicity of roles women, men, boys, and girls play in relation to small arms violence, use, and control. Even though CEDAW and the Beijing Declaration and PfA set a precedent for international policies on women to begin to address these issues, the first five UNSCRs on women, peace, and security make no reference to 'small arms', the 'arms trade', or 'weapons'. Despite this lacuna within the official text of these resolutions, the UN Secretary-General and CSOs have made clear arguments for why small arms control is relevant to the provisions focusing on the protection of civilians, participation of women, supporting local women's peace and security initiatives, and DDR.

A true convergence of the two agendas on a normative level only began in 2012, after many years of NGO activism. With respect to small arms, the outcome of the 2012 PoA Review Conference refers to women's participation and victimization, the 2013 ATT requires a risk assessment for gender-based violence prior to any export of arms, and the UNSCR of September 2013 emphasizes women's participation in combating the illicit transfer and misuse of small arms. In relation to women, peace, and security, the UNSCRs of June and October 2013 both contain language on the ATT; the latter includes an operative paragraph on ensuring women's participation in eradicating the illicit transfer and misuse of small arms. Also in 2013, the CEDAW Committee asked member states to enact small arms laws to prevent violence against women and their general recommendation on women in conflict prevention, conflict, and post-conflict situations calls for arms control to prevent gender-based violence. These are important but piecemeal achievements that could be the basis for progressive regional and national policies. They reinforce the ongoing work of NGOs to raise awareness of the impacts of small arms on men, women, girls, and boys—NGOs whose research, projects, and activism can support the development and implementation of such policies.

At the national level, progress in harmonizing policy concerning small arms control and women, peace, and security has so far been very limited. Just one-quarter of 1325 NAPs contain references to small arms, but rarely do they translate them into action. Even where action is mandated, as the development of the Philippines' new firearms legislation demonstrates, sustained focus by civil society is nonetheless needed to keep women on the small arms agenda. In a number of countries, however, domestic violence has been prioritized in the licensing of civilian small arms and other protocols, with some success.

Focusing on preventing domestic violence, removing arms from communities, and consulting with women's CSOs are proven ways in which small arms controls can be strengthened by a women, peace, and security perspective. Women's networks and organizations have been, and can continue to be, partners in policy and legislative development, in the monitoring of implementation, and in small arms reduction and education processes. Indeed, the UNSCRs on women, peace, and security—and now the UNSCR on small arms—call for women to be full participants in all aspects of small arms control. Now that the international policy framework linking small arms with women, peace, and security is growing in substance and visibility, concrete action and robust accountability are needed at the national and local levels to ensure implementation. ◼

LIST OF ABBREVIATIONS

1325 NAP	National action plan for the implementation of United Nations Security Council Resolution 1325
ATT	Arms Trade Treaty
CEDAW	United Nations Convention on the Elimination of All Forms of Discrimination against Women
CSO	Civil society organization
CSW	Commission on the Status of Women
DCAF	Geneva Centre for the Democratic Control of Armed Forces
DDR	Disarmament, demobilization, and reintegration
DRC	Democratic Republic of the Congo
ECOWAS	Economic Community of West African States
IANSA	International Action Network on Small Arms

MALAO	Mouvement contre les Armes Légères en Afrique de l'Ouest
NAP	National action plan
NGOs	Non-governmental organizations
PfA	Platform for Action
PoA	United Nations Programme of Action to Prevent, Combat and Eradicate the Illicit Trade in Small Arms and Light Weapons in All Its Aspects
UN Action	United Nations Action against Sexual Violence in Conflict
UNIFEM	United Nations Development Fund for Women
UNSCR	United Nations Security Council Resolution

ENDNOTES

1   See Otto (2009, pp. 11–12) and Appiagyei-Atua (2011).

2   This assertion is based on a review of the 'field updates' published on the UN Action website, the most recent of which covers to August 2010 (UN Action, n.d.a).

3   The Committee has urged states such as the Czech Republic, Germany, Lebanon, Myanmar, Serbia, and Timor-Leste to develop a 1325 NAP.

4   The intention of this discussion is to focus on how 1325 NAPs may contribute to the control of small arms. The references to DDR in 1325 NAPs primarily focus on women's access to DDR programmes, and particularly on ensuring that women who are not arms-bearers can access such programmes. Thus, DDR references have not been included.

5   Correspondence from Jasmin Nario-Galace, national coordinator, Women Engaged in Action on 1325 and Steering Committee, Philippine Action Network to Control Arms, 30 September 2013.

6   This section draws on correspondence from Jasmin Nario-Galace, national coordinator, Women Engaged in Action on 1325 and Steering Committee, Philippine Action Network to Control Arms, 30 September 2013.

7   This section draws upon a telephone interview with Georges Ndiaye, executive director, MALAO, 8 November 2013.

8   See also UNGA (2012a, para. I.14).

9   See, for example, IANSA (2009) and AI (2012b).

10   Correspondence from Sarah Masters, former coordinator of the IANSA Women's Network, 17 October 2013.

11   The phrase 'women and children' is used here as this is the language in the text of the ATT. Placing women and children in the same category has been criticized as both incorrect, since women and children have different legal statuses, and discriminatory, since it infantilizes women by equating their experiences, needs, and capacities with those of children. See IANSA (2011).

12   In 2003, the Security Council had adopted a declaration on 'Proliferation of Small Arms and Light Weapons and Mercenary Activities: Threat to Peace and Security in West Africa', which makes no reference to gender, women, or UNSCR 1325 (UNSC, 2003).

BIBLIOGRAPHY

Abrahams, Naeemah, et al. 2012. *Every Eight Hours: Intimate Femicide in South Africa 10 Years Later!* Tygerberg: South African Medical Research Council.

AI (Amnesty International). 2012a. 'Amnesty International Philippines Calling for a Bulletproof Arms Trade Treaty on Its Quarterlife Anniversary.' 28 April.
  <http://www.amnesty.org.ph/news.php?item=news&id=231>

—. 2012b. *'If You Resist, We'll Shoot You': The Democratic Republic of the Congo and the Case for an Effective Arms Trade Treaty.* London: AI.
  <http://www.amnesty.org/en/library/asset/AFR62/007/2012/en/cdd8cdd9-913f-4dc5-8418-71d2eedbdde0/afr620072012en.pdf>

—, IANSA (International Action Network on Small Arms), and Oxfam International. 2005. *The Impact of Guns on Women's Lives.* Oxford: AI, IANSA, and Oxfam International.

Appiagyei-Atua, Kwadwo. 2011. 'United Nations Security Council Resolution 1325 on Women, Peace, and Security: Is It Binding?' *Human Rights Brief,* Vol. 18, Iss. 3, pp. 2–6.

Australia. 2012. Australian National Action Plan on Women, Peace and Security 2012–2018. Canberra: Department of Families, Housing, Community Services and Indigenous Affairs.
  <http://www.dss.gov.au/sites/default/files/documents/05_2012/aus_nap_on_women_2012_2018.pdf>

Bastick, Megan and Daniel de Torres. 2010. 'Implementing the Women, Peace and Security Resolutions in Security Sector Reform.' In Megan Bastick and Kristin Valasek, eds. *Gender and Security Sector Reform Toolkit.* Geneva: Geneva Centre for the Democratic Control of Armed Forces, Organization for Security and Co-operation in Europe Office for Democratic Institutions and Human Rights, United Nations International Research and Training Institute for the Advancement of Women.

Bathily, Abdoulaye Diop, Hawa Deb Diouf Keita and Salie Thiam Labou. 2012. *Problématique de la dissémination des armes légères et de petit calibre au Sénégal.* Dakar: Mouvement contre les Armes Légères en Afrique de l'Ouest.

BCPR (Bureau for Crisis Prevention and Recovery). 2008. *How to Guide: Small Arms and Light Weapons Legislation.* Geneva: United Nations Development Programme.

Belgium. 2009. *Women, Peace and Security: Belgian Action Plan on the Implementation of UN Security Council Resolution 1325.* Brussels: Federal Public Service Foreign Affairs, Foreign Trade and Development Cooperation. <http://www.peacewomen.org/assets/file/belgium_nap_2009.pdf>

Calica, Aurea. 2013. 'New Law Gets Strict on Gun Ownership.' *Philippine Star.* 2 June.

CEDAW Committee (Committee on the Elimination of Discrimination against Women). 2012. 'Statement of the Committee on the Elimination of Discrimination against Women on the Need for a Gender Perspective in the Text of the Arms Trade Treaty.' <http://www2.ohchr.org/english/bodies/cedaw/docs/statements/StatementGenderPerspective.pdf>

—. 2013a. *Concluding Observations on the Fourth Periodic Report of Pakistan, Adopted by the Committee at Its Fifty-fourth Session (11 February– 1 March 2013).* CEDAW/C/PAK/CO/4 of 27 March. New York: UN. <http://www.un.org/en/ga/search/view_doc.asp?symbol=CEDAW/C/PAK/CO/4>

—. 2013b. *Concluding Observations on the Combined Sixth and Seventh Periodic Reports of the Democratic Republic of the Congo.* CEDAW/C/COD/ CO/6-7 of 23 July. New York: UN. <http://www.un.org/en/ga/search/view_doc.asp?symbol=CEDAW/C/COD/CO/6-7>

—. 2013c. General Recommendation No. 30 on Women in Conflict Prevention, Conflict and Post-conflict Situations. CEDAW/C/GC/30 of 18 October. New York: UN. <http://www.ohchr.org/Documents/HRBodies/CEDAW/GComments/CEDAW.C.CG.30.pdf>

Cheikhomar, Ammar and Henry Austin. 2013. '"They Can't Succeed without Us": Women Take Front-line Role in Syria Conflict.' NBC News (New York). 23 June.

Cohn, Carol. 2007. *Mainstreaming Gender in UN Security Policy: A Path to Political Transformation?* Working Paper No. 204. Boston: The Consortium on Gender, Security and Human Rights.

Dehesa, Cynthia and Sarah Masters. 2010. *Joined-Up Thinking: International Measures for Women's Security and SALW Control.* Surrey, UK: IANSA Women's Network. <http://www.iansa-women.org/sites/default/files/newsviews/en_iansa_1325_anniversary_paper_2010_final.pdf>

Denmark. 2008. National Action Plan for Implementation of UN Security Council Resolution 1325 on Women, Peace and Security 2008–2013. Copenhagen: Ministry of Foreign Affairs. <http://www.peacewomen.org/assets/file/NationalActionPlans/nap_danish1325actionplan2008-2013_2010.pdf>

Dharmapuri, Sahana. 2013. 'New Political Will Links Women, Peace and Security Agenda to International Humanitarian Law.' *Global Observatory* (New York/Vienna). 23 April.

DRC (Democratic Republic of the Congo). 2011. *Plan d'action national de contrôle et de gestion des armes légères et de petit calibre en RDC, 2012–2016.* Kinshasa: Ministère de l'Intérieur et Sécurité de la République Démocratique du Congo. <http://www.reseau-rafal.org/sites/reseau-rafal.org/files/document/externes/Plan%20d'action%20national%20ALPC%202012-2016.pdf>

Drost, Nadja. 2011. 'To Win the War, Colombia Needs Female Fighters to Lay Down Their Arms.' *Global Post* (Boston). 1 June.

Dube, Joseph. 2010. 'Impact of Resolution 1325 on Small Arms: 10 Years Later.' *Arms Control: Africa,* Vol. 2, Iss. 5. November, p. 4.

Farr, Vanessa. 2006. 'Scared Half to Death: The Gendered Impacts of Prolific Small Arms.' *Contemporary Security Policy.* Vol. 27, No. 1, pp. 45–59.

—, Henri Myrttinen, and Albrecht Schnabel, eds.. 2009. *Sexed Pistols: The Gendered Impacts of Small Arms & Light Weapons.* Tokyo: United Nations University Press.

FEIM (Fundación para Estudio e Investigación de la Mujer) et al. 2011. 'Written Statement Submitted to CEDAW on the Occasion of the General Discussion on Women in Conflict and Post-Conflict Situations.' 18 July. <http://www.peacewomen.org/assets/file/PWandUN/CEDAW/2011/cedaw_gr_iansajointstatement_2011.pdf>

Feuerschütz, Susann. 2012. *Gender and Urban (In)Security in Fragile and Conflict-Affected States.* Ottowa: North–South Institute. December. <http://www.nsi-ins.ca/publications/gender-and-urban-insecurity-in-fragile-and-conflict-affected-states/>

Frattaroli, Shannon. 2009. *Removing Guns from Domestic Violence Offenders: An Analysis of State Level Policies to Prevent Future Abuse.* Baltimore: Johns Hopkins Center for Gun Policy and Research.

Freedom House. 2011. 'Countries at the Crossroads: Eritrea.' <http://www.freedomhouse.org/report/countries-crossroads/2011/eritrea>

Galace, Jasmin. 2010. '1325 and the Violent World of Small Arms.' Opendemocracy.net. <http://www.opendemocracy.net/5050/jasmin-galace/1325-and-violent-world-of-small-arms>

Geneva Declaration Secretariat. 2011. *Global Burden of Armed Violence 2011: Lethal Encounters.* Cambridge: Cambridge University Press. December.

Germany. 2012. Action Plan of the Government of the Federal Republic of Germany on the Implementation of United Nations Security Council Resolution 1325 for the Period 2013–2016. Berlin: Federal Government of Germany.
<http://www.peacewomen.org/assets/file/germany_nationalactionplan_dec2012.pdf>

Global Gender Program. n.d. National Action Plan chart. Washington, DC: Elliott School of International Affairs, George Washington University. Accessed 16 January 2014. <http://www.peacewomen.org/naps/>

GNWP (Global Network of Women Peacebuilders). 2012. Women Count—Security Council Resolution 1325: Civil Society Monitoring Report 2012.
<http://www.gnwp.org/wp-content/uploads/2010/02/Global_Monitoring_Report.pdf>

—. 2013a. 'Mavic Cabrera-Balleza's Presentation at the Panel "Resolution 1325 in Action: Lessons Learned and Reflections on 1325 NAPs."' 8 July.
<http://www.gnwp.org/wp-content/uploads/2010/02/Mavic-Cabrera-Ballezas-Presentation-at-the-NAP-1325-Panel-Discussion-with-Japan-Mission_July-8th-2013.pdf>

—. 2013b. 'Secretary Dharandhir Khatiwda's Presentation at the Panel "Resolution 1325 in Action: Lessons Learned and Reflections on 1325 NAPs."' 8 July. <http://www.gnwp.org/wp-content/uploads/2010/02/Secretary-Khatiwadas-Presentation-at-the-NAP-1325-Panel-Discussion-with-Japan-Mission_July-8th-2013.pdf>

Green, Caroline, et al. 2013. 'Gender-based Violence and the Arms Trade Treaty: Reflections from a Campaigning and Legal Perspective.' Gender & Development, Vol. 21, No. 3, pp. 551–62.

Gumru, F. Belgin and Jan Marie Fritz. 2009. 'Women, Peace and Security: An Analysis of the National Action Plans Developed in Response to UN Security Council Resolution 1325.' Societies without Borders, Vol. 4, No. 2, pp. 209–25.

IANSA (International Action Network on Small Arms). 2008. 'Women in the Crossfire: UN SCR 1325 and Small Arms.'
<http://www.iansa-women.org/sites/default/files/newsviews/en-1325-small-arms.pdf>

—. 2009. Women, Peace and Security: The Role of an ATT. <http://www.iansa-women.org/sites/default/files/en_iansa_wn_att_wps_2009_web.pdf>

—. 2011. Including Gender in the Arms Trade Treaty. IANSA Women's Network Policy Paper. Version 2. 13 July.
<http://www.iansa-women.org/sites/default/files/ATT_Precom_3_iansa_wn_pp_130711.pdf>

ICRC (International Committee of the Red Cross). 1999. Arms Availability and the Situation of Civilians in Armed Conflict. Geneva: ICRC.
<http://www.icrc.org/eng/assets/files/other/icrc_002_0734_arms_availability.pdf>

IRC (International Rescue Committee). 2012. Let Me Not Die before My Time: Domestic Violence in West Africa. New York: IRC.
<http://www.rescue.org/sites/default/files/resource-file/IRC_Report_DomVioWAfrica.pdf>

—. 2013. Syria: A Regional Crisis. New York: IRC Commission on Syrian Refugees. January.
<http://www.rescue.org/sites/default/files/resource-file/IRCReportMidEast20130114.pdf>

Ireland. 2011. National Action Plan for Implementation of UNSCR 1325, 2011–2014. Dublin: Department of Foreign Affairs and Trade.
<https://www.dfa.ie/media/dfa/alldfawebsitemedia/ourrolesandpolicies/int-priorities/National-Action-Plan-UNSCR-1325.pdf>

Kalitowski, Susanna. 2006. Survivors: Women Affected by Gun Violence Speak Out. London: International Action Network on Small Arms Women's Network. <http://www.seesac.org/res/files/failovi/215.pdf>

Kenya. 2006. National Action Plan for Arms Control and Management. Nairobi: Kenya National Focal Point on Small Arms and Light Weapons.
<http://www.isn.ethz.ch/Digital-Library/Publications/Detail/?ots591=0c54e3b3-1e9c-be1e-2c24-a6a8c7060233&lng=en&id=124869>

Kosovo. 2009. National Small Arms Light Weapons Control and Collection Strategy and Action Plan. Pristina: Government of Kosovo.
<http://www.mpb-ks.org/repository/docs/Strategjia%20per%20Kontroll%20dhe%20Grumbullim%20te%20Armve-English-Final.pdf>

Liberia. 2009. National Action Plan for the Implementation of United Nations Resolution 1325. Monrovia: Ministry of Gender and Development.
<http://www.un.org/womenwatch/ianwge/taskforces/wps/nap/LNAP_1325_final.pdf>

Masters, Sarah. 2010. 'UN Business: Women, Guns and Small Arms Control.' OpenDemocracy. 25 October.
<http://www.opendemocracy.net/5050/sarah-masters/un-business-women-guns-and-small-arms-control>

McWilliams, Monica. 1998. 'Violence against Women in Societies under Stress.' In Rebecca Emerson Dobash and Russell P. Dobash, eds. Rethinking Violence against Women. Thousand Oaks, CA: Sage Publications, pp. 111–40.

NGOWG (NGO Working Group on Women, Peace and Security). 2013. 'Monthly Action Points on Women, Peace and Security: September 2013.'
<http://womenpeacesecurity.org/media/pdf-MAP_September2013.pdf>

Norway. 2006. The Norwegian Government's Action Plan for the Implementation of UN Security Council Resolution 1325 (2000) on Women, Peace and Security. Oslo: Ministry of Foreign Affairs. <http://www.peacewomen.org/assets/file/NationalActionPlans/norway-nationalactionplan_march2006.pdf>

—. 2011. Women, Peace and Security: Norway's Strategic Plan 2011–13. Oslo: Ministry of Foreign Affairs.
<http://www.peacewomen.org/assets/file/NationalActionPlans/nor_updatednap_2011-13.pdf>

Onuoha, Freedom. 2013. 'Porous Borders and Boko Haram's Arms Smuggling Operations in Nigeria.' Al Jazeera Center for Studies. 8 September.

Otto, Dianne. 2009. 'The Exile of Inclusion: Reflections on Gender Issues in International Law Over the Last Decade.' Melbourne Journal of International Law, Vol. 10, Iss. 1, pp. 11–26.

Panapress. 2008. 'Les femmes du Sénégal se mobilisent contre les armes légères.' 28 April.
<http://www.panapress.com/Les-femmes-du-Senegal-se-mobilisent-contre-les-armes-legeres--12-677586-99-lang2-index.html>

Patten, Pramila. 2012. 'Women's Human Rights: The Arms Trade Treaty and CEDAW.' Paper presented at a panel discussion, International Alliance of Women. 20 July. <http://womenalliance.org/old/pdf/IAW%20Talking%20Point%20_%20The%20Arms%20Trade%20Treaty%20and%20CEDAW.pdf>

PeaceWomen. n.d. 'National Implementation.' Accessed November 2013. <http://peacewomen.org/naps/>

Philippines. 2010. National Action Plan on Women, Peace & Security. Manila: Office of the President. <http://www.opapp.gov.ph/sites/default/files/The%2520Philippine%2520National%2520Action%2520Plan%2520on%2520Women%252C%2520Peace%2520%2526%2520Security.pdf>

Portugal. 2009. Plano Nacional de Acção para implementação da Resolução CSNU 1325 (2000) sobre Mulheres, Paz e Segurança (2009–2013). <http://www.peacewomen.org/assets/file/NationalActionPlans/portugal_nationalactionplan_august_2009.pdf>

Schroeder, Emily, Vanessa Farr, and Albrecht Schnabel. 2005. *Gender Awareness in Research on Small Arms and Light Weapons: A Preliminary Report.* Working Paper No. 1. Bern: Swisspeace.

Senegal. 2011. Plan d'action national: mise en œuvre au Sénégal de la résolution 1325 (2000) du conseil de sécurité des nations unies. Dakar: Ministère du Genre et des Relations avec les Associations féminines Africaines et Etrangères. <http://www.peacewomen.org/assets/file/NationalActionPlans/senegal_nationalactionplan_may2011.pdf>

Serbia. 2010. National Action Plan for the Implementation of United Nations Security Council Resolution 1325: Women, Peace and Security in the Republic of Serbia (2010–2015). Belgrade: Ministry of Defence. <http://www.peacewomen.org/assets/file/NationalActionPlans/serbia_nap.pdf>

Small Arms Survey. 2002. *Small Arms Survey 2002: Counting the Human Cost.* Geneva: Small Arms Survey.

—. 2007. *Small Arms Survey 2007: Guns and the City.* Cambridge: Cambridge University Press.

Suerte Felipe, Cecille. 2013. 'Implementing Rules of New Gun Control Law Ready.' *Philippine Star.* 20 September.

Uganda. 2007. *Mapping the Small Arms Problems in Uganda: The Development of Uganda's National Action Plan on Small Arms and Light Weapons.* Kampala and Tshwane: Uganda National Focal Point on Small Arms and Light Weapons, Saferworld, SaferAfrica. <http://www.saferworld.org.uk/downloads/pubdocs/Uganda_Mapping.pdf>

—. 2008. Action Plan on UN Security Council Resolutions 1325 & 1820 and the Goma Declaration. Kampala: Ministry of Gender, Labour and Social Development. <http://www.peacewomen.org/assets/file/NationalActionPlans/uganda_nationalactionplan_december2008.pdf>

UN (United Nations). 1995. Beijing Declaration and Platform of Action. Adopted 15 September. A/CONF.177/20 and A/CONF.177/20/Add.1 of 27 October. <http://www.un.org/womenwatch/daw/beijing/pdf/BDPfA%20E.pdf>

—. 2001. Programme of Action to Prevent, Combat and Eradicate the Illicit Trade in Small Arms and Light Weapons in All Its Aspects. A/CONF.192/15. New York: UN. July. <http://www.un.org/events/smallarms2006/pdf/192.15%20(E).pdf>

—. 2002. *Women, Peace and Security: Study Submitted by the Secretary-General Pursuant to Security Council Resolution 1325 (2000).* New York: UN. <http://www.un.org/womenwatch/daw/public/eWPS.pdf>

—. 2006. *Integrated Disarmament, Demobilization and Reintegration Standards.* New York: UN. <http://www.unddr.org/iddrs.aspx>

—. 2011. *UN Strategic Results Framework on Women, Peace and Security: 2011–2020.* New York: UN. July. <http://www.un.org/womenwatch/ianwge/taskforces/wps/Strategic_Framework_2011-2020.pdf>

UN Action (UN Action against Sexual Violence in Conflict). n.d.a. 'UN Action Updates from the Field.' Accessed January 2014. <http://www.stoprapenow.org/field-updates>

—. n.d.b. *Comprehensive Strategy on Combating Sexual Violence in the Democratic Republic of the Congo.* <http://stoprapenow.org/uploads/features/CSonDRCforweb.pdf>

UNGA (United Nations General Assembly). 2012a. Outcome Document on the Programme of Action to Prevent, Combat and Eradicate the Illicit Trade in Small Arms and Light Weapons in All Its Aspects. Adopted 7 September. A/CONF.192/2012/RC/4 of 18 September (Annex I). <http://www.poa-iss.org/RevCon2/Documents/RevCon-DOC/Outcome/PoA-RevCon2-Outcome-E.pdf>

—. 2012b. *Women, Disarmament, Non-proliferation and Arms Control.* Adopted 3 December. A/RES/67/48 of 4 January 2013. <http://www.un.org/en/ga/search/view_doc.asp?symbol=A/RES/67/48>

—. 2013a. Arms Trade Treaty. 'Certified true copy (XXVI-8).' May. <https://treaties.un.org/Pages/ViewDetails.aspx?src=TREATY&mtdsg_no=XXVI-8&chapter=26&lang=en>

—. 2013b. *Report on Women, Disarmament, Non-proliferation and Arms Control.* A/68/166. 22 July. <http://www.un.org/ga/search/view_doc.asp?symbol=A/68/166>

UNIFEM (United Nations Development Fund for Women). 2004. *Getting It Right, Doing It Right: Gender and Disarmament, Demobilisation and Reintegration.* New York: UNIFEM. October. <http://www.unwomen.org/~/media/Headquarters/Media/Publications/UNIFEM/GettingitRightDoingitRight.pdf>

UNMIN (United Nations Mission in Nepal). 2008. 'JMCC 61st Meeting Signs Off on Verification Figures.' 1 March. <http://www.un.org.np/unmin-archive/?d=activities&p=activity_detail&aid=54>

UNODA and IANSA (United Nations Office for Disarmament Affairs and International Action Network on Small Arms). 2010. *Mainstreaming Gender for the Effective Implementation of the UN PoA*. New York: UNODA and IANSA.
<http://www.iansa-women.org/sites/default/files/un_poa_gender_guidelines_UNODA-RDB_IANSA_2010.pdf>

UNSC (United Nations Security Council). 2000. Resolution 1325. S/RES/1325 of 31 October.
<http://daccess-dds-ny.un.org/doc/UNDOC/GEN/N00/720/18/PDF/N0072018.pdf?OpenElement>

—. 2002a. *Report of the Secretary-General on Women, Peace and Security*. S/2002/1154 of 16 October. New York: UN.
<http://www.un.org/womenwatch/ods/S-2002-1154-E.pdf>

—. 2002b. *Statement by the President of the Security Council*. S/PRST/2002/32 of 31 October. New York: UN.
<http://daccess-dds-ny.un.org/doc/UNDOC/GEN/N02/671/80/PDF/N0267180.pdf?OpenElement>

—. 2003. Resolution 1467. S/RES/1467(2003) of 18 March. <http://www.un.org/en/ga/search/view_doc.asp?symbol=S/RES/1467%282003%29>

—. 2005. *Statement by the President of the Security Council*. S/PRST/2005/52 of 27 October. New York: UN.
<http://www.un.org/womenwatch/ods/S-PRST-2005-52-E.pdf>

—. 2006. *Report of the Secretary-General on Women, Peace and Security*. S/2006/770 of 27 September.
<http://www.un.org/en/ga/search/view_doc.asp?symbol=S/2006/770>

—. 2009. Resolution 1889. S/RES/1889 of 5 October. <http://www.un.org/en/ga/search/view_doc.asp?symbol=S/RES/1889(2009)>

—. 2010. *Women and Peace and Security: Report of the Secretary-General*. S/2010/173 of 6 April. New York: UN.
<http://www.un.org/ga/search/view_doc.asp?symbol=S/2010/173>

—. 2011a. *Report of the Secretary-General on Women, Peace and Security*. S/2011/598 of 29 September. New York: UN.
<http://www.un.org/en/ga/search/view_doc.asp?symbol=S/2011/598>

—. 2011b. *Report of the Secretary-General on Small Arms*. S/2011/255 of 5 April. New York: UN.
<http://www.poa-iss.org/poa/S-2011-255-smallarms-en.pdf>

—. 2012. *Report of the Secretary-General on Women, Peace and Security*. S/2012/732 of 2 October. New York: UN.
<http://www.un.org/en/ga/search/view_doc.asp?symbol=S/2012/732>

—. 2013a. *Sexual Violence in Conflict: Report of the Secretary-General*. S/2013/149 of 14 March. New York: UN.
<http://www.un.org/ga/search/view_doc.asp?symbol=S/2013/149>

—. 2013b. Resolution 2106. S/RES/2106 of 24 June. <http://www.un.org/en/ga/search/view_doc.asp?symbol=S/RES/2106(2013)>

—. 2013c. *Report of the Secretary-General on Small Arms*. S/2013/503 of 22 August. New York: UN.
<http://www.un.org/en/ga/search/view_doc.asp?symbol=S/2013/503>

—. 2013d. Resolution 2122. S/RES/2122 of 18 October. <http://www.un.org/en/ga/search/view_doc.asp?symbol=S/RES/2122(2013)>

—. 2013e. Resolution 2117. S/RES/2117 of 26 September. <http://www.un.org/en/ga/search/view_doc.asp?symbol=S/RES/2117(2013)>

USIP (United States Institute of Peace). 2013. 'Men, Peace and Security Symposium: Agents of Change.' 28–30 October.
<http://www.usip.org/events/men-peace-and-security-symposium-agents-of-change>

WE Act 1325 (Women Engaged in Action on 1325). 2013. 'Stakeholders Meeting on the Comprehensive Firearms Regulation Law.'
<http://weact1325.org/2013/08/20/stakeholders-meeting-on-the-comprehensive-firearms-regulation-law>

WHO (World Health Organization). 2001. *Small Arms and Global Health*. Geneva: WHO. <http://whqlibdoc.who.int/hq/2001/WHO_NMH_VIP_01.1.pdf>

WILPF (Women's International League for Peace and Freedom). 2011. *Women, Disarmament, Non-proliferation and Arms Control*. International Women's Day Seminar Outcome Document. Geneva: WILPF.
<http://www.peacewomen.org/assets/file/disarm_womendisarmamentnonproliferationandarmscontrol_wilpf_march2011.pdf>

ACKNOWLEDGEMENTS

Principal authors

Megan Bastick and Kristin Valasek, Geneva Centre for the Democratic Control of Armed Forces (DCAF)

Contributors

Veerle Triquet and Callum Watson, DCAF; Jasmin Nario-Galace; and the Mouvement contre les Armes Légères en Afrique de l'Ouest (MALAO)

WOMEN behind the GUN
Aiming for Equality and Recognition

Illustrations by ZAZA U. Röttgers

The women and girls who are featured in this section have something in common: at some point in their lives, whether as adults or as children, legally or illicitly, they all became intimately familiar with firearms. Not all of them have actually had to fire their guns in the line of duty, yet most hold or carry a weapon as a demonstration of force. Most also reflect a desire to be recognized for their contributions–as combatants, as professionals, as equals.

Sexism and the threat of sexual assault can profoundly threaten the self-esteem and security of women in the military. A Dutch soldier recalls that she was advised to carry a gun to the toilets at night to protect herself from her male peers while stationed in Afghanistan. A former US Marine recollects that, during her first tour of duty in Iraq, she began to question her will to live as male Marines repeatedly demeaned her to signal their superiority. She welcomes US plans to integrate women in combat roles as a means of removing the 'last gender-specific definition of performance' in the military.

Former and current rebels also speak of an ongoing need for gender equality. A group of demobilized *guerrilleras* in Colombia seeks to prevent ex-combatant women from being forgotten, mischaracterized, and vilified. They recall facing a lack of trust from male combatants, some of whom disobeyed or even abandoned their female commanders–an act unheard of among *guerrilleros*. In Iran, *peshmergas* (fighters) in the Komalah, a Kurdish armed movement, rank the pursuit of gender equality and the promotion of women's rights high among the objectives of the movement, although they note that the number of women in decision-making roles is in decline despite 'good policy'.

A call for respect also characterizes the account of a prison guard in South Africa, who laments that many people–including her own daughter–cannot understand why a woman would do such work, be in charge of men, or carry a gun.

There are signs of change, however. A veteran policewoman in Kenya explains that civilian men have become increasingly willing to work with female officers, that addressing gender-based violence gradually became part of the police mandate, and that her daughter also joined the police and now works in a gender unit.

For policewomen in United Nations peacekeeping missions, being female can be beneficial. A Rwandan policewoman in the UN Operation in Côte d'Ivoire points out that Ivorian women are more likely to approach a policewoman than a policeman with their problems and concerns. Similarly, in the UN Mission in Liberia, the commander of the Indian Formed Police Unit argues that policewomen have easier 'emotional access' to Liberians and that they have succeeded in demonstrating that a police officer can also be female.

Women are also part of the Syrian insurgency. A female sniper in the Free Syrian Army claims many Syrian men 'want their wives and sisters to learn how to use weapons'. Yet a former child soldier with the Lord's Resistance Army, in Uganda, reveals that the group's leaders would force young mothers who had been abducted and trained as fighters to carry their infants on their backs 'so that our hands were free to carry and fire weapons'.

In short, the picture is mixed–as further illustrated by the story of an Irish bodyguard. She considers being female an asset in her line of work, as she guards mostly women and children who 'do not want attention'. In that context, she essentially aims to look inconspicuous.

– Tania Inowlocki

Sexual harassment is something I could have encountered, having been deployed twice to Afghanistan in an international environment. At one base they told me, 'If you go to the toilets at night, take your pistol to protect yourself against colleagues.' That was completely new to me, something I had never encountered.

When you are on patrol as a woman, Afghans perceive you as a third gender, as something new, something interesting. In my experience, Afghan men do not see us as they see their own women because they see that women from their society have a different role and the men have to protect the women. Therefore, they are very willing to engage with us and talk to us. It comes down to masculinity in general–they tend to discuss different topics with male colleagues than with me. To me they talk about more feminine things, like feelings and the current situation–more emotional things. And that was something we saw throughout the whole unit, the Provincial Reconstruction Team.

We were the first unit that focused on having females in each of our engagement teams. We had a minimum of one female in each of those teams. We gave them gender training beforehand, and we implemented gender policies throughout our whole mission.

As the only female officer in my engineer battalion, I was tasked with making sure that the PRT engaged women in the local population. It's about how you improve your situational awareness and your operational effectiveness by engaging 100 per cent of the population. After our mission, NATO requested an investigation of how UN Resolution 1325 on gender and security could be implemented. Having done that, I just stayed with the gender topic.

As gender advisers for military operations, we advise on the implications of gender and the gender perspective within the mission, about operational effectiveness. When I teach I tend to focus more on the operational side. If you look at the implementation of Resolution 1325, it has an internal and an external focus. Looking at the external focus is how you improve your mission, how you focus on the host nation. The internal aspect is about the diversity of the army, men and women in the army. I think that is connected to culture in general and your national view on gender roles.

I have been in the army now for 12 years and you can see a big difference between now and when I started. Men and women are more equal in society, so there are more women in the army in different and higher positions. Ten years ago there were no female generals; now women are rising in the ranks, more and more.

Source: interview by Alexander Buehler

Captain in the Royal Netherlands Army, instructor with the Civil–Military Co-operation Centre of Excellence, former deputy commander of the Dutch-led Provincial Reconstruction Team (PRT) in Tarin Kowt, Afghanistan

Mentor for US
veterans, former
sergeant in the
US Marine Corps
reserves, including
as a machine gunner
on convoy security
in Iraq*

A Marine operates within a squad and a fire team, and trusts every other member with her safety, because every other Marine relies on her for their safety. If a woman experiences rape, she can no longer rely on this. A mentor or representative of Veterans Affairs can help to retrain this trust and provide an opportunity for the patient to regain the value of seeking and receiving help. Military sexual trauma creates a specific need for care, regardless of the victim's gender.

During my first tour of duty, gender differences were used more as a control method, rather than as a means of barring me from combat; the men verbally demeaned and abused me, due to my gender, as a method of reminding me that the men were in charge, and that at any time they could remove me from the gunner position. My performance and critical thinking were constantly questioned and I was accused of being a failure at everything. My self-esteem was at an all-time low, and I questioned my desire to remain alive.

Gender was also an issue when we observed the Islamic restrictions on interactions with the opposite sex. Other women and I were on hand, during patrols, to search women for contraband weapons and devices. As a female, I could thor-oughly search an Iraqi woman while respecting her culture. Often, fellow male Marines would say that the only reason female Marines were allowed on patrol was to respect the Islamic restrictions. My response was always, so what if that's the only reason? It provides female Marines the opportunity to prove that they can operate in combat environments with distinction, and that the more common reasons for restricting service women are false. If the door to gender equality in the armed forces opens with respecting gender politics of an occupied country, then I'll take it.

The removal of the combat ban on women was a step in the right direction, because it removes the last gender-specific definition of performance within the military. No longer can men, theoretically, use a woman's biological differences to justify her exclusion from certain roles, and thus from career advancement. I speculate that the successful integration of women into combat roles will drastically reduce the rate of military sexual trauma, because there will no longer be a reason for men to feel superior to women. Full gender integration will create an environment where men can no longer say, 'You aren't allowed in combat, so you are, by default, weaker than me.'

Note: * This text is an excerpt from a longer submission. For the complete version, see http://www.smallarmssurvey.org/publications/by-type/yearbook/small-arms-survey-2014.html.

Source: responses to questions sent by Tania Inowlocki

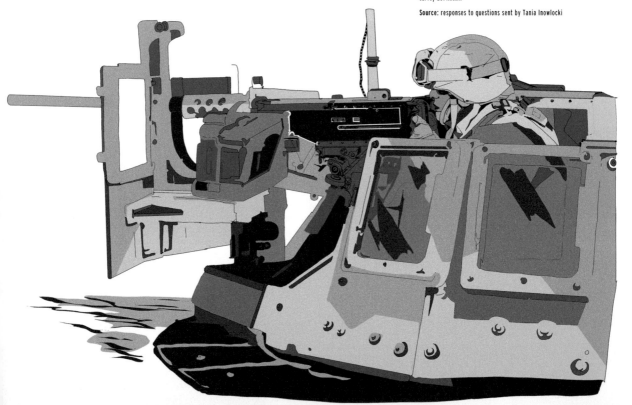

Social memory is a battlefield in Colombia. The role of women combatants has been erased and there are attempts to delegitimize our contributions to our country's history. The images of women in war are full of stereotypes. It is common to hear that women joined armed groups to flee domestic violence or forced marriage, as a result of forced recruitment or for the love of a soldier. Traditional representations also depict women as less inclined to violence and more peaceful than men. Thus, because we fought as men, carrying and using weapons, we are considered monsters. We must approach with caution both overly glorified and degrading representations of combatant women as well as representations that view us merely as victims.

As women combatants we were stronger, more disciplined, and more committed than men, because our engagement was a thought-out decision, considering that we had stepped out from the traditional role assigned to us by our society. The price to pay was that it would take us double the time and effort to get to the same positions as men although we had the same capacities. To exert power as a woman commander was particularly difficult: we faced a lack of trust from male combatants. Some refused to obey and others would abandon their female commander during a harsh fight while they would have died for their commander if she had been a man.

For the few of us who managed to have command positions, we did not have any feminine model to guide us in this role. The only model we had was from male commanders and anyway we had to abide by the rules of the organization and its ethics. We did not aim at changing the way these groups were functioning because they were organized as political spaces, with a view to changing society. We shared this objective and so we did not advocate any change. We were only women who transited into these groups and became empowered from this participation.

As women, we conducted the war in the same manner as men, with the same strength and determination. But we managed to carry out our activities in a manner that would avoid harm against civilians. It is not that men were more brutal but that, as women, we were more sensitive to this issue and more strategic about it. We were particularly outstanding in our capacity to create trust among the community, gain their support, and ensure protection of women and children in the midst of war.

Note: *These women are members of the Network of Women Ex-combatants from the Insurgency (Red Nacional de Mujeres Excombatientes de la Insurgencia), which was established in 2000 to raise awareness of the experience of women ex-combatants and enhance their role in Colombian society. The Network comprises women who were formerly affiliated with the armed groups that signed peace agreements between 1990 and 1994–Movimiento 19 de Abril (M19), Ejército Popular de Movimiento Indígena Armado Quintín Lame, and Corriente de Renovación Socialista–as well as ex-combatants from the Fuerzas Armadas Revolucionarias de Colombia-Ejército del Pueblo (FARC-EP) and the Ejército de Liberación Nacional (ELN), who joined the network after recent individual demobilizations.

Source: portrait supplied by Geneva Call

Demobilized
guerrillas in
Colombia*

Peshmergas (fighters) in the Komalah, a Kurdish armed movement in Iran

My movement deeply believes in gender equality and equality between men and women. We also believe in positive discrimination. We take extra care to support women's roles and values that promote women's rights within the organizations. We have an excellent background in this. In all Kurdish regions, the movement is known for its support and its belief in the equality of women and men.

It was the first movement in the Middle East that managed to attract hundreds of courageous and politically motivated women. However, it is difficult for women today to join the movement because many of us live in exile in other countries.

Women receive the same training as men when they join the movement. Everyone is entitled to carry a weapon, but not everyone participates in combat. The role of the movement is not just military, but also political. The movement's media and Internet presence play a big role in promoting the roles of women. Women are very active in the media work.

We can talk about a double repression that affects women: because they are Kurdish and because they are women. Women do not have the same opportunities and freedom as men in the society, throughout their lives. Therefore, they need much more time and education to achieve the same status as men.

In the movement, women are allowed to create their own organizations. Women can gather and fight for their rights; they take courses on women's rights, in which they can learn to be more independent and how to develop themselves more.

The movement tries to encourage women to be more active, which means women can get priority access to conferences and courses. Yet, this is still not enough. The movement also has problems and limitations, which hinder it from reaching all the objectives set regarding women. In spite of good policy, the number of women participating in decision-making processes is decreasing these days.

Women remain as involved as men in the movement. Some get married, want to have children and a calmer life; some migrate to other countries because of family pressure. Yet, overall, women do not leave the organization before men. In joining the movement, they find a certain form of freedom and many other opportunities.

Source: portrait supplied by Geneva Call

There wasn't money to study so I joined the Department of Correctional Services in 1996, when I was 25 years old. I work in the Emergency Support Team within Pollsmoor. We are mostly called in for serious situations like a gang fight or a conflict incident. We also handle all the high-security exercises, like transporting an offender to court. Inmates try to intimidate me but you have to be firm. Over the years you learn survival techniques.

There are 25 guards per unit, with smaller teams of approximately six persons per team. Within the 25-person unit there are three women. For six years I was the only woman in the unit–at least now there are three of us. We work 11 days on and then have three days off. I only get nervous if I cannot choose my team. I am confident in my ability and, if I know my team's abilities, then it's ok. But if I have unknown people on my team then I am worried as you don't know how they will react.

Many women don't join because they are not comfortable with firearms. I carry a firearm every day. A Glock 19. I use it to intimidate but not to fire. We use batons, teargas, and shock-shields. I take the gun home as I can be on call and then I need it.

The hardest part of the job is being accepted by other people. They don't understand why women would do this work. They don't understand that women can be in charge of men. That I can carry a gun. People judge me for doing this work and they see me as different. My ex-husband was too intimidated by me and so we got divorced. My eight-year-old likes my job, he is proud of his Mom. My daughter is 21 and she wishes I would get another job. I do what I do and I can do it well. I love my job and I would not change it for anything, but sometimes it can be lonely because people don't understand.

The experience that most stands out for me happened when I was on maternity leave in 2005. My unit was involved in escorting an offender to court and they walked into an ambush. There was a shoot-out and one of my team members was killed. I felt so guilty because I wasn't there. If I was there I could have prevented it. I have lost a child, I have been through a divorce, but this was much, much worse. This was the most significant. I could have prevented it, if I was there. I was a mess for a long time and I had to pay for my own counselling. The Department of Correctional Services did not make any psychologists available for us.

Source: interview by Natalie Jaynes

Guard at Pollsmoor Maximum Security Prison, South Africa

Officer Command-
ing Police Division,
Kenya Police Service
Division in Embu,
Eastern Province

My service with the Kenyan Police is a god-chosen career. I was 17 years old when I was recruited, in 1975. There was an ad in a magazine, from the commissioner of police, calling for people to join. There was no history of my family in the police at that time, but I took the test and they selected me. After six months of training I was posted in Kitale.

As a female police officer then it was difficult to interact with civilian men. It was hectic for us female officers, and people did not want to interact with us and so we had big challenges. But things are very different now. Civilian men are more willing today to work with female officers.

Early on, addressing gender-based violence (GBV) was not part of the police mandate. But today we have come to understand it as part of what we do.

We work closely with NGOs and other organizations with a focus on GBV. There is a GBV commissioner within the police now, a sign that we have really picked it up. Before my current position, I was based in Nairobi for many years working on GBV issues. It is important to keep talking to people, to get information from them about GBV. Many cases of GBV have been opened up

and this has added trust in the police among the people. Work on GBV is a commitment of the police now.

I was trained to use many different types of firearms–sub-machine guns, AK-47s, G3s, and others. Today, at the managerial level, I no longer carry larger weapons, but instead I carry a 9 mm pistol. This is common for officers in similar positions to mine.

Early on we didn't have very sophisticated weapons. Civilians had many, primarily supplied by neighbouring countries experiencing civil wars. We didn't have the types of firearms necessary to confront them, but we are catching up.

In Kenya, it is always necessary for the police to carry firearms. I have been involved in many instances where firearms were necessary. One such incident involved a number of armed criminals who had killed some people on the road near Nakuru. We were well armed, we had the same firearms as the criminals, and we apprehended all of them.

I have a family of four and my daughter joined the police over 12 years ago. She is doing very well. I have been a mentor to her and today she is part of a gender unit within the police.

Source: interview by Khristopher Carlson

As a policewoman, it's important that I carry a firearm. Our mission is to protect civilians and sometimes you encounter individuals who can threaten security, which is why we need arms to protect ourselves and others. Since we share one mission, there is no difference between the men and women who carry arms. And we are all working in the same conditions, so I don't see any differences.

I am the focal point for child protection at UNOCI headquarters and am the mission's liaison officer to the National Police of Côte d'Ivoire. I also coordinate our focal points in the field. We have mixed teams on the ground and our female staff members are well trained to approach women and children, since in the local culture it is easier for women to approach another woman than a man with problems and concerns. But when it comes to efficiency, again, I see no difference between UNPOL women and men.

In my career, I have focused on the protection of vulnerable persons because my country–Rwanda–has experienced exactly these problems.

We had war, genocide. I have seen children suffering as well as the violence of conflict. I have seen in my country that there is a necessity to protect children and other vulnerable persons. Because children can die due to the effects of conflict, or of poor hygiene, or as a result of being separated from their families. Children are more vulnerable than adults. In armed conflicts there are more civilian victims and children are especially vulnerable.

I wanted to share my experience and have a possibility to intervene for the others, since that is required by the international community when there are conflicts.

Before 1994 I was member of the Gendarmerie Nationale of Rwanda, so I was trained to use firearms. But it was a strange feeling that whenever I wore the uniform, I had to carry a firearm. I was asked a lot of questions, like 'What are you doing there?' or 'If you use the firearm, isn't that going to have negative consequences for us?' I told people that firearms must always be used very carefully because they destroy lives.

Source: interview by Alexander Buehler

Rwandan United Nations Police (UNPOL) Officer, United Nations Operation in Côte d'Ivoire (UNOCI)

Commander of the
Indian Formed
Police Unit (FPU) of
the United Nations
Mission in Liberia
(UNMIL), Monrovia

Our FPU contingent is composed of 124 women and we receive logistics support from 21 men. Even though our contingent is an all-female FPU, our tasks are not gender-specific. Our primary tasks are to guard the Ministry of Foreign Affairs of Liberia and to assist the UN Police and the Liberian National Police during night patrols. But we also carry out other mandated tasks, such as providing security for UN personnel and anti-riot control.

As a female UNMIL peacekeeper, it's easier to get emotional access to the people of Liberia. The response is very positive from the people here. In the initial period of our deployment, seven years ago, we attracted attention, but now the people are used to seeing us.

We have many outreach programmes, we encourage the women to participate in the law and order process and to get enlisted in the police. Our contingent medical officer assists during the recruitment of women to the Liberian National Police. We help in stepping up awareness–we show that a police officer can also be female. I think we have been able to send a message to the people.

Many women have recently graduated from the academy, so in the future there will be a higher proportion of women in the Liberian National Police. From the data for 2007 to 2013, it is clear that the proportion of women registered in the Liberian National Police has increased from 6 per cent to 15 per cent.

When I joined the service in India, a formerly male-dominated force, they were already used to having women around. In my particular service, the department first started to enlist women in 1988. And I joined in 1997. So female recruits were not new when I joined. In India, my department has three battalions that are composed exclusively of women; it includes 1,200 staff.

The police service gives you a sense of purpose, of joining a profession, which is very important in maintaining the order of the country. In India, the services are a very respectable profession. People respect the uniformed services because you are seen as serving the nation. The uniform gives a sense of security and you literally feel empowered. And this is also something we are promoting in Liberia.

Source: interview by Alexander Buehler

When the revolution erupted two years ago, I was taking photos and recording videos. I came here to Aleppo not to fight, but to help people, around September 2012. But when I saw that the FSA fighters were very happy to defend the land, to fight the regime, to defend the people, I found myself able to hold a weapon. I wasn't accurate with my aim, so I asked my husband–he's the leader of a *katiba* (battalion)– to train me.

It's very easy. I am sure that all Muslim women could help by taking up arms. Our men, a lot of them, want their wives and sisters to learn how to use weapons. It is common for us here, not something strange. If you want to learn how to shoot, that's okay. We have a Muslim rule, a saying: 'Teach your children how to shoot, ride horses, and swim.'

Today we are at war in Syria. And what do you need? Weapons. You need to defend yourself and the others around you. I want the people to be safe.

The goal with me is not the number of killings. The goal is to stop the regime from proceeding towards us, to the checkpoint of our katiba. In my katiba we are three snipers. I watch the streets around the front. If I see men coming towards us, I know the regime asked them to go to this area, and this area is very dangerous. So I shoot in the street. When I see a soldier–click–I will kill him. The soldiers are like our men, they are 18-21, 22.

Source: interview by Alexander Buehler

Free Syrian Army (FSA) sniper in Aleppo

Former child soldiers of the Lord's Resistance Army (LRA), Uganda

I was abducted when I was 15. I gave birth to a baby while I was in the LRA. Many times we were forced to carry our infant children on our backs so that our hands were free to carry and fire weapons (Lira District, 2003).

I asked for a weapon to fight with. I wanted to be away from the LRA camps as it was the only way to escape. I did escape. During a fight with the Uganda People's Defence Force I pretended to be dead, and when everyone was gone, I left the gun and ran (Gulu District, 2003).

Most of the girls taken by the LRA were trained as fighters, except the youngest ones. One commander who had many wives made those without children take guns and fight. He said it was necessary for them to contribute their part to the LRA's effort to defeat the government (Lira District, 2005).

My husband had eight wives and there were four children among them. I had one child from the bush. He made one of his wives fight even when she was pregnant. If pregnant wives refused to fight, they would be killed (Lira District, 2005).

Source: interviews by Khristopher Carlson

I trained in firearms mostly for jobs, because they would look for a firearms licence–it's something for your CV. And if you're going to a more high-risk area, you'd need it. I've gotten jobs just because of my certificate.

Having a military background in this field can be a hindrance in some situations. I've worked with ex-military people and they tend to present themselves differently. They have a more aggressive approach, putting hands out and smashing camera lenses. Coming from a civilian background, you can take a softer approach–things don't need to be elevated to another level. The first weapon of defence is your brain, first and foremost. The last line of defence is confrontation–everything else is just avoidance.

Being female and not coming from a military background definitely helps with the type of work that I do. I work with a lot with women and children. The people I work with do not want attention–it's not like Madonna jogging through Central Park surrounded by five huge bodyguards. So you try to look like one of their friends or a secretary. You look inconspicuous. When people ask if I'm a bodyguard, I say, 'I'm the secretary.' And people get really disinterested.

Firearms are sometimes a problem in crowds. All bodyguards are looking at the first three rows because you can get a shot in from there. But after the third row, it's likely you're not going to hit your target. Surveillance teams are looking for stretched-out hands trying to touch VIPs, and if there aren't two hands out, they're looking for that. And if they think there's a problem they'll move the VIP off the red carpet.

When I started training, there were very few female bodyguards. But about ten years ago the demand for female bodyguards started to increase because of the growing number of Arab clients. Arab men didn't want men around their women. When I was fully trained and worked with other female bodyguards for the first time, I was shocked–I could not believe the standards. I was the only female bodyguard who had been properly trained. So I reported back and said there was a need for training.

Slowly, there's been an increase in the number of women who get training. Women come for training from Japan, Russia, and Eastern Europe. I fought against women-only courses because you might as well make it natural. Men can be sexist in this line of work–but even in the training environment, there's no point in sugar-coating it.

Source: interview by Tania Inowlocki

Bodyguard and director of the Women's Bureau of the International Bodyguard Association, Ireland

ARMS FOR ATROCITIES

Activists supporting the Arms Trade Treaty lie in fake body bags in front of the UN building,
New York, 2 July 2012. © Andrew Kelly/Control Arms Coalition/Reuters

Breaking New Ground?

THE ARMS TRADE TREATY

3

INTRODUCTION

'[T]he world has decided to finally put an end to the free-for-all nature of international weapons transfers', UN Secretary-General Ban Ki-moon asserted when the Arms Trade Treaty (ATT) opened for signature on 3 June 2013 (UNDPI, 2013b). Sixty-seven countries signed the treaty during the signing ceremony at UN Headquarters in New York that day, with states continuing to sign—and in several cases ratify—the ATT at a brisk pace during the last half of 2013.[1] To date, UN member states have demonstrated broad support for the ATT, suggesting that they see it as a game changer.

In fact, different stakeholders perceive different benefits as arising from the ATT. For some, it is a means of levelling the playing field and ensuring that emerging arms exporters and those that do not already participate in existing export control regimes are subject to international norms and standards. For others, it represents a chance, through a legally binding instrument, to fulfil the promise of the UN Programme of Action (PoA) to curb the illicit small arms trade. For others, it is the beginning of the end of the human suffering brought about by irresponsible arms transfers. As the excitement following the adoption subsides, the question becomes: what does the ATT do and what will it change?

The central aim of the treaty is to establish the highest possible common international standards to regulate the international trade in conventional arms. This chapter evaluates the standards established by the treaty and considers what its provisions mean for arms transfer practices. Drawing on the treaty itself, UN documents, and the author's observations of the ATT negotiations, the chapter reviews the provisions of the ATT, situates the treaty within the current arms transfer control framework, and assesses its potential impact on state practice. Its main conclusions include:

- The compromises necessary for agreement on the treaty text have left the ATT with few unqualified legal obligations.
- The ATT covers a broad range of transfer-related activities, as well as items, but an absence of definitions and a lack of prescriptive detail may result in uneven and inconsistent implementation.
- The ATT makes a significant contribution to existing legal frameworks by introducing new standards for the international transfer of conventional arms. These gains are, however, more modest in comparison with existing small arms control measures.
- Given the universal scope of the treaty, non-exporting states have been and will continue to be involved in ATT-related arms transfer discussions as well as in the development of global norms to curb irresponsible arms transfers.
- The ATT process has raised the level of attention and scrutiny given to this issue at the global level and will undoubtedly continue to do so. This trend, in turn, has the potential to change state behaviour.

The chapter begins with a brief history of the ATT process. Next, it analyses the nature and content of the provisions of the treaty, including via a selective comparison of the ATT with other arms transfer commitments. A section exploring the possible impact of the ATT follows. The conclusion summarizes the chapter's main themes and findings.

A SHORT HISTORY

The journey towards the ATT began with a series of civil society initiatives. The first was the 1997 International Code of Conduct on Arms Transfers developed by Óscar Arias, former president of Costa Rica and winner of the Nobel Peace Prize, together with a group of fellow Nobel Peace laureates (Arias Foundation, 2008, p. 1). The Code stipulated that countries aiming to purchase arms meet certain criteria, including the promotion of democracy, the protection of human rights, and transparency in military spending (NPL ICoC, 1997, para. 2). This original set of standards was seen to be overly ambitious,[2] mainly because it sought to impose a de facto arms embargo on any state that did not comply with any one of its criteria rather than assessing exports on a case-by-case basis.

In 2001, a group of non-governmental organizations (NGOs)[3] circulated a revised version of the text, based on states' international obligations; it became known as the draft Framework Convention on International Arms Transfers (Framework Convention, 2001, n. i). In October 2003, Amnesty International, Oxfam, and the International Action Network on Small Arms (IANSA) launched the Control Arms campaign and set about gathering support for an ATT of global scope. As part of this effort, they delivered a petition called 'Million Faces' to UN Secretary-General Kofi Annan on 26 June 2006 (UN News Centre, 2006). In 2009, the campaign developed and launched the Global Principles for International Arms Transfers based on the draft Framework Convention. It put forward a conceptual framework for an arms trade treaty, rather than draft treaty text (Control Arms, 2009).

Although the concept of an ATT enjoyed widespread NGO support, it was not until national governments—specifically, Costa Rica and the UK—began pushing the idea that it gained traction among states. In September 2004, Foreign Secretary Jack Straw announced that the UK supported the idea of an ATT (Vollmer, 2008, p. 3).

The permanent representative of Syria to the UN addresses the Final UN Conference on the ATT, expressing his country's opposition to the draft treaty, New York, 28 March 2013. © Rick Bajornas/UN Photo

By October 2006, a group of seven governments[4] that became known as the 'co-authors' had co-drafted an initial ATT resolution and submitted it to the UN General Assembly. In December 2006, 153 UN member states voted in favour of the resolution, with 24 states abstaining[5] and 1 voting against[6] (UNGA, 2006a, p. 31). Resolution 61/89 instructed the Secretary-General to seek the views of member states on 'the feasibility, scope and draft parameters for a comprehensive, legally binding instrument establishing common international standards for the import, export and transfer of conventional arms' and to establish a group of governmental experts (GGE) to examine the same question (UNGA, 2006b, paras. 1–2). After three sessions in 2008,[7] the GGE, comprising experts from 28 countries, produced a report that was endorsed by the UN General Assembly in Resolution 63/240 (UNGA, 2008b, para. 1). The resolution also established an open-ended working group (OEWG) to facilitate further consideration of UN efforts to address the international arms trade, as the GGE had recommended (UNGA, 2008b, para. 3; 2008a, para. 27).

The OEWG, open to all UN member states, delivered its report in July 2009 (UNGA, 2009a). In December 2009 the UN General Assembly decided to convene a conference in 2012—namely the United Nations Conference on the Arms Trade Treaty—to elaborate an international treaty on conventional arms transfers (UNGA, 2009b, paras. 4–5). The resolution also mandated that the three remaining OEWG sessions, scheduled for 2010 and 2011, be treated as preparatory committee meetings (PrepComs) for the ATT Conference (para. 6).

The United Nations Conference on the Arms Trade Treaty was held in New York from 2 to 27 July 2012, but was unable to reach consensus on a final treaty text. In December 2012 the UN General Assembly voted, by a wide margin,[8] to convene the Final United Nations Conference on the ATT in March 2013. Resolution 67/234 A specified that the draft ATT text submitted by the president of the 2012 ATT Conference 'shall be the basis for future work' on the ATT (UNGA, 2012a, paras. 2–3).

The Final United Nations Conference on the Arms Trade Treaty, held in New York on 18–28 March 2013, produced a treaty text that could not be adopted by consensus, as Conference rules required, because of opposition from Iran, North Korea, and Syria. The matter was swiftly transferred back to the UN General Assembly, which, on 2 April 2013, voted to adopt the same ATT text through resolution 67/234 B—by 154 votes to 3,[9] with 23 abstentions[10] (UNGA, 2013c; UNGA, 2013e).

Box 3.1 ATT timeline: the UN process

2006

18 October Co-authors submit resolution 'Towards an Arms Trade Treaty: Establishing Common International Standards for the Import, Export and Transfer of Conventional Arms' to UN General Assembly (UNGA)

December UNGA adopts Resolution 61/89

2007

September GGE appointed

2008

11–15 February First GGE session

12–16 May Second GGE session

28 July–8 August Third GGE session

August GGE submits its report

December UNGA adopts Resolution 63/240, establishing OEWG

2009

23 January Organizational session of OEWG

2–6 March First substantive session of OEWG

13–17 July Second substantive session of OEWG

July OEWG delivers its report

December UNGA adopts Resolution 64/48, establishing a treaty negotiating conference

2010

12–23 July First ATT PrepCom

2011

28 February–4 March Second ATT PrepCom

11–15 July Third ATT PrepCom

2012

13–17 February Fourth ATT PrepCom

2–27 July United Nations Conference on the ATT

November UNGA adopts resolution 67/234 A

2013

18–28 March Final United Nations Conference on the ATT

2 April UNGA adopts the ATT through Resolution 67/234 B

3 June ATT opens for signature

THE NATURE OF THE TREATY

While the ATT carries the word 'trade' in its title,[11] there was never any question of negotiating it at the World Trade Organization (WTO), the established forum for international trade negotiations. First, agreements governing the transfer of arms, ammunition, and other 'implements of war' fall outside the WTO's remit (GATT, 1947, XXI(b)(ii)). Second, and more importantly, the humanitarian objectives pursued by ATT supporters appeared incompatible with the WTO goal of facilitating and liberalizing global trade. The consideration and negotiation of the ATT was instead assigned to the UN's principal forum for the regulation of conventional arms: the First Committee of the UN General Assembly, which deals with disarmament and international security.

ATT obligations are many and varied, in content and nature.
The ATT contains introductory text ('preamble' and 'principles') and 28 articles. States parties' ATT obligations are many and varied, in both their content and nature. The binding or non-binding nature of a treaty provision is signalled by the use of terms, such as 'shall', 'shall not', 'may', and 'encouraged', as well as the presence or absence of qualifying language, such as 'where feasible', 'where appropriate', or 'pursuant to its national laws'. Some treaty provisions create legal obligations that require a state party to take or refrain from a specific action. Other treaty provisions merely encourage a state party to take certain action or give it the option of taking such action; they do not create legal obligations.

In fact, there are relatively few legal obligations in the ATT. The ones that exist are often general—even subjective—in nature, such as the requirement that each state party 'implement this Treaty in a consistent, objective and non discriminatory manner' (UNGA, 2013a, art. 5(1)). In some instances, this lack of prescriptive detail reflects the reality that states regulate and control arms transfers in different ways, depending on the nature of their legal and political systems, and the nature and scale of transfers involving them.[12] In other instances, however, the lack of detail reflects the desire of some exporting states to limit their ATT obligations to what they are already doing under their current control frameworks, as well as the concerns of small, non-exporting states regarding the use of scarce resources to establish complex export control systems that they do not need.

SCOPE

The scope of the treaty refers to the categories of conventional arms and types of activities to which the treaty applies.

Conventional arms

The discussions regarding the conventional arms to be covered by the treaty revolved around the question of whether to adhere to the categories of the UN Register of Conventional Arms. Under the UN Register, established in 1992, UN member states are 'called upon' or 'requested' to provide data on the import and export of seven categories of conventional arms (UNGA, 1991, para. 9; annexe, para. 2(a)); in addition, they are 'invited' to report on small arms transfers (UNGA, 2005c, para. 3). Ultimately, states agreed to apply the UN Register's categories, such that the ATT explicitly applies to all conventional arms within the following categories:

- Battle tanks;
- Armoured combat vehicles;
- Large-calibre artillery systems;
- Combat aircraft;

- Attack helicopters;
- Warships;
- Missiles and missile launchers; and
- Small arms and light weapons (UNGA, 2013a, art. 2(1)).

During the negotiations, this list of categories was referred to as '7 plus 1' because it included the seven categories of the UN Register—listed in ATT Article 2(1)(a)–(g)—as well as small arms and light weapons. The treaty does not include definitions of the conventional arms covered, but rather makes reference to existing descriptions in other instruments. With respect to the arms listed in Article 2(1)(a)–(g), the definitions that states must adopt as part of their national control lists 'shall not cover less than the descriptions used in the United Nations Register of Conventional Arms at the time of entry into force of this Treaty' (UNGA, 2013a, arts. 5(2)–(3)).

The descriptions applied to the categories have been amended by various groups of experts that have met eight times since the UN Register was established;[13] they are likely to undergo further modification by future groups of experts. As suggested above, states parties to the ATT are bound to adopt, at a minimum, the descriptions used in the UN Register 'at the time of entry into force' of the treaty (UNGA, 2013a, art. 5(3))—in essence fixing the ATT-related definitions in time.[14] Such static definitions are more palatable to states seeking certainty as to the arms they must regulate. However, the definitions will not be aligned with those in the UN Register if the latter evolve—unless states

A police officer guards a container holding parts and components of conventional arms seized from a North Korean ship travelling from Cuba back to North Korea, in Colon City, Panama, July 2013. © Carlos Jasso/Reuters

Box 3.2   Definitions of small arms and light weapons in the International Tracing Instrument

For the purposes of this instrument, 'small arms and light weapons' will mean any man-portable lethal weapon that expels or launches, is designed to expel or launch, or may be readily converted to expel or launch a shot, bullet or projectile by the action of an explosive, excluding antique small arms and light weapons or their replicas. Antique small arms and light weapons and their replicas will be defined in accordance with domestic law. In no case will antique small arms and light weapons include those manufactured after 1899:

(a) 'Small arms' are, broadly speaking, weapons designed for individual use. They include, inter alia, revolvers and self-loading pistols, rifles and carbines, sub-machine guns, assault rifles and light machine guns;

(b) 'Light weapons' are, broadly speaking, weapons designed for use by two or three persons serving as a crew, although some may be carried and used by a single person. They include, inter alia, heavy machine guns, hand-held under-barrel and mounted grenade launchers, portable anti-aircraft guns, portable anti-tank guns, recoilless rifles, portable launchers of anti-tank missile and rocket systems, portable launchers of anti-aircraft missile systems, and mortars of a calibre of less than 100 millimetres (UNGA, 2005a, para. II.4).

parties voluntarily incorporate the new definitions in their national control lists or the ATT is amended to reflect changes in the UN Register. More broadly, linking the scope of the ATT to the UN Register categories means that the treaty will be left behind if Register categories are amended and updated to reflect the development of new types of conventional arms.

With respect to small arms and light weapons, the ATT specifies that national definitions 'shall not cover less than the descriptions used in relevant United Nations instruments at the time of entry into force of this Treaty' (UNGA, 2013a, art. 5(3)). The 2005 International Tracing Instrument, which is cited in the ATT preamble, is the only UN instrument that includes a definition of 'small arms and light weapons'[15] (UNGA, 2005a; see Box 3.2).

'Ammunition/munitions' and 'parts and components'

Certain provisions of the treaty also apply to 'ammunition/munitions'[16] (UNGA, 2013a, art. 3), as well as 'parts and components' (art. 4). As a result, certain transfers of ammunition and parts and components are prohibited (art. 6) and states parties must conduct a risk assessment before exporting these items (art. 7). Yet—in contrast to their obligations with respect to conventional arms more broadly—states parties are not obliged to regulate the import, transit, transhipment, or brokering of ammunition/munitions or parts and components under the treaty, nor to keep records of their export or report on the import or export of such items (arts. 8–13). The disparity in the treatment of these items reflects the compromise necessary to accommodate opposition from the Russian Federation, the United States, and others to the inclusion of ammunition in particular in the scope of the treaty (Casey-Maslen, Giacca, and Vestner, 2013, p. 21).

As with conventional arms, the treaty itself does not include definitions of 'ammunition/munitions' or 'parts and components'. Moreover, in this case, it includes no reference to other definitions or descriptions outside the ATT. The treaty offers some guidance on these items, however, specifying that ammunition/munitions are to be 'fired, launched or delivered by the conventional arms covered under Article 2(1)' (art. 3) and referring to parts and components 'where the export is in a form that provides the capability to assemble the conventional arms covered under Article 2(1)' (art. 4).

The Firearms Protocol is the only UN instrument that includes definitions of ammunition and parts and components[17] (UNGA, 2001a, art. 3(b)–(c)), but only insofar as they relate to firearms. States that are parties to the Wassenaar Arrangement may also look to the Wassenaar Munitions List[18] for guidance in implementing Articles 3 and 4. Nevertheless, the issue of definitions in the treaty—or their absence—is something that states parties could revisit after its entry into force, when control lists have been devised and exchanged, and gaps and weaknesses in the scope of the ATT are identified.

Activities

With respect to the activities that comprise the 'international trade' in conventional arms under the treaty, Article 2(2) stipulates that these consist of export, import, transit, transhipment, and brokering; throughout the treaty, the term 'transfer' refers to these activities collectively. An early version of the draft treaty text included references to other activities, such as 'manufacture under foreign licence' and 'technology transfer' (UNGA, 2011, para. IV.2(e)–(f)); another informal document circulated in July 2012 also called for the inclusion of references to leases, loans, gifts, re-export, and 'production by major producers/exporters' (UNGA, 2012c, para. B(1)(e)–(g)). However, these were not included in the final list of activities comprising international trade under the treaty.

The activities listed in Article 2(2) are not defined under the treaty, although early drafts of the treaty text attempted to define international arms transfer—adapting the description proffered by the 1992 Panel of Experts on the UN Register (UNGA, 1992, para. 10)—as involving 'the transfer of title or control over the equipment as well as the physical movement of the equipment into or from a national territory' (UNGA, 2011, annexe A, para. 1(a)). Such a definition—as well as explicit references to gifts and loans mentioned in earlier drafts—made it clear that financial consideration or payment was not a prerequisite for a delivery of goods to qualify as a 'transfer' under the treaty. Yet China, in particular, resisted explicit references to 'gifts' and 'loans' within a definition of transfer, and such references were ultimately omitted from the treaty.[19]

> It is unclear whether a 'transfer' includes non-commercial transactions.

In the absence of a definition, or explicit references to gifts and loans, it remains unclear whether the activities that comprise a 'transfer' under the treaty include non-commercial transactions or only sales and (financial) leases, leaving states parties some discretion. However, rules of treaty interpretation—which require consideration of a treaty's object and purpose—suggest that states parties should apply the ATT's provisions to all trade, regardless of whether it is commercial in nature. Indeed, on 22 October 2013 Switzerland circulated a model interpretative declaration, which asserts that:

> the terms 'export', 'import', 'transit', 'trans-shipment' and 'brokering' in Article 2, paragraph 2, [include], in light of the object and purpose of this Treaty and in accordance with their ordinary meaning, gifts, loans and leases and [. . .] therefore these activities fall under the scope of this Treaty (Switzerland, 2013, p. 1).

The treaty stipulates that its provisions do not apply to the international movement of conventional arms by, or on behalf of, a state party for its own use, as long as the arms remain under that state's ownership (UNGA, 2013a, art. 2(3)). In other words, if a state sends weapons to its own forces overseas, the shipment does not constitute a 'transfer' within the meaning of the treaty. This provision is consistent with discussions under the UN Register (UNGA, 1992, para. 11) and was most likely included to put the matter beyond doubt. But the fact that its inclusion was deemed necessary suggests that the mere movement of conventional arms (without a change in title or monetary payment) *is* regarded as a 'transfer' under Article 2(2). Thus, its inclusion supports the interpretation that a transaction does not have to involve financial payment or a change in title to constitute a 'transfer' under the treaty.

TRANSFER CRITERIA

The provisions in Articles 6 and 7 of the treaty, which include prohibitions on transfers in certain circumstances and require states parties to conduct a risk assessment before exporting conventional arms, ammunition, and parts and components, comprise the heart of the treaty.

Prohibitions

Under Article 6 of the treaty, a state party shall not transfer—that is, export, import, transit, tranship, or permit brokering of—conventional arms, ammunition/munitions, or parts and components in the following circumstances:

1. [. . .] if the transfer would violate its obligations under measures adopted by the United Nations Security Council acting under Chapter VII of the Charter of the United Nations, in particular arms embargoes.

2. [. . .] if the transfer would violate its relevant international obligations under international agreements to which it is a Party, in particular those relating to the transfer of, or illicit trafficking in, conventional arms.

3. [. . .] if it has knowledge at the time of authorization that the arms or items would be used in the commission of genocide, crimes against humanity, grave breaches of the Geneva Conventions of 1949, attacks directed against civilian objects or civilians protected as such, or other war crimes as defined by international agreements to which it is a Party (UNGA, 2013a, art. 6).

The interpretation of Article 6(3) will form the subject of further discussions.

The requirements that a state party refuse to authorize a transfer if it would violate an arms embargo (UNGA, 2013a, art. 6(1)) or an existing obligation under an international agreement to which it is a party (art. 6(2)) do not create 'new' obligations with respect to arms transfers, but simply codify existing obligations. UN member states are already bound to 'accept and carry out the decisions of the Security Council' under Article 25 of the UN Charter (UN, 1945); moreover, by definition, all states are obliged to fulfil relevant international obligations under international agreements to which they are parties.

There are differences of opinion regarding the exact scope of Article 6(3). First, it is not clear what threshold is set by the requirement that a state party have 'knowledge' that arms to be transferred would be used to commit certain crimes. The language in Article 6(3) was inspired by Article 16 of the Draft Articles on Responsibility of States for Internationally Wrongful Acts, which stipulate that a state that aids or assists another state to commit an internationally wrongful act is 'internationally responsible for doing so' if, among other things, 'that State does so with knowledge of the circumstances of the internationally wrongful act' (ILC, 2001, art. 16). The commentary to the draft article indicates that the latter phrase reflects a requirement that the assisting state 'be aware of the circumstances making the conduct of the assisted State internationally wrongful' (ILC, 2001, commentary to art. 16, para. 3).[20]

Similarly, in the context of determining the mental element required for individual criminal responsibility, the Rome Statute provides that '"knowledge" means awareness that a circumstance exists or a consequence will occur in the ordinary course of events' (ICC, 1998, art. 30(3)). But, in its model interpretative declaration, Switzerland indicates that the term 'knowledge' implies that the state party concerned shall not authorize the transfer 'if it has reliable information that provide[s] substantial grounds' for believing that the arms would be used in the commission of the crimes listed (Switzerland, 2013, p. 1), establishing a higher threshold for determining that a state has 'knowledge' than 'awareness'.

Furthermore, Article 6(3) does not specifically cover all war crimes. For instance, it does not refer to serious violations of Common Article 3 to the four Geneva Conventions, which covers prohibited acts that have been recognized in the Rome Statute and the case law of international criminal tribunals as amounting to war crimes in *non-international armed conflict*[21] (Doermann, 2013, p. 5). In other words, uncertainties with respect to the interpretation and coverage of Article 6(3) will undoubtedly form the subject of further discussions among states parties and in potential treaty development.[22]

Export and export assessment

If an export of conventional arms, ammunition, or parts and components is not prohibited under Article 6, an exporting state must conduct a risk assessment before authorizing the export of such arms or items, to assess the potential that they:

- would contribute to or undermine peace and security;
- could be used to commit or facilitate:
  - a serious violation of international humanitarian law (IHL);
  - a serious violation of human rights law;
  - an offence under terrorism conventions or protocols[23] to which the exporting state is a party; or
  - an offence under transnational organized crime conventions or protocols to which the exporting state is a party (UNGA, 2013a, art. 7(1)).

In making this assessment, exporting states must also 'take into account' the risk of the arms or items being used to commit or facilitate serious acts of gender-based violence or serious acts of violence against women and children (UNGA, 2013a, art. 7(4)). In addition, they must evaluate the risk of diversion of the export (art. 11(2)).

Assessment must be undertaken 'in an objective and non-discriminatory manner'.

If any of the risks in Article 7(1) or a risk of diversion is identified, states parties are required to consider whether there are 'measures that could be undertaken to mitigate' such risks (UNGA, 2013a, arts. 7(2), 11(2)). In other words, states must consider if the risks can be reduced, lessened, or alleviated. The treaty does not specify what mitigation measures should or could be taken, though it does suggest 'confidence-building measures or jointly developed and agreed programmes' by the importing and exporting states (arts. 7(2), 11(2)).

If the exporting state has conducted the risk assessment and considered available mitigating measures, and if it determines that there is an 'overriding risk' of any of the negative consequences listed in Article 7(1), it 'shall not authorize the export' (UNGA, 2013a, art. 7(3)). While exporting states must consider the risk of diversion, and the risk of use in gender-based violence or serious acts of violence against women and children, they are not required to deny such exports if an 'overriding risk' of any of these consequences exists—unless such risks have the potential to lead to one of the consequences in Article 7(1).

If an exporting state authorizes an export and later becomes aware of 'new relevant information', it is encouraged—but not obliged—to reassess the authorization (UNGA, 2013a, art. 7(7)). Common sense suggests the state party should take into account the same criteria as in the original assessment to determine whether an 'overriding risk' of any of the consequences in Article 7(1) now exists, though this is not stipulated in Article 7(7). An exporting state could thus change its decision and withdraw or revoke a previously granted export authorization, although such a reversal will depend on the state's own procedures and the terms of any agreement between the exporting state and importing state or entities involved in the transaction.

Article 7(1) tries to limit states' discretion by requiring them to make the Article 7(3) assessment 'in an objective and non-discriminatory manner' and to take into account 'relevant factors', including information provided by the importing state (UNGA, 2013a, art 7(1)). The treaty does not elaborate on what information exporting states should rely on when making an assessment or what 'relevant factors' must be taken into account (other than information provided by the importing state), although in the context of assessing the diversion risk of an export, exporting states are encouraged to consider examining the parties involved in the export, and requiring additional documentation (art. 11(2)).

Table 3.1 Overview of instruments that include transfer criteria

Scope (geography)	Instrument[a]	Nature		Scope (arms)				Scope (activities)			
		Legally binding	Politically binding	Major conventional arms	Small arms and light weapons	Ammunition	Other	Export	Import	Transit/transhipment	Brokering
Global	ATT	✓		✓	✓	(✓)		✓	(✓)	(✓)	(✓)
Multilateral	Wassenaar BPG		✓		✓			✓			✓
	Wassenaar Elements		✓	✓	✓	✓		✓			
Regional	Central African Convention	✓			✓	✓		✓	✓	✓	✓
	ECOWAS Convention	✓			✓	✓		✓	✓	✓	✓
	EU Common Position	✓		✓	✓	✓	✓ (software, technology)	✓	✓	✓	✓
	OSCE Document		✓	✓	✓		✓ (related technology)	✓	✓	✓	✓
	OSCE Principles		✓	✓	✓	n.s.	✓ (related technology)	n.s.[b]	n.s.[b]	n.s.[b]	n.s.[b]
	SICA Code of Conduct		✓	✓	✓	✓		n.s.[b]	n.s.[b]	n.s.[b]	n.s.[b]

Notes:

(a) For a list of complete instrument names and adoption dates, see endnote 24.

(b) The transfer criteria apply to 'transfers', but this term is undefined.

n.s. = not specified; (✓)=partially covered.

At least eight multilateral and regional instruments[24]—some legally binding, some politically binding—include provisions that require participating states to conduct a risk assessment with respect to proposed exports of arms or apply certain considerations ('transfer criteria'). Table 3.1 provides an overview of relevant instruments that include transfer criteria, indicating whether the instruments are legally or politically binding, and what types of arms and transactions are covered. Annexe 3.1 provides a comparative overview of the transfer criteria entailed in these instruments, including the nature of the obligation, the threshold to be applied to a risk assessment, and the consequence or risk to be assessed.

A comparison of transfer criteria in the ATT and in other instruments reveals several unique features. For example, the ATT's use of the term 'serious' to describe violations of IHL or human rights law arguably creates a higher threshold than most equivalent existing provisions[25] that do not place a qualifier on the nature or scale of the violations. There is no settled international agreement on what constitutes a 'serious' violation of human rights law, although a review shows that 'describing a violation of human rights as "serious" is generally assessed by the nature of the right violated and the scale or pervasiveness of the violation' (da Silva, 2009, p. 31).

The ATT provision regarding terrorism is also narrower in scope than its equivalent in existing instruments, although it is potentially more meaningful. While other instruments require states to consider whether a proposed transfer might be used to support or encourage 'terrorism' generally,[26] the ATT is limited to terrorist acts that constitute offences under international terrorism conventions to which the exporting state is a party (UNGA, 2013a, art. 7(1)iii). It thus provides a reference point for what constitutes 'terrorism', for which no internationally agreed definition exists.

Inclusion of gender-based violence as part of a risk assessment is unique.

The abovementioned obligation in the ATT to consider the risk of arms, ammunition/munitions, and parts and components being used to commit or facilitate gender-based violence or violence against women and children is unprecedented. No other instrument or regime specifically mentions gender-based violence as a component of a risk assessment. In this sense, the inclusion of the phrase in the ATT is an unequivocal success for those who lobbied for its incorporation, especially given the strong resistance to its inclusion by several states (WOMEN, PEACE, AND SECURITY).[27]

However, the insistence on a separate, specific reference to 'gender-based violence' in the ATT inevitably led the term to be distinguished from the category of 'risks' that it might otherwise belong to: serious violations of IHL and human rights law. The inclusion of gender-based violence as an example of a serious violation of IHL or human rights law in Article 7(1) would instead have underlined the relationship and prompted states parties to deny exports where the overriding risk of such violence was detected.

While the use of the phrase 'overriding risk' is also unprecedented in arms control agreements, its meaning is unclear. Indeed, it appears to have posed significant challenges to those tasked with translating the treaty into the official UN languages (see Box 3.3). Other relevant instruments tend to stipulate that the risk be 'clear' or that the misuse of weapons is 'likely', thus focusing on the magnitude of the risk rather than a comparison against other factors. The vast majority of states that spoke to the issue argued for the replacement of 'overriding' with 'substantial' during the ATT negotiations, with several states contending that the term 'overriding' was somewhat vague.[28]

To describe a risk as 'overriding' normally means that it is 'more important than any other considerations' (Oxford Dictionaries, n.d.a). In the context of the ATT, the question is: what should the risk be compared to? What must it outweigh? There are at least two possible interpretations or applications: 1) the risk (or potential) that one of the negative consequences in Article 7(1) may occur outweighs the possibility or likelihood that it will not occur; or 2) there is a risk (or potential) that one of the negative consequences in Article 7(1) will occur, and this outweighs any *positive* contribution that the arms or items could make to 'peace and security', which is mentioned in Article 7(1)(a) as a possible positive consequence of an export.

Box 3.3   Lost in translation: 'overriding' risk

In the original translation of the ATT into Russian, the term 'overriding risk' was translated as 'significant risk' ('значительного риска'), and in the Spanish version it was translated as 'clear risk' ('un riesgo manifiesto'), but both terms were subsequently corrected (UNGA, 2013d; UNGA, 2013f). The corrections illustrate the difficulty in reaching a clear understanding of the term 'overriding'. The terms used are now closer to the English word 'preponderant', derived from the Latin word *praeponderare*, which means to 'weigh, consider' (Oxford Dictionaries, n.d.b; see Table 3.2).

Table 3.2   Translation of 'overriding risk' in official treaty texts

Language	Official text	Unofficial English translation
Arabic	خطرا كبيرا	high risk
Chinese	高于一切的风险	overriding risk, above all risks
French	un risque prépondérant	preponderant risk
Russian	безусловного риска возникновения	absolute risk
Spanish	un riesgo preponderante	preponderant risk

Source: UNGA (2013a)

The use of the term 'overriding' received strong support from the United States, which aimed for the treaty to acknowledge the legitimacy of international arms transfers that have the potential 'to enhance, rather than undermine, peace and security' (US, 2013, p. 2). In other words, the United States appeared to envisage circumstances when the possible security benefits of a transfer would outweigh the possible human rights or other violations.

Some commentators see this usage as a significant loophole in the treaty.[29] Many states, it seems, will interpret the word 'overriding' to mean 'substantial'. For instance, following the adoption of the treaty on 2 April, New Zealand formally stated that it would interpret the concept of 'overriding' risk as a 'substantial' risk when applying the treaty (UNDPI, 2013a). The model interpretative declaration circulated by Switzerland indicates that the term 'overriding risk' entails an obligation not to authorize an export when the state party assesses the likelihood of any of the negative consequences in Article 7(1) materializing 'as being higher than the likelihood of them not materializing' (Switzerland, 2013, p. 1).

OTHER TRANSFER CONTROLS

General implementation

Article 5 of the treaty contains a series of general implementation measures, under which states parties are required to:

- implement the treaty in a 'consistent, objective and non discriminatory manner' (UNGA, 2013a, art. 5(1));
- establish and maintain a national control system (art. 5(2));
- establish a national control list (art. 5(2)) and provide it to the UN Secretariat, which will make it available to other states parties (art. 5(4));
- take the measures necessary to implement the treaty and designate a competent national authority 'in order to have an effective and transparent national control system'[30] (art. 5(5)); and
- designate one or more national points of contact to exchange information on matters related to treaty implementation (art. 5(6)).

States are also encouraged to make their control lists publicly available (UNGA, 2013a, art. 5(4)).

Dell Higgie, New Zealand's Disarmament Ambassador to the UN, signs the ATT, New York, 3 June 2013. © Keith Bedford/Insider Images

Import

The import obligations in Article 8 of the treaty require importing states to 'take measures' to provide information, if requested, to exporting states parties when conducting an export assessment (UNGA, 2013a, art. 8(1)); further, they task states with regulating imports of conventional arms (not ammunition/munitions nor parts and components) 'where necessary' (art. 8(2)). Under Article 8(3) importing states are entitled to request information from an exporting state party regarding an export decision (pending or complete).

The treaty only requires states parties to take measures to regulate imports 'where necessary' and does not specify what measures should be taken, except to note that 'such measures may include import systems' (UNGA, 2013a, art. 8(2)). Accordingly, states have discretion to determine whether and how they wish to regulate or control the importation of conventional arms, including whether to adopt a system of licensing or authorization.

This lack of prescription stands in contrast to the two international[31] and seven regional instruments[32] that include commitments to regulate the import of small arms—and, in some instances, ammunition and parts and components— most of which require importing states to establish a system of import licensing or authorization.[33] Some instruments also include:

- details of the procedure to be followed: for example, a requirement that an import licence be issued by the import-ing state before an export licence is issued by the exporting state (UNGA, 2001a, art. 10(2); Nairobi Protocol, 2004, art. 10(b)(i)) or a condition that a shipment not be authorized until an import licence has been received by the exporting state (OSCE, 2000, para. III(B)(3); OAS, 1997, art. IX(3));

- details regarding the nature and contents of import documentation: such as specifying the place and the date of issuance, the date of expiration, the country of export, the country of import, the final recipient, and a description and the quantity of the arms (OSCE, 2000, para. III(C)(1); ECCAS, 2010, art. 6); and

- a requirement that the importing state notify the exporting state upon receipt or delivery of the arms, generally when requested to do so.[34]

The ATT transit provision is broadly consistent with existing small arms instruments. In short, all UN member states have undertaken to adopt laws, regulations, and administrative procedures to exercise 'effective control' over the import of small arms (UNGA, 2001b, para. II.2); some are under a legal obligation to implement more specific small arms import controls that are stronger than their ATT equivalent. Consequently, while the ATT import obligations may represent a strengthening of states' existing commitments with respect to the broad spectrum of conventional arms, the same cannot be said with respect to the specific category of small arms and light weapons.

Transit or transhipment

The ATT requires states parties to take appropriate measures to regulate the transit and transhipment of conventional arms (not ammunition/munitions nor parts and components) (UNGA, 2013a, art. 9). The treaty does not specify what 'measures' are appropriate;[35] accordingly, states parties have discretion to adopt such measures as they deem appro-priate. The obligation to regulate the transit and transhipment of arms is qualified by two caveats: 'where necessary and feasible' and 'in accordance with relevant international law' (art. 9). The former caveat acknowledges that there may be instances when it is not possible for a state to regulate or control goods in transit, due to resource or practical constraints, or out of a desire not to interrupt commercial operations, since controlling goods in transit can delay goods from reaching their intended destination. The latter caveat acknowledges that states have commitments under inter-national law that may inhibit their ability to interfere with goods in transit (see Box 3.4).

For the most part, the ATT transit provision is consistent with commitments in existing small arms instruments. Under the PoA, for example, UN member states have committed to establishing 'adequate laws, regulations and administrative procedures' to control the transit of small arms (UNGA, 2001b, paras. II.2, II.12); meanwhile, states parties to the Firearms Protocol must establish or maintain a system of 'measures on international transit' for the transfer of firearms, their parts and components, and ammunition (UNGA, 2001a, art. 10(1)) and must ensure that transit states have given notice in writing, prior to shipment, that they have no objection to the transit (art. 10(2)(b)). The 1997 Inter-American Convention against the Illicit Manufacturing of and Trafficking in Firearms, Ammunition, Explosives, and Other Related Materials goes somewhat further, requiring states to establish a system of transit licences or authorizations for the transit of firearms, ammunition, explosives, and other related materials (OAS, 1997, art. IX(1)).

However, instruments that include commitments on the part of transit states only cover small arms. Accordingly, the creation of a legally binding obligation—albeit qualified—to establish measures to regulate the transit of conven-tional arms does constitute a contribution to the current control system.

Brokering

The ATT requires each state party to take measures to regulate brokering taking place under its jurisdiction with respect to conventional arms (but not ammunition/munitions or parts and components) 'pursuant to its national laws' (UNGA, 2013a, art. 10). This provision could be interpreted several ways. It could imply that states need not do more than is already being done under existing national law, a reading supported by the fact that the original drafting used the phrase 'within its national laws' (UNGA, 2012b, art. 8). Or it could mean that states parties must regulate brokering in a way that is consistent with related national legislation regarding, for example, the possible imposition of criminal sanctions against corporations. The treaty also offers the following suggestions for what measures may be taken to regulate brokering: requiring brokers to register or obtain written authorization before engaging in brokering (UNGA, 2013a, art. 10).

The brokering provision of the ATT echoes equivalent provisions in international instruments on small arms. It is slightly stronger than the Firearms Protocol, which includes a non-mandatory provision whereby states parties 'shall consider' a system for regulating brokers (UNGA, 2001a, art. 15(1)). But it is slightly weaker than the PoA, which includes a clear, unqualified commitment to 'develop adequate national legislation or administrative procedures' regulating brokers, and stronger, more detailed language regarding the components of such regulation, which 'should' include registration of brokers, licensing, or authorization of brokering transactions, and appropriate penalties for all illicit brokering activities 'performed within the State's jurisdiction and control' (UNGA, 2001b, para. II.14).

Box 3.4 'Relevant international law' with respect to transit

Transit states may face restrictions on their ability to regulate all goods in transit through their territories under existing international commitments.

The United Nations Convention on the Law of the Sea gives states parties a right of innocent passage,[36] which precludes coastal states from hampering the innocent passage of foreign ships through their territorial sea–such as by imposing requirements on foreign ships that have the practical effect of denying or impairing the right of innocent passage–except in specified circumstances (UNCLOS, 1982, art. 24).

Under the Convention on Civil Aviation, all *scheduled* flights over the territory of a contracting state require special permission or other authorization of that state (ICAO, 1944, art. 6); in contrast, contracting states have agreed that *non-scheduled* aircraft (such as charter flights) shall have the right 'to make flights into or in transit non-stop across its territory and to make stops for non-traffic purposes without the necessity of obtaining prior permission, and subject to the right of the State flown over to require landing' (art. 5).

The 1965 New York Convention on Transit Trade of Land-locked States recognizes the right of landlocked states to free access to the sea as an essential principle for the expansion of international trade and economic development, and grants freedom to traffic in transit (UNGA, 1965, principle 1; art. 2(1)). However, the convention notes that it does not affect measures a contracting state may have to take under another convention (existing or concluded later) if they relate to export or import or transit of particular kinds of articles including 'arms' (art. 11(3)) or any action necessary for the protection of its essential security interests (art. 11(4)). The provisions of this convention have been largely superseded by the Convention on the Law of the Sea, which gives landlocked states freedom of transit through the territory of transit states by all means of transport with the terms and modalities for exercising freedom of transit to be agreed between the concerned states (UNCLOS, 1982, art. 125).

Member states[37] of the 1980 Convention Concerning International Carriage by Rail have agreed to 'adopt all appropriate measures in order to facilitate and accelerate international rail traffic' (COTIF, 1980, art. 5); they have also decided to eliminate any 'useless' procedures, simplify and standardize existing formalities, and simplify frontier checks (art. 5(1)(a)-(c)). Further, Article 12(5) provides that a transit state may only seize a railway vehicle transiting its territory under a judgment given by the judicial authority of that state. Similarly, states parties[38] to the International Convention on the Harmonization of Frontier Controls of Goods have undertaken to 'provide simple and speedy treatment for goods in transit', for example by 'limiting their inspections to cases where these are warranted by the actual circumstances or risks' (UNECE, 1982, ch. III, art. 10(1)).

Anna Macdonald, head of the Control Arms campaign, addresses a press conference at the opening for signatures of the ATT, New York, 3 June 2012. © Evan Schneider/UN Photo

In 2003, participating states of the Wassenaar Arrangement agreed a set of common Elements for Effective Legislation on Arms Brokering (WA, 2003). That same year, the European Union (EU) adopted a Common Position specifically on brokering (EU, 2003). In addition to requiring the registration of brokers, the licensing of brokering activities, record-keeping and information exchange, and the adoption of penalty provisions, each of these agreements requires that applications for brokering licences or authorizations be assessed in accordance with specified transfer criteria. The EU Common Position on brokering also encourages member states to consider controlling brokering activities *outside* of their territory (art. 2(1)); in essence, it encourages them to establish extraterritorial controls.[39]

The weak language of the final ATT text on brokering can in part be attributed to Canada, which claimed that states should not be required to 'regulate' brokering, but rather should choose their own processes for controlling brokers. Canada also raised concerns over the extraterritorial application of brokering measures (Canada, 2011, p. 3). As a consequence of such resistance to stronger language, the ATT brokering provisions are weak and even the measures that states 'may' adopt are very limited. In addition, the treaty fails to define the terms 'broker' and 'brokering' and, importantly, lacks stipulations on extraterritorial jurisdiction. Given the attention the issue of brokering has gained at the international[40] and regional levels over the past decade, the weakness of the ATT brokering provision signals a missed opportunity.

Diversion

Article 11 of the ATT is dedicated exclusively to the issue of diversion. While the term 'diversion' is not defined in the ATT, it is generally understood to refer to a breakdown in the transfer control chain such that, either before or after arriving at their intended destination, exported weapons come under the control of unauthorized end users or are used in violation of commitments made by end users prior to export (McDonald, 2008, p. 156).

The requirements of Article 11, which apply only to transfers of conventional arms and not to ammunition/munitions or parts and components, are:

- for states parties to take measures to prevent diversion (UNGA, 2013a, art. 11(1));
- for exporting states to prevent diversion by assessing the risk of diversion of exports of conventional arms, and potentially not authorizing the export (art. 11(2));
- for states parties to cooperate and exchange information in order to mitigate the risk of diversion of conventional arms (art. 11(2)–(3));
- for states parties to take appropriate measures to address diversion when detected, including by alerting potentially affected states parties, examining diverted shipments, and taking follow-up measures through investigation and law enforcement (art. 11(4)); and
- for states parties to share information on effective measures to address diversion (art. (11(5)).

> Article 14 is a reminder that implementation means more than adopting laws.

In addition, states parties are encouraged to report to each other on measures taken in addressing the diversion of transferred conventional arms (UNGA, 2013a, art. 11(6)).

Enforcement

Article 14 obliges states parties to 'take appropriate measures' to enforce national laws and regulations that implement the provisions of the treaty, which implies an obligation to adopt such national laws and regulations.[41] Except for the word 'appropriate', which may stem from the desire to reflect different national approaches to enforcement, the obligation in Article 14 is strong, given that it is unqualified. But its lack of detail, including the absence of a specific reference to penal sanctions, is a source of weakness.

Nevertheless, Article 14 is an important reminder that it is not sufficient for states parties simply to adopt laws and establish control systems to implement the treaty. They must also *enforce* the measures adopted to implement the treaty. There are other examples of enforcement-related commitments in the treaty, such as the suggestion in Article 11(4) that measures taken to address diversion may include 'investigation and law enforcement' and the requirement in Article 15(5) that states parties 'afford one another the widest measure of assistance in investigations, prosecutions and judicial proceedings in relation to violations of national measures established pursuant to this Treaty' if, for example, they have mutual legal assistance provisions in place.

International cooperation and assistance

The ATT includes an article on international cooperation (UNGA, 2013a, art. 15) and a separate article on international assistance (art. 16). As with similar articles in other treaties, these provisions are designed to promote and facilitate information sharing between states, mutual legal cooperation to prosecute individuals engaged in criminal activities relating to the arms trade, and the provision and reception of assistance—including technical, financial, and legislative assistance as well as institutional capacity building—for ATT implementation. States parties that are 'in a position to do so shall provide' assistance on request (art. 16(1))—though they cannot be compelled to provide assistance as states parties themselves will determine if they are 'in a position to do so'. States parties are also encouraged to contribute to the voluntary trust fund to be established under the treaty (art. 16(3)).

The inclusion of provisions on international cooperation and assistance is important, particularly for countries that are not major exporters or importers of arms, but that frequently feel the effects of arms trafficking and misuse. Regional organizations such as the Caribbean Community (CARICOM)[42] and the Pacific Islands Forum[43] stressed the importance of including such provisions to facilitate implementation efforts.

TRANSPARENCY

Record-keeping

A legal obligation to record conventional arms transfers sets a precedent. Under Article 12 of the treaty, states parties are required to keep records of export authorizations or actual exports of conventional arms (not ammunition/munitions or parts and components) (UNGA, 2013a, art. 12(1)); they are also encouraged to keep records of imported arms and arms that are authorized to transit their territories (again, excluding ammunition/munitions and parts and components) (art. 12(2)). The treaty urges states parties to include the following information in these records: quantity, value, model/type, authorized transfers of conventional arms, conventional arms actually transferred, details of exporting state(s), importing state(s), transit and transhipment state(s), and end users, 'as appropriate' (art. 12(3)).

The obligation to keep records of export authorizations or actual exports is qualified by the phrase 'pursuant to its national laws and regulations'. This language may be designed to acknowledge the need to abide by national laws regarding the keeping of private or sensitive information. In any case, in many countries record-keeping requirements are not incorporated in national legislation, but rather in policy documents and other directives applicable to the agency responsible for export controls.

Lastly, the treaty requires records to be kept for a minimum of ten years (UNGA, 2013a, art. 12(4)). However, at the international level, in 2005 UN member states undertook to keep information on the transfer of small arms 'indefinitely' (to the extent possible) or at least 20 years under the International Tracing Instrument (UNGA, 2005a, para. IV.12). The ATT's requirement that states parties keep records for only ten years is reminiscent of the timeframe adopted in the Firearms Protocol (UNGA, 2001a, art. 7)—12 years prior to the adoption of the ATT—and represents a step backwards from emerging best practice under small arms instruments. That said, a legally binding provision obliging states parties to keep records of their *conventional* arms transfers is a precedent in international arms control.

Reporting

The ATT includes commitments for states parties to report on diversion, implementation, and exports and imports (UNGA, 2013a, arts. 11(6), 13). A summary of reporting commitments under the ATT is provided in Table 3.3.

States parties are required to report annually on their authorized or actual exports and imports of conventional arms (not ammunition/munitions or parts and components), although the reports 'may exclude commercially sensitive or national security information' (UNGA, 2013a, art. 13(3)).

Table 3.3 **Reporting commitments under the ATT**			
Theme	**Content and information**	**Nature of commitment**	**Frequency**
Diversion	Measures taken to address diversion (art. 11(6))	Encouraged	Ad hoc
	Measures proven effective in addressing diversion (art. 13(2))	Encouraged	Ad hoc
Implementation	Initial report on implementation (art. 13(1))	Mandatory	Within one year of entry into force for the state
	Ad hoc reports as new implementation measures are taken (art. 13(1))	Mandatory	When appropriate/ ad hoc
Transfers	Authorized or actual exports of arms (art. 13(3))	Mandatory	Annual (by 31 May)
	Authorized or actual imports of arms (art. 13(3))	Mandatory	Annual (by 31 May)

Source: UNGA (2013a)

One issue surrounding reporting that remained contentious throughout the ATT deliberations was whether and to what extent reports submitted to a dedicated ATT secretariat would be made publicly available. Given that one of the stated purposes of the ATT is to promote transparency in the international arms trade (UNGA, 2013a, art. 1), this was an important issue for many states. Ultimately, states agreed that reports on implementation and transfers 'shall be made available, and distributed to States Parties by the Secretariat' (arts. 13(1), 13(3); see Table 3.3). While the provision clearly stipulates that the secretariat will distribute reports to other states parties to the treaty, there is some ambiguity in the phrase 'shall be made available' and the placement of the comma. Whether reports *may* or *are to be* 'made available' to a wider audience beyond states parties is open to interpretation.

UN member states are already 'called upon' to provide data on an annual basis on imports and exports of the seven categories of conventional arms to the UN Register (UNGA, 1991). The 2003 GGE agreed that interested states could include transfers of small arms in their annual report to the Register as part of additional background information, and the 2006 GGE established a standardized reporting format to be used on an optional basis (UNDDA, 2007, p. 16). In the event, the ATT specifies that the report submitted by states parties to the ATT secretariat:

> *may contain the same information submitted by the State Party to relevant United Nations frameworks, including the United Nations Register of Conventional Arms* (UNGA, 2013a, art. 13(3)).[44]

Part of the reason for the latter provision was to allay concerns among states that they would be overburdened by reporting obligations.[45] The major difference is that states parties to the ATT have a *legally binding* obligation to report rather than simply being 'called upon' to report—although the treaty does allow them to exclude commercially sensitive or national security information.

Secondly, the ATT provision enhances states' commitment with respect to reporting on small arms transfers since they are included in the scope of the treaty. This is much stronger than 'inviting' states to report on small arms transfers under the UN Register. The creation of a legal obligation to report transfers of conventional arms, including small arms, to an ATT secretariat should increase the level of reporting and information exchange on such transfers (TRADE UPDATE).

BOOKENDS

The ATT also includes introductory provisions, in the form of a preamble and principles, as well final provisions, which set out the procedural elements of the treaty.

Introductory provisions

Generally speaking, the preamble of an international treaty is designed to introduce the main text by providing information on its background and purpose. It may also contain political statements as well as references to issues whose inclusion in the body of the treaty could not be secured by negotiating states (Aust, 2013, p. 367).

The provisions in the preamble help states interpret and apply the treaty.

The ATT preamble does both of these things. It includes references to the purposes of the treaty, such as 'the need to prevent and eradicate the illicit trade in conventional arms'[46] (UNGA, 2013a, preambular para. 3); further, it acknowledges certain issues that could not be addressed in the main text of the treaty, such as lawful civilian access to and use of arms (preambular para. 13).[47] The latter consideration also led to a restatement of certain principles, including the inherent right to self-defence under Article 51 of the UN Charter, in the introductory part of the treaty.

While the provisions of a preamble are not legally binding, they can aid in the interpretation and application of the treaty, and they may reflect certain understandings states have regarding how to interpret and apply the treaty. For example, while there is no definition of 'diversion' in the treaty, the reference in the third paragraph of the preamble to preventing diversion 'to the illicit market, or for unauthorized end use and end users', including terrorists, provides some guidance to the application of the term in the context of the ATT.

The object of the treaty—as echoed in the title of the ATT resolutions—is to 'establish the highest possible common international standards for regulating or improving the regulation of the international trade in conventional arms' (UNGA, 2013a, art. 1) as well as to prevent and eradicate the illicit trade in conventional arms and prevent diversion. The ATT's purpose is threefold: to contribute to international and regional peace, security, and stability; reduce human suffering; and promote cooperation, transparency, and responsible action by states parties in the international arms trade, thereby building confidence among states parties (UNGA, 2013a, art. 1).

Final provisions

Generally speaking, the final provisions of a treaty, or final clauses, as they are commonly called, relate to procedural aspects rather than substance. They generally include articles governing the establishment of treaty infrastructure, future meetings, the settlement of disputes, treaty amendments, the requirements for the treaty to enter into force, and reservations (UNOLA, 2003, p. 1).

The central elements of the ATT's final provisions can be summarized as follows:

- A Conference of States Parties will be convened no later than one year following the entry into force of the treaty. The first such conference will determine the frequency with which future meetings are held and the rules of procedure governing such meetings (UNGA, 2013a, art. 17(1)–(2)).
- Article 18 establishes a secretariat to 'assist States Parties in the effective implementation of this Treaty'. Article 18(3) indicates the secretariat should operate 'within a minimized structure'. This wording reflects a desire expressed by many states during negotiations that the secretariat be relatively small and inexpensive. Presumably, however, the size of the secretariat will ultimately depend on the tasks that are allocated to it.
- Proposed amendments to the treaty can first be made six years after its entry into force, and thereafter every three years (art. 20(1)).

- When a proposed amendment is under consideration, states parties must make every effort to achieve consensus on the amendment; if consensus cannot be achieved, the amendment may be adopted by a three-quarters majority vote of the states parties present and voting at the meeting (art. 20(3)). Any amendment that is adopted will only bind those states parties that deposit an instrument of acceptance for the amendment with the depositary (art. 20(4)).[48]
- The treaty only enters into force—that is, it becomes legally binding for states parties—90 days after the day on which the 50th state has submitted its instrument of ratification, acceptance, or approval[49] to the Secretary-General of the United Nations (art. 22(1)).
- States may declare that they will provisionally apply Articles 6 and 7 of the treaty at the time they sign or deposit an instrument of ratification, acceptance, approval, or accession,[50] even before the treaty comes into force (art. 23). Of the states that signed the treaty when it was opened for signature on 3 June 2013, only Spain declared that it would provisionally apply Articles 6 and 7. States may also formulate reservations at the time of signature, ratification, acceptance, approval, or accession, provided such reservations are compatible with the object and purpose of the treaty (art. 25).

One of the most contested and controversial articles in the final provisions is Article 26, which governs the relationship between the ATT and other international agreements. The article is composed of two paragraphs: the first notes that treaty implementation 'shall not prejudice obligations undertaken by States Parties with regard to existing or future international agreements, to which they are parties', provided those obligations are consistent with the treaty (UNGA, 2013a, art. 26(1)); the second stipulates that the treaty 'shall not be cited as grounds for voiding defence cooperation agreements concluded between States Parties' (art. 26(2)).

The impact of the ATT will depend on more than words on a page.

In its original form, the first paragraph created a significant potential loophole, since there was no requirement that obligations under other agreements be consistent with the ATT (UNGA, 2012b, art. 5(2)). With respect to the second paragraph, India, in particular, as a major importer of arms, sought to ensure that exporting states that enter long-term arrangements to supply arms to it would not be able to use the treaty to break such agreements. In essence, Article 26 confirms that states parties may honour existing or future arrangements for the supply of weapons to allies, provided the latter are 'consistent with' the treaty.

IMPACT

The preceding analysis of ATT provisions offers a partial answer to the question: what impact will the ATT have? The brief comparison with some of the international and regional instruments that already restrict or at least affect states' freedom to transfer conventional arms reveals what difference the ATT makes on paper: it expands and strengthens some existing commitments and introduces some new commitments, but it also weakens some existing norms and emerging practice, in particular with respect to small arms and light weapons.

Ultimately, however, the question of what difference the ATT will make in practice and whether it will achieve its objectives probably does not depend on words on a page. It depends on the extent to which states apply the treaty's obligations and recommendations. As noted by the Secretary-General: 'its effectiveness will depend on the willingness of States to ensure its full implementation' (UNDPI, 2013c). This includes states' willingness to implement the treaty themselves, as well as to ensure implementation by other states through cooperation and assistance, and through closer scrutiny of states' decisions to export arms, ammunition, and parts and components in light of the ATT transfer criteria.

John Kerry, US Secretary of State, signs the ATT, New York, 25 September 2013. © Spencer Platt/Getty Images

A willingness to implement the treaty is apparent from the number of states that have already started the process of reviewing their existing national frameworks to determine what needs to be done to comply with the ATT; in some instances, states are already translating the ATT into national legislation.[51] Furthermore, many states have expressed an intention to take a progressive approach to their interpretation of the treaty. As pointed out by several states[52] following its adoption, the ATT creates a 'floor, not a ceiling' (UNDPI, 2013a); states that wish to do more than the ATT strictly requires them to are free to do so. Many states parties—including the ones that pushed for stronger treaty language and that are likely to be among the first to ratify the treaty—may take a maximalist approach, implementing provisions even if they are only 'encouraged' or 'optional'.

A willingness to facilitate implementation by other states through the provision of assistance has already been demonstrated through the establishment of the multi-donor UN Trust Facility Supporting Cooperation on Arms Regulation (UNSCAR) in June 2013. Hosted by the UN Office for Disarmament Affairs, UNSCAR is to support ATT implementation with support from Australia, Denmark, Germany, the Netherlands, and Spain (UNDPI, 2013d).[53] Other states are providing funding for ATT projects on a bilateral basis to support implementation at both the national and regional levels.

It is too early to assess states' willingness to ensure implementation of the ATT transfer criteria by other states through closer scrutiny of export authorization decisions. Although the ATT itself does not include a mechanism for monitoring arms transfers or reviewing exporters' decisions to authorize exports, it unequivocally provides the framework for closer examination of states' decisions by outlining the risks that should be assessed. In the absence of a formal monitoring mechanism, civil society and the media will probably undertake such examination in the early years after entry into force. But, in the longer term, states parties themselves are likely to take up the mantle, formally or informally.

Monitoring by states will probably not take the form of public condemnation of export licensing decisions or a resort to formal dispute resolution regarding the application of the treaty (although this is possible under Article 19). It is more likely to take the form of bilateral consultations and requests for clarification of decisions taken, including, possibly, within meetings of the Conference of States Parties. Even states that do not become states parties to the ATT and that are not legally bound by its terms will experience pressure to apply its standards and will find their export licensing decisions scrutinized against the ATT backdrop.

While not all states are behind the treaty and certainly not all states will sign and ratify it, the evidence to date indicates that the majority of states are willing and intend to implement it and are looking for ways to assist other states to do the same. The ATT is already prompting states to take stock of their existing transfer control systems—be they exporting, importing, or transit states—and to identify weaknesses and gaps. Improvements to existing control systems and an increase in the number of countries that have control systems should boost the fight against the illicit arms trade.

Most states are willing and intend to implement the ATT.

In this sense, the ATT has raised awareness of the importance of transfer controls and opened up discussions on and scrutiny of the arms trade. Most major arms exporters are already committed to applying transfer criteria similar to the ATT's under existing export control regimes. But the majority of UN member states are importers or transit states and are not members of such regimes, which largely excludes them from the consideration of export control issues and the development of transfer criteria. The participation of non-exporting states in a global regulatory system—which the ATT offers—means that those that have traditionally not been in the exporters 'club' but that more frequently experience the adverse effects of irresponsible arms transfers will have a legitimate forum in which to raise their concerns and work to improve ATT standards.

From the commercial—as opposed to the humanitarian—perspective, the ATT is the first multilateral treaty that creates a level playing field for the international arms trade (Saferworld, 2013). Moreover, it is believed that '[i]ncreasing the number of countries operating under common standards of control will provide more predictability and confidence for organizations that operate in a global market place and with global supply chains' (de Vries, 2013). In other words, the ATT may bring improvements to the arms industry by ensuring that arms manufacturers throughout the world are subject to the same degree of governmental regulation (Youngman, 2013).

The adoption of the ATT also sends a positive message about multilateral arms control, which has had a less than impressive track record in recent decades. For example, the last agreement successfully negotiated by the Conference on Disarmament[54] was the 1996 Comprehensive Nuclear-Test-Ban Treaty (UNGA, 1996). Since then, conference members have been locked in a procedural stalemate, unable to agree on a programme of work. Both the Mine Ban Treaty and the Convention on Cluster Munitions were negotiated outside of the UN[55] after discussions within the auspices of the Convention on Certain Conventional Weapons at the United Nations in Geneva failed to make progress on the issues. In contrast, the successful negotiation of an ATT within a UN framework sends a signal that the UN can still deliver new arms treaties.

That said, the ATT also has the potential to detract attention from ongoing processes, such as the PoA and the Firearms Protocol, as states turn their focus—and donors turn their wallets—to ATT implementation and compliance. There are many overlaps and opportunities for synergies between the ATT and these existing processes, but there is also a danger that UN member states will perceive the ATT as replacing, or at least taking priority over, implementation of other commitments. A related danger is that, as part of efforts—and pressure—to sign and ratify the treaty, non-exporting states will pour energy and scarce resources into developing national control systems for weapons that are rarely traded to or from their territories, at the expense of investing in measures that would do more to prevent diversion, such as improved stockpile management and surplus destruction.

CONCLUSION

The negotiation of an Arms Trade Treaty was a complex and ambitious undertaking, involving the reconciliation of humanitarian objectives with commercial and security considerations in a disarmament forum, all this while trying to balance the interests of arms suppliers and recipients alike. The ATT is, inevitably, an imperfect document that reflects the compromises necessary to achieve agreement. It contains a comprehensive array of regulatory measures, but its lack of detail and its reliance on national discretion increase the risk of inconsistent implementation by states parties.

In the coming months and years, lawyers will grapple with some of the ambiguities of ATT language as they seek to translate treaty provisions into national legislation and policy. That said, the ATT does establish *legally binding* common standards for the international trade in conventional arms, which, judging from the protracted and difficult treaty negotiations, are the 'highest possible' that the UN membership has been able to attain to date. This fact alone makes a significant difference from the perspective of international law. The ATT codifies some existing responsibilities relating to international arms transfers and helps develop other norms in an area that has hitherto been stubbornly resistant to such development.

The process towards an ATT has demonstrated impressive political momentum among states and civil society alike. The perceived success of that process can be expected to yield positive political ramifications. The ATT has already had an impact on the level of awareness of, and attention to, arms transfer decisions. This will undoubtedly lead to closer scrutiny of arms transfer decisions by states parties and non-state parties alike. Whether it translates into more responsible decisions being made in the longer term, and fewer arms getting into the hands of the wrong people, depends on several factors, including states' long-term commitment to converting words on paper into concrete action.

The ATT cannot be expected to stop all arms exports that breach treaty norms. But it does promise greater scrutiny of arms transfer decisions by the international community. It has provided a universal benchmark against which all transfer decisions will be assessed and provides the framework for all states to engage on the issue of responsible arms transfers. The ATT negotiations and the implementation process that is just beginning have shone a light on an issue routinely considered a matter of 'national security'. Until now. ◾

LIST OF ABBREVIATIONS

ATT	Arms Trade Treaty
CARICOM	Caribbean Community
ECOWAS	Economic Community of West African States
EU	European Union
GGE	Group of governmental experts
IHL	International humanitarian law

NGO	Non-governmental organization
OEWG	Open-ended working group
OSCE	Organization for Security and Co-operation in Europe
PoA	United Nations Programme of Action to Prevent, Combat and Eradicate the Illicit Trade in Small Arms and Light Weapons in All Its Aspects
PrepCom	Preparatory committee
UNGA	United Nations General Assembly
UNSCAR	United Nations Trust Facility Supporting Cooperation on Arms Regulation
WTO	World Trade Organization

ANNEXE

Online annexe at <http://www.smallarmssurvey.org/publications/by-type/yearbook/small-arms-survey-2014.html>

Annexe 3.1. A comparative overview of transfer criteria in multilateral and regional instruments on conventional arms

ENDNOTES

1 For up-to-date information on ATT signatures and ratifications, see UNODA (n.d.a).

2 Author interview with a participant in the Code initiative, New York, 22 October 2013.

3 The group was comprised of Amnesty International, the Arias Foundation, the British American Security Information Council, the Federation of American Scientists, Oxfam, Project Ploughshares, and Saferworld.

4 The seven states were Argentina, Australia, Costa Rica, Finland, Japan, Kenya, and the United Kingdom.

5 The abstaining states were Bahrain, Belarus, China, Egypt, India, Iran, Iraq, Israel, Kuwait, Laos, Libya, the Marshall Islands, Nepal, Oman, Pakistan, Qatar, the Russian Federation, Saudi Arabia, Sudan, Syria, the United Arab Emirates, Venezuela, Yemen, and Zimbabwe.

6 The United States voted against.

7 The sessions were held on 11–15 February, 12–16 May, and 28 July–8 August 2008.

8 There were 133 votes in favour, 17 abstentions, and no votes against.

9 Iran, North Korea, and Syria voted against.

10 After the official vote, the delegations of Angola (which had abstained) and Cape Verde (which had not voted) informed the UN Secretariat that they had intended to vote in favour of the resolution (UNGA, 2013b, p. 13). Accordingly, 156 states voted in favour of the resolution, 3 voted against it, and 22 abstained from voting.

11 The US statement on the ATT stressed that 'this is not an arms control treaty, not a disarmament treaty—it is a trade treaty regulating a legitimate activity' (US, 2013, p. 2).

12 Canada noted: 'On the issue of treaty implementation, States Parties should take the necessary legislative and administrative measures to implement the treaty, but there must be national discretion on how such measures are put in place. There is no "one-size-fits-all" model' (Canada, 2011, p. 3).

13 Expert meetings were held in 1992, 1994, 1997, 2000, 2003, 2006, 2009, and 2013. The reports of the various expert meetings on the UN Register, including amendments to the descriptions of the seven categories of conventional arms, are available at UNODA (n.d.b).

14 The current descriptions adopted by the UN Register are available at UNODA (n.d.c).

15 The Firearms Protocol includes a definition of 'firearm', which covers all small arms but only applies to a narrow range of light weapons; see McDonald (2005, p. 126).

16 The term 'munitions' was added to the term 'ammunition' to ensure that the ATT covers bombs and shells. Furthermore, there is no word for 'ammunition' in Spanish, making negotiations using the English term difficult. The exact scope of the phrase is unclear, but given the require-ment that ammunition/munitions be 'fired, launched or delivered' by the conventional arms the ATT covers (UNGA, 2013a, art. 3), items such as hand grenades and landmines appear to be excluded.

17 Yet the International Tracing Instrument does give the following as examples of elements of a small arm that constitute 'parts': 'the barrel and/or slide or cylinder of the weapon' (UNGA, 2005, para. III.10). In addition, the international Ammunition Technical Guidelines includes definitions for ammunition, munitions, missiles, and other terms (UNODA, 2011).

18   The list is available at WA (n.d.).

19   See also Doermann (2013) and Casey-Maslen (2013).

20   During the negotiations, states disagreed over whether the commentary to Article 16 was authoritative, especially since it deviates from the actual text of the article. Eventually, the negotiators elected not to align the ATT with Article 16 (author correspondence with a participant in the ATT negotiations, December 2013)

21   This refers to armed conflicts in which one or more non-state armed groups are involved, in contrast to 'international armed conflicts', in which the opposing sides are states. See ICRC (2008) for more details.

22   For more details on Article 6(3), see Casey-Maslen, Giacca, and Vestner (2013, p. 25) and Clapham (2013, p. 2).

23   The ATT provision makes reference only to 'international conventions or protocols' and thus implicitly excludes regional instruments. A listing of the 16 major international legal instruments and additional amendments dealing with terrorism can be found on the Security Council Counter-Terrorism Committee website at CTC (n.d.).

24   The eight instruments are: (1) Wassenaar BPG: the Wassenaar Best Practice Guidelines for Exports of Small Arms and Light Weapons (SALW), adopted 2002, amended 2007 (WA, 2002); (2) Wassenaar Elements: the Wassenaar Elements for Objective Analysis and Advice Concerning Potentially Destabilising Accumulations of Conventional Weapons, adopted 1998, amended 2004 (WA, 1998); (3) Central African Convention: the Central African Convention for the Control of Small Arms and Light Weapons, Their Ammunition and All Parts and Components That Can Be Used for Their Manufacture, Repair and Assembly, 2010, not yet in force (ECCAS, 2010); (4) ECOWAS Convention: the Economic Community of West African States' Convention on Small Arms and Light Weapons, Their Ammunition and Other Related Materials, 2006, in force 2009 (ECOWAS, 2006); (5) EU Common Position: the European Union's Common Position of 2008 (EU, 2008); (6) OSCE Document: the Organization for Security and Co-operation in Europe (OSCE) Document on Small Arms and Light Weapons, adopted 2000, reissued 2012 (OSCE, 2000); (7) OSCE Principles: the OSCE Principles Governing Conventional Arms Transfers, 1993 (OSCE, 1993); and (8) SICA Code of Conduct: the Code of Conduct of Central American States on the Transfer of Arms, Ammunition, Explosives and Other Related Materiel, 2005 (SICA, 2006).

25   However, the EU Common Position makes reference to 'major' violations in providing that member states should deny transfers if there is a clear risk they may be used for 'internal repression', defined to include torture and other cruel, inhuman, and degrading treatment or punishment, summary or arbitrary executions, disappearances, arbitrary detentions, and 'other *major* violations of human rights and fundamental freedoms' as set out in relevant instruments (EU, 2008, art. 2, criterion 2, emphasis added).

26   For example, the OSCE Document and the Wassenaar BPG call on states to 'avoid' transfers where there is a 'clear risk' that the arms 'might' support or encourage terrorism (OSCE, 2000, para. III(A)(2)(b)(ix); WA, 2002, para. 2(a)).

27   For example, the Holy See argued that 'the reference to gender-based violence was ambiguous and that it could not accept this inclusion' in the relevant article (Nielsen, 2012, p. 4).

28   Liechtenstein was among those states (UNDPI, 2013a).

29   See Clapham (2013, p. 4).

30   Article 5(5) stipulates that states parties must have an effective and transparent national control system 'regulating the transfer of conventional arms covered under Article 2(1) and of items covered under Article 3 and Article 4'. The use of the term 'transfer', combined with the references to Articles 3 and 4, implies that states parties have an obligation to regulate the *transfer* (that is, the export, import, transit, transhipment, and brokering) of ammunition/munitions and parts and components. This contradicts the text of Articles 3 and 4, which requires only that states parties regulate the *export* of these items.

31   The two international instruments are the Firearms Protocol and the PoA.

32   The regional instruments are the Andean Plan (2003); the ECOWAS Convention (ECOWAS, 2006); the Inter-American Convention against the Illicit Manufacturing of and Trafficking in Firearms, Ammunition, Explosives, and Other Related Materials (OAS, 1997); the Nairobi Protocol (2004); the OSCE Document (2000); and the Protocol on the Control of Firearms, Ammunition and Other Related Materials in the Southern African Development Community Region (SADC, 2001).

33   ECCAS (2010, ch. II, art. 6); ECOWAS (2006, art. 4(2)); Nairobi Protocol (2004, art. 10(a)); OAS (1997, art. IX(1)); OSCE (2000, para. III(B)(2)); UNGA (2001a, art. 10(1)).

34   Nairobi Protocol (2004, art. 10(d)); OAS (1997, art. IX(4)); OSCE (2000, para. III(B)(4)); UNGA (2001a, art. 10(4)).

35   Nevertheless, the reference to the keeping of records of conventional arms that are 'authorized to transit or trans-ship territory' in Article 12(2) suggests that a system of authorization would be an appropriate measure to regulate transit and transhipment.

36   The Convention on the Law of the Sea stipulates that 'ships of all States, whether coastal or land-locked, enjoy the right of innocent passage through the territorial sea' (UNCLOS, 1982, art. 17).

37   A list of member states is available at OTIF (n.d.).

38   A list of states parties is available at UN (n.d.).

39   Attempts to control brokers and brokering activities outside states' territories are important since such activities are often conducted in a country other than the broker's country of nationality, residence, or registration. In addition, the arms in question do not necessarily pass through the territory of the country where the brokering activity is conducted.

40   For example, a GGE to consider further steps to enhance international cooperation in preventing, combating, and eradicating illicit brokering in small arms and light weapons was established under General Assembly Resolution 60/81 in 2005 (UNGA, 2005b). The GGE met in 2007 and produced a report that included recommendations on the regulation of brokers at the national level (UNGA, 2007, p. 18).

41   Article 5(2) requires states parties to establish a national control system but does not specify that this should include laws and regulations.

42   In a statement, the Caribbean Community noted that 'international cooperation and assistance is another vital area for CARICOM, provisions for which must find its way into the treaty' (CARICOM, 2012, p. 4).

43   The Pacific Islands Forum stressed that 'effective national implementation of the ATT will be contingent on the availability of technical assistance [. . .]. It is important that the ATT provide a comprehensive framework for international cooperation and assistance' (PIF, 2012, p. 4).

44   The date for submission of ATT reports on imports and exports—31 May—coincides with the date by which states are requested to provide information to the UN Register each year.

45   Throughout the ATT process, states stressed that reporting should not be overly burdensome and noted that 'reporting fatigue from too frequent, detailed and technical reporting should be avoided' (Kytömäki, 2012, pp. 78–79).

46   This reference is echoed in Article 1 of the ATT.

47   Several states tried to exclude civilian small arms from the ATT. For example, Italy argued that the treaty should not apply to sports shooting or hunting weapons (Italy, 2012, p. 3).

48   As the ATT depositary, the UN Secretary-General's offices will be responsible for keeping custody of the treaty and receiving notice of any amendments.

49   A state that has signed the ATT has an obligation to refrain, in good faith, from acts that would defeat the object and purpose of the treaty, but it is not legally bound by the treaty until it enters into force for that state. In ratifying a treaty, a state expresses its consent to be bound by the treaty (VCLT, 1969, art. 14(1)). Alternatively, it can express its consent by acceptance or approval, equivalent processes that are subject to similar conditions (art. 14(2)).

50   Accession is the equivalent of ratification, except that it takes place after a treaty has entered into force.

51   Author's observation derived from statements and interventions made by UN member states during UN and regional follow-up meetings in 2013 after the adoption of the ATT.

52   These states include Japan and the United States.

53   The UK has also pledged support to UNSCAR.

54   The Conference on Disarmament was established in 1979 as the single multilateral disarmament negotiating forum of the international community. It is based in Geneva and currently has 65 members.

55   The Mine Ban Treaty was negotiated through the Canadian-led 'Ottawa Process' and the Convention on Cluster Munitions was negotiated through the Norwegian-led 'Oslo Process'.

BIBLIOGRAPHY

Andean Plan (Andean Plan to Prevent, Combat and Eradicate Illicit Trade in Small Arms and Light Weapons in All Its Aspects). 2003. Quirama Recinto, Colombia, 25 June. <http://www.comunidadandina.org/ingles/normativa/D552e.htm>

Arias Foundation (for Peace and Human Progress). 2008. *Viability of the Arms Trade Treaty: Comparative Legal Analysis Exercise*. San José, Costa Rica: Arias Foundation.
    <http://controlarms.org/wordpress/wp-content/uploads/2011/03/Towards-an-Arms-Trade-Treaty-Perspective-of-Countries-in-Latin-America.pdf>

Aust, Anthony. 2013. *Modern Treaty Law and Practice*, 3rd edn. Cambridge: Cambridge University Press.

Canada. 2011. 'Statement by the Delegation of Canada: Arms Trade Treaty PrepCom.' 14 July.
    <http://www.un.org/disarmament/convarms/ATTPrepCom/Documents/Statements-MS/PrepCom3/2011-July-14/2011-07-14-Canada-EL.pdf>

CARICOM (Caribbean Community). 2012. 'Statement by the Honourable Winston Dookeran Minister for Foreign Affairs of the Republic of Trinidad and Tobago on behalf of the Caribbean Community (CARICOM) in the High Level Segment of the Diplomatic Conference on the Arms Trade Treaty (ATT).' 2 July. <http://www.un.org/disarmament/ATT/statements/docs/20120705/Regional%20Groups/20120705_CARICOM_E.pdf>

Casey-Maslen, Stuart. 2013. 'The Arms Trade Treaty: A Major Achievement.' 8 April. <blog.oup.com/2013/04/un-arms-trade-treaty-pil/>

—, Stuart, Gilles Giacca, and Tobias Vestner. 2013. *The Arms Trade Treaty*. Academy Briefing No. 3. Geneva: Geneva Academy of International Humanitarian Law and Human Rights. June. <http://www.geneva-academy.ch/docs/publications/Arms%20Trade%20Treaty%203%20WEB(2).pdf>

Clapham, Andrew. 2013. 'The Arms Trade Treaty: A Call for an Awakening.' *ESIL Reflections*, Vol. 2, Iss. 5. Florence: Home European Society of International Law. 6 May. <http://www.esil-sedi.eu/sites/default/files/Clapham%20Reflection_0.pdf>

Control Arms. 2009. 'Global Principles for the Parameters of an ATT.' Position Paper No.1. London: NGO Arms Trade Treaty Steering Committee. July. <http://www.saferworld.org.uk/downloads/pubdocs/Global%20Principles%20of%20an%20ATT.pdf>

COTIF (Convention Concerning International Carriage by Rail). 1980. Of 9 May 1980 as amended by the Vilnius Protocol of 3 June 1999. <http://www.itg-rks.com/repository/docs/COTIF_381179.pdf>

CTC (Security Council Counter-Terrorism Committee). n.d. 'International Laws.' <http://www.un.org/en/sc/ctc/laws.html>

da Silva, Claire. 2009. 'Creating a Human Rights Standard for the Arms Trade Treaty.' *Disarmament Forum*, Nos. 1–2, pp. 27–36.

de Vries, Wendela. 2013. 'We Have an Arms Trade Treaty: What Difference Does It Make?' *War Profiteers' News*, No. 38. 23 April. <http://www.wri-irg.org/fr/node/21654>

Doermann, Knut. 2013. *Adoption of a Global Arms Trade Treaty: Challenges Ahead*. International Law Summary. London: Chatham House. 16 April. <http://www.chathamhouse.org/sites/default/files/public/Research/International%20Law/160413summary.pdf>

ECCAS (Economic Community of Central African States). 2010. Central African Convention for the Control of Small Arms and Light Weapons, Their Ammunition and All Parts and Components that Can Be Used for Their Manufacture, Repair and Assembly. Kinshasa, Democratic Republic of the Congo, 30 April. <http://www.poa-iss.org/revcon2/Documents/PrepCom-Background/Regional/ECCAS_Kinshasa%20Convention.pdf>

ECOWAS (Economic Community of West African States). 2006. ECOWAS Convention on Small Arms and Light Weapons, Their Ammunition and Other Related Materials. Abuja, Nigeria, 14 June. <http://www.poa-iss.org/RegionalOrganizations/ECOWAS/ECOWAS%20Convention%202006.pdf>

EU (European Union). 2003. Council Common Position 2003/468/CFSP of 23 June 2003 on the Control of Arms Brokering. *Official Journal of the European Union*. Notice No. L 156/79. 23 June. <http://eur-lex.europa.eu/LexUriServ/LexUriServ.do?uri=OJ:L:2003:156:0079:0079:EN:PDF>

—. 2008. Council Common Position 2008/944/CFSP of 8 December 2008 Defining Common Rules Governing Control of Exports of Military Technology and Equipment. *Official Journal of the European Union*. Notice No. L 335/99. 13 December. <http://eur-lex.europa.eu/LexUriServ/LexUriServ.do?uri=OJ:L:2008:335:0099:0099:EN:PDF>

Framework Convention (on International Arms Transfers). 2001. <http://seesac.org/sasp2/english/publications/2/4_1_Framework.pdf>

GATT (General Agreement on Tariffs and Trade). 1947. Legal Texts: GATT 1947. <http://www.wto.org/english/docs_e/legal_e/gatt47_02_e.htm#articleXXI>

ICAO (United Nations International Civil Aviation Organization). 1944. Convention on Civil Aviation. Chicago, 7 December. <http://www.icao.int/publications/Documents/7300_orig.pdf>

ICC (International Criminal Court). 1998. Rome Statute of the International Criminal Court. A/CONF.183/9 of 17 July 1998, with corrections. <http://www.icc-cpi.int/nr/rdonlyres/ea9aeff7-5752-4f84-be94-0a655eb30c16/0/rome_statute_english.pdf>

ICRC (International Committee of the Red Cross). 2008. *How Is the Term 'Armed Conflict' Defined in International Humanitarian Law?* ICRC Opinion Paper. March. <http://www.icrc.org/eng/assets/files/other/opinion-paper-armed-conflict.pdf>

ILC (International Law Commission). 2001. *Report of the International Law Commission on the Work of its Fifty-third Session: Draft Articles on Responsibility of States for Internationally Wrongful Acts, with Commentaries*. Geneva: United Nations, 2008. <http://legal.un.org/ilc/texts/instruments/english/commentaries/9_6_2001.pdf>

Italy. 2012. 'Statement by H.E Ambassador Cesare Maria Ragaglini, Permanent Representative of Italy to the United Nations, Plenary Meeting of the General Assembly United Nations Conference on the Arms Trade Treaty.' 5 July. <http://www.un.org/disarmament/ATT/statements/docs/20120709/20120709_Italy_E.pdf>

Kytömäki, Elli. 2012. *Supporting the Arms Trade Treaty Negotiations through Regional Discussions and Expertise Sharing: Final Report of the EU–UNIDIR Project*. Geneva: United Nations Institute for Disarmament Research. <http://www.unidir.org/files/medias/pdfs/final-report-eng-0-255.pdf>

McDonald, Glenn. 2005. 'Locking onto Target: Light Weapons Control Measures.' In Small Arms Survey. *Small Arms Survey 2005: Weapons at War*. Oxford: Oxford University Press, pp. 123–41.

—. 2008. 'Who's Buying? End-user Certification.' In Small Arms Survey. *Small Arms Survey 2008: Risk and Resilience*. Cambridge: Cambridge University Press, pp. 154–81.

Nairobi Protocol. 2004. The Nairobi Protocol for the Prevention, Control and Reduction of Small Arms and Light Weapons in the Great Lakes Region and the Horn of Africa. Nairobi, 21 April. <http://www.recsasec.org/pdf/Nairobi%20Protocol.pdf>

Nielsen, Rørdam. 2012. 'News in Brief.' *Arms Trade Treaty Monitor*, Vol. 5, No. 18. 27 July. <http://reachingcriticalwill.org/images/documents/Disarmament-fora/att/monitor/ATTMonitor5.18.pdf>

NPL ICoC (Nobel Peace Laureates' International Code Of Conduct On Arms Transfers). 1997. May. <http://www.wagingpeace.org/articles/1997/05/00_nobel-code-conduct.htm>

OAS (Organization of American States). 1997. Inter-American Convention against the Illicit Manufacturing of and Trafficking in Firearms, Ammunition, Explosives, and Other Related Materials. Washington, DC, 14 November. <http://www.oas.org/juridico/english/treaties/a-63.html>

OSCE (Organization for Security and Co-operation in Europe). 1993. Principles Governing Conventional Arms Transfers.
<http://www.osce.org/documents/fsc/1993/11/4269_en.pdf>

—. 2000. Document on Small Arms and Light Weapons. FSC.DOC/1/00/Rev.1, originally adopted 24 November 2000, reissued 20 June 2012. Vienna: Forum for Security Co-operation, OSCE. <http://www.osce.org/fsc/20783>

OTIF (Intergovernmental Organisation for International Carriage by Rail). n.d. 'List of Member States.'
<http://www.otif.org/en/about-otif/list-of-member-states.html>

Oxford Dictionaries. n.d.a. 'Overriding.' <http://www.oxforddictionaries.com/definition/english/overriding?q=overriding>

—. n.d.b. 'Preponderant.' <http://www.oxforddictionaries.com/definition/english/preponderant>

PIF (Pacific Islands Forum). 2012. 'Common Principles on the Key Elements of the Arms Trade Treaty: Statement of Behalf of the Members of the Pacific Islands Forum in New York—Statement by H.E. Dell Higgie, Ambassador for Disarmament.' 3 July.
<http://www.un.org/disarmament/ATT/statements/docs/20120709/Regional/20120706_PIF_E.pdf>

SADC (Southern African Development Community). 2001. Protocol on the Control of Firearms, Ammunition and Other Related Materials in the Southern African Development Community Region. 14 August. <http://www.sadc.int/index/browse/page/125>

Saferworld. 2013. 'Turning Words into Action: The Arms Trade Treaty Deserves the World's Full Support.' 15 October.
<http://www.saferworld.org.uk/news-and-views/comment/112>

SICA (Central American Integration System). 2006. Code of Conduct of Central American States on the Transfer of Arms, Ammunition, Explosives and Other Related Materiel. A/CONF.192/2006/RC/WP.6. 30 June. <http://www.un.org/events/smallarms2006/pdf/rc.wp.6-e.pdf>

Switzerland. 2013. Model interpretative declaration. 22 October.

UN (United Nations). 1945. Charter of the United Nations. 24 October. <https://www.un.org/en/documents/charter/>

—. n.d. 'United Nations Treaty Collection.' <https://treaties.un.org/Pages/ViewDetails.aspx?src=TREATY&mtdsg_no=XI-A-17&chapter=11&lang=en>

UNCLOS (United Nations Convention on the Law of the Sea). 1982. <http://www.un.org/depts/los/convention_agreements/texts/unclos/unclos_e.pdf>

UNDDA (United Nations Department of Disarmament Affairs). 2007. United Nations Register of Conventional Arms: Information Booklet 2007. New York: UNDDA. <http://www.un.org/disarmament/convarms/Register/DOCS/ReportingGuides/InfoBooklet2007/MOD%20ENGLISH.PDF>

UNDPI (United Nations Department of Public Information). 2013a. 'Overwhelming Majority of States in General Assembly Say "Yes" to Arms Trade Treaty to Stave Off Irresponsible Transfers that Perpetuate Conflict, Human Suffering.' GA/11354. 2 April.
<http://www.un.org/News/Press/docs/2013/ga11354.doc.htm>

—. 2013b. 'Arms Trade Treaty Will End "Free-For-All" Nature of Transfers, Secretary-General Says at Signing Ceremony, Noting All Eyes on Traders, Producers, Governments.' DC/3434 L/T/4428 of 3 June. <http://www.un.org/News/Press/docs/2013/dc3434.doc.htm>

—. 2013c. 'As Arms Trade Treaty Opens for Signature, Secretary-General Says It Will Deter Destabilizing Arms Flows, Particularly in Conflict-Prone Regions.' SG/SM15075 of 3 June. <http://www.un.org/News/Press/docs/2013/sgsm15075.doc.htm>

—. 2013d. 'New Trust Fund Facility Adds Momentum to Arms Trade Treaty.' Press release. DC/3437 of 7 June.
<http://www.un.org/News/Press/docs//2013/dc3437.doc.htm>

UNECE (United Nations Economic Commission for Europe). 1982. International Convention on the Harmonization of Frontier Controls of Goods. 21 October. ECE/TRANS/55/Rev.2. <http://www.unece.org/fileadmin/DAM/trans/conventn/harmone.pdf>

UNGA (United Nations General Assembly). 1965. Convention on Transit Trade of Land-locked States. New York, 8 July.
<http://treaties.un.org/pages/ViewDetails.aspx?src=TREATY&mtdsg_no=X-3&chapter=10&lang=en>

—. 1991. Resolution 46/36 L: Transparency in Armaments. Adopted 6 December. A/RES/46/36/L of 9 December.
<http://www.un.org/depts/ddar/Register/4636.html>

—. 1992. General and Complete Disarmament: Transparency in Armaments—Report on the Register of Conventional Arms. A/47/342 of 14 August.
<http://www.un.org/ga/search/view_doc.asp?symbol=A/47/342>

—. 1996. Comprehensive Nuclear-Test-Ban Treaty. Resolution 50/245, adopted 10 September. A/RES/50/245 of 17 September.
<http://www.ctbto.org/fileadmin/content/treaty/treaty_text.pdf>

—. 2001a. Protocol against the Illicit Manufacturing of and Trafficking in Firearms, Their Parts and Components and Ammunition, Supplementing the United Nations Convention against Transnational Organized Crime ('Firearms Protocol'). Resolution 55/255, adopted 31 May. A/RES/55/255 of 8 June. <http://www.unodc.org/pdf/crime/a_res_55/255e.pdf>

—. 2001b. Programme of Action to Prevent, Combat and Eradicate the Illicit Trade in Small Arms and Light Weapons in All Its Aspects ('UN Programme of Action'). Adopted 21 July. A/CONF.192/15 of 20 July. <http://www.poa-iss.org/PoA/PoA.aspx>

—. 2005a. International Instrument to Enable States to Identify and Trace, in a Timely and Reliable Manner, Illicit Small Arms and Light Weapons ('International Tracing Instrument'). Adopted 8 December. A/60/88 of 27 June (Annexe).
<http://www.poa-iss.org/InternationalTracing/ITI_English.pdf>

—. 2005b. Resolution 60/81, adopted 8 December 2005. A/RES/60/81 of 11 January 2006.
    <http://www.un.org/en/ga/search/view_doc.asp?symbol=A/RES/60/81>

—. 2005c. Resolution 60/226, adopted 23 December. A/RES/60/226 of 11 January 2006.
    <http://www.un.org/ga/search/view_doc.asp?symbol=A/RES/60/226>

—. 2006a. *Official Records of the Sixty-first Session, 67th Plenary Meeting.* A/61/PV.67 of 6 December 2006. New York.
    <http://www.un.org/ga/search/view_doc.asp?symbol=A/61/PV.67&Lang=E>

—. 2006b. Resolution 61/89—Towards an Arms Trade Treaty: Establishing Common International Standards for the Import, Export and Transfer of
    Conventional Arms. Adopted 6 December. A/RES/61/89 of 18 December 2006.
    <http://www.un.org/en/ga/search/view_doc.asp?symbol=A/RES/61/89&Lang=E>

—. 2007. *Report of the Group of Governmental Experts Established Pursuant to General Assembly Resolution 60/81 to Consider Further Steps to Enhance
    International Cooperation in Preventing, Combating and Eradicating Illicit Brokering in Small Arms and Light Weapons.* A/62/163 of 30 August.
    <http://www.poa-iss.org/BrokeringControls/English_N0744232.pdf>

—. 2008a. *Report of the Group of Governmental Experts to Examine the Feasibility, Scope and Draft Parameters for a Comprehensive, Legally Binding
    Instrument Establishing Common International Standards for the Import, Export and Transfer of Conventional Arms.* Adopted 26 August 2008.
    A/63/334 of 26 August 2008. <http://www.poa-iss.org/CASAUpload/ELibrary/A-63-334.pdf>

—. 2008b. Resolution 63/240, adopted 24 December. A/RES/63/240 of 8 January.
    <http://www.un.org/en/ga/search/view_doc.asp?symbol=A/RES/63/240&Lang=E>

—. 2009a. *Report of the Open-ended Working Group towards an Arms Trade Treaty: Establishing Common International Standards for the Import,
    Export and Transfer of Conventional Arms.* Adopted 20 July. A/AC.277/2009/1 of 20 July 2009.
    <http://daccess-dds-ny.un.org/doc/UNDOC/GEN/N09/412/00/PDF/N0941200.pdf?OpenElement>

—. 2009b. Resolution 64/48: The Arms Trade Treaty. Adopted 2 December 2009. A/RES/64/48 of 12 January 2010.
    <http://www.un.org/en/ga/search/view_doc.asp?symbol=A/RES/64/48>

—. 2011. Chairman's Draft Paper. 14 July.
    <http://reachingcriticalwill.org/images/documents/Disarmament-fora/att/prepcom3/docs/ChairPaper-14July2011.pdf>

—. 2012a. Resolution 67/234: The Arms Trade Treaty ('Resolution 67/234 A'). Adopted 24 December. A/RES/67/234 of 4 January 2013.
    <http://www.un.org/en/ga/search/view_doc.asp?symbol=A/RES/67/234>

—. 2012b. Draft of the Arms Trade Treaty Submitted by the President of the Conference. A/CONF.217/CRP.1. 1 August.
    <http://www.un.org/ga/search/view_doc.asp?symbol=A/CONF.217/CRP.1&Lang=E>

—. 2012c. Elements of Provision on Scope in an ATT. Unpublished document. 13 July.
    <http://reachingcriticalwill.org/images/documents/Disarmament-fora/att/negotiating-conference/documents/elements-scope.pdf>

—. 2013a. Arms Trade Treaty. 'Certified true copy (XXVI-8).' May.
    <https://treaties.un.org/Pages/ViewDetails.aspx?src=TREATY&mtdsg_no=XXVI-8&chapter=26&lang=en>

—. 2013b. *Official Records of the 77th Session, 71st Plenary Meeting.* A/67/PV.71 of 2 April 2013.
    <http://www.un.org/ga/search/view_doc.asp?symbol=A/67/PV.71>

—. 2013c. ATT Voting Record. 2 April 2013.
    <http://reachingcriticalwill.org/images/documents/Disarmament-fora/att/negotiating-conference-ii/documents/UNGA-voting-results.pdf>

—. 2013d. Arms Trade Treaty: Proposal of Corrections to the Original Text of the Treaty (French and Spanish Authentic Texts) and the Certified True
    Copies. C.N.279.2013.TREATIES-XXVI.8 (Depositary Notification). 16 May.
    <http://treaties.un.org/doc/Publication/CN/2013/CN.279.2013-Eng.pdf>

—. 2013e. Resolution 67/234 B: The Arms Trade Treaty. Adopted 2 April. A/RES/67/234 B of 11 June 2013.
    <http://www.un.org/en/ga/search/view_doc.asp?symbol=A/RES/67/234%20B>

—. 2013f. Arms Trade Treaty: Proposal of Corrections to the Original Text of the Treaty (Russian Authentic Text) and the Certified True Copies.
    C.N.548.2013.TREATIES-XXVI.8 (Depositary Notification). 13 September. <http://treaties.un.org/doc/Publication/CN/2013/CN.584.2013-Eng.pdf>

UN News Centre. 2006. 'Annan Receives Arms Petition by One-millionth Signer, Vows to Transmit Call Onward.' 26 June.
    <http://www.un.org/apps/news/story.asp?NewsID=18997#.UptcpODEVVA>

UNODA (United Nations Office for Disarmament Affairs). 2011. *Ammunition Technical Guidelines: Glossary of Terms, Definitions and Abbreviations.*
    IATG 01.40. 1 October. <http://www.un.org/disarmament/convarms/Ammunition/IATG/docs/IATG01.40.pdf>

—. n.d.a. 'The Arms Trade Treaty.' <http://www.un.org/disarmament/ATT/>

—. n.d.b. 'UN Register of Conventional Arms.' <http://www.un.org/disarmament/convarms/Register/>

—. n.d.c. 'The Global Reported Arms Trade: The UN Register of Conventional Arms.' <http://www.un-register.org/Background/Index.aspx>

UNOLA (United Nations Office of Legal Affairs). 2003. *Final Clauses of Multilateral Treaties: Handbook.* New York: United Nations. <http://treaties.un.org/doc/source/publications/FC/English.pdf>

US (United States). 2013. 'Statement of Assistant Secretary of State Thomas Countryman.' Arms Trade Treaty Conference, Morning Plenary Session. 25 March. <http://www.un.org/disarmament/ATT/statements/docs/20130325/20130325_USA%20Statement.pdf>

VCLT (Vienna Convention on the Law of Treaties). 1969. <http://untreaty.un.org/ilc/texts/instruments/english/conventions/1_1_1969.pdf>

Vollmer, Patrick. 2008. 'Debate 15th May: Development of the International Arms Trade Treaty.' House of Lords, Library Note, LLN 2008/013. 12 May.

WA (Wassenaar Arrangement on Export Controls for Conventional Arms and Dual-Use Goods and Technologies). 1998. Elements for Objective Analysis and Advice Concerning Potentially Destabilising Accumulations of Conventional Weapons. 3 December. <http://www.ehu.es/ceinik/tratados/2TRATADOSSOBREDESARMAMEYCONTROLDEARMAMENTOS/21Desarmedearmamentosconvencionales/DCA216ING.pdf>

—. 2002. 'Best Practice Guidelines for Exports of Small Arms and Light Weapons (SALW).' December. <http://www.ehu.es/ceinik/tratados/2TRATADOSSOBREDESARMAMEYCONTROLDEARMAMENTOS/21Desarmedearmamentosconvencionales/DCA216ING.pdf>

—. 2003. Elements for Effective Legislation on Arms Brokering. <http://www.wassenaar.org/guidelines/docs/Elts_for_effective_legislation_on_arms_brokering.pdf>

—. n.d. 'Control Lists: Current.' <http://www.wassenaar.org/controllists/>

Youngman, D. Allen. 2013. 'The Arms Trade Treaty and American's Rights: An Insider Look at the Arms Trade Treaty and How It Developed.' *Small Arms Defense Journal.* 17 April. <http://sadefensejournal.com/wp/?p=1891>

ACKNOWLEDGEMENTS

Principal author

Sarah Parker

Following the MV Faina's release from Somali pirates, a military officer in Mombasa guards the ship which was carrying tanks and weapons destined for South Sudan, February 2009.
© Tony Karumba/AFP Photo

Trade Update
TRANSFERS, RETRANSFERS, AND THE ATT

4

INTRODUCTION

Given the complex dynamics of the small arms trade, the impact of the Arms Trade Treaty (ATT) is difficult to predict. Yet this chapter, building on the considerable advances made in our understanding of the small arms trade in recent years, examines some of the factors that will determine the treaty's future impact on transfers, retransfers, and transparency. After reviewing the main actors of the authorized trade and global trends from 2001 to 2011, using the United Nations Commodity Trade Statistics Database (UN Comtrade), the chapter considers some of the possibilities—and opportunities—the ATT offers for addressing unauthorized retransfers. One of the main purposes of the ATT is to increase transparency in the international arms trade. After presenting the 2014 edition of the Transparency Barometer, this chapter reflects on how the ATT can build upon existing instruments to achieve this goal.

The main findings of the chapter include:

- In 2011, the top exporters of small arms and light weapons (those with annual exports of at least USD 100 million), according to available customs data, were (in descending order) the United States, Italy, Germany, Brazil, Austria, Switzerland, Israel, the Russian Federation, South Korea, Belgium, China, Turkey, Spain, and the Czech Republic.

- In 2011, the top importers of small arms and light weapons (those with annual imports of at least USD 100 million), according to available customs data, were (in descending order) the United States, Canada, Germany, Australia, Thailand, the United Kingdom, France, and Italy.

- The value of the global trade in small arms and light weapons almost doubled between 2001 and 2011, according to UN Comtrade. The category of small arms ammunition has seen the greatest increase (USD 959 million or 205 per cent).

- While the ATT does not specifically refer to unauthorized retransfers, other instruments and good practice guidelines outline relevant measures. Guidance is scarce, however, on how to respond to suspected or detected cases of unauthorized retransfers.

- The 2014 edition of the Transparency Barometer identifies Switzerland, Germany, Serbia, and the United Kingdom as the most transparent of the major exporters, while Iran, North Korea, Saudi Arabia, and the United Arab Emirates are the least transparent.

- Although overall transparency improved slightly since last year, with more countries improving or maintaining their level of transparency than not, the Barometer shows that more than half of the countries under review do not provide any information on licences granted or refused, despite the categories overall importance to transparency.

- The ATT offers an important opportunity to increase transparency in small arms transfers. Yet, to achieve this goal, ATT reporting needs to take its inspiration not only from the UN Register of Conventional Arms (UN Register), but also from UN Comtrade and national arms export reports.

AUTHORIZED SMALL ARMS TRANSFERS

Since 2001, the Small Arms Survey has provided annual information on authorized small arms transfers. This year, the authorized transfers update presents data provided by states for trade conducted in 2011, as reported in UN Comtrade. A decade's worth of Comtrade data helps to identify key trends in the global trade.

Definitions and sources

For the purposes of this section, 'authorized transfers' are 'international transfers that are authorized by the importing, exporting, or transit states' (Dreyfus et al., 2009, p. 9). The term 'small arms' refers to small arms and light weapons, including their parts, accessories, and ammunition. While there is no single comprehensive source of data on small arms transfers, the trend analysis for 2001–11 uses exclusively UN Comtrade data so as to ensure comparability.[1]

UN Comtrade compiles customs data submitted annually by exporters and importers worldwide.[2] It remains the most extensive source of data on global transfers for pistols and revolvers, small-calibre ammunition, sporting rifles, and sporting shotguns.[3] Yet it provides only partial coverage of the trade in military firearms, firearm parts and accessories, and light weapons and their ammunition—partly because some Comtrade categories include a mix of small arms and larger-calibre weapons and ammunition. At the same time, several major small arms exporters do not report to UN Comtrade at all, while others under-report or omit categories.[4]

Military and security officials look at weapons at the Bahrain International Air Show, Sakir, January 2014. © Hamad I Mohammed/Reuters

Although UN Comtrade can be used to map trends in the global small arms trade over time, it does not capture the total value of the trade, or its undocumented component. The Small Arms Survey estimates the total value of the global small arms trade at approximately USD 8.5 billion, based on an analysis of sources such as national arms export reports, the UN Register, and UN Comtrade (Grzybowski, Marsh, and Schroeder, 2012, p. 251).

Top and major exporters and importers in 2011

This year, the authorized transfers update presents UN Comtrade data provided by states for trade conducted in 2011, contrasting these figures with their 2010 equivalents.[5]

In 2011, the number of top exporters (exporting at least USD 100 million[6] of small arms annually) rose to 14, from 12 in 2010. They were, in descending order, the United States, Italy, Germany, Brazil, Austria, Switzerland, Israel, the Russian Federation, South Korea, Belgium, China, Turkey, Spain, and the Czech Republic (see Table 4.1). The new top exporters in 2011 were China (whose exports increased from USD 89 million in 2010 to USD 112 million in 2011), Turkey (from USD 98 million to USD 108 million), and the Czech Republic (USD 91 million to USD 104 million).

Sweden moved from the top exporter category to that of 'major exporter', as its exports decreased from USD 132 million in 2010 to USD 44 million in 2011. The number of top and major exporters (exporting at least USD 10 million annually) was 39 in 2011, four more than in 2010. The new major exporters in 2011 were Pakistan (from USD 4

Table 4.1 **Exporters of small arms based on UN Comtrade, 2011**			
Category		**Value (USD)**	**Countries (listed in descending order of value exported)**
Top exporters	Tier 1	≥500 million	1: United States
	Tier 2	100–499 million	13: Italy, Germany, Brazil, Austria, Switzerland, Israel, Russian Federation, South Korea, Belgium, China, Turkey, Spain, Czech Republic
Major exporters	Tier 3	50–99 million	8: Japan, Canada, Norway, United Kingdom, France, Pakistan, Finland, Croatia
	Tier 4	10–49 million	17: Sweden, Portugal, Mexico, India, Serbia, Taiwan, Philippines, Singapore, Cyprus, Ukraine, Australia, Denmark, Argentina, Hong Kong, Romania, Poland, Hungary

Table 4.2 **Importers of small arms based on UN Comtrade, 2011**			
Category		**Value (USD)**	**Countries (listed in descending order of value imported)**
Top importers	Tier 1	≥500 million	1: United States
	Tier 2	100–499 million	7: Canada, Germany, Australia, Thailand, United Kingdom, France, Italy
Major importers	Tier 3	50–99 million	14: Norway, Switzerland, Colombia, Côte d'Ivoire, Netherlands, Afghanistan, Russian Federation, Belgium, Israel, Sweden, Spain, Austria, Denmark, Mexico
	Tier 4	10–49 million	42: Poland, Jordan, Turkey, United Arab Emirates, South Korea, Singapore, Philippines, Portugal, Morocco, Cambodia, Indonesia, Saudi Arabia, Iraq, Japan, Finland, Pakistan, Lebanon, New Zealand, Brazil, Estonia, Argentina, South Africa, Chile, Czech Republic, Ukraine, Sudan, India, Kenya, Kuwait, Peru, Cyprus, Honduras, Malaysia, Greece, Hungary, Bulgaria, Venezuela, Oman, Slovakia, China, Luxembourg, Dominican Republic

million in 2010 to USD 76 million in 2011),[7] Ukraine (from USD 3 million to USD 21 million), Hong Kong (from USD 1 million to USD 13 million), and Poland (USD 8 million to USD 12 million). Overall, the United States remains the largest exporter of small arms, with at least USD 917 million exported in 2011, almost 100 million more than in 2010 (when it reported USD 821 million).

In 2011, the top importers (importing at least USD 100 million of small arms annually) were, in descending order, the United States, Canada, Germany, Australia, Thailand, the United Kingdom, France, and Italy (see Table 4.2). Their identity and number (eight) underwent limited changes between 2010 and 2011. Only South Korea dropped from the list of top importers (with a decrease from USD 130 million in 2010 to 40 million in 2011), whereas Italy joined the list (with an increase from 68 million in 2010 to USD 108 million in 2011). In contrast, the number of top and major importers (importing at least USD 10 million annually) rose significantly: from 56 in 2010 to 64 in 2011. Almost all of the new major importers were Tier 4 countries, with imports of between USD 10 million and USD 49 million (Cambodia, Sudan, India, Kenya, Honduras, Hungary, Oman, China, Luxembourg, Dominican Republic; see Table 4.2).[8]

A worker prepares for the opening of the Chinese pavilion at the Eurosatory Defense Exhibition, Villepinte, France, June 2010. © Jacques Brinon/AP Photo

International trends: 2001-11

Global trends by total value

As captured by UN Comtrade, between 2001 and 2011 the global value of the small arms trade increased by approximately USD 2.254 billion in constant 2011 dollars—a total increase of 95 per cent over the decade (see Figure 4.1 and Table 4.3).[9] As noted in the 2009 edition of the *Small Arms Survey*, this increase has not been constant from year to

Figure 4.1 **Changes in the value of the global small arms trade based on UN Comtrade (USD billion*), 2001-11**

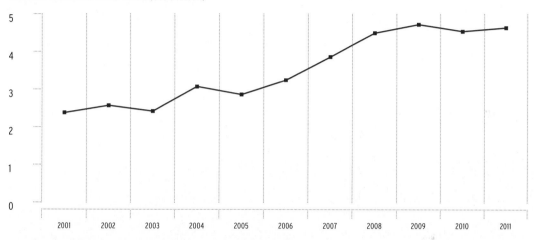

VALUE OF THE SMALL ARMS TRADE (USD BILLION)

Notes: * All values are expressed in constant 2011 US dollars; all figures have been rounded to the nearest million.
Sources: NISAT (n.d.); UN Comtrade (n.d.)

Table 4.3 **Trends in small arms transfers per category, as reported to UN Comtrade, 2001-11**

Types of weapons	2001 value (USD million*)	2011 value (USD million)	Absolute change 2001-11 (USD million)	% change
Small arms ammunition (≤12.7 mm)	468	1,427	959	205
Pistols and revolvers	275	653	378	138
Sporting rifles	198	475	277	140
Sporting shotguns	349	552	203	58
Shotgun cartridges	223	374	151	68
Parts and accessories for pistols or revolvers	57	190	133	232
Parts and accessories for shotguns or rifles	171	302	131	77
Military small arms and light weapons**	593	605	13	2
Shotgun barrels	46	55	9	19
Total	2,380	4,634	2,254	95

Notes: * All values are expressed in constant 2011 US dollars; all figures have been rounded to the nearest million. ** Broadly speaking, this category reflects the trade in small arms designed to military specifications. It includes three specific Comtrade categories: military weapons (930100), rocket and grenade launchers (930120), and military firearms (930190).

Sources: NISAT (n.d.); UN Comtrade (n.d.)

year.[10] Since 2001 there have been decreases, rather than increases, in 2003, 2005, and 2010, with annual drops of 6, 7, and 4 per cent, respectively (see Figure 4.1).

Global trends by weapon category

Regarding changes by weapon category, from 2001 to 2011 the international trade in small arms ammunition saw the greatest absolute increase: an absolute growth of USD 959 million (see Table 4.3). In 2011 it was the most exported category of materiel, with exports worth USD 1.427 billion, marking a surge of 205 per cent since 2001.

The three other categories that have experienced the largest increases in traded values since 2001 are pistols and revolvers, sporting rifles, and sporting shotguns. The value of exported parts and accessories for pistols and revolvers has seen the greatest relative change, with a 232 per cent increase since 2001, but the magnitude of its trade remains low compared to most other categories: USD 190 million in 2011. Although it fluctuated during the period, the trade in military small arms and light weapons increased by only 2 per cent from 2001 to 2011, remaining at around USD 600 million.

Figure 4.2 shows changes in traded values for six selected small arms categories. The value of the trade in small arms ammunition increased from 2001 to 2011, with two slight decreases in 2005 and 2009.

9 mm bullets at an outlet for sport shooting supplies, Pennsylvania, April 2013. © Keith Srakocic/AP Photo

Figure 4.2 Changes in traded values for six categories of small arms and light weapons based on UN Comtrade (USD million*), 2001-11

■ Small arms ammunition (≤12.7 mm) ■ Pistols and revolvers ■ Military small arms and light weapons ■ Sporting shotguns ■ Sporting rifles
■ Parts and accessories for pistols or revolvers

VALUE OF TRADE (USD MILLION)

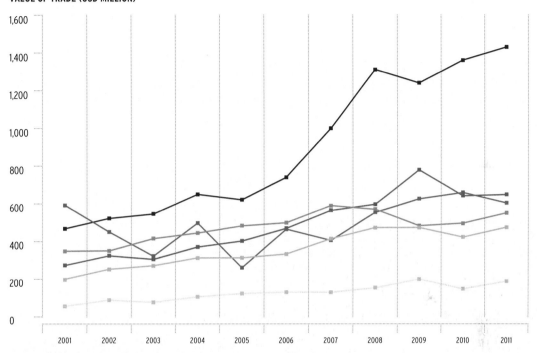

Notes: * All values are expressed in constant 2011 US dollars; all figures have been rounded to the nearest million.
Sources: NISAT (n.d.); UN Comtrade (n.d.)

The rise in ammunition transfers accounts for a large portion (42.5 per cent) of the overall increase in the small arms trade since 2001. In 2011 ammunition alone represented 30.8 per cent of the total trade. Table 4.4 examines some of the dynamics of this trade, presenting the ten largest exporters of ammunition between 2001 and 2011, along with changes in their exports during that period.

The United States is the most important exporter of small arms ammunition, capturing 26 per cent of the global trade in this category between 2001 and 2011. Yet several other countries have contributed to the global rise in ammunition exports, with dramatic increases in exports from, in descending order, Germany (537 per cent), Norway (517 per cent), Switzerland (412 per cent), Brazil (397 per cent), and the Russian Federation (332 per cent) during the decade. All told, the top ten exporters presented in Table 4.4 accounted for 71 per cent of the ammunition trade during this period.

An analysis of top importers sheds further light on the ammunition market during the decade. As illustrated in Table 4.5, several countries have seen large relative increases in their imports of small arms ammunition. These include the Netherlands (up 888 per cent since 2001) and Israel (728 per cent), as well as the United Kingdom (486 per cent), Switzerland (386 per cent), and Norway (338 per cent). Although the United States had a lower percentage increase (266 per cent), it imported far more ammunition than any other state during the decade—almost four times the value of the second most important importer.

Table 4.4 **Changes in the exports of the ten largest exporters of small arms ammunition as reported to UN Comtrade (USD million*), 2001–11**

Exporter	Average exports (USD million)	% of all exports in this category	Absolute change in exports (USD million)	% change
United States	237	26	221	136
Germany	77	9	115	537
Switzerland	64	7	93	412
South Korea	50	6	46	155
Russian Federation	49	5	61	332
Canada	43	5	27	177
Norway	42	5	65	517
Brazil	28	3	34	397
Sweden	28	3	13	62
Czech Republic	25	3	9	37
Total ammunition	**901**	**100**	**959**	**205**

Notes: * All values are expressed in constant 2011 US dollars; all figures have been rounded to the nearest million.

Sources: NISAT (n.d.); UN Comtrade (n.d.)

Table 4.5 **Changes in the imports of the ten largest importers of small arms ammunition as reported to UN Comtrade (USD million*), 2001–11**

Importers	Average imports (USD million)	% of all imports in this category	Absolute change in imports (USD million)	% change
United States	211	23	209	266
Australia	57	6	66	183
Germany	54	6	48	176
Canada	42	5	61	282
United Kingdom	40	4	48	486
Israel	28	3	39	728
France	27	3	20	183
Netherlands	27	3	40	888
Switzerland	26	3	46	386
Norway	24	3	41	338
Total ammunition	**904**	**100**	**986**	**211**

Notes: * All values are expressed in constant 2011 US dollars; all figures have been rounded to the nearest million.

Sources: NISAT (n.d.); UN Comtrade (n.d.)

As captured by customs data, the value of the authorized small arms trade reflects a clear upward trend from 2001 to 2011, with an especially pronounced rise for ammunition.[11] As the global small arms trade picks up, the Arms Trade Treaty, which covers small arms and, to some extent, their parts, components, and ammunition, retains all its importance. That said, the increasing importance of the ammunition trade poses a problem for the ATT, which, as discussed in the next section, does not cover the diversion, including unauthorized retransfers, of this materiel.

PROFILING UNAUTHORIZED RETRANSFERS

An unauthorized retransfer is a type of diversion in which the arms are retransferred by the authorized importer or end user to an end user in another state (unauthorized re-export) or within the same state, in violation of commitments made by the authorized importer or end user prior to export.[12] Unauthorized retransfers can lead to the same negative consequences as other types of diversion, such as the supply of arms to undesirable end users, including criminals and terrorists, or for fuelling conflict and the commission of human rights abuses. Although the Arms Trade Treaty does not explicitly mention unauthorized retransfers, it contains several provisions that could be utilized to address the problem (see Box 4.1).

The challenges posed by unauthorized retransfers are not new and are not confined to any particular region of the world. They occur after delivery to the authorized importer or end user, but at very different times and in different forms after such delivery. For example, it is reported that the tanks, artillery, small arms, and ammunition delivered by Ukraine to Kenya in 2007–08 were quickly sent to South Sudan without the authorization of the Ukrainian government (Lewis, 2009). It appears that the tanks were used against opposition forces in South Sudan in 2011,

Box 4.1   The ATT and unauthorized retransfers

The Arms Trade Treaty represents a significant development in international efforts to improve regulation of the international arms trade and combat the illicit arms trade (UNGA, 2013b; ARMS TRADE TREATY). Nevertheless, the lack of a specific reference to unauthorized retransfers or to measures designed to address the problem—and the fact that the diversion article does not apply to ammunition, parts and components, or licensed production—limit the ATT's utility in this area. As the cases described in this section demonstrate, the latter items and arrangements are particularly susceptible to unauthorized retransfers. ATT negotiators, drawing upon existing regional instruments and guidelines, could have taken the opportunity to reflect good practices in preventing unauthorized retransfers. That said, the ATT can still be utilized to combat the problem by taking the following measures:

- **Risk assessment:** Articles 6 and 7 require exporters, including re-exporters, to prohibit particular arms exports and undertake risk assessments designed to prevent arms exports from having certain negative consequences.
- **Preventing diversion:** Article 11(1) requires all states parties to take measures to prevent the diversion of arms, including, at least implicitly, unauthorized retransfer. However, the provision only applies to the eight ATT arms categories, which exclude ammunition, parts and components, and licensed production arrangements.
- **Record-keeping:** Article 12 on record-keeping, particularly by importing states, could prove useful to exporting states seeking to investigate suspected or detected unauthorized retransfers.
- **Reporting:** Article 13 on reporting requires states parties to report on authorized or actual imports and exports—including re-exports—and encourages them to report on effective measures to prevent diversion, presumably including unauthorized retransfer.
- **International cooperation:** Article 15(5) on international cooperation can provide a basis for assistance with investigations, prosecutions, and judicial proceedings after unauthorized retransfers have been detected.
- **Information sharing:** Article 17 on Conferences of States Parties could provide a forum for states parties to share information on diversion risks, including information on detected and suspected unauthorized retransfers, as well as on measures to prevent, detect, and respond to unauthorized retransfers.

Source: UNGA (2013b)

President of Venezuela Hugo Chavez shows a Swedish-made anti-tank rocket as an example of weapons allegedly stolen by FARC from the Venezuelan military, before their subsequent seizure by the Colombian military, Caracas, August 2009. © Thomas Coex/AFP Photo

with civilian casualties also reported (AI, 2012, pp. 18–20). Unauthorized retransfers can also take place decades after initial delivery, as in the case of the Carl Gustav (AT-4) anti-tank ammunition, which Sweden had delivered to Venezuela in 1988, but which the Colombian government discovered in a camp of the Revolutionary Armed Forces of Colombia (FARC) in 2008 (AFP, 2009; BBC, 2009).

Unauthorized retransfers of parts and components that are supposed to be incorporated into weapons systems produced by the recipient are another challenge. For example, parts and components supplied by China to Iran for the production of surface-to-air missiles and PG-7-AT1 rocket-propelled grenades were reportedly transferred to armed groups in Iraq and then used against Coalition and Iraqi forces, as well as civilians (Rayner, 2011). Concerns have also been raised with regard to the unauthorized retransfer of arms and ammunition produced under licence, in particular the G-3, FN FAL, and Kalashnikov rifles. FN FAL rifles produced under licence in Argentina in the early 1990s, though officially destined for Panama and Venezuela, were in fact delivered to Ecuador during its conflict with Peru (Vranckx, 2005, pp. 13–14).

Since 2011, considerable media attention has focused on a number of cases of unauthorized retransfers of arms and ammunition from European suppliers to Libyan and Syrian non-state armed groups via members of the Gulf Cooperation Council. Another case in point is Col. Muammar Qaddafi's Libya, which, prior to the regime's collapse, had a reputation for undertaking unauthorized retransfers to armed groups in Africa (see Box 4.2).

Although several high-profile cases have come to light in recent years, it remains difficult to know how common unauthorized retransfers are and how many are detected. Even in cases of suspected or detected unauthorized retransfers, both exporting and importing states may deny that an unauthorized retransfer has taken place. When Somali pirates hijacked the merchant vessel *Faina* in September 2008, Kenyan, South Sudanese, and Ukrainian officials insisted that its cargo of military equipment was destined for end users in Kenya (Solomko and Stroginov, 2008). There was, however, substantial evidence indicating that it would follow previous Ukrainian shipments and be retransferred to South Sudan (Lewis, 2009). Kenyan officials

---

Box 4.2 Weapons flows to and from Libya

Libya has been a concern with regard to unauthorized retransfers of arms since the Qaddafi era. The country provided Soviet-supplied man-portable air defence systems (MANPADS) to the Irish Republican Army and Saharawi armed forces in the late 1980s and Belgian-supplied 106 mm recoilless rifle cartridges to armed groups in Sudan in the 21st century (Lutterbeck, 2009, pp. 510–11; UNSC, 2008, paras. 217–25). Unauthorized retransfers to embargoed entities in Liberia and Sierra Leone continued while Libya was itself subject to a UN arms embargo (Fruchart et al., 2007). After the lifting of the UN arms embargo in 2003 Libya imported small arms from a wide range of European suppliers, as well as China and the United States (NISAT, n.d.).

At the same time, however, there were signs that the leopard had not changed its spots. In 2006, the Italian police revealed that Libyan authorities were purchasing 500,000 Chinese-made Type-56 rifles in a deal brokered by Italian organized criminals. The weapons were to be shipped to Libya and then retransferred, most likely to the government of Chad or rebels in Sudan (Mampaey and Santopinto, 2009). The UK cited the risk of re-export to unauthorized end users as the reason for its denial of a brokering licence that a UK-based company had requested for the transfer of 130,000 Kalashnikov rifles from Ukraine to Libya (Bromley, 2012, p. 12).

In early 2012, investigators documented in Libya 1980s vintage Pakistani-made 7.62 x 51 mm ammunition and Swiss-made M-80 ammunition, which Pakistan and Switzerland had initially exported to Qatar in 1981–82 and 2009, respectively (UNSC, 2012, paras. 97–102; 2013, paras. 62–73; AMMUNITION PROFILING). In both cases it appears that Qatar breached its agreements not to re-export these items without authorization from the original exporting states (UNSC, 2012, para. 98; UNSC, 2013, para. 69). The Pakistani-made ammunition has since been found in shipments from Libya to the Syrian opposition (UNSC, 2013, paras. 70, 171).

---

did eventually inform US officials of Kenya's role in retransferring Ukrainian arms imports to South Sudan (Gettleman and Gordon, 2010), but apparently not their Ukrainian counterparts. Even in 2010 the former head of the Ukrainian state arms exporter, Ukrspetsexport, stated that arms deliveries to Kenya were staying there (Shevchenko, 2010).

When presented with evidence of an unauthorized retransfer, major exporters in Europe and Asia tend to use the same refrain—that there are limited options available for responding to such incidents and that responsibility ends at the original exporter's border. The first signs that Yugoslav-origin M79 anti-tank weapons were being used by Syrian rebels appeared in January 2013 (Brown Moses Blog, 2013). Investigative journalists revealed that 3,000 tons of weapons—including M79 Osa anti-tank weapons, RPG-22s, RBG-6s, and M60 recoilless rifles—had been transported by air from Croatia to Jordan between November 2012 and February 2013, with unknown quantities retransferred by Jordan to Syrian rebels (Žabec, 2013). When questioned on the unauthorized retransfer, Croatian president Ivo Josipović stated that, 'what third countries or countries that we or someone else export weapons to do with (arms) afterward, we unfortunately cannot control' (Hina, 2013).

The remainder of this section presents some of the main features of the problem, as well as some of the measures that can be used to address it.

A Syrian rebel holds a Serbian-made grenade launcher, allegedly shipped by the Saudi Arabian government to support rebel groups, Kfar Nbouda, February 2013.
© David Enders/MCT/Getty Images

International and regional instruments: an overview

Several international and regional instruments and good practice guidelines outline steps that exporting and re-exporting states can or should take to prevent the risk of unauthorized retransfer, with several focusing on MANPADS (see Table 4.6). The politically binding UN Programme of Action (PoA) explicitly addresses unauthorized retransfers of small arms, asking states:

> to make every effort, in accordance with national laws and practices, without prejudice to the right of States to re-export small arms and light weapons that they have previously imported, to notify the original exporting State in accordance with their bilateral agreements before the retransfer of those weapons (UNGA, 2001, para. II.13).

Usefully, the PoA provisions on unauthorized retransfers address retransferring states directly; yet they are relatively weak in that they merely encourage those states to notify the original exporting state before a retransfer.

The regional instruments referenced in Table 4.6 contain measures exporting states can take to prevent unauthorized retransfers, with an emphasis on the pre-shipment stage. Guidelines have been produced to assist states with the implementation of the European Union (EU) Common Position, the Nairobi Protocol, and the Document on Small Arms and Light Weapons of the Organization for Security and Co-operation in Europe (OSCE), all of which also include options for post-delivery measures. The Wassenaar Arrangement has produced several best practice guidelines, including one that specifically addresses unauthorized re-exports.

Table 4.6 International and regional instruments that address unauthorized retransfers

Scope	Instruments	Pre-shipment measures		Post-delivery measures	
		For initial exporter	For re-exporter	For initial exporter	For re-exporter
International	PoA (UNGA, 2001, para. II.13)		•		
Regional and export control	ECOWAS Convention (ECOWAS, 2006, art. 6.5)	•			
	EU Common Position (EU, 2008, arts. 2.7, 6) and *User's Guide* (EU, 2009)	•		•	
	Kinshasa Convention (2010, art. 5.5.a)	•			
	Nairobi Protocol (2004, art. 3) and Nairobi Best Practices Guidelines (2005)	•			•
	OSCE Document (OSCE, 2000, ss. III.A.2.b.vii, III.B.6, III.C) and *Handbook of Best Practices* (OSCE, 2003)	•	•	•	
	OSCE Standard Elements (OSCE, 2004b, art. 1)	•			
	Wassenaar Arrangement (WA, 2005, elements 5-6; 2011, arts. 1-3)	•	•	•	
MANPADS	APEC Guidelines (APEC, 2003, point 3)	•			
	OAS resolution (OAS, 2005, appendix, art. 3)	•			
	OSCE Principles (OSCE, 2004a, arts. 1.2, 2)	•			
	Wassenaar Arrangement Elements (WA, 2003, arts. 2.7-2.9)	•		•	

Pre-shipment controls

Under Article 11(2) of the ATT, exporting states parties 'shall seek to prevent' diversion—and therefore also unauthorized retransfers—by undertaking risk assessments. For this purpose, they are to consider the establishment of mitigation measures such as 'examining parties involved in the export, requiring additional documentation, certificates, assurances, not authorizing the export or other appropriate measures', normally in cooperation with importing states parties (UNGA, 2013b, art. 11.2).

A number of regional instruments require exporting state authorities to conduct a risk assessment to determine the likelihood that arms or ammunition will be retransferred without authorization. The OSCE Document calls upon each participating state to:

avoid issuing licences for exports where it deems that there is a clear risk that the small arms in question might [. . .] be either re-sold (or otherwise diverted) within the recipient country or re-exported for purposes contrary to the aims of this document' (OSCE, 2000, s. III, para. A.2.b.vii).

The 2006 Convention of the Economic Community of West African States and Kinshasa Convention of 2010 contain stronger provisions, obliging states parties to deny an export application if the risk assessment determines that the small arms or ammunition are likely to be retransferred to unauthorized end users in the recipient state or a third country (ECOWAS, 2006; Kinshasa Convention, 2010). Such assessments focus on several areas:

- the accuracy of the information contained in end-use or end-user documentation (McDonald, 2008; Wood and Danssaert, 2011, p. 10);
- the identity of the end user and/or importer, paying particular attention to the appropriateness of the items to be transferred and the end user's record of compliance with non-retransfer undertakings; and
- the importing state's export control policies and the effectiveness of its export control system, particularly if parts and components are to be exported or a licence for production is to be granted.

In practice, the end user and importing state authorities are primarily responsible for preventing unauthorized retransfers—as reflected in their provision of assurances to abide by the requirements of the original exporting state in this regard (Wood and Danssaert, 2011, pp. 28–29). These assurances are contained in the contract, end-use or end-user certificate (EUC), or other documentation provided by the intended recipient and/or end user. States currently utilize a variety of measures to hinder retransfer, including by:

- prohibiting retransfers;
- permitting retransfers only with the written authorization of the original exporting state; or
- granting the right to retransfer to states that are identified in the EUC, contract, or other relevant documentation (EU, 2009, p. 19).[13]

Figure 4.3 provides examples of two types of non-re-export clauses, one from Germany and one from Finland. The German EUC template is one of several the German export control agency asks

Figure 4.3 **Examples of non-re-export clauses in end-user documents: Germany and Finland**

Letterhead of
the consignee in the
country of destination

Einzelabnehmer-EVE
für Güter der
Antifolter Verordnung

Name/Address of the supplier
in the Federal Republic of Germany

END-USE CERTIFICATE
For presentation to the Export Control Authorities
of the Federal Republic of Germany

In accordance with the regulations of the Federal Republic of Germany which state that granting of an individual export licence is dependent on the presentation of an end-use certificate, we (I) certify that the goods supplied by

Name of the supplier ______

Description of the goods ______

Quantity/Weight ______

Value ______

are intended for consumption/will remain in ______
(country of final destination)

and will be used only for ______

We (I) certify that the above-mentioned goods will not be used for the purpose of torture, the execution of capital punishment, slavery or cruel and inhumane punishment.

Re-exporting the goods is definitely excluded.

Place, Date ______ Original signature of the end-user ______

Company stamp/official seal ______ name and title of signer in block letters ______

SAMPLE

Finnish Ministry of Defence; EUC form 2

DECLARATION BY END-USER
TO THE GOVERNMENT OF FINLAND

WE, ...
(name and address of purchaser)

HEREBY CERTIFY THAT THE EQUIPMENT LISTED BELOW AND ORDERED BY

US FROM ......
(name and address of supplier)

IS FOR THE EXCLUSIVE USE OF

......

......
(name and address of end-user, description of end-use)

AND WILL NOT BE EXPORTED OR RE-EXPORTED WITHOUT A PRIOR WRITTEN CONSENT OF THE GOVERNMENT OF FINLAND.

We confirm that the equipment will not be used in any activities related to the development nor production of chemical or biological or nuclear weapons.

PURCHASER: ......

CONTRACT NUMBER: ......

CONTRACT DATE: ......

EQUIPMENT: TYPE: QUANTITY:

Upon request by the competent Finnish authorities we undertake to confirm the receipt of the equipment listed above. When requested by the competent Finnish authorities, this confirmation shall include an on-site inspection of the receipt of the goods performed by representatives authorized by the Government of Finland.

......
(date, name and signature)

......
(name of purchaser and official stamp, contact information)

Note
The Declaration by End User should be signed by a person authorized to sign on behalf of the purchaser and confirmed by an official stamp of the purchaser.

Sources: Germany (n.d.); Finland (n.d.)

exporters and end users to fill out (Germany, n.d.). In this particular example, Germany authorizes the importer to retransfer without seeking its prior approval if the controlled items are to be retransferred to a designated state. The Finnish EUC template requires the importer to obtain prior written consent from Finland before any retransfer is undertaken (Finland, n.d.). Nevertheless, as indicated above, experience shows that the provision of such assurances is not sufficient to prevent unauthorized retransfers.

Post-delivery controls

The ATT makes no provision for post-delivery controls. In fact, they do not always feature among the tools states use to prevent diversion or unauthorized retransfers. For example, the UK government states that an export licensing system is sufficient for preventing diversion and unauthorized retransfers since licences will be denied if there is a high risk of retransfer (UK, 2012, para. 57). In addition, the UK government argues that 'it is not feasible for the Government to track all UK origin goods once they have been exported', noting that such a system could deter customers (para. 56).

Nevertheless, the EU *User's Guide to Council Common Position* (EU, 2009), the OSCE Document (OSCE, 2000), and the Wassenaar Arrangement's consolidated list of common end-user assurances (WA, 2005) all provide exporting states with optional provisions they can include in EUCs to grant them the right to conduct on-site inspections of transferred arms in the recipient state after delivery. Finland, Norway, Romania, Sweden, and Switzerland include such provisions in their EUCs (Wood and Danssaert, 2011, p. 22; see Figure 4.3). These provisions are most

The Qadaffi government shows journalists confiscated weapons and ammunition which they claim was bound for rebels, Janzur, Libya, July 2011. © Mahmud Turkia/AFP Photo

often activated when there is an allegation of diversion or an unauthorized retransfer (McDonald, 2008, p. 163). A number of European countries have shown greater interest in the issue of post-delivery controls as a result of the Arab Spring and the armed conflicts in Libya and Syria.

The United States maintains two comprehensive end-use monitoring programmes that include post-delivery controls to ensure that recipients are in compliance with US laws and regulations, in particular those relating to the prevention of diversion and unauthorized retransfers. The US Department of Defense is responsible for the Golden Sentry programme, which covers equipment provided under government-to-government contracts (DSCA, 2012). Depending on the type of arms, and the physical security environment and other potential threats in the recipient country, Golden Sentry applies one of two types of end-use monitoring—routine or enhanced. Routine monitoring consists of reporting on misuse or unapproved retransfers, visits to installations, and the gathering of other sources of information, with the results entered into a database. Enhanced monitoring is for a limited set of items, of which MANPADS are the only type of small arm or light weapon; the approach includes an annual on-site physical inventory check as well as record-keeping of reported recipient use, loss, or destruction.

The US Department of State is responsible for the Blue Lantern programme, which calls for comprehensive end-use monitoring of direct commercial sales of arms to provide 'reasonable assurance' that the recipient is complying with applicable US requirements, including declared end use (DDTC, 2013).

On-site post-delivery checks are conducted based on the potential risk of diversion, including unauthorized retransfers, or misuse.

At the post-delivery stage, the importing state is supposed to abide by any non-retransfer assurances it has given the original exporting state. If the end-user assurances are comparable to those contained in the Finnish EUC shown in Figure 4.3, the importing state could seek authorization to retransfer the items if, for example, it deemed them surplus to requirements at some point. The Wassenaar Arrangement best practice guidelines on re-export controls call on participating states to review such requests 'as expeditiously as possible and on a non-discriminatory basis', but still to apply the same criteria they would use to assess potential exports from their own territory (WA, 2011, art. 3).

Box 4.3 Switzerland's prevention measures and responses to unauthorized retransfers

Switzerland has made information on unauthorized retransfers publicly available, issuing reports on three cases detected since 2004 and putting in place new preventive measures. The first case concerns the export of 40 M-109 howitzers to the United Arab Emirates (UAE), as authorized in 2004. The UAE signed a non-re-export declaration but subsequently retransferred the howitzers as a 'gift' for 'training purposes' to Morocco (SFC, 2006). At the time, gifts were not covered by Swiss non-re-export declarations. Switzerland responded, first, by imposing a one-year moratorium on arms exports to the UAE and, second, by strengthening its non-re-export declaration to cover gifts (SFC, 2007, p. 2021; SECO, 2012).

In 2011, Swiss media reported that insurgent forces in Libya were using Swiss-produced M80 7.62 x 51 mm ammunition. The ammunition had been exported to the Qatar Armed Forces in 2009 after Qatar signed a non-re-export declaration for the ammunition (UNSC, 2012, paras. 97–102). While Qatar denied that it had provided arms and ammunition to Libyan rebels, military authorities from the Libyan opposition told the UN Panel of Experts on Libya that Qatar was providing them with these materials (UNSC, 2012, para. 101; 2013, paras. 62–66). The Qatari ambassador to Switzerland informed Swiss authorities that the unauthorized retransfer 'was a misadventure' and that Qatar had taken 'appropriate measures to prevent similar errors in the future' (UNSC, 2012, para. 98).

The third case came to light in 2012, when Swiss-made hand grenades were identified in Syria. They were supplied to the UAE in 2003 and retransferred to Jordan in 2004. A preliminary investigation conducted by the Swiss export control agency concluded that the UAE had retransferred the grenades without Swiss authorization, although, as in the howitzer case, as a gift (CCNC, 2012). Switzerland responded with a range of measures. It introduced a temporary moratorium on arms exports to the UAE and lent a set of 2006 rules on non-re-export declarations firmer legal footing, incorporating them in the Ordinance on War Material (SFC, 2013, art. 5a.2). Switzerland will also require future non-re-export declarations with the UAE to be signed by a high-level government representative and will reserve the right to conduct on-site inspections in the country after any arms delivery (SECO, 2012; SFC, 2013).

Responding to unauthorized retransfers after the fact

While regional instruments and best practice guidelines outline a number of measures that can help states prevent and detect unauthorized retransfer cases, they do not provide guidance on possible responses to such suspected or confirmed cases. This section examines existing national practices that could help to fill this gap at the regional and international levels.

At a minimum, evidence of unauthorized retransfers will factor into assessments of future applications for the export of similar items to the same end user or importing state. Such evidence can also lead to the revocation or suspension of export licences that have been granted but not implemented, in the sense that deliveries have not begun or are incomplete. States may also impose a temporary moratorium on export licence applications for a particular destination (see Box 4.3).

States investigate suspected or detected unauthorized retransfers using several different approaches. First, the recipient state government may undertake an investigation in response to a request from its parliament, the exporting state, or a UN panel or group of experts. In practice, this approach yields mixed results. For example, Swedish authorities were dissatisfied with the response from

Venezuela to their request for an investigation into how FARC acquired Carl Gustav anti-tank ammunition, but satisfied with the results of an Indian investigation into Carl Gustav anti-tank weapons that had been delivered to India in 2003 and detected in Myanmar in 2012.[14] Second, the exporting state may carry out its own investigation, via either its embassy or experts from its licensing authority. Third, authorities in the exporting and recipient states may undertake a joint investigation. Fourth, in very rare instances, an independent team of experts may be asked to investigate the case. For example, at the request of the Ukrainian government, a UK–US team conducted an independent investigation into allegations of a Ukrainian export of a Kolchuga radar system to Iraq when the latter was subject to a UN arms embargo (USEU, 2002). The ATT could also be of assistance in this area as it provides for states parties to 'afford one another the widest measure of assistance in investigations, prosecutions and judicial proceedings in relation to violations of national measures established pursuant to this Treaty' (UNGA, 2013b, art. 15(5)).

Not only can the results of such investigations feed into the export or import licensing decisions of states that are directly affected, but they can also be shared with other states. At present, exporting states can use the Wassenaar Arrangement and the EU Working Group on Conventional Arms Exports, known as COARM, as forums in which to share information on end users and importing states that do not abide by non-retransfer guarantees. Once established, the ATT Conference of States Parties could provide another forum for such exchanges. In addition, Articles 11(6) and 13(2) of the ATT encourage states parties to report on measures they have taken to prevent diversion, which would include unauthorized retransfers.

Certain unauthorized retransfer cases have led to the imposition of UN sanctions. The unauthorized retransfer of arms and ammunition by Liberia, under Charles Taylor, to the Revolutionary United Front in Sierra Leone and by the current government of Eritrea to armed groups in Somalia were among the factors cited for the imposition of UN sanctions on both of these regimes (UNSC, 2001; 2009).

> Unauthorized transfers are a form of diversion that many states seem reluctant to acknowledge.

Conclusions on unauthorized retransfers

Unauthorized retransfers are a form of diversion that many states seem reluctant to acknowledge. They can occur very shortly after delivery to the authorized importer or end user, or take place decades later.

Existing international and regional instruments and best practice guidelines tend to emphasize preventive measures, in particular risk assessments and the inclusion of non-retransfer provisions in end-use and end-user documentation. Although such standards are now common in sub-Saharan Africa and Europe, a reliance on documentation provided by importers and on past records of compliance with end-user and end-use assurances is not always a good indication of the future intentions of end users and importers. The best preventive measure remains, in fact, the denial of an export licence where there is a high risk of unauthorized retransfer.

Despite their importance to the prevention and detection of unauthorized retransfers, post-delivery controls remain under-utilized. Even the provision in EUCs of a right to conduct post-delivery on-site checks remains the exception, rather than the norm, although some of the states that opposed such provisions most vocally are now accommodating these requests. For example, India has expressed considerable resistance to post-delivery controls by exporters but has nonetheless agreed to US end-use monitoring arrangements (Chellaney, 2009; Lakshmanan, 2009).

There could also be a greater focus on the development of international and regional standards for responding to suspected or confirmed cases of unauthorized retransfer. This is currently something of a 'missing element' for many regional control regimes, as well as for the Wassenaar Arrangement. National practices that have proven effective in responding to unauthorized retransfer could be codified in the form of multilateral measures and suggested best practice documents.

As unauthorized retransfers are not explicitly addressed in the ATT, it is not evident that the treaty will help states overcome their seeming reluctance to acknowledge and respond to suspected and detected cases. Nevertheless, as indicated above, the ATT contains a series of provisions that could be utilized to prevent unauthorized retransfers and address them when detected. Yet, if the ATT is to make a difference in this area, states parties will have to make it clear that they understand their responsibilities under the ATT to include the prevention of unauthorized retransfers. Sharing experiences, information, and best practices via ATT reporting mechanisms and Conferences of States Parties would help a wide range of states to utilize the treaty to this end.

THE 2014 TRANSPARENCY BAROMETER

The most transparent countries are Switzerland, Germany, Serbia, and the United Kingdom.

This section presents the 2014 edition of the Small Arms Trade Transparency Barometer, designed to assess countries' transparency in reporting on their small arms and light weapons exports. The Barometer examines countries that claim—or are believed—to have exported USD 10 million or more of small arms and light weapons, including their parts, accessories, and ammunition, during at least one calendar year between 2001 and 2012. The three main sources used to assess state transparency are: (1) national arms export reports;[15] (2) the UN Register; and (3) UN Comtrade (see Table 4.7). The Barometer does not assess the veracity of the data states provide. The 2014 edition assesses national transparency in small arms export activities undertaken in 2012, generally based on state reporting in 2013.[16] Like the 2013 Barometer, it reviews the reporting practices of 55 countries.[17]

For the second consecutive year, the Barometer identifies Switzerland, Germany, and Serbia as the most transparent countries, although this year the United Kingdom joins Serbia in a tie for third place.[18] The least transparent countries are Iran, North Korea, Saudi Arabia, and the United Arab Emirates, all scoring zero points.

Compared to the last edition, the top ten has remained unchanged with two exceptions: Norway and Montenegro have replaced Belgium and Spain. Having gained 2.25 points, Norway slightly exceeded its all-time highest score, reached in 2005, to place 7th, tied with Croatia; the increase is attributable to enhanced information on transfer control and brokering legislation and to more comprehensive reporting to the UN Register. Montenegro broke into the top ten thanks to its relatively recent contributions to all three reporting mechanisms for the first time since its inclusion in the Barometer, thus advancing from the 31st to the 9th position (with a 6.75-point increase).

The Russian Federation and Egypt also improved their scores in the last year, with 4.75- and 2.50-point increases, respectively; both countries reported transfers of small arms, parts, accessories, and ammunition to UN Comtrade, in contrast to previous years.

Austria, Bosnia and Herzegovina, and Hungary lost points. Neither Austria[19] nor Bosnia Herzegovina[20] published a national report in 2013, and neither submitted new background information on small arms transfers to the UN Register. These omissions resulted in a loss of 3.75 and 2.50 points, respectively. Hungary's score fell by 2.75 points, mainly due to a less comprehensive submission to the UN Register.

Overall transparency improved slightly since last year. While the average score increased by only 1.2 per cent, from 10.75 to 10.88 out of a maximum of 25 points, more countries improved or maintained their level of transparency than not. The Barometer reveals specific improvements with regard to the comprehensiveness of information provided in various areas (+5 per cent) and on licences refused (+4 per cent). Nevertheless, 51 per cent and 65 per cent of the countries under review do not provide any information on licences granted and refused, respectively, despite this category's overall importance to transparency.

Table 4.7 Small Arms Trade Transparency Barometer 2014, covering major exporters*

	Total (25.00 max)	Export report**/ EU Annual Report***	UN Comtrade	UN Register	Timeliness (1.50 max)	Access and consistency (2.00 max)	Clarity (5.00 max)	Comprehensiveness (6.50 max)	Deliveries (4.00 max)	Licences granted (4.00 max)	Licences refused (2.00 max)
Switzerland	20.00	X	X	X	1.50	1.50	4.00	5.00	3.00	4.00	1.00
Germany	19.75	X/EU Report	X	X	1.50	1.50	4.25	4.00	3.50	3.50	1.50
Serbia[1]	19.50	X(11)	X	X	1.50	1.50	3.75	4.75	3.50	2.50	2.00
United Kingdom	19.50	X/EU Report	X	X	1.50	2.00	4.50	5.25	3.50	1.50	1.25
Netherlands	19.25	X/EU Report	X	X	1.50	2.00	4.25	5.00	2.50	2.50	1.50
Romania	19.00	X/EU Report	-	X	1.50	2.00	2.50	5.00	3.00	3.00	2.00
Croatia	17.25	X(11)	X	X	1.50	1.50	3.25	3.50	3.00	3.00	1.50
Norway	17.25	X	X	X	1.50	1.50	4.75	4.75	3.00	1.00	0.75
Italy	16.25	X/EU Report	X	-	1.50	1.50	3.50	6.00	2.50	1.25	0.00
Montenegro	16.25	X	X	X(11)	1.50	1.00	2.50	5.25	3.00	2.00	1.00
Spain	16.25	X/EU Report	X	X	1.50	1.50	2.50	3.75	3.50	2.00	1.50
Belgium[a2]	16.00	X/EU Report	X	X	1.50	2.00	3.25	2.25	2.50	2.50	2.00
Slovakia	16.00	X/EU Report	X	X	1.50	1.50	2.50	3.50	3.00	2.00	2.00
United States[3]	15.75	X	X	X	1.50	1.50	4.25	4.00	2.50	2.00	0.00
France[a]	15.00	X/EU Report	X	X	1.50	1.50	4.00	3.75	2.50	1.25	0.50
Sweden	15.00	X/EU Report	X	X	1.50	1.50	2.75	4.25	2.50	1.50	1.00
Denmark	14.75	X(11)EU Report	X	X	1.50	1.00	4.25	3.50	2.50	2.00	0.00
Finland	14.75	X/EU Report	X	X	1.50	1.50	3.00	3.50	3.00	2.00	0.25
Czech Republic	14.50	X/EU Report	X	X	1.50	1.50	2.50	4.00	3.00	2.00	0.00
Poland	14.25	X/EU Report	X	X	1.50	1.00	3.00	3.75	3.00	1.50	0.50
Bulgaria	13.25	X/EU Report	-	X	1.50	1.50	2.25	3.25	3.00	1.50	0.25
Portugal	12.75	X/EU Report	X	X	1.50	1.50	3.00	2.50	3.00	1.00	0.25
Greece	11.75	EU Report	X	X	1.50	1.00	2.00	2.50	3.00	1.50	0.25
Australia	11.25	-	X	X	1.50	1.00	1.50	3.75	3.50	0.00	0.00
Hungary	11.00	X/EU Report	X	X	1.50	1.50	1.50	2.50	2.50	1.50	0.00
Austria	10.50	X(10)EU Report	X	X	1.50	1.00	2.25	1.75	2.50	1.50	0.00
Canada	10.25	-	X	X	1.50	0.50	1.50	3.75	3.00	0.00	0.00
Lithuania	10.25	EU Report	X	X	1.50	1.00	1.50	2.25	2.50	1.50	0.00

	Total (25.00 max)	Export report**/ EU Annual Report***	UN Comtrade	UN Register	Timeliness (1.50 max)	Access and consistency (2.00 max)	Clarity (5.00 max)	Comprehensiveness (6.50 max)	Deliveries (4.00 max)	Licences granted (4.00 max)	Licences refused (2.00 max)
Russian Federation	10.25	–	X	X	1.50	1.00	1.50	3.25	3.00	0.00	0.00
South Korea	10.00	–	X	X	1.50	1.00	1.50	3.50	2.50	0.00	0.00
Luxembourg△	9.75	EU Report	X	X	1.50	0.50	1.50	2.75	2.00	1.50	0.00
Thailand	9.75	–	X	–	1.50	0.50	1.50	3.25	3.00	0.00	0.00
Pakistan	9.00	–	X	X	1.50	0.50	1.50	3.00	2.50	0.00	0.00
Israel	8.75	–	X	–	1.50	0.50	1.50	3.25	2.00	0.00	0.00
Colombia	8.50	–	X	–	1.50	0.50	1.25	2.25	3.00	0.00	0.00
Turkey	8.50	–	X	X	1.50	0.50	1.50	2.50	2.50	0.00	0.00
India△	8.25	–	X	X	1.50	0.50	1.50	2.25	2.50	0.00	0.00
Mexico	8.25	–	X	X	1.50	1.00	1.50	1.75	2.50	0.00	0.00
Philippines	8.25	–	X	–	1.50	0.50	1.50	2.25	2.50	0.00	0.00
Argentina	8.00	–	X	X	1.50	1.00	1.50	1.50	2.50	0.00	0.00
Cyprus	8.00	–	X	X	1.50	1.00	1.00	2.00	2.50	0.00	0.00
Ukraine	8.00	X	–	X	1.50	1.50	1.00	2.00	2.00	0.00	0.00
Brazil△	7.00	–	X	X	1.50	0.50	1.00	1.50	2.50	0.00	0.00
China	7.00	–	X	–	1.50	0.50	1.00	1.50	2.50	0.00	0.00
Japan	7.00	–	X	X	1.50	1.00	1.25	2.25	1.00	0.00	0.00
Egypt	6.75	–	X	–	1.50	0.50	1.50	1.25	2.00	0.00	0.00
Singapore	6.50	–	X	X	1.50	1.00	1.00	1.00	2.00	0.00	0.00
Taiwan	4.75	–	X(11)	–	1.00	0.00	1.00	0.75	2.00	0.00	0.00
Malawi	3.75	–	X(11)	–	1.00	0.00	0.75	0.75	1.25	0.00	0.00
South Africa	3.50	X	–	X	1.50	1.50	0.50	0.00	0.00	0.00	0.00
Bosnia and Herzegovina	1.50	–	–	X	1.50	0.00	0.00	0.00	0.00	0.00	0.00
Iran	0.00	–	–	–	0.00	0.00	0.00	0.00	0.00	0.00	0.00
North Korea	0.00	–	–	–	0.00	0.00	0.00	0.00	0.00	0.00	0.00
Saudi Arabia	0.00	–	–	–	0.00	0.00	0.00	0.00	0.00	0.00	0.00
United Arab Emirates	0.00	–	–	–	0.00	0.00	0.00	0.00	0.00	0.00	0.00

Note: The online version of the Transparency Barometer incorporates updates and corrections, all of which affect states' scores as well as their rankings. For these reasons, the online editions–rather than the printed version–should be considered definitive. See Small Arms Survey (n.d.).

* Major exporters are countries that export–or are believed to export–at least USD 10 million worth of small arms, light weapons, their parts, accessories, and ammunition in a given year. The 2014 Barometer includes all countries that qualified as a major exporter at least once during the 2001-12 calendar years.

** X indicates that a report was issued; X(year) indicates that, as a report was not issued by the cut off-date, the country was evaluated on the basis of its most recent submission, covering activities for the period reported in brackets.

*** The Barometer assesses information provided in the EU's Fifteenth Annual Report (CoEU, 2014), reflecting military exports by EU member states in 2012.

Δ The country submitted data to the UN Register for its 2012 activities, but its contribution was not available for analysis by the cut-off date (UNODA, 2013; UNGA, 2013d; 2013e). It is therefore evaluated on the basis of its most recent submission, when available, covering activities in 2011.

Scoring system

The scoring system for the 2014 Barometer remains the same as in 2013. The Barometer's seven categories assess: timeliness, access and consistency in reporting, clarity, comprehensiveness, and the level of detail provided on actual deliveries, licences granted, and licences refused. For more complete information on the scoring guidelines, see Small Arms Survey (n.d.).

Explanatory notes

Note A: The 2014 Barometer is based on each country's most recent arms export report, made publicly available between 1 January 2012 and 31 December 2013.

Note B: The 2014 Barometer takes account of national submissions to the UN Register from 1 January 2012 to 31 August 2013, as well as information states have submitted to UN Comtrade on their 2012 exports up to and including 29 November 2013.

Note C: The fact that the Barometer is based on three sources–national arms export reports, UN Register submissions, and UN customs data–works to the advantage of states that publish data in all three outlets. Barometer scores reflect the information provided to each of the three sources. The same information is not credited twice, however.

Country-specific notes

1. Serbia published a national arms export report in 2013 that was limited to 2011 activities.

2. In addition to the national report issued by the Belgian federal government, each Belgian region (Brussels, Flanders, and Wallonia) reports separately on its arms exports. As the Brussels and Flanders regions did not issue their arms export reports by the cut-off date, Belgium's 2014 score is derived from the Belgian national report and the report issued by Wallonia.

3. For the purposes of the Barometer, the US annual report refers to the State Department report, issued pursuant to Section 655 of the Foreign Assistance Act on direct commercial sales, and the report on foreign military sales, which is prepared by the US Department of Defense.

Sources: Small Arms Survey (2014)

TRANSPARENCY ON SMALL ARMS TRANSFERS UNDER THE ATT

The Arms Trade Treaty (ATT) is the first global legally binding instrument for the control of the international transfer of conventional arms, including small arms and light weapons, and promoting transparency in the international arms trade is one of its declared purposes (UNGA, 2013b, art. 1). To meet this goal, the ATT requires states parties to make available: (a) an initial, one-off report on measures undertaken to implement the treaty, including national laws, regulations, and administrative measures, and (b) an annual report on authorized or actual exports and imports of conventional arms (art. 13). States parties are also encouraged to share information on good practices in combating diversion (arts. 11(6), 13(2)).

The ATT does not indicate what specific types of information should be provided in the annual report. The UN Secretary-General's 1991 report on 'ways and means of promoting transparency in international transfers of conventional arms' identifies ten types of information:

a. the supplier and recipient;

b. the type of arms transferred;

c. the number of units;

d. a description of the item, components, knowledge, or services transferred;

e. the final end user or end use;

Figure 4.4 **Percentage of states providing information on small arms and light weapons exports undertaken in 2011, by type of weapon and reporting mechanism**

■ National report (N=25)   ■ UN Register (N=34)   ■ UN Comtrade (N=47)

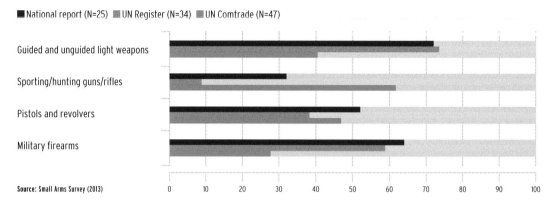

Source: Small Arms Survey (2013)

f.   the dates of agreement and deliveries;

g.   the condition of the weapons;

h.   the financial value of the transfer;

i.   how the transfer is being carried out; and

j.   any technical support and training provided (UNGA, 1991, para. 116).

This study influenced the content of the UN Register and it remains an important reference point for arms transfer reporting.

Article 12 of the ATT requires states parties to maintain national records of export authorizations or actual exports; it encourages record-keeping for conventional arms that are transferred to, or authorized to transit across, their territory. While the ATT does not dictate the specific content of those records, it does encourage states parties to include information on 'the quantity, value, model/type' and authorizations of international transfers of conventional arms covered under Article 2(1) (with the exception of ammunition and parts and components), along with 'conventional arms actually transferred, details of exporting State(s), importing State(s), transit and trans-shipment State(s), and end users' for conventional arms covered under Article 2(1) (UNGA, 2013b, art. 12).

The ATT seeks to address reporting burden concerns by noting that the annual report on arms transfers 'may contain the same information submitted by the State Party to relevant United Nations frameworks, including the United Nations Register of Conventional Arms' (UNGA, 2013b, art. 13). Other frameworks for small arms transfer reporting, both UN-related and not, include UN Comtrade and national arms export reports (see Figure 4.4).[21] Even when these different frameworks are taken into account, public reporting on small arms transfers by UN member states remains limited. The following sections consider the example of these instruments, along with their implications for meaningful ATT reporting on small arms.

The United Nations Register of Conventional Arms

The UN Register was established in 1991 to promote transparency in conventional arms transfers and holdings. It includes seven of the eight categories of conventional arms covered by the ATT: small arms is the only ATT category that does not have a counterpart in the UN Register. However, since 2003 some light weapons are included in the large-calibre artillery category and MANPADS are included in the missiles and missile launchers category. Since 2003 states have also been invited to provide 'background information' on their international small arms transfers (UNGA, 2003, paras. 112–13). In 2006 a standardized form, which is identical to the form used for reporting to the UN Register, was introduced to facilitate such reporting. A definition of small arms was not provided, but the form contains six subcategories for small arms and seven subcategories for light weapons.[22]

The UN Secretary-General appoints a group of governmental experts (GGE) every three years to consider the operation and further development of the UN Register. The inclusion of small arms in the UN Register has been considered at length and the abovementioned developments of 2003 and 2006 are the result of recommendations made by GGEs. The 2009 GGE was expected to recommend the creation of an eighth category for reporting on small arms transfers, but the Russian expert opposed this move (Holtom, 2010, p. 81). The 2009 GGE recommended that member states submit their views on the inclusion of a small arms category. As of July 2013, ten states had submitted their views, nine of them favouring such a category (UNGA, 2013c, para. 25). The issue of a small arms category was also considered by the 2013 GGE, which met shortly after the adoption of the ATT. This time, the Chinese and Cuban experts objected (Morley, 2013). The group repeated the earlier recommendation for states to submit their views on such a category. As a result, states will continue to report on small arms transfers as background information to the UN Register.

Since 2004, 80 UN member states have provided background information on their small arms transfers at least once (UNGA, 2013c, para. 24). At the same time, the overall level of participation in the UN Register declined from 126 states in 2001 to an all-time low of 52 states in 2012 (Holtom et al., 2011, p. 2; UNGA, 2013c, para. 16). In 2012, 32 states provided background information on international small arms transfers, down from 49 states in 2011 (UNGA, 2013c, para. 21, table 2).

> A robust ATT template would enhance the UN Register's contribution to transparency.

The UN Register invites states to provide information on actual transfers, yet some countries only report on authorizations. For example, Germany previously indicated that its background information on small arms exports was derived from data on authorizations (UNGA, 2007, p. 104); it is not alone in this regard (Holtom, 2008, p. 26). This practice probably explains why ATT states parties were given a choice of reporting either authorizations or actual exports and imports. States could, however, routinely require those authorized to export or import small arms to report their actual exports and imports to national licensing authorities. Poland, for example, has indicated that this is its preferred option for collecting data on actual exports (Poland, 2011, p. 15). As described below, customs practices offer further scope for improved reporting on actual exports and imports.

The ATT balances the goal of greater transparency with negotiated language that appears to act as a constraint on the same. For example, the ATT states that '[r]eports may exclude commercially sensitive or national security information' (UNGA, 2013b, art. 13(3))—language that is not found in the UN Register. There is an obvious risk that this phrase could be used as a blanket justification for non-reporting. It will also be important to confirm that the phrase, 'Reports shall be made available, and distributed to States Parties by the Secretariat' (art. 13(3)), means that ATT reports will be made available to the public.

Such uncertainties notwithstanding, the ATT could draw upon existing good practices in reporting to fulfil its stated goal of enhanced arms trade transparency. Most of the states that report small arms transfers to the UN Register provide information on subcategories of small arms transferred, suppliers, recipients, and the number of items transferred. Several states have provided a description of the small arms and additional types of information (see Table 4.8); in some cases, they indicate the type of end user or end use when reporting small arms imports.[23] This additional information— such as on the type of end user—could be incorporated into an ATT reporting template along with the elements of the UN Register template. To the extent that ATT states parties provided the same information to the UN Register, a robust ATT template would also enhance the UN Register's contribution to arms trade transparency.

Table 4.8 Background information on international exports of small arms and light weapons provided by states to the UN Register on 2010 and 2011 activities[24]

State	Year of activities	Category#	Final importer state(s)	No. of items	State of origin (if not exporter)	Intermediate location (if any)	Description of item	Comments on transfer	Additional comment	UNGA source+
Australia	2011	-	-	Yes^	Yes	-	General description	General	List of aggregated totals of licences granted by state	2012b
Austria	2010	Yes (2)	Yes	Yes	Yes	-	-	-	-	2011
Bosnia and Herzegovina	2010	Yes (5)	Yes	Yes	-	-	-	-	-	2011
Bulgaria	2011	Yes (8)	Yes	Yes	Selected	-	Selected	-	-	2012c
Canada	2010	Yes (5)	Yes	Yes	-	-	Selected	Donations and demilitarized	-	2011
Croatia	2010	Yes (1)	Yes	Yes	-	-	Yes	-	-	2011*
Denmark	2010	Yes (5)	Yes	Yes	Yes	-	Yes	Temporary exports	-	2012a
France	2011	Yes (3)	Yes	Yes	-	-	Yes	-	-	2012b
Germany	2011	Yes (7)	Yes	Yes	-	-	-	United Nations end user	German arms transfer policy	2013a
Hungary	2011	Yes (6)	Yes	Yes	Yes	-	Yes	Surplus export	-	2013a
Italy	2010	Yes (2)	Yes	Yes	-	-	-	-	-	2012a
Lithuania	2011	Yes (3)	Yes	Yes	Yes	-	-	Temporary import	-	2012b
Montenegro	2011	Yes (5)	Yes	Yes	Yes	-	Yes	-	-	2013a
Netherlands	2011	Yes (4)	Yes	-	Selected	-	-	Destruction	-	2012b

State	Year of activities	Category#	Final importer state(s)	No. of items	State of origin (if not exporter)	Intermediate location (if any)	Description of item	Comments on transfer	Additional comment	UNGA source+
Norway	2011	Yes (3)	Yes	Yes^X	Selected	-	-	-	-	2012b
Poland	2011	Yes (11)	Yes	Yes	-	-	-	-	-	2012b
Portugal	2011	Yes (11)	Yes	Selected	-	-	-	Government end user	-	2013a
Romania	2011	Yes (11)	Yes	Yes	-	-	Selected	Export of kits; hunting and sporting exports	-	2012c
Serbia	2010	Yes (10)	Yes	Yes	Yes	Yes	-	Information on transit states	-	2011
Slovakia	2011	Yes (11)	Yes	Yes	-	-	-	Re-export	-	2012b
South Korea	2011	Yes (4)	Yes	Yes	-	-	Yes	-	-	2013a
Sweden	2011	Yes (2)	-	-	-	-	Yes	Classified information	-	2012c
Switzerland	2011	Yes (5)	Yes	Yes	-	-	Selected	-	-	2013a
Turkey	2010	Yes (3)	Yes	Yes	-	-	-	-	-	2011
Ukraine	2010	Yes (8)	Yes	Yes	-	-	-	-	-	2011
United Kingdom	2011	Yes (4)	Yes	Yes	-	-	Selected	-	-	2012b

Notes: + For a full listing of sources, see the bibliography.
The number in brackets indicates on how many small arms and light weapons categories the state reports.
^ The state provides the total number of licences granted.
X The state provides aggregated totals per arms category.
* The state contributed to the UN Register for 2011, but its contribution was not available for analysis at the time of writing.

UN Comtrade

Every year, countries around the world report standardized customs data to UN Comtrade. The database is considered the most comprehensive repository of trade data, as it contains detailed information on commodity imports and exports for almost all UN member states since 1962. Customs data is collected by national statistics authorities and reported according to the Harmonized Commodity Description and Coding System, now at its fourth revision. Some states use customs data as one of the sources of information for their national arms exports reports (AI, 2011; Holtom and Bromley, 2011). They report arms data to UN Comtrade under the overarching category 93—'Arms and ammunition, parts and accessories thereof'—and its seven subcategories. Although Comtrade does not have a specific subcategory for small arms and is not traditionally regarded as a transparency instrument, states provide a considerable amount of information on their small arms transfers to it (see Table 4.9). Crucially, Comtrade information is publicly available.

That said, a number of limitations restrict the potential use of Comtrade data for reporting small arms transfers to the ATT. First, as with the UN Register, the information states provide varies in its level of detail. Another problem, specific to Comtrade, is that a number of major arms-exporting states do not report to Comtrade on arms, including small arms, that are delivered to military and security forces, whether commercially or as gifts, loans, or donations. Further, Comtrade contains considerably more information on transfers of sporting and hunting firearms in comparison to items that only military forces are likely to use, such as light weapons (including MANPADS and mortars; see Table 4.9).

Table 4.9 Percentage of states that report to UN Comtrade on the value and quantity of small arms and light weapons exports, by arms category for 2011 activities (n=47)*

UN Comtrade categories		% of states reporting	
		Value	Quantity
Guided and unguided light weapons	930111	12.8	8.5
	930120	27.7	14.9
	930119	27.7	12.8
	Average	22.7	12.1
Sporting and hunting guns and rifles	930320	70.2	72.3
	930330	76.6	78.7
	Average	73.4	75.5
Revolvers and pistols	930200	57.4	59.6
	Average	57.4	59.6
Military weapons	930190	38.3	19.1
	Average	38.3	19.1
Small arms and light weapons ammunition	930621	66.0	0
	930690	68.1	0
	930630	74.5	0
	930629	76.6	0
	Average	71.3	0
Parts and accessories of small arms and light weapons	930590	0	0
	930521	44.7	0
	930591	53.2	0
	930510	66.0	0
	930529	74.5	0
	930599	74.5	0
	Average	52.15	0

Note: * Under UN Comtrade, states can report on quantities in units and by weight. The categories marked in red contain exclusively small arms and light weapons while the others also contain other conventional weapons.

Sources: NISAT (n.d.); UN Comtrade (n.d.)

Despite these shortcomings, a large number of states are willing to provide customs data on their actual arms exports and imports to UN Comtrade. Customs data could also be used to report on actual exports and imports under the ATT, although several questions would need to be resolved beforehand. First, ATT reporting would need to permit information on either the number of units being transferred or the declared customs value of the transfer, as per Comtrade practice. Second, Comtrade arms classifications preclude the easy identification of small arms. The ATT's existence would argue for a revision of the Harmonized Commodity Description and Coding System to reflect the eight categories of the ATT, as well as ammunition and parts and components, thus allowing states parties to utilize customs data for ATT reporting on actual exports and imports. If states parties use customs data in this way, they would still need to ensure that any arms transfers not recorded in customs statistics were also reported to the ATT.

National arms export reports

Governments publish regular national reports on arms exports to provide information to the public on their export control systems and their arms export licensing decisions, including actual exports in some cases. As of January 2014, 35 states had produced at least one national report on arms exports, with 32 states submitting at least one report since 2009. Of these 32 countries, all but two—South Africa and the United States—are European.

> Customs data could be used to report on exports and imports.

A prime reason for the large number of European reports is undoubtedly that the EU Common Position, adopted in 2008, requires EU member states to produce a national report on arms exports if they have authorized conventional arms exports. These reports must contain information on the number of licences issued and the value of licences for all items covered by the EU Military List, disaggregated by destination and military list category. This information is compiled and published in the EU Annual Report on Arms Exports (CoEU, 2008).[25] The EU Report also reflects data provided by some EU member states on the value of actual exports, licence denials, and brokering authorizations—although the state that has denied a licence is not identified. Non-EU states in South-eastern Europe have also produced national reports, with prospective EU membership a key driver of this process (Bromley, 2011).

Broadly speaking, states take one of three approaches when reporting on their authorizations and/or actual exports of small arms and light weapons: small arms-specific national reports (as is the case for Switzerland); sections on international small arms transfers in national reports (as provided by e.g. the Czech Republic, Germany, Norway, Sweden, and the UK); and reporting to other transparency instruments that use the Wassenaar Arrangement Military List (such as the EU Annual Report), which includes not only small arms, but also large-calibre artillery in the same category. In addition to these differences in format, the national reports are characterized by considerable variety in terms of the types of information on small arms transfers.

During the ATT negotiations, some states proposed sharing information on denials, as is the case, for example, under the EU Common Position and in the Wassenaar Arrangement. In the event, the ATT does not require states to provide information on denials, but such information would undoubtedly help elucidate the application of ATT prohibitions and licensing criteria, as well as the treaty's provisions on diversion. In fact, information on denials often signals potentially problematic transfers (Lazarevic, 2012, p. 304). Nevertheless, some countries are reluctant to share this information—as demonstrated by interventions states made on this issue during the ATT negotiations. First, these countries cite the potential harm to exporter–importer relations. Second, they claim that the exporting state risks revealing a potential business opportunity to unscrupulous suppliers. Finally, they assert that sharing denial information can damage an importing state's reputation, even if it concerns a delivery of conventional arms to a company or dealer—as opposed to the importing state's armed or security forces— if the prospective end user is not identified.

In reporting on their small arms transfers, some states include information on registered arms brokers or licences for brokering transactions that they have granted or denied. Nearly one-third of the national reports captured by the Barometer provide information on brokering, but the level of detail varies as much as it does for exports.

National arms export reports also demonstrate that a significant number of major exporters, including many of the states that have signed the ATT, are able and willing to provide the public and peers with information on temporary exports, as well as applicable laws, regulations, and multilateral instruments (see Table 4.10). It remains to be seen whether the ATT will build on these efforts— or instead undermine them by encouraging lowest-common-denominator reporting.

Table 4.10	Information on small arms and light weapons provided by national reports (n=25)		
Type of information provided		No. of states	% of states
Small arms distinguished from other conventional arms		20	80
Multilateral commitments relating to the control of international small arms transfers, including brokering		19	76
Small arms ammunition distinguished from ammunition for other conventional arms		16	64
Measures to prevent and detect the diversion of international small arms transfers		13	52
Government transactions distinguished from those involving private industry		12	48
Temporary exports		6	24
Brokering control legislation covering small arms		7	28
Authorized (small) arms brokers		6	24
Transfer control legislation (covering small arms export, transit, and/or import)		5	20

Source: Small Arms Survey (2014)

Conclusions on transparency under the ATT

In line with its stated purposes, the ATT offers a unique opportunity to boost transparency in the international transfer of conventional arms, including small arms. Yet there is a risk that the reports of many ATT states parties simply duplicate their submissions to the UN Register's seven categories—excluding small arms. At a minimum, states parties will need to supplement such submissions with information on their international transfers of small arms (UNGA, 2013b, art. 13(3)), perhaps using the corresponding UN Register reporting form. This measure alone would lead to an increase in the number of states providing information on small arms transfers, yet ATT reporting practices that stop at the UN Register would fall well short of what is possible and feasible.

The UN Register—and in particular its standardized reporting template—offers an established basis on which the ATT can build. A standardized reporting template will probably be one of the first items that ATT states parties consider once the treaty enters into force, with the Register undoubtedly exerting a strong influence on its development. Yet, as this section has explained, ATT reporting can also harness other practice to maximize broader transparency gains—such as by synchronizing the subcategories of the Comtrade category for 'arms, ammunition, parts and components thereof' with the ATT arms categories. This would allow states that provide arms data to Comtrade to use the same information to report on actual exports and imports under the ATT. As noted above, states parties could also require recipients of arms export and import authorizations to report to national licensing authorities on actual exports and imports.

States parties will need to address several other questions as they consider what form ATT reporting should take. These include: whether a single category for small arms is sufficient; whether the subcategories of the UN Register reporting template for small arms should be retained or revisited; which national reporting practices should be introduced into the ATT; whether state parties should be encouraged to provide additional information on ammunition and parts and components; and what additional information states parties should provide on brokering, transit, denials, and measures to prevent diversion. The ATT reporting provisions offer only the most basic guidance on arms transfer reporting. If the ATT is to fulfil its goal of enhanced transparency in the international arms trade, states parties will need to draw inspiration from the full range of current reporting practices. ∎

LIST OF ABBREVIATIONS

ATT	Arms Trade Treaty
EU	European Union
EUC	End-use(r) certificate
FARC	Revolutionary Armed Forces of Colombia (Fuerzas Armadas Revolucionarias de Colombia)
GGE	Group of governmental experts
MANPADS	Man-portable air defence system
NISAT	Norwegian Initiative on Small Arms Transfers
OSCE	Organization for Security and Co-operation in Europe
PoA	United Nations Programme of Action to Prevent, Combat and Eradicate the Illicit Trade in Small Arms and Light Weapons in All Its Aspects
UAE	United Arab Emirates
UN Comtrade	United Nations Commodity Trade Statistics Database
UN Register	United Nations Register of Conventional Arms

ANNEXES

Online annexes at <http://www.smallarmssurvey.org/publications/by-type/yearbook/small-arms-survey-2014.html>

Annexe 4.1. Annual authorized small arms and light weapons exports for major exporters (annual exports of at least USD 10 million), 2011

Annexe 4.2. Annual authorized small arms and light weapons exports imports for major importers (annual imports of at least USD 10 million), 2011

ENDNOTES

1   The figures may differ from the values given in previous editions of the *Small Arms Survey* as countries sometimes revise their submissions to UN Comtrade. See Dreyfus et al. (2009, p. 54, n. 10).

2   The Small Arms Survey relies on the analysis of customs data provided by the Norwegian Initiative on Small Arms Transfers (NISAT) project at the Peace Research Institute Oslo. NISAT considers countries' self-reported exports as well as 'mirror data'—reported imports by destination countries—to generate a single value by transaction. See Marsh (2005).

3   See Dreyfus et al. (2009, p. 29, table 1.22); Grzybowski, Marsh, and Schroeder (2012, p. 247); and Figure 4.4 in this chapter.

4   In 2010, top exporters that did not report on their military firearm transfers to UN Comtrade were: Austria, Belgium, Brazil, China, Germany, Italy, the Russian Federation, Spain, and Sweden (Rigual, 2013). For an overview of UN Comtrade reporting, see the 2014 Transparency Barometer (Table 4.7).

5   Data for 2010 is not adjusted for inflation given the short (two-year) review period.

6   All values presented in this section are rounded to the nearest USD 1 million.

7   This increase, as well as the new status of Côte d'Ivoire as a major importer, reflects a single transaction: Côte d'Ivoire reported an import of
     USD 73 million worth of small arms ammunition from Pakistan in 2011.

8   The exception was Côte d'Ivoire, whose imports rose from around USD 5 million in 2010 to USD 77 million in 2011. See the previous note.

9   The UN Comtrade categories used to calculate the global small arms trade are presented in Annexes 4.1 and 4.2, available online. All figures
     from 2001 to 2011 are expressed in constant 2011 US dollars.

10   See Dreyfus et al. (2009, pp. 11–25) for an analysis of global trends from 2000 to 2006.

11   For an explanation for the increase in the value of the ammunition trade, see Corney and Marsh (2013, pp. 9–13).

12   This section uses the term 'unauthorized retransfer' to refer to both 'unauthorized re-export' and unauthorized retransfer to end users in the import-
     ing state in violation of commitments made by the authorized importer or end user prior to export.

13   For examples of non-re-export clauses in EUCs, see Wood and Danssaert (2011, table 3, pp. 82–84).

14   Author communication with the Swedish Agency for Non-Proliferation and Export Controls (Inspektionen för Strategiska Produkter), 12 December 2013.

15   This includes information EU states have contributed to the EU Annual Report on military exports (CoEU, 2014).

16   There are important exceptions to these yearly timeframes. See Lazarevic (2010) for full details of the scoring methodology and for a description
     of the changes to the Transparency Barometer scoring system since its introduction in 2004.

17   The Small Arms Survey relies on the NISAT Database of Small Arms Transfers to determine which states meet the minimum export threshold for
     inclusion (Marsh, 2005; NISAT, n.d.). Peru was not considered a 'major exporter' this year since the Survey counted two similar UN Comtrade
     transactions, reported separately by Peru (exporter) and the United States (importer), as a single transaction.

18   In the 2013 Barometer, Romania tied with Serbia for third place (Small Arms Survey, n.d.).

19   Since 2011, Austria has not issued a national arms export report, but it makes information on arms exports available in the EU Annual Report.

20   Bosnia and Herzegovina does not issue a national report but reports to the South Eastern and Eastern Europe Clearinghouse for the Control of
     Small Arms and Light Weapons (SEESAC), whose latest report covers 2011 activities.

21   Of the 14 countries whose small arms exports match or exceed USD 100 million in value, eight have issued national export reports and/or con-
     tributed to the EU Annual Report: Austria, Belgium, the Czech Republic, Germany, Italy, Spain, Switzerland, and the United States.

22   For the full list of categories, see the reporting template in annexes I and II of the 2006 GGE report (UNGA, 2006).

23   In 2011 and 2012 the following states provided such information on their arms imports: Albania, Grenada, Hungary, Portugal, Switzerland, and
     Trinidad and Tobago (UNGA, 2011; 2012b).

24   The table employs the same terms as those in the UN Register template.

25   As of January 2014, only Cyprus had not yet filed an EU report.

BIBLIOGRAPHY

AFP (Agence France-Presse). 2009. 'Sweden Asks Venezuela to Explain FARC Weapons Find.' 27 July.
    <http://www.google.com/hostednews/afp/article/ALeqM5jgmUhszbB9C53sLHMP2Pea4c9CfQ?hl=en>

AI (Amnesty International). 2011. *Our Right to Know: Transparent Reporting under an Arms Trade Treaty.*
    <http://www.amnesty.org/en/library/asset/ACT30/116/2011/en/c6a0310e-81fa-47eb-be10-87e596823f16/act301162011en.pdf>

—. 2012. *South Sudan: Overshadowed Conflict.* London: AI.

APEC (Asia Pacific Economic Cooperation). 2003. *APEC Guidelines on Control and Security of Man-Portable Air Defence Systems (MANPADS).*
    <http://www.fas.org/asmp/campaigns/MANPADS/APECguidelines1.pdf>

BBC (British Broadcasting Corporation). 2009. 'Swedes Quiz Venezuela on Weapons.' 27 July. <http://news.bbc.co.uk/2/hi/8171580.stm>

Bromley, Mark. 2011. *The Development of National and Regional Reports on Arms Exports in the EU and South Eastern Europe.* Belgrade: South Eastern
    and Eastern Europe Clearinghouse for the Control of Small Arms and Light Weapons. September.
    <http://www.sipri.org/research/armaments/transfers/transparency/research/armaments/transfers/publications/other_publ/other%20publications/
    the-development-of-national-and-regional-reports-on-arms-exports-in-the-eu-and-south-eastern-europe-seesac>

—. 2012. *The Review of the EU Common Position on Arms Exports: Prospects for Strengthened Controls.* EU Non-Proliferation Consortium Non-
    Proliferation Papers No. 7. January. <http://www.sipri.org/research/disarmament/eu-consortium/publications/publications/non-proliferation-paper-7>

Brown Moses Blog. 2013. 'Are Yugoslavian Anti-tank Weapons Being Smuggled into Syria?' 16 January.
    <http://brown-moses.blogspot.se/2013/01/are-yugoslavian-anti-tank-weapons-being.html>

CCNC (Control Committee of the National Council). 2012. 'Utilisation de grenades à main de fabrication suisse dans le conflit syrien—Déclarations de
    non-réexportation de matériel de guerre: mesures adéquates du Conseil fédéral.' Bern: Swiss Parliament. 12 November.
    <http://www.parlament.ch/e/mm/2012/pages/mm-gpk-n-2012-11-12b.aspx>

Chellaney, Brahma. 2009. 'End-use Monitoring Woes for India.' *Hindu.* 27 July. <http://www.hindu.com/2009/07/27/stories/2009072755490800.htm>

CoEU (Council of the European Union). 2008. Council Common Position Defining Common Rules Governing Control of Exports of Military Technology
    and Equipment. 2008/944/CFSP. Adopted 8 December. <http://eur-lex.europa.eu/LexUriServ/LexUriServ.do?uri=OJ:L:2008:335:0099:0103:EN:PDF>

—. 2014. *Fifteenth Annual Report According to Article 8(2) of Council Common Position 2008/944/CFSP Defining Common Rules Governing Control of Exports of Military Technology and Equipment.* 2014/C 18/01. 21 January.
<http://eur-lex.europa.eu/LexUriServ/LexUriServ.do?uri=OJ:C:2014:018:FULL:EN:PDF>

Corney, Neil and Nicholas Marsh. 2013. *Aiming for Control: The Need to Include Ammunition in the Arms Trade Treaty.* Oslo: Peace Research Institute Oslo.

DDTC (Directorate of Defense Trade Controls). 2013. *End-Use Monitoring of Defense Articles and Defense Services Commercial Exports FY 2012.* Washington, DC: United States Department of State. <http://www.pmddtc.state.gov/reports/documents/End_Use_FY2012.pdf>

Dreyfus, Pablo, et al. 2009. 'Sifting the Sources: Authorized Small Arms Transfers.' In Small Arms Survey. *Small Arms Survey 2009: Shadows of War.* Cambridge: Cambridge University Press, pp. 6–59.

DSCA (Defence Security Cooperation Agency). 2012. 'End-Use Monitoring.' In DSCA. *Security Assistance Management Manual (SAMM).* Washington, DC: United States Department of Defense, ch. 8. 30 April. <http://www.samm.dsca.mil/chapter/chapter-8>

ECOWAS (Economic Community of West African States). 2006. ECOWAS Convention on Small Arms and Light Weapons, Their Ammunition and Other Related Materials. Adopted in Abuja, Nigeria, 14 June. Entered into force 29 September 2009.
<http://www.poa-iss.org/RegionalOrganizations/ECOWAS/ECOWAS%20Convention%202006.pdf>

EU (European Union). 2008. Council Common Position 2008/944/CFSP of 8 December 2008 Defining Common Rules Governing Control of Exports of Military Technology and Equipment. *Official Journal of the European Union.* L 335/99 of 13 December 2008.
<http://eur-lex.europa.eu/LexUriServ/LexUriServ.do?uri=OJ:L:2008:335:0099:0103:EN:PDF>

—. 2009. *User's Guide to Council Common Position 2008/944/CFSP of 8 December 2008 Defining Common Rules Governing Control of Exports of Military Technology and Equipment, 9241/09.* 29 April. <http://register.consilium.europa.eu/pdf/en/09/st09/st09241.en09.pdf>

Finland. n.d. 'Declaration by End User to the Government of Finland.' Helsinki: Ministry of Defence of Finland.
<http://www.defmin.fi/files/1228/VNS6_2004_Liite_EUC2_nuclear_OCI.pdf>

Fruchart, Damien, et al. 2007. *United Nations Arms Embargoes: Their Impact on Arms Flows and Target Behaviour.* Stockholm and Uppsala: Stockholm International Peace Research Institute and Uppsala University.

Germany. n.d. 'End-Use Certificate for Presentation to the Export Control Authorities of the Federal Republic of Germany.' Eschborn: Bundesamt für Wirtschaft und Ausfuhrkontrolle (Federal Office of Economics and Export Control).
<http://www.bafa.de/ausfuhrkontrolle/de/antragstellung/endverbleibsdokumente/formularmuster_zu_endverbleibserklaerungen.pdf >

Gettleman, Jeffrey and Michael Gordon. 2010. 'Pirates' Catch Exposed Route of Arms in Sudan.' *The New York Times.* 8 December.
<http://www.nytimes.com/2010/12/09/world/africa/09wikileaks-tank.html?pagewanted=all&_r=0>

Grzybowski, Janis, Nicholas Marsh, and Matt Schroeder. 2012. 'Piece by Piece: Authorized Transfers of Parts and Accessories.' In Small Arms Survey. *Small Arms Survey 2012: Moving Targets.* Cambridge: Cambridge University Press, pp. 240–81.

Hina. 2013. '"We Sold Weapons to Jordan but Not to Syria!" Josipovic Confirmed that He Knew about the Export of 200 Tons of Weapons [translated from the Croatian].' *Jutarnji List* (Zagreb). 6 April. <http://www.jutarnji.hr/ivo-josipovic--hrvatska-je-prodala-oruzje-jordanu--a-ne-siriji/1095377/>

Holtom, Paul. 2008. *Transparency in Transfers of Small Arms and Light Weapons: Reports to the United Nations Register of Conventional Arms, 2003–2006.* SIPRI Policy Paper No. 22. Stockholm: Stockholm International Peace Research Institute. July. <http://books.sipri.org/files/PP/SIPRIPP22.pdf>

—. 2010. 'Nothing to Report: The Lost Promise of the UN Register of Conventional Arms.' *Contemporary Security Policy,* Vol. 31, No. 1, pp. 61–87.

— et al. 2011. 'Reporting to the United Nations Register of Conventional Arms.' SIPRI Fact Sheet. Stockholm: Stockholm International Peace Research Institute. May. <http://books.sipri.org/files/FS/SIPRIFS1105.pdf>

— and Mark Bromley. 2011. *Implementing an Arms Trade Treaty: Lessons Learned on Reporting and Monitoring from Existing Mechanisms.* SIPRI Policy Paper 28. Stockholm: Stockholm International Peace Research Institute. July. <http://books.sipri.org/files/PP/SIPRIPP28.pdf>

Kinshasa Convention (Central African Convention for the Control of Small Arms and Light Weapons, Their Ammunition, Parts and Components that Can Be Used for Their Manufacture, Repair and Assembly). 2010. Adopted in Kinshasa, Democratic Republic of the Congo, 30 April.
<http://www.iansa.org/system/files/Pages%20from%20Convention%20de%20Kinshasa%20certifi%C3%A9e_low_eng.pdf>

Lakshmanan, Indira. 2009. 'India Agrees on Monitoring of US Defense Purchases.' Bloomberg. 20 July.
<http://www.bloomberg.com/apps/news?pid=newsarchive&sid=ajPF_JTWoDn4>

Lazarevic, Jasna. 2010. *Transparency Counts: Assessing States Reporting on Small Arms Transfers, 2001–08.* Occasional Paper 25. Geneva: Small Arms Survey. June.

—. 2012.'Point by Point: Trends in Transparency.' In Small Arms Survey. *Small Arms Survey Yearbook 2012: Moving Targets.* Cambridge: Cambridge University Press, pp. 283–91. <http://www.smallarmssurvey.org/fileadmin/docs/A-Yearbook/2012/eng/Small-Arms-Survey-2012-Chapter-09-EN.pdf>

Lewis, Mike. 2009. *Skirting the Law: Sudan's Post-CPA Arms Flows.* Human Security Baseline Assessment Working Paper 18. Geneva: Small Arms Survey. September.

Lutterbeck, Derek. 2009. 'Arming Libya: Transfers of Conventional Weapons Past and Present.' *Contemporary Security Policy,* Vol. 30, No. 3, pp. 505–28.

Mampaey, Luc and Federico Santopinto. 2009. *'Opération Parabellum': Enquête sur un trafic d'armes aux sommets de l'État libyen.* Brussels: Groupe de Recherche et d'Information sur la Paix et la Sécurité. 13 December.
<http://www.grip.org/sites/grip.org/files/NOTES_ANALYSE/2009/NA_2009-11-13_FR_L-MAMPAEY_F-SANTOPINTO.pdf>

Marsh, Nicholas. 2005. *Accounting Guns: The Methodology Used in Developing Data Tables for the Small Arms Survey.* Unpublished background paper. Oslo: Norwegian Initiative on Small Arms Transfers/Peace Research Institute, Oslo. 14 November.

McDonald, Glenn. 2008. 'Who's Buying? End-User Certification.' In Small Arms Survey. *Small Arms Survey 2008: Risk and Resilience.* Cambridge: Cambridge University Press, pp. 154–81.

Morley, Jefferson. 2013. 'UN Experts Call for Drone Reporting.' *Arms Control Today,* Vol. 43, No. 7. September . <http://www.armscontrol.org/act/%252F2013_09/UN-Experts-Call-for-Drone Reporting%20>

Nairobi Best Practice Guidelines (*Best Practice Guidelines for the Implementation of the Nairobi Declaration and the Nairobi Protocol on Small Arms and Light Weapons*). 2005. Approved by the Third Ministerial Review Conference of the Nairobi Declaration. Nairobi, June. <http://www.recsasec.org/pdf/Best%20Practice%20Guidlines%20Book.pdf>

Nairobi Protocol (Nairobi Protocol for the Prevention, Control and Reduction of Small Arms and Light Weapons in the Great Lakes Region and the Horn of Africa). 2004. Adopted in Nairobi, Kenya, 21 April. Entered into force 5 May 2006. <http://www.recsasec.org/pdf/Nairobi%20Protocol.pdf>

NISAT (Norwegian Initiative on Small Arms Transfers). n.d. 'NISAT Database of Small Arms Transfers: Researcher's Database.' Oslo: NISAT, Peace Research Institute Oslo. Accessed November 2013. <http://nisat.prio.org/Trade-Database/Researchers-Database/>

OAS (Organization of American States). 2005. 'Denying MANPADS to Terrorists: Control and Security of Man-portable air Defense Systems (MANPADS).' AG/RES. 2145 (XXXV-O/05). Adopted 7 June. <http://www.fas.org/asmp/campaigns/MANPADS/2005/OASmanpads.pdf>

OSCE (Organization for Security and Co-operation in Europe). 2000. Document on Small Arms and Light Weapons. FSC.DOC/1/00/Rev.1, originally adopted 24 November 2000, reissued 20 June 2012. Vienna: Forum for Security Co-operation, OSCE. <http://www.osce.org/fsc/20783>

—. 2003. *Handbook of Best Practices on Small Arms and Light Weapons.* Vienna: Forum for Security Co-operation, OSCE. <http://www.osce.org/fsc/item_11_13550.html>

—. 2004a. Principles for Export Controls Of Man-Portable Air Defence Systems (MANPADS). FSC.DEC/3/04 of 26 May. <http://www.osce.org/fsc/32593>

—. 2004b. Standard Elements of End-User Certificates and Verification Procedures for SALW Exports. Decision No. 5/04. FSC.DEC/5/04 of 17 November. <http://www.osce.org/fsc/16941>

Poland. 2011. *Exports of Arms and Military Equipment from Poland: Report for 2010.* Warsaw: Ministry of Foreign Affairs of Poland. <http://www.sipri.org/research/armaments/transfers/transparency/national_reports/Poland/poland_2010.pdf>

Rayner, Gordon. 2011. 'Chinese Weapons Fall into Hands of Insurgent.' *Daily Telegraph* (UK). 3 February. <http://www.telegraph.co.uk/news/worldnews/wikileaks/8299388/WikiLeaks-Chinese-weapons-fall-into-hands-of-insurgents.html>

Rigual, Christelle. 2013. 'Annexes 8.1 and 8.2: Major Exporters and Importers.' Geneva: Small Arms Survey. <http://www.smallarmssurvey.org/fileadmin/docs/A-Yearbook/2013/en/Small-Arms-Survey-2013-Chapter-08-Annexes-8.1-8.2-EN.pdf>

SECO (Swiss State Secretariat for Economic Affairs). 2012. 'Swiss Hand Grenade in Syria: Conclusion of Investigations and Measures.' Press release. Bern: Federal Counci, SECO. 21 September. <http://www.seco.admin.ch/aktuell/00277/01164/01980/index.html?lang=en&msg-id=46075>

SFC (Swiss Federal Council). 2006. *Exécution de la législation sur le matériel de guerre: décisions du Conseil fédéral du 29 juin 2005 et réexportation d'obusiers blindés vers le Maroc: Rapport de la Commission de gestion du Conseil national.* 2006-2883 of 7 November. Feuille fédérale No. 13 of 27 March 2007, pp. 1993–2012. <http://www.admin.ch/f/ff/2007/1993.pdf>

—. 2007. *Exécution de la législation sur le matériel de guerre: décisions du Conseil fédéral du 29 juin 2005 et réexportation d'obusiers blindés vers le Maroc—Rapport du 7 novembre 2006 de la Commission de gestion du Conseil national: Avis du Conseil fédéral.* 2006–3005 of 21 February. Feuille fédérale n° 13 of 27 Mars 2007, pp. 2013–2024. <http://www.admin.ch/opc/fr/federal-gazette/2007/2013.pdf>

—. 2013. War Material Ordinance of 25 February 1998 (Status as of 1 January 2013). Document 514.511. <http://www.admin.ch/opc/en/classified-compilation/19980112/201301010000/514.511.pdf>

Shevchenko, Artem. 2010. 'Sergei Bondarchuk: Yes, We Are Also Known around the World as Arms Dealers, but It Is Not Necessary to be Ashamed of This [translated from the Russian].' *Levyi bereg* (Kiev). 13 August. <http://lb.ua/news/2010/08/13/60799_sergey_bondarchuk_mire.html>

Small Arms Survey. 2013. *Small Arms Trade Transparency Barometer 2013: Sources.* Unpublished background paper. Geneva: Small Arms Survey.

—. 2014. *Small Arms Trade Transparency Barometer 2014: Sources.* Unpublished background paper. Geneva: Small Arms Survey.

—. n.d. 'The Transparency Barometer.' <http://www.smallarmssurvey.org/weapons-and-markets/tools/the-transparency-barometer>

Solomko, Irina and Konstantin Stroginov. 2008. 'The Authorities of Sudan: T-72 Tanks Are Not for Us, but for Kenya [translated from the Russian].' *Segodnya* (Kiev). 8 October. <http://www.segodnya.ua/ukraine/vlacti-cudana-tanki-t-72-shli-ne-k-nam-a-v-keniju.html>

UK (United Kingdom). 2012. *Scrutiny of Arms Exports (2012): UK Strategic Export Controls Annual Report 2010—Quarterly Reports for July to December 2010 and January to September 2011, the Government's Review of Arms Exports to the Middle East and North Africa, and Control Issues.* 13 July. <http://www.publications.parliament.uk/pa/cm201213/cmselect/cmquad/419/41902.htm>

UN Comtrade (United Nations Commodity Trade Statistics Database). n.d. 'United Nations Commodity Trade Statistics Database.' Accessed November 2013. <http://comtrade.un.org/db/>

UNGA (United Nations General Assembly). 1991. *Study on Ways and Means of Promoting Transparency in International Transfers of Conventional Arms: Report of the Secretary-General.* A/46/301 of 9 September 1991.

—. 2001. Programme of Action to Prevent, Combat and Eradicate the Illicit Trade in Small Arms and Light Weapons in All Its Aspects ('UN Programme of Action'). Adopted 21 July. A/CONF/192/15 of 20 July. <http://www.poa-iss.org/poa/poahtml.aspx>

—. 2003. *Continuing Operation of the United Nations Register on Conventional Arms and its Further Development.* A/58/274 of 13 August. <http://www.un.org/ga/search/view_doc.asp?symbol=A/58/274>

—. 2006. *Continuing Operation of the United Nations Register on Conventional Arms and Its Further Development.* A/61/261 of 15 July.
<http://www.un.org/en/ga/search/view_doc.asp?symbol=A/61/261>

—. 2007. *United Nations Register of Conventional Arms: Report of the Secretary-General.* A/62/170 of 27 July.
<http://www.un.org/en/ga/search/view_doc.asp?symbol=A/62/170>

—. 2011. *United Nations Register of Conventional Arms: Report of the Secretary-General.* A/66/127 of 12 July.
<http://www.un.org/ga/search/view_doc.asp?symbol=A/66/127>

—. 2012a. *United Nations Register of Conventional Arms: Report of the Secretary-General—Addendum.* A/66/127/add.1 of 18 June.
<http://www.un.org/ga/search/view_doc.asp?symbol=A/66/127/Add.1>

—. 2012b. *United Nations Register of Conventional Arms: Report of the Secretary-General.* A/67/212 of 30 July. <http://undocs.org/A/67/212>

—. 2012c. *United Nations Register of Conventional Arms: Report of the Secretary-General—Addendum.* A/67/212/Add.1 of 21 September.
<http://www.un.org/ga/search/view_doc.asp?symbol=A/67/212/Add.1>

—. 2013a. *United Nations Register of Conventional Arms: Report of the Secretary-General—Addendum.* A /67/212/Add.2 of 30 January.
<http://www.un.org/ga/search/view_doc.asp?symbol=A/67/212/Add.2>

—. 2013b. Arms Trade Treaty. Adopted 2 April 2013. 'Certified true copy (XXVI-8).' May.
<https://treaties.un.org/Pages/ViewDetails.aspx?src=TREATY&mtdsg_no=XXVI-8&chapter=26&lang=en>

—. 2013c. *Continuing Operation of the United Nations Register on Conventional Arms and Its Further Development.* A/68/140 of 15 July.
<http://www.un.org/en/ga/search/view_doc.asp?symbol=A/68/140>

—. 2013d. *United Nations Register on Conventional Arms: Report of the Secretary-General.* A/68/138 of 15 July.
<http://www.un.org/ga/search/view_doc.asp?symbol=A/68/138>

—. 2013e. *United Nations Register on Conventional Arms: Report of the Secretary-General.* A/68/138.Add.1 of 17 September. Unpublished report.

UNODA (United Nations Office for Disarmament Affairs). 2013. 'United Nations Register on Conventional Arms: Reporting by Member States in 2013.'
Accessed 11 December. <http://www.un.org/disarmament/convarms/Register/>

UNSC (United Nations Security Council). 2001. Resolution 1343 adopted 7 March. S/RES/1343 of 7 March.
<http://www.un.org/en/ga/search/view_doc.asp?symbol=S/RES/1343%282001%29>

—. 2008. *Report of the Panel of Experts Established Pursuant to Resolution 1591 (2005) Concerning the Sudan.* S/2008/647 of 11 November.
<http://www.un.org/ga/search/view_doc.asp?symbol=S/2008/647>

—. 2009. Resolution 1907 adopted 23 December. S/RES/1907 of 23 December.
<http://www.un.org/ga/search/view_doc.asp?symbol=S/RES/1907%282009%29>

—. 2012. *Final Report of the Panel of Experts Established Pursuant to Resolution 1973 (2011) Concerning Libya.* S/2012/163 of 20 March.
<http://www.un.org/ga/search/view_doc.asp?symbol=S/2012/163>

—. 2013. *Final Report of the Panel of Experts Established Pursuant to Resolution 1973 (2011) Concerning Libya.* S/2013/99 of 9 March.
<http://www.un.org/ga/search/view_doc.asp?symbol=S/2013/99>

USEU (United States Embassy in Ukraine). 2002. *Kolchuga Report: Report of the Experts Team Visit to Ukraine.* Kiev: United States and United Kingdom.
20 October. <nuclearno.ru/text.asp?4499>

Vranckx, An. 2005. *European Arms Exports to Latin America: An Inventory.* Background report. Antwerp: International Peace Information Service. March.

WA (Wassenaar Arrangement on Export Controls for Conventional Arms and Dual-Use Goods and Technologies). 2003. Elements for Export Controls of
Man-Portable Air Defence Systems (MANPADS). <http://www.wassenaar.org/2003Plenary/MANPADS_2003.htm>

—. 2005. 'End-User Assurances Commonly Used: Consolidated List.'
<http://www.wassenaar.org/publicdocuments/docs/End-user_assurances_as_updated_at_the_December_2005_PLM.pdf>

—. 2011. 'Best Practice Guidelines on Subsequent Transfer (Re-export) Controls for Conventional Weapons Systems Contained in Appendix 3 to the
WA Initial Elements.' 14 December. <http://www.wassenaar.org/guidelines/docs/3%20-%20Re-export.pdf>

Wood, Brian and Peter Danssaert. 2011. *Study on the Development of a Framework for Improving End-use and End-user Control Systems.* UNODA
Occasional Paper No. 21. New York: United Nations.
<http://www.un.org/disarmament/HomePage/ODAPublications/OccasionalPapers/PDF/OP21.pdf>

Žabec, Krešimir. 2013. 'Jutarnji Reveals that in 4 Months 75 Aircraft Carried 3000 Tonnes of Weapons from Pleso Airport in Zagreb to Syria [translated from
the Croatian].' *Jutarnji List* (Zagreb). 7 March. <http://www.jutarnji.hr/u-4-mjeseca-za-siriju-s--plesa--otislo-75-aviona-sa-3000-t-oruzja/1089573/>

ACKNOWLEDGEMENTS

Principal authors

Paul Holtom, Irene Pavesi, and Christelle Rigual

The epicentre of the blasts at the Mpila munitions depot, in which military barracks and surrounding civilian buildings were destroyed or damaged and at least 300 people killed, 9 March 2012, Brazzaville, Republic of the Congo.
© United Nations Mine Action Team (UNMAT)

Countdown to Catastrophe

THE MPILA AMMUNITION DEPOT EXPLOSIONS

5

INTRODUCTION

On 4 March 2012, a series of explosions destroyed several military barracks in the Mpila area of Brazzaville, Republic of the Congo (RoC). The blasts devastated two surrounding, densely populated districts of the capital, claiming hundreds of lives, injuring thousands, and displacing well over 100,000 people.

The international community swiftly contributed significant emergency funding and coordinated explosive ordnance disposal (EOD) and humanitarian relief activities with non-governmental organizations (NGOs). The magnitude of the event—particularly its immediate consequences—drew considerable media coverage as well as efforts to tackle the underlying problem of poor stockpile management. Since then, however, national priorities and international donor funding have moved on. The root causes of the explosions have still not been properly addressed, nor have their broad socio-economic consequences been fully remedied.

In January 2013 the Small Arms Survey participated in an evaluation funded by the European Union (EU) and led by the Geneva International Centre for Humanitarian Demining (GICHD). The assessment focused on (i) the effectiveness of the clearance activities, (ii) the coordination between the national authorities and the implementation partners, and (iii) the risk education provided to communities around Mpila concerning the potential danger of unexploded ordnance (UXO). The evaluation team travelled to Brazzaville from 14 to 23 January 2013 and published its report in March 2013 (EU, 2013).

The Survey subsequently sought to complement the findings of the evaluation report, which only addresses UXO clearance and risk education efforts, by focusing on other cross-cutting issues, namely: (i) the long-term ammunition procurement and stockpiling practices that led to the explosions, and (ii) the direct and indirect consequences of the blasts on the city's population, the country's finances, and government policy.

The research used a wide range of mostly internal documents obtained during the initial EU-funded evaluation, including reports from the Forces Armées Congolaises (Congolese Armed Forces, FAC), international organizations, NGOs, and the EOD coordination centre. The Survey complemented these sources with (i) follow-up interviews with a broad range of field actors, (ii) expert background papers, (iii) the United Nations Commodity Trade Statistics Database (UN Comtrade),[1] (iv) Survey research, including the Unplanned Explosions at Munitions Sites (UEMS) project, and (v) other open source and media reports. The Survey also submitted more than 1,700 ammunition photos[2] to EOD specialist Alex Diehl for identification of ammunition types.

The chapter's main findings are:

- In a matter of minutes, the explosions killed at least 300 people, injured more than 2,500, and left more than 121,000 homeless. The number of dead probably far exceeds 300 since the Ministry of Defence (MoD) did not officially report military fatalities.

- According to ammunition technicians and EOD specialists familiar with the event, inadequate ammunition stockpile management is the root cause of the Mpila ammunition depot explosions.

- The quantity of ammunition originally contained in the depots before the blasts is unknown, yet EOD teams destroyed more than 200 tonnes of UXO—representing more than 39 tonnes in net explosive content—during the subsequent clearance efforts between March 2012 and April 2013.

- The ammunition types destroyed, which were not recent, included a mix of pyrotechnics, small arms ammunition, grenades, mines, large-calibre projectiles, rockets, missiles, and aircraft bombs amassed haphazardly in the Mpila depot's explosive storehouses in the late 1970s and 1980s, during the RoC's internal conflicts in the 1990s, and during subsequent disarmament, demobilization, and reintegration (DDR) programmes.

- The unchecked expansion of the civilian population around an explosive storage area containing such types and quantities of ammunition places more people at higher risk in the case of an explosion.

- The total impact of the explosions was partially estimated—mostly in terms of direct physical damage to the private sector—at more than XAF 336 billion (USD 672 million). Broader economic impacts were significant and long-lasting, with macroeconomic repercussions felt throughout the country.

- The tragedy was preventable. Prior to the explosion, a number of warning signs were ignored by the international donor community or, in the case of the FAC, simply not recognized due to its lack of stockpile management expertise.

- At the time of writing, post-explosion progress in stockpile management practices was slow, indicating a lack of buy-in from RoC authorities, as well as donor fatigue and wariness from potential sponsors.

This chapter begins by looking back. A chronological description of the Mpila ammunition depot explosions—and their root causes—leads to a discussion on the types and quantities of ammunition that were in the depot prior to the explosion, as well as the probable origins of this ordnance. The second section details the impact of the explosions on the local population and infrastructure, government finances, and the country's socio-economic development. The third and final section highlights the opportunities the RoC had to avoid the explosion, the country's multilateral commitments for stockpile management, and future perspectives.

ANATOMY OF AN EXPLOSION

This section provides a chronological description of the Mpila ammunition depot explosions. It discusses the root causes of the explosions, the types and quantities of ammunition that were in the depot before the explosions, and the probable origins of this ordnance.

Chronology of the blasts

The EU-funded evaluation report details the chronology of the emergency efforts, rubble excavation, and clearance operations that followed the Mpila explosions (EU, 2013, annexe 5). This section of the chapter discusses the sequence of the explosions themselves. It draws on interview notes gathered during the assessment team's visit to Brazzaville in January 2013, as well as on an unpublished background paper authored by technical team member John Rawson of the GICHD (Rawson, 2013a–d).

The first explosion occurred between 7:30 a.m. and 8:10 a.m. on Sunday, 4 March 2012. Photographic evidence and witness accounts indicate that this first explosion was not a detonation but a deflagration.[3] Since this first explosion was

A plume of smoke billowing over the site of the explosions at the munitions depot in Mpila, Brazzaville, is visible from across the river, 4 March 2012, Kinshasa, Democratic Republic of the Congo. © Marc Hofer/AFP Photo

not accompanied by a blast wave, it drew the local population, which gathered at the scene as though to see a spectacle. Casualties were limited. Around 120 soldiers from the FAC barracks located next to the depot, eventually accompanied by the fire brigade and police, tried to fight the fire and organize evacuation. As the fire persisted, many small items of burning ammunition were probably kicked out, causing smaller fires to burn around them.

Some of the kick-outs from the deflagrating store landed in one or several trailers of ammonium nitrate/fuel oil (ANFO)[4] that were reportedly parked inside the barracks, as discussed below. Unpublished amateur videos showing people fleeing just before the large blast suggest that it may have been at this point that some began to appreciate the danger and started to move away from the area.

By 8:40 a.m. the fire had transferred enough heat energy to detonate the ANFO, resulting in a high-order explosion. In turn, the latter caused a sympathetic detonation among other stocks of larger high-explosive items located nearby. These included high-explosive fragmentation aircraft bombs, 120 mm mortar rounds, 122 mm (Grad) rockets, and other large-calibre ammunition (see Annexe 5.1). This resulted in a huge explosion with an accompanying blast wave that flattened buildings up to 1 km around the site, causing the majority of the casualties. While the exact figure is unknown, a large percentage of the military personnel assisting the officer from the Direction générale de l'équipement (General Directorate of Logistics and Equipment, DGE) or fighting the fires were killed or injured in this explosion, along with many civilian bystanders. Some who survived then began to rescue the injured who lay among the rubble, recovering bodies. Once the FAC regained a semblance of control after this explosion, they started to move people outwards, away from the immediate area of the blast, and set up a 1-km safety cordon around the site (see Map 5.2).

A third large explosion occurred at approximately 9:40 a.m. (Rawson, 2013b). By this stage, most of the bystanders had fled the area, leaving behind those who were rescuing victims at the scene. Local press reported irregular secondary explosions until midday on 6 March (N'Zobo and Mavanga Balaka, 2012).

Causes

The primary cause that triggered the first explosion is a sensitive issue.

Ammunition depot explosions can be triggered by a variety of factors, including lightning, rough handling, electrical faults, and the auto-ignition of propellant (spontaneous combustion). Within the framework of the UEMS project, the Small Arms Survey refers to these triggers as 'primary causes', meaning the specific event or condition that caused the ammunition to ignite (Berman and Reina, 2014, p. 26).

In the case of Mpila, the primary cause that triggered the first explosion is a sensitive issue. The authorities sent mixed messages. A few hours after the blasts, RoC authorities officially reported that the initial blast had been caused by a fire stemming from an electrical fault (MAG, 2012b, p. 2; Nsoni and Yabbat-Ngo, 2012). For months, a government-appointed commission of inquiry worked under the assumption that the fire was set intentionally (Nsoni, 2012a; 2012b). As discussed below, on 9 September 2013 the national criminal court convicted a FAC non-commissioned officer of the crime of having deliberately set fire to the Mpila depot (*Jeune Afrique*, 2013a). No independent, technical assessment has yet been commissioned to identify the primary causes of the explosions.

Beyond the immediate, primary cause of the Mpila depot explosions, there were underlying structural conditions that facilitated the explosion. This chapter, in line with the UEMS project, uses the term 'root causes' to refer to the broader, structural conditions that, in combination with the primary cause, led to the explosion (Berman and Reina, 2014, p. 24). Understanding how root causes relate to the Mpila context is fundamental to identifying corrective actions.

According to ammunition stockpile management specialists, the most common root causes of UEMS can be grouped into five main categories (Berman and Reina, 2014, table 8):

- lack of surveillance leading to ammunition deterioration;
- inappropriate storage systems and infrastructure;
- handling errors and inappropriate work practices;
- failure to take into account external, environmental influences and events; and
- poor security.

In the case of Mpila, field reports, research notes, and interviews with ammunition and EOD specialists familiar with the explosions indicate that ammunition stockpile management deficiencies falling under many of these categories paved the way to the disaster. Ammunition was reportedly stacked to the ceilings; there was no effort to separate ammunition by type, compatability grouping, or hazard classification; many of the armoured vehicles on the site were fully loaded with fuzed ammunition, ready to be fired (MAG, 2012a, p. 4); and there was no fence around the site, nor had any effective safety distances been imposed (AOAV, 2012, p. 2).

Alone the scale of damage to military infrastructure suggests exceptionally poor risk management of the ammunition stockpile. The explosions resulted in the destruction of the barracks of six FAC units based in Mpila:

- the 1er Régiment du Génie (1st Engineer Regiment);
- the Bataillon de réparation automobiles et engins blindés (Automobile and Armoured Vehicle Maintenance Batallion);
- the Direction centrale du matériel et du commissariat (Central Directorate of Logistics and Maintenance);
- the 1er Régiment blindé (1st Armoured Regiment);
- the 4ème Bataillon de chars légers (4th Light Armoured Regiment); and
- the Etablissement central de réparation, de rechange et de réserve en armement et munitions (Central Office for Weapons and Ammunition Repair, Replacement, and Reserves, ECRRRAMU), which served as the main barracks and storage area, and was the site of the first explosions.

Each of these units contained several explosive storehouses. For instance, the Groupement du Régiment Blindé de Mpila (Mpila Armoured Group), composed of the 1er Régiment blindé and 4ème Bataillon de chars légers, used four explosive storehouses. One of the four collapsed entirely, burying a large quantity of ammunition underneath the rubble. The three other ones were seriously damaged, with unexploded ammunition still inside (MAG, 2012a, p. 3). The scale of destruction suggests that the depot's explosive storehouses were either not segregated or protected by blast walls or earthworks, or that the stockpiles that were being stored exceeded the capacity of the infrastructure.

Yet an additional factor amplified the explosions. Observers reported during field interviews that, prior to the blast, several[5] containers filled with ANFO had been parked temporarily by an unidentified foreign road building firm on the premises of the ECRRRAMU barracks. It is unclear how and why the FAC allowed this ANFO to be stored temporarily within the perimeter of the barracks (Rawson, 2013b). The ANFO did not cause the initial blast, but it was probably responsible for the second (main) explosion. It is unclear how many tonnes of ANFO had been stored on site, and

Bags of ammonium nitrate, a fertilizer often used in the manufacture of explosives, contributed significantly to the force of the second blast at the Mpila munitions site, March 2012, Brazzaville. © UNMAT

whether part of this ANFO was already mixed. After the explosion, sacks of Orange Label ammonium nitrate were found scattered around one of the craters (AOAV, 2012, p. 4), and the US EOD team from the Office of Weapons Removal and Abatement subsequently destroyed 20 tonnes of ANFO left over from the ECRRRAMU site (RoC MoD, 2012b; 2012c).

Depot contents

While numerous unknown variables preclude an accurate extrapolation of the quantity of ammunition that was in the Mpila depot prior to the blasts, the FAC reportedly suggested that more than seven million items of munitions were stored in the ECRRRAMU's explosive storehouse *alone* (MAG, 2012a, p. 3; Skilling, 2013). Yet there was apparently no previous accounting of the tonnage of ammunition originally stored in the depot, nor was there any technical assessment of how much ammunition exploded during or burned after the blasts. Consequently, this section is limited to identifying the types and quantities of ammunition that were recovered during clearance operations and subsequently destroyed.

It is difficult to determine what types of ammunition and pyrotechnics were in the depot prior to the blasts. It is unclear whether the FAC ever provided an official list of the types of munitions stored in the depot to assist EOD operators in gauging the level of risk posed to neighbouring communities, or of the types of objects that were likely to be present in contaminated zones. A Survey researcher's field interview notes suggest that, as of April or early May 2012, FAC had not yet provided accurate descriptions or figures to the clearance teams (Lazarevic, 2012). According to the French NGO Demeter, the FAC provided a basic list of ammunition types (not quantities) to the joint EOD coordination centre to standardize the clearance procedures among the various EOD teams of disparate training (Demeter, 2012). The list was reportedly used to determine which items should be moved to the temporary storage location, and which had to be destroyed on site.

To obtain a clearer picture of what types of ammunition and pyrotechnics were in the depot, the Survey compiled the monthly reports of the Mines Advisory Group (MAG)[6] from the joint ammunition destruction site in Bambou.[7]

A fragmentation aircraft bomb, flung out during the explosions, is incorrectly identified as a rocket with a handwritten sign warning local civilians of danger: 'Unexploded rocket; Beware; Danger', March 2012, Brazzaville. © UNMAT

Table 1 of Annexe 5.1 presents the results, listing the categories, types, descriptions, and cumulative quantities of ammunition recovered and destroyed during the clearance activities undertaken from March 2012 to April 2013. To confirm and complement the contents of this list, the author submitted more than 1,700 field photos and videos[8] to EOD specialist Alex Diehl for further identification. Further analysis of the field photos taken during clearance operations revealed additional ammunition types that were destroyed by the EOD teams but not inventoried in the monthly destruction reports, probably as a result of incomplete or inadequate reporting. These items are listed in Table 2 of Annexe 5.1.

As indicated in Tables 1 and 2 of Annexe 5.1:

- The EOD clearance teams destroyed more than 200 tonnes of ammunition from March 2012 to April 2013, representing a total weight of more than 39 tonnes in net explosive content.
- The depot stored a mixed selection of ammunition and pyrotechnics that was not necessarily relevant to the FAC units' functions, such as aircraft bombs and submunitions stored in light armoured cavalry and engineer regiments.
- It is unclear whether the depot contained surplus or operational ammunition stockpiles. As discussed below, the ammunition types listed in Tables 1 and 2 are not recent. The few items for which markings were visible and legible on field photographs were not of recent manufacture.
- According to Table 1, small arms ammunition represented almost 21 per cent (almost 42 tonnes) of the total weight destroyed. However, it must be stressed that in general small arms cartridges (Hazard Division 1.4S) do not contribute to the effects of an explosion and can, on the contrary, be used as emergency traverses or barricades in ammunition storage areas (UNODA, 2011a; 2011d, s. 9.2.1.).
- More importantly, medium- and large-calibre projectiles represented just under 42 per cent (almost 84 tonnes) of the total weight destroyed; free flight rockets almost 26 per cent; and missiles nearly 10 per cent. Table 1 of Annexe 5.1 shows a large number of high-explosive projectiles with a calibre exceeding 100 mm, some of which were found with sensitive fuzing systems. This had important consequences for the speed and efficiency of clearance operations because International Mine Action Standards require specific EOD levels for all operators handling UXO with these calibres (UNMAS, 2013, s. 4.2.).

> The Mpila depot stored a mixed selection of ammunition and pyrotechnics.

Provenance of the ammunition

It is difficult to ascertain the origin and provenance of this large, centralized stockpile of ammunition. Research suggests three non-exclusive possibilities; specifically, the Mpila depot may have contained ammunition that was:

- collected during previous DDR programmes;
- transferred by and inherited from neighbouring countries and their troops during the conflicts of the 1990s; but mainly
- procured externally before and—to a lesser extent—during and after the conflicts.

The legacy of militias

During the conflicts of the 1990s, most fighting took place among three militias (the Cobra, Cocoye, and Ninja) that enjoyed political and military primacy—and that effectively replaced the official armed forces. Total militia force levels were low—not exceeding 2,000—during the conflict of 1993–94 but increased with the mass militia recruitments during the conflicts of 1997 and 1998–99. For 2002, Survey researchers estimate lower and upper thresholds of total militia force levels at 26,000–36,400 combatants, with an average total militia force level of 31,200 (Demetriou, Muggah, and Biddle, 2002, p. 14.; Biddle et al., 2003, p. 264).

The militias acquired most of their weapons and ammunition by looting government arsenals, including police and military weapons depots as well as military academies (Demetriou, Muggah, and Biddle, 2002, annexe 4; Biddle et al., 2003, p. 258; Muggah and Nichols, 2007, p. 39).

After the conflicts, a significant number of these weapons and munitions were unsecured. The government undertook several DDR programmes, often in collaboration with international partners, to disarm and reintegrate militia members. According to data provided by the DDR Commission, the RoC led five DDR programmes between 1999 and 2011, all of which were largely concentrated in the Pool region. During this period, 366,500 items labelled 'ammunition and explosives' (unspecified) were reportedly collected during voluntary surrender operations (Small Arms Survey

Box 5.1   Timeline of key events in the RoC: 1970–2012

1970

Marien Ngouabi proclaims the RoC a Marxist People's Republic with the Parti Congolais du Travail (Congolese Labour Party, PCT) as its sole legitimate party.

1977

March: Ngouabi is assassinated. Joachim Yhombi-Opango becomes president.

1979

The PCT forces Yhombi-Opango to resign and elects Denis Sassou Nguesso as his successor.

1981

The RoC signs a treaty of friendship and cooperation with the Soviet Union.

1990

The PCT abandons Marxism.

1992

Establishment of a multi-party system. Pascal Lissouba, former prime minister and head of the Union panafricaine pour la démocratie sociale (Pan-African Union for Social Democracy), becomes president in the RoC's first democratic election. A power struggle ensues with Sassou Nguesso, head of the PCT, and Bernard Kolélas, head of a coalition known as the Union pour le renouveau démocratique (Union for Democratic Renewal).

1993

November: Disputed parliamentary elections deteriorate into violent conflict between rival militias. The crisis militarizes the RoC's political culture. Brazzaville and environs experience numerous armed confrontations at the end of the year.

1994

January: The belligerents agree to a ceasefire. Peace gradually returns after a period of insecurity lasting for the whole of 1994 and most of 1995, particularly in Brazzaville.

1997

June: Tensions rise in the run-up to the July presidential elections. On 5 June, government troops raid Sassou Nguesso's home in Mpila to arrest suspects in the murder of four of his opponents. His Cobra militia resists and the fighting spreads. By 9 June the Cobras are in control of some two-thirds of the capital.

October: On 15 October Sassou Nguesso's Cobra rebels, backed by troops sent by Angola, prevail, driving Lissouba into exile.

1998

The Congolese government uses the FAC, the national police, and Cobra forces to pacify the southern regions of the country and disarm the Cocoye and Ninja militias. This sparks rebellions in the Bouenza and Pool regions in late 1998; the unrest culminates in full-scale fighting throughout the south of the country and Brazzaville.

1999

November: Rebels have lost all their key positions to the government forces, who are backed by Angolan troops. On 16 November, the Sassou Nguesso administration announces an amnesty for the three warring militias. A ceasefire accord follows in December 1999.

2000

January: A committee is established to demobilize the ex-combatants—mainly the Cobra, Cocoye, and Ninja militiamen—and to collect weapons in circulation.

2002

January: The Congolese approve a new constitution by referendum.

March: Sassou Nguesso is re-elected while Lissouba and Kolélas are forced into exile. The political situation deteriorates precipitously, following the abrupt termination of negotiations between the DDR commission and the leader of the remaining Ninja militia in the Pool region. The RoC army and air force proceed to increase military pressure on the region. Armed violence quickly spreads to Brazzaville.

2003

17 March: The Congolese government signs a peace agreement with the Ninja rebels of the clergyman known as Pastor Ntumi.

2009

July: Sassou Nguesso is re-elected.

2012

March: Explosions rock the Mpila depot.

Sources: BBC News (n.d.); Demetriou, Muggah, and Biddle (2002); Biddle et al. (2003); Muggah and Nichols (2007)

and GRIP, 2013, p. 27; HC, 2013). This figure certainly includes any large-calibre, high-explosive, and incendiary projectiles used by the warring parties. Among them is the RPO-A 'Shmel', a rocket-propelled incendiary projectile launcher produced in the Russian Federation (since 1988) and China (since 1998). As mentioned in previous Survey research, this launcher was imported en masse and was used extensively during the 1997 conflict (Demetriou, Muggah, and Biddle, 2002, p. 12.; Biddle et al., 2003, p. 262). Table 1 of Annexe 5.1 confirms that at least 15 RPO-A 'Shmel' launchers were stockpiled in the Mpila depot prior to the explosions and subsequently destroyed by the EOD teams.

While a portion of the collected ammunition was neutralized, burned, and destroyed, it is likely that many of the items that were collected by the government and by the DDR implementation committee were reinstated in FAC stockpiles (Biddle et al., 2003, p. 269; Muggah, Maughan, and Bugnion, 2003, p. 15; Small Arms Survey and GRIP, 2013, p. 27).

The role of neighbouring countries and their troops

Since the Portuguese decolonization of Angola in the mid-1970s, Brazzaville has been a major weapons and ammu-nition transit hub. During the Angolan civil war, the Russians opened up a new route for arms deliveries via the RoC, whereby weapons and munitions were either shipped to the Congolese port of Pointe-Noire and then smuggled into the Cabinda enclave by truck, or flown into the Maya Maya air base, in Brazzaville, before being transported into Angola (Moss, 1977; see Map 5.1).

Later, in 1994, following the signing of the Lusaka Protocol, the Angolan rebel movement União Nacional para a Independência Total de Angola (UNITA) of Jonas Savimbi moved weapons and ammunition from Angola into President Pascal Lissouba's Congo in order to avoid UN monitoring of the disarmament and demobilization efforts that were

Map 5.1 Brazzaville, Republic of the Congo

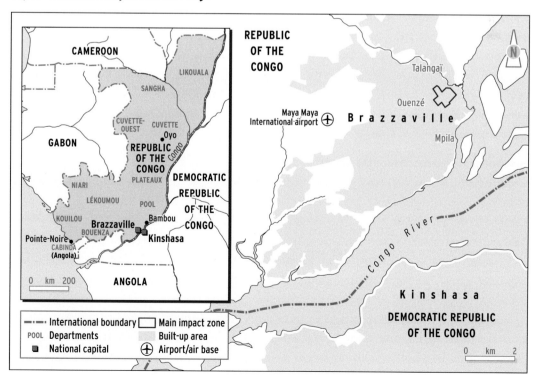

Based on: © OpenStreetMap contributors (open database licence)

to follow the peace agreement. The weapons were then progressively transported back into UNITA territory from Pointe-Noire. Lissouba reportedly retained a portion of these weapons and ammunition as a fee for their storage. During this period, the RoC was a major sanctions-busting hub for hundreds of tonnes of UNITA weaponry, which were transported from Bulgaria to UNITA-held territories via then Zaire and Pointe-Noire in the RoC (Small Arms Survey, 2001, p. 118.; Biddle et al., 2003, ns. 16, 27; UNSC, 2000).

During the conflict years, neighbouring countries, wishing to tip the balance of forces in favour of their preferred side, also transferred weapons and ammunition. In September 1997, for instance, Angola and Gabon facilitated a turn in the tide of conflict by supplying at least two major shipments of conventional weapons, munitions, and armoured vehicles to Cobra forces, which were supporting Denis Sassou Nguesso against Pascal Lissouba. The Angolan shipment was allegedly air-dropped north of Brazzaville. The Gabonese shipment was reportedly flown into the town of Oyo and then transported by road to Brazzaville (Demetriou, Muggah, and Biddle, 2002, p. 13).

It is difficult to ascertain the provenance of this large ammunition stockpile.

Regular and irregular troops from Angola, Burundi, the Democratic Republic of the Congo (DRC), Gabon, and Rwanda participated in the RoC's conflicts and brought their share of large-calibre ammunition. The fighting in Brazzaville in 1997 occurred after the fall of Kinshasa to the forces of Laurent-Désiré Kabila in May. Former members of Mobutu Sese Seko's Forces Armées Zaïroises and the special presidential division as well as other units fled across the Congo river to Brazzaville. Members of Rwanda's armed forces and the Hutu Interahamwé militia were also present. The groups sided with either Lissouba or Sassou Nguesso (IRIN, 1997; Le Pape and Salignon, 2001, p. 70; *Africa Confidential*, 2004).

The major weapons systems that seem to have influenced the conflict belonged not to the FAC but to foreign—in particular Angolan—units supporting the rebels that had ousted the government in 1997 (Wezeman and Wezeman, 1998, p. 15). The Angolan army's intervention reportedly tilted the balance in mid-October 1997. In 2002, Sassou Nguesso's soldiers were again backed by around 1,000 Angolan troops protecting airports and other key points in Brazzaville and the port of Pointe-Noire.[9]

It appears that at least some of the ammunition originally transferred or brought in from neighbouring countries during the conflicts was stored indefinitely in the stocks of the FAC, including in the Mpila depot. During a recent baseline study on the fight against the illicit accumulation and trafficking of firearms in Africa, RoC officials from the Interior and Defence ministries verbally confirmed that weapons and ammunition seized from combatants fleeing the DRC had in fact been stockpiled in Mpila (Small Arms Survey and GRIP, 2013).[10]

External procurement before the blasts

Research suggests that the Mpila depot also contained large-calibre ammunition that was procured abroad prior to the blasts. Some ammunition transfers were officially declared and recorded, either by the RoC as a recipient, or by its suppliers. For this section of the chapter, the Norwegian Initiative on Small Arms Transfers (NISAT) provided the Survey with raw data[11] on recorded weapons and ammunition imports and exports into the RoC during the period 1962 to 2011. Countries reported data via several sources, including UN Comtrade, consolidated EU reports, Eurostat, and national arms export reports. The Survey isolated the reporting categories that encompassed large-calibre ammunition types most pertinent to a depot explosion and similar to the ammunition types found in Tables 1 and 2 of Annexe 5.1.

Analysis focused on large-calibre ammunition, and included various reporting categories.[12] Efforts were made to avoid double counting, which occurs when the same shipment is recorded in two (or more) ways. The following criteria were used to determine if a duplicate entry exists: provenance, currency valuation, timeframe, and export category. For details on the categories and on the methodology used to process the data, see Annexe 5.2.

Figure 5.1 **Declared values of large-calibre ammunition exports to the RoC, 1978-2011**

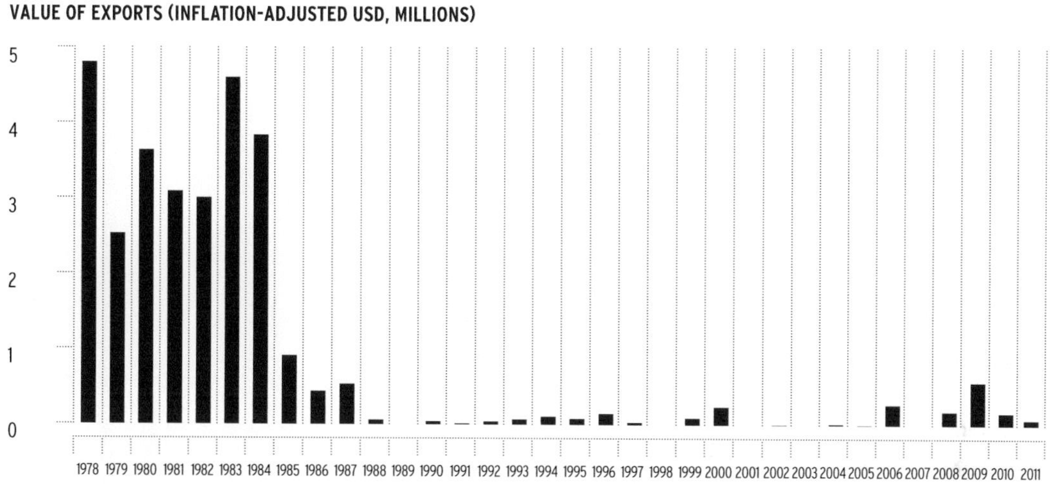

VALUE OF EXPORTS (INFLATION-ADJUSTED USD, MILLIONS)

Note: See endnote 12 and Annexe 5.2 for a detailed listing of reporting categories.

Figure 5.1 provides an overview of the cumulated values of declared large-calibre ammunition exports to the RoC between 1978 and 2011, as reported by category to the various instruments and sources. While data exists from 1962 to 2011, the period between 1962 and 1977 contains very little declared import activity for large-calibre ammunition and is thus omitted.

According to the declared values shown in Figure 5.1, the RoC imported the bulk of its large-calibre, high-explosive ammunition arsenal between the late 1970s and the mid-1980s, more than ten years before the conflicts of the early and late 1990s, during which some of this ammunition was certainly used. The bulk was stored indefinitely by RoC authorities in various FAC units and was probably centralized in and around the seat of government, Brazzaville. As mentioned earlier, the ammunition types sampled in Tables 1 and 2 of Annexe 5.1 are not recent either, suggesting that they were procured more than 30 years before the blasts and, in some cases, subsequently stored in the Mpila explosive storage area.

Figure 5.1 corroborates the claim that inadequate ammunition stockpile management is the root cause of the Mpila depot explosions. Under optimal storage and surveillance conditions, the effective service life of most ammunition is at least 20 years (UNODA, 2011c, p. 6). Yet environmental factors and inadequate storage conditions influence the ageing process. The service life will be significantly reduced if the ammunition is stored in climatic conditions for which it was not designed. In the case of Mpila, high and fluctuating temperatures, direct sun, and high humidity undoubtedly led to a rapid degradation of the performance and safety of inadequately stored explosives.

One impact that such storage conditions may have had on ammunition is the chemical deterioration of propellant. According to the International Ammunition Technical Guidelines (IATG), the rate of chemical deterioration of stored propellant is approximately doubled for every 10°C rise in temperature above 30°C. Most propellants have a shelf life of at least 15 to 40 years when stored at a constant 30°C, and they will last much longer in temperate climates (UNODA, 2011e, p. 5). In high-heat environments such as the RoC, the stabilizer depletes far more rapidly, increasing the chances of spontaneous combustion due to autocatalytic ignition.

Figure 5.1 shows that declared exports to the RoC of categories comprising large-calibre ammunition dropped sharply from the late 1980s onwards. Yet it also reveals that the RoC continued to import certain materiel, particularly (i) during periods preceding tension, (ii) during phases of conflict, and (iii) after the conflicts.

Figure 5.2 **Declared values of large-calibre ammunition exports to the RoC, 1988–2011**

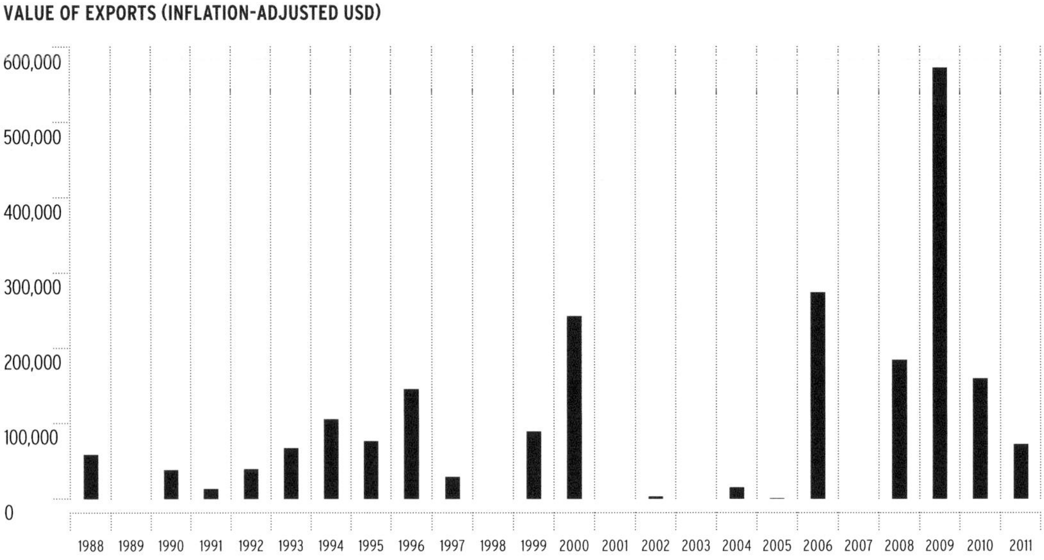

VALUE OF EXPORTS (INFLATION-ADJUSTED USD)

Note: See endnote 12 and Annexe 5.2 for a detailed listing of reporting categories.

Like Figure 5.1, Figure 5.2 shows export values for materiel imported into the RoC, but it focuses on the years 1988–2011. Declared, post-conflict transfers of large-calibre ammunition occurred despite (i) ongoing DDR programmes in the RoC in 1999–2011, (ii) international capacity building efforts in the field of EOD and stockpile management, and (iii) field reports documenting the country's difficulties with ammunition stockpile management, as discussed below.

Figure 5.2 provides but a partial overview of the RoC's external ammunition procurement in the years that preceded the blasts. Most importantly, the data fails to capture munitions transfers that were poorly recorded—or simply not declared—by the RoC or by its suppliers. Previous Survey research indicates, for example, that the 1997 conflict involved significant arms purchases from abroad, in contrast to the conflict of 1993–94, which was fought primarily with weapons pillaged from government depots (Demetriou, Muggah, and Biddle, 2002, p. 11; Biddle et al., 2003, p. 261). Survey research also documents the brokering activities of Belgian national Jacques Monsieur, a former army officer who supplied surplus ammunition and weapons—some of them from Iran[13]—to the RoC in 1997 (Servenay, 2004; Small Arms Survey, 2001, box 3.5). From June to September 1997, Lissouba reportedly ordered from Monsieur 12 consignments of weapons and munitions worth USD 61.4 million, including 'rockets, missiles and bombs' (Lallemand, 2002; Biddle et al., 2003, n. 21).

Similarly, Figure 5.2 fails to highlight the significance of Chinese and South African exports to the RoC during the 1997 conflict (Biddle et al., 2003, ns. 22, 23; Batchelor, 2010, tables 2, 3). Research shows that China was still the number one supplier of conventional arms to the RoC in 2006–2010 (Wezeman, Wezeman, and Béraud-Sudreau, 2011, table 2.4).

THE CONSEQUENCES OF THE BLASTS

This section assesses the impact of the blasts on the population, government, and city infrastructure as well as on the country's socio-economic development. It draws heavily on data provided by Ricardo Zapata-Marti (2013), regional adviser of the Disaster Evaluation Unit at the United Nations Economic Commission for Latin America and the Caribbean

(ECLAC), who participated in a damage and loss assessment (DaLA) workshop sponsored and conducted by the World Bank in Brazzaville from 23 to 31 July 2012.

The goal of the DaLA workshop was to (i) assess the monetary cost and social and environmental implications of the explosion, (ii) enhance national capacities to undertake such an assessment, and (iii) teach and promote the methods and tools to evaluate damage, loss, and reconstruction needs in post-explosion Mpila. The event gathered more than 150 Congolese participants (civil servants and members of the private sector as well as international organizations). Organizers divided participants into 13 working subgroups and tasked them with sector-specific data gathering (World Bank, 2012a; 2012c). They compiled the limited field data into a rough estimate of direct damage and indirect loss[14] incurred in the various sectors.

Table 5.1 summarizes the limited, unofficial assessment made during the training mission, by sector, in terms of direct damage and indirect loss. No data was available for the sectors of commerce, environment, health, industry, public infrastructure, or social affairs. Consequently, Table 5.1 presents only a partial estimate of the total damage and loss—mainly in terms of direct physical impact on the private sector—which nevertheless exceeds XAF 336 billion (USD 672 million).

The major limitation of the DaLA methodology in assessing the impact of the Mpila explosions is linked to a general lack of field data that should have been contributed by the national bodies involved in the evaluation. Some government agencies did not provide data that they deemed sensitive or confidential. The Ministry of Defence, for instance, did not provide the stockpile value of the weapons and ammunition destroyed in the blasts. More generally, the figure reported under 'public sector' includes neither military damage or loss, nor government compensation to the affected population, which was budgeted at XAF 3 million (USD 6,000) per beneficiary, as discussed below. Important contributors, such as the Ministry of Finance, did not participate in the workshop.

The workshop did not produce a definitive evaluation document. The RoC government committed to (i) collecting the missing field data from the various government stakeholders and (ii) acquiring the required resources and personnel to finalize the report (World Bank, 2012c, p. 8). At the time of writing, RoC authorities had not yet finalized a full assessment report. The following sections thus attempt to break down, and, whenever possible, supplement, this rough assessment of impacts by focusing on specific sectors.

Table 5.1 **Impact summary: partial estimate as of 27 July 2012, in XAF (millions) and USD (millions)**			
Sector	**Damage**	**Loss**	**Total**
Agriculture	XAF 2,200 (USD 4.4)	n/a	XAF 2,200 (USD 4.4)
Education	XAF 2,034 (USD 4.1)	n/a	XAF 2,034 (USD 4.1)
Energy	XAF 339 (USD 0.7)	XAF 182 (USD 0.4)	XAF 521 (USD 1.0)
Fishing	XAF 250 (USD 0.5)	XAF 422 (USD 0.8)	XAF 672 (USD 1.3)
Housing	XAF 315,220 (USD 630.4)	n/a	XAF 315,220 (USD 630.4)
Transport	XAF 10,911 (USD 21.8)	XAF 473 (USD 1.0)	XAF 11,384 (USD 22.8)
Water and sanitation	XAF 4,000 (USD 8.0)	n/a	XAF 4,000 (USD 8.0)
TOTAL	**XAF 334,954 (USD 669.9)**	**XAF 1,077 (USD 2.2)**	**XAF 336,031 (USD 672.1)**

Note: n/a = not available.

Source: Zapata-Marti (2013, table 3)

Damage radius of the blasts

Protecting the public from the effects of an explosive event involves the use of separation distances, which ensure that the population is always at a reasonably safe distance from explosives during storage and handling. The greater the separation distance, the greater the protection (UNODA, 2011b, p. v). Given the abovementioned contents of the depot, the gradual expansion of Brazzaville's civilian population towards the explosive storage area of Mpila was extremely dangerous.

The blast radius of the Mpila explosions is indicative of the damage caused in the context of urban sprawl. Despite a formal government ban on housing in the immediate surroudings of the depot, the area had been steadily urbanized into a dense grid of houses and small trading entities, built erratically without prior planning, safety restrictions, or government approval. There was no buffer zone to protect the population from the blasts.

Figure 5.3 **Distribution and concentration of ordnance scattered during the Mpila explosions, 22 March 2012**

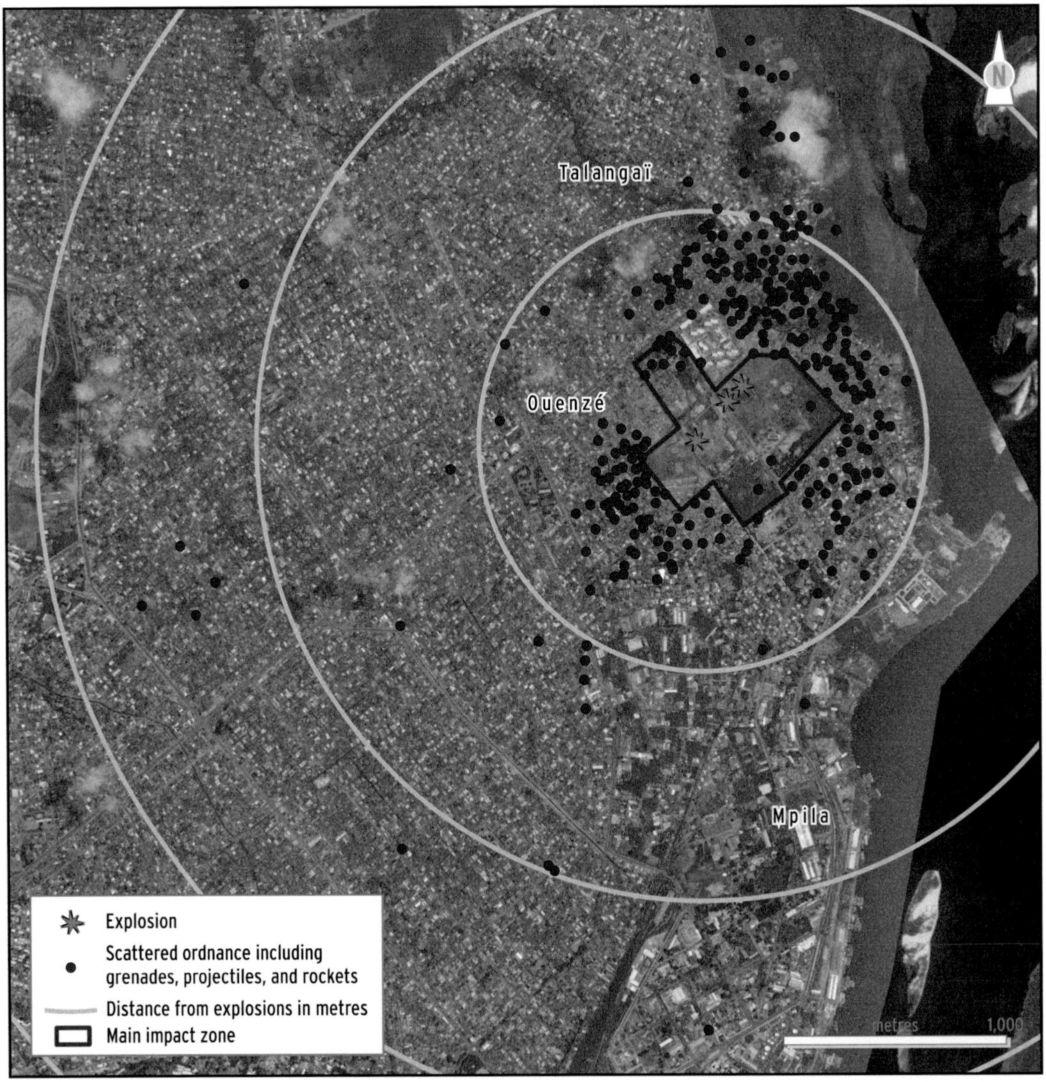

Source: © MapAction, 2012

Contamination by UXO was extremely high within a 1-km radius of the affected area (UNMAS, 2012b). The impact zone, the most highly contaminated area, had a surface area of 50–60 hectares and extended to a radius of 500 m. This area was predominantly dedicated to homes and offices of military personnel. Within this zone, clearance teams delineated Sector 4—nicknamed 'ground zero'—which covered a surface area of 40.8 hectares. It comprised four high-impact locations: the ECRRRAMU site (the epicentre of the blasts), the schools complex (high school, primary school, and kindergarten), two armoured battalion compounds, and two craters formed by the explosions (MAG, 2012c) (see Map 5.2).

The blasts projected rockets complete with warhead and fuze out to a 1-km radius, with the fuzes armed by the propulsive effects of the blast causing the warheads to detonate on impact, resulting in further casualties. Expended rocket motors with no warhead

Map 5.2 Mpila munitions depot explosions

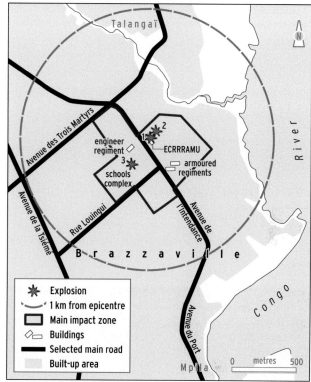

Based on: © OpenStreetMap contributors (open database licence)

attached were found up to 3 km from the epicentre, while larger expended 122 mm rocket (Grad) motors landed up to 5 km away (see Figure 5.3; Rawson, 2013b–d).

The human toll

Based on information provided by the UN Office for the Coordination of Humanitarian Affairs (OCHA) and the Ministère des affaires sociales, de l'action humanitaire et de la solidarité (Ministry of Social Affairs, Humanitarian Action, and Solidarity, MASAHS), the DaLA workshop presented an initial estimate of the human toll of the explosions (see Tables 5.2 and 5.3).

The districts of Talangaï and Ouenzé, which cover a surface area of about 26.5 km² and were home to more than 520,000 people before the blasts, suffered the most damage (World Bank, 2012b, p. 2; see Table 5.3). Subdistricts 54, 59, 61, 63, and 64, where more than 93,000 inhabitants resided, were entirely destroyed. Of nearly 62,000 people who lived in Subdistricts 56 and 62, 50 per cent and 45 per cent, respectively, were directly affected. This population includes mostly small merchants, independent workers, day labourers, and artisans with a relatively significant, although unknown, percentage of immigrants from neighbouring countries.

Following the workshop, these figures were often increased on revision. For instance, the total affected population was later estimated at 121,841 (Zapata-Marti, 2013). Estimates of the number of injured came in at 1,500, 3,000, and 3,277 (UNMAT, 2012b; Skilling, 2013; IFRC, 2012, p. 2). The number of reported deaths first increased to 286 and then to 292 (IFRC, 2012, p. 2; AOAV, 2012, p. 4); yet even the latter estimate remains an underestimate since the MoD

Table 5.2 Estimated human toll of the explosions, as recorded by OCHA on 16 March 2012

Category	Total/%
Deceased	232
Injured	2,500
Displaced population (including in public and private shelters, and staying with family and friends)	121,654
Total population in the affected communities (estimated in 2010)	520,043
% affected over total affected communities	23.39%
Brazzaville total population	1,373,382
% affected over total urban area (Brazzaville)	8.86%
Total population of RoC	3,697,490
% affected in country	3.29%

Source: Zapata-Marti (2013)

Table 5.3 Estimated human toll of the explosions in the districts of Ouenzé and Talangaï, as recorded by OCHA on 16 March 2012

Category	Total	Ouenzé district			Talangaï district			
		S54 and S59*	S56	Subtotal**	S61 and S64	S62	S63	Subtotal**
Affected population	121,654	25,343	7,311	32,654	53,187	21,239	14,574	89,000
Total population in the affected communities (2010 estimate)	520,043	25,343	14,622	182,057	53,187	47,197	14,574	337,986
% affected over total affected communities	23%	100%	50%	18%	100%	45%	100%	26%

Notes: * S = subdistrict; ** Including other subdistricts.

Source: Zapata-Marti (2013)

did not report military casualties. Local press mentioned the (unconfirmed) figure of 200–300 dead among the military, indicating that most of these fatalities occurred during the second explosion, while military personnel were assisting the DGE officer after the initial deflagration (*La Semaine Africaine*, 2012a; Rawson, 2013b).

In March 2012, between 13,000 and 17,000 people found shelter in at least 11 public and private camps[15] (Zapata-Marti, 2013, table 1; EU, 2013, p. 14). The number decreased over time,[16] but managing the camps remained a significant sanitation and security challenge. The camps were overcrowded as they attracted numerous refugees, including from the DRC (Lazarevic, 2012). Sanitary conditions quickly deteriorated, with reported cases of cholera, malaria, and infectious respiratory diseases (Yabbat-Ngo, 2012b; Zapata-Marti, 2013, p. 5).

Civilian unrest grew. The blasts caused long-lasting psychological trauma among the population (Lazarevic, 2012). The people blamed the government and were angered at Charles Zacharie Bowao, the minister of defence, for initially

Workers construct graves for people killed in the Mpila blasts, in preparation for a mass burial service, to be held a week after the explosions, 9 March 2012, Brazzaville. © Guy-Gervais Kitina/AFP Photo

trying to understate the extent of the damage (Bowao, 2012; Nsoni and Yabbat-Ngo, 2012, p. 3). At the national burial ceremony, on Sunday, 11 March 2012, Congolese police and gendarmerie units were reinforced to anticipate demonstrations and prevent public order disturbance (Yabbat-Ngo, 2012a). Later, EOD operations were suspended several times because of riots or demonstrations (AOAV, 2012, p. 11; Lazarevic, 2012). Ultimately, the lingering presence of large quantities of UXO prevented thousands of people from returning to their homes and schools for more than one year.

Government spending

On 17 April 2012, the government and parliament voted for a supplemental budget to fund the post-blast emergency response and recovery. The minister of economy indicated that the funds were specifically earmarked to address the consequences of the explosions; that is, to provide cash to affected families, to pay for camps for people displaced from their homes, and to deliver education services to ensure children did not lose the entire school year. Figures provided in a press declaration indicate that just over XAF 400 billion (USD 800 million) were earmarked for this purpose (Yabbat-Ngo, 2012c; 2012d).

The supplemental budget also foresaw the creation of two separate emergency funds, one for victim compensation (XAF 25 billion or about USD 50 million), funded directly by the state, and another for the reconstruction of affected districts (XAF 60 billion or USD 120 million), funded largely by external loans and donations (*La Semaine Africaine*, 2012b; Yabbat-Ngo, 2012c; RoC, 2012, pp. 33, 36).

The government reportedly earmarked more than XAF 90 billion (USD 180 million) for allowances, compensation, and social support (Yabbat-Ngo, 2012c). On 8 March the government decided to allocate XAF 3 million (USD 6,000) to the heads of households affected by the explosion (Doko and N'Kouka-Koudissa, 2012), to help them move out of the camps and settle elsewhere. In total, 20,333 affected households reportedly received about XAF 61 billion (USD 122 million) allocated as 'emergency funds' (Untitled, 2013). The allocation of allowances was not without problems, however. There were a high number of irregularities in the drafting of the lists, as well as discontent with the allocation process (*La Semaine Africaine*, 2012c).

It is difficult to estimate government spending on UXO clearance activities. The EU-funded evaluation explicitly deplores the poor participation of the RoC, now considered a middle-income country, in the direct funding of the rubble excavation, clearance, and risk education operations (EU, 2013, p. 39). The government reportedly earmarked an estimated XAF 2 billion (USD 4 million) for UXO clearance activities (Yabbat-Ngo, 2012c), yet it is unclear how or whether this sum was spent.

As an in-kind contribution, the government seconded between 140 and 180 military personnel to work in collaboration with EOD operators (GICHD, 2012, p. 5; RoC MoD, 2012d, p. 8). The FAC hosted the clearance coordination centre as of 8 March 2012, with

Recoilless rifle rounds (75 mm), collected from the debris of the Mpila explosions, are grouped together by clearance teams prior to safe destruction, March 2012, Brazzaville. © UNMAT

support from the UN Mine Action Service (UNMAS), responsible for coordinating the activities of Demeter, Handicap International, and MAG (EU, 2013, annexe 5). The RoC MoD had reportedly allocated XAF 578 million (USD 1.2 million) for the clearance coordination centre (in addition to international contributions). As of 31 August 2012, they reported having spent XAF 230 million (USD 460,000), or 40 per cent of the funds (RoC MoD, 2012d, p. 10).

Although unconfirmed, additional spending may have included the rental of the Bambou open burning/open detonation site—for XAF 200,000 (USD 400) per trimester, paid to the village leader (RoC MoD, 2012e, p. 3), as well as the rental fees for the Swedish Civil Contingencies Agency's armoured excavator once the international organizations had left in January 2013.

The post-explosion investigation incurred unknown administrative costs, as well as significant legal consequences. Throughout the proceedings, the press reported that a number of officials had been officially questioned by the commission of enquiry, including: the defence minister (Charles Zacharie Bowao), the deputy general secretary of the National Security Council (Col. Marcel Ntsourou), the commanding officer of the 4ème Bataillon de chars légers (Col. André Joseph Sahouss), and the DGE's commanding officer (Col. Germain Ickonga Akindou) as well as two of its officers (Cols. Jean-Claude Mopita and Frédéric-Noël Ingani) (Bowao, 2012; Nsoni, 2012a; 2012b). At the time of the investigation, Col. Ickonga Akindou and Col. Mopita were assigned to the clearance coordination centre as national supervisor and national coordinator, respectively (EU, 2013, p. 25). By early May, a total of 23 individuals (22 military and 1 civilian) had reportedly been arrested and presented to the attorney general's office (Nsoni, 2012c; 2012d).

On 9 September 2013, the court delivered six judgements. The main defendant, Master Corporal Kakom Kouack Blood, was found guilty of having set fire deliberately to the Mpila depots and sentenced to 15 years of forced labour. Col. Marcel Ntsourou, Col. Ikonga Akindou, and three FAC non-commissioned officers were fined and sentenced to various terms of prison and forced labour (*Jeune Afrique*, 2013a; RFI, 2013). The high-profile trial had a dramatic conclusion. On 16 December 2013, after a violent four-hour siege, government forces raided Col. Ntsourou's residence, which resulted in 55 arrests, more than 40 deaths, and Ntsourou's surrender to the security forces (*Jeune Afrique*, 2013c; 2013d).

City infrastructure

Urban lots and parcels affected by the explosions numbered 5,000–6,000.

The DaLA workshop established that between 5,000 and 6,000 urban lots of various sizes were affected by the explosions (Doko, 2012; Loutoumba, 2012). These lots contained private property (with several individual dwellings per lot) and parcels of land or urban areas comprising entities such as homes, shops, businesses, and warehouses. The impact is thus reflected over both the private and public sectors. Damage to transport and energy was estimated at nearly XAF 11 billion (USD 22 million) and XAF 339 million (USD 678,000), respectively (see Table 5.1).

The most affected sector was private housing. The 2012 supplemental budget earmarked XAF 200 billion (USD 400 million) for housing reconstruction projects on first-, second-, and third-perimeter districts in Brazzaville (Yabbat-Ngo, 2012c). Yet more than 17,700 homes were either partially or completely destroyed, with the resulting damage assessment exceeding XAF 315 billion (USD 630 million) (Zapata-Marti, 2013). The DaLA workshop estimated that the combined costs of construction of new housing and rehabilitation of damaged housing amounted to almost XAF 500 billion (USD 1 billion) (Zapata-Marti, 2013). In one example of reconstruction and relocation, the government set out to build 5,000 houses on 350 hectares in Kintélé, about 15 km from Brazzaville. Although the cost of the Kintélé housing project was reportedly estimated at XAF 29 billion (USD 58 million) (Loutoumba, 2012), in November 2013 Congolese authorities contracted a Moroccan company to build 3,250 houses for more than four times that amount (EUR 195 million or USD 267 million) (*Jeune Afrique*, 2013b).

Many school buildings were either partially damaged or totally destroyed. The Lycée de la Révolution, located next to the military barracks, was completely destroyed. Five thousand students normally attend the high school. If the explosion had occurred on a Monday instead of on a Sunday, the school would have been packed with children and the casualty toll would have been far higher. Although the students were transferred to another site, the transport allowance provided by the government was only sufficient to cover fares for ten days (AOAV, 2012, p. 10; Gac, 2012, p. 8). The Pierre Nsiété School, located only 800 m from the main blast, suffered considerable damage, and some UXO was found in the compound (MAG, 2012f). The Ecole du 31 Juillet was 60 per cent destroyed by the blast (Gac, 2012, p. 8). In total, 18,000 to 20,000 students were affected (World Bank, 2012b, p. 2; Lazarevic, 2012).

Defence spending was also earmarked for the reconstruction of military installations outside cities. One feature of urban sprawl has been the expansion of many residential areas towards military installations. Starting in 2010, additional funds were reportedly spent on stepping up the relocation process of hundreds of FAC members stationed at Mpila (IMF, 2012b, p. 11). The government said it was committing XAF 35 billion (USD 70 million) to the contruction of new military barracks, XAF 1.5 billion (USD 3 million) to the rehabilitation of existing barracks, and XAF 50 billion (USD 100 million) to the restoration of the 'operational capacity' of the security forces (Yabbat-Ngo, 2012c). It is unclear what 'operational capacity' encompasses. The MoD did not provide the actual value of the ammunition destroyed in the blasts, but the XAF 50 billion (USD 100 million) could potentially be used to buy new ammunition to replace the destroyed stockpile.

Socio-economic development

The RoC has a population of more than 4.3 million people, 1.5 million of whom live in Brazzaville; it is considered a lower-middle-income country with a gross national income of USD 2,550 per capita in 2012 (World Bank, n.d.). However, it scores very low on the leading measures of socio-economic development. In the UN's 2013 *Report on Human Development*, the RoC occupies the 142nd place out of 187 countries (UNDP, 2013). The country occupies the

A resident of Mpila raises her hands in dismay as she surveys the debris of her former neighbourhood, 5 March 2012, Brazzaville. © Patrick Fort/AFP Photo

154th place out of 177 in Transparency International's Corruption Perceptions Index and holds 185th place out of 189 in the World Bank's Doing Business 2014 ranking (TI, 2013; World Bank, 2014).

The country's economy is very dependent on the oil sector, which represented 68 per cent of the gross domestic product (GDP) in 2010 (*Africa Confidential*, 2012b). Non oil exports are minimal (IMF, 2011, p. 10). In its Article IV report, the International Monetary Fund (IMF) highlights that, while the economy was relatively stable, 'growth had not been inclusive, the private sector was not diversified and public spending was still subject to the vagaries of the oil price' (*Africa Confidential*, 2012b; IMF, 2012b).

The explosions had macroeconomic effects throughout the country. In 2010, the Central African Economic and Monetary Community and the IMF predicted that inflation would stabilize at 3–4 per cent (IMF, 2011, p. 3). In 2012, the RoC's economic activity was dominated by the emergency budgetary measures taken to face the consequences of the depot explosions. Direct cash transfers to the families affected by the explosions and reconstruction plans boosted the demand for domestic goods. However, additional imports quickly overwhelmed the limited transport facilities between the port of Pointe-Noire and Brazzaville roughly 500 km to the east (IMF, 2012b, p. 34). Additional spending spurred growth, yet the low level of economic diversification and limited domestic capacity to increase supply in response to increased demand fuelled inflation. In other words, although the emergency budget voted in April was aimed at reconstruction, it did little more than kindle import-intensive inflation (*Africa Confidential*, 2012b).

The IMF then announced a GDP growth of 3.8 per cent with inflation reaching 7.5 per cent, up from approximately 5 per cent in 2010 and 2011 (IMF, 2013a; 2011, p. 2). Higher inflation affected vulnerable groups through higher prices and scarcity of staple goods (IMF, 2012b, p. 34). Activity in non-oil related sectors, the weakest link of the RoC economy, was artificially supported by the recovery compensation and the increase in public expenditure. In addition to inflation, the rapid increase in expenditures made the primary fiscal deficit climb to 64.3 per cent of GDP excluding oil, in comparison to 46.3 per cent in 2011 (IMF, 2012a, tables 1, 3b; 2013a). Inflation rates decreased only a year later, and the IMF announced a GDP growth of 5.8 per cent in May 2013 (IMF, 2013b).

The explosions had macroeconomic effects throughout the country.

The international response

Initially, some donor countries were reluctant to fund the emergency response efforts. This is partly because donors regard the RoC as a relatively wealthy country that should allocate funding for emergency response efforts from the national budget (EU, 2013, p. 15). Nevertheless, donor countries and international organizations contributed significant funding, technical expertise (such as damage assessment and UXO clearance), and material aid (such as water, food, sanitation, and logistical support).[17]

In fact, the success of the clearance and risk education[18] activities owes much to the rapid funding. On 30 April 2011, the Central Emergency Response Fund provided nearly USD 7 million to seven UN agencies for emergency risk education, UXO clearance, and the provision of various health, hygiene, and sanitation services and equipment (OCHA, 2012). The EU devoted EUR 2.5 million (USD 3.4 million) to rubble excavation, clearance, and risk education efforts, directly funding the three main implementation partners—Demeter, Handicap International, and MAG (EU, 2013, p. 15).

On a bilateral basis, a host of other donor countries also contributed funds and EOD teams, as well as technical and material support. The EU-funded evaluation report describes the mobilization and the key role of embassies and national representatives, noting the flexibility of the implementation partners, which frequently provided their own funding in order to start field work while awaiting external financing (EU, 2013, p. 15).

STOCKPILE MANAGEMENT: LESSONS LEARNED?

The Mpila depot explosions reflect the global, persistent, and growing threat of UEMS. The Survey has recorded 508 unplanned explosions that took place worldwide between 1980 and 2013. Not one year has passed without a UEMS (Berman and Reina, 2014, p. 10); in more than half of the past 35 years, at least ten UEMS incidents have taken place per year. The greatest number of incidents—37 events—were registered in 2011. Almost 60 per cent of the events recorded in the Survey's UEMS database for the period under review occurred in the years 2003–13.

This section highlights the RoC's history of UEMS, as well as its efforts to improve ammunition stockpile management before and after the Mpila explosions. In addition, it reviews the RoC's multilateral commitments in relation to ammunition management.

Early warning

The Survey's UEMS database contains records of four unplanned explosions at various munitions sites in Pointe-Noire and Brazzaville before the Mpila explosions in March 2012 (Small Arms Survey, n.d.).

> Before the Mpila explosions, RoC had a history of UEMS.

In 1997 an ammunition depot exploded in the district of La Poudrière, contaminating 26 hectares of land adjacent to Brazzaville's Maya Maya International Airport. The explosion was probably initiated by a targeted attack, such as shelling, bombardment, or sabotage during fighting, which also caused underground structures to collapse. MAG was still clearing the area with EU funding when the Mpila depot exploded in March 2012 (EC–ECHO, 2012; MAG, 2012g; EU, 2013, p. 16). Three other explosions occurred: in 2008 (details unknown); in April 2009 in Mpila's Camp de l'Intendance (Intendance military barracks) (Nsoni and Yabbat-Ngo, 2012; N'Zobo and Mavanga Balaka, 2012); and in May 2010 in the private depot of a FAC general's residence in Talangaï (Dombe Bemba, 2012; Mouébara, 2013).

Prior to the Mpila blasts, the international community had launched several initiatives to improve stockpile management and secure a number of storage sites, yet activities focused on small arms and light weapons management rather than large-scale, large-calibre ammunition storage. In the process, a few organizations reported having accessed the depots that exploded in March 2012.[19]

In March 2010 and March 2011, the Defense Threat Reduction Agency (DTRA) of the US Department of Defense organized physical security and stockpile management (PSSM) courses. There was reportedly another one planned for March 2012. These summary courses are designed to provide guidance on how to move and store munitions. The DTRA staff apparently never obtained permission to inspect the ECRRRAMU depot that exploded in March 2012 (Rawson, 2013b).

In September 2011, MAG conducted a survey to assess the PSSM conditions in five storage buildings identified by the FAC as requiring the most support, including the ammunition depot that exploded in March. The FAC invited and granted access to MAG. Following its survey, MAG prepared a proposal for technical support to the FAC for stockpile management; that is, guidance, training, and recommended action. However, although MAG tried to raise awareness of the urgent need for ammunition stockpile management in the RoC, it was unable to secure funding for this activity before the Mpila explosion (*Africa Confidential*, 2012a; GICHD, 2012, p. 6; EU, 2013, p. 22).[20] MAG's post-explosion efforts were geared towards emergency response.

International assistance and capacity building

One of the post-emergency priorities was to help the FAC develop an autonomous EOD capacity—that is, a stand-alone unit capable of working without supervision according to best practice and international standards—before international operators left in December 2012 and January 2013. For this reason, most of the operators trained dozens of FAC members on several occasions at EOD levels 1, 2, and 3, as well as in basic first aid. One FAC officer was instructed in the use of the Information Management System for Mine Action (IMSMA) software in order to collect and analyse the data provided by the operators (UNMAT RoC, 2012a; EU, 2013, p. 37).

The EU evaluation notes that serious weaknesses remained as of January 2013, characterizing the FAC's organic EOD capacity as insufficient and understaffed. The assessment team also mentions the apparent loss of the laptop computer with the IMSMA software, as well as the loss of data recorded during the clearance and risk education activities (EU, 2013, p. 38). Despite such shortfalls, progress was made, as signalled by the creation of a 75-strong EOD platoon under the supervision of an EOD level-3 officer (RoC MoD, 2012a; 2012d).

RoC authorities were less receptive to suggested improvements in ammunition stockpile management. The UN Mine Action Team (UNMAT) commenced dialogue with the FAC in relation to ammunition stockpile management in early April 2012 (UNMAS, 2012c; 2012d). Following the initial emergency assessment missions after the blasts, the plans were discussed with the RoC government—including long-term operational capacity building to respond to stockpile management needs at remaining munitions sites in the RoC, to reduce the likelihood of future events of this kind (MAG, 2012d).

Several unfruitful stockpile management initiatives were attempted after the explosions.

There were several ad hoc, bilateral, and often simultaneous initiatives. In April 2012 Handicap International proposed an 18-month stockpile management programme that was not implemented (HI, 2012). In a field update dated 7 July 2012, UNMAS mentions its intention to launch an assessment of ammunition storage facilities from 15 July to 30 September 2012. The plan was to access all stockpiles in order to identify needs for immediate rehabilitation of existing facilities and for the construction of new facilities, with a view to launching a training programme on ammunition management based on the IATG (UNMAS, 2012e). In parallel, the FAC reportedly approached MAG to request stockpile management assistance in munitions depots in Pointe-Noire. MAG sought funds to carry out this essential work, but failed to secure them, despite considerable effort (MAG, 2012f). In October–November 2012, the Belgian Embassy and the United States Africa Command organized stockpile management training courses for almost 30 FAC personnel (RoC MoD, 2012e).

Throughout September and October 2012, UNMAT held regular meetings with the FAC and with the MoD to discuss the ongoing activities and next steps of the Mpila project, with an emphasis on stockpile management (UNMAT, 2012b). Yet there was clearly no buy-in from RoC authorities, nor was there the desired donor response (UNMAS, 2012a). In December 2012, UNMAT was still investigating 'possible funds and strategy for a potential PSSM project' for 2013 (UNMAT, 2012c; 2013). In this context, UNMAT conducted a stockpile management technical visit with an RoC delegation in Côte d'Ivoire in December 2012 (UNMAT, 2013). Upon its return, the RoC delegation was asked to draft a document laying out the country's stockpile management policy requirements. As of November 2013, it was unclear whether the document had been drafted or finalized.

Progress has been slow since the publication of the EU evaluation report. A report of the UN Office for Disarmament Affairs mentions an assistance proposal from the RoC to construct and improve applicable storage facilities and to build operational capacity for stockpile management through training and the establishment of standard operating procedures (UNODA, 2012). However, the proposed activities appear focused on small arms and light weapons management rather than large-calibre ammunition storage. Potential implementing partners include the United

Nations Regional Centre for Peace and Disarmament in Africa (UNREC)[21] and the UN Development Programme RoC (UNODA, 2012; UNGA, 2012, p. 9).

The normative framework

In the RoC's 2010 report outlining its implementation of the UN Programme of Action (PoA), the government identifies capacity building in stockpile management and weapons destruction as a priority area (RoC, 2010, p. 7). Since 2008, UN-hosted follow-up meetings, in particular the outcome document of the Third Biennial Meeting of States, have stressed the importance of stockpile management and surplus disposal, identifying improperly managed stockpiles as an important security threat (UNGA, 2008).

The management of surplus weapons and ammunition is relatively new to the RoC.

While the PoA does not clearly cover ammunition, certain provisions, such as those pertaining to stockpile management and surplus destruction, could arguably apply to ammunition. This is left to the discretion of UN member states (Bevan, McDonald, and Parker, 2009, p. 145).

The RoC's regional stockpile management commitments also pertain to small arms and light weapons, not to large-scale storage of explosive ammunition. RoC is a signatory to the Nairobi Protocol for the Prevention, Control and Reduction of Small Arms and Light Weapons in the Great Lakes Region and the Horn of Africa, adopted in 2004. In addition, the RoC ratified the Kinshasa Convention on 5 December 2012 (Small Arms Survey and GRIP, 2013a, p. 15; 2013b, p. 23).

As a category, light weapons technically include various explosive weapons, such as light mortar systems or portable missiles and rocket launchers. In Annexe 5.1, Tables 1 and 2 show that light weapons ammunition was present in the Mpila depot, yet UEMS are typically caused by much larger ammunition.

Developed in 2011, the IATGs currently provide the only global framework for large-calibre ammunition stockpile management. The guidelines reflect accepted notions of international best practice, while taking differing national capacities into account.

That said, in many countries with low levels of infrastructure and capacity, it is a lack of political will, not capacity, that prevents compliance with the minimum stockpile standards contained in the IATGs, namely risk reduction process level 1. In the RoC, priorities for the future include:

- dedicating funds to ammunition stockpile management;
- isolating or relocating depots away from urban areas; and
- revising standard operating procedures and ensuring their implementation.

Standard operating procedures for stockpile identification, management, and disposal are currently inadequate and, moreover, poorly implemented. According to a DGE officer, two structures are officially tasked with ammunition depot maintenance and technical surveillance: the Commandement de la logistique (under the responsibility of the FAC chief of staff) and the Direction des armements (under the responsibility of the DGE). Meanwhile, the Inspection générale des armées et de la gendarmerie also appears to have certain responsibilities in this area (EU, 2013, n. 36). Yet the EU field assessment team was unable to confirm the relevant structures and procedures during their visit.

There is also a lack of awareness among those in the RoC who work with ammunition stockpiles. The management of surplus weapons and ammunition is a relatively new concept in the country. When asked about the plans for future ammunition safety management and the ammunition stockpile, a DGE officer said that the stockpile would be built back up to the level it was before the explosions. According to this officer, the explosions had occurred not because they had too much ammunition but because they lacked storage capacity (Rawson, 2013a; 2013b).

CONCLUSION

The explosions that rocked the government ammunition depot located in Brazzaville's Mpila area on 4 March 2012 are symptomatic of the global problem of UEMS. They serve as a warning to many governments that still consider large, excess ammunition stockpiles as assets rather than the liabilities they often are—especially when located in the middle of large, urban residential areas.

This chapter has discussed the various root causes that led to the Mpila explosions, reviewing the extensive impacts incurred by the city, its population, and the RoC as a whole. The nature of the primary cause of the Mpila explosions—reportedly a fire, either accidental or deliberate—is of secondary importance. Of far greater relevance is the fact that the fire triggered a series of powerful blasts that levelled six military barracks and two surrounding, heavily populated districts in a matter of minutes. This was almost certainly due to the lack of basic ammunition management at the depot's multiple explosive storehouses and because the civilian population had not been prevented from settling close to an explosive storage area.

Several factors led to the Mpila depot disaster. Analysis of the types and quantities of ammunition destroyed by EOD teams during the emergency clearance effort reveals an ageing mix of pyrotechnics, small arms ammunition, grenades, mines, large-calibre projectiles, rockets, missiles, and aircraft bombs that were probably procured in the late 1970s and 1980s, transferred and used during the RoC's internal conflicts in the 1990s, and ultimately centralized for indefinite storage in the Mpila barracks. The evidence indicates that these items were amassed with little concern for basic ammunition management and security standards.

The Mpila explosions tragically link dangerous ammunition management practices with severe human and economic harm. Following the explosion, assessments of the damage to health, housing, and infrastructure yielded only partial estimates, and compensation was thus likewise partial. Full reconstruction, to the extent it occurs, will prove costly. Other economic variables affected by the event—such as reductions in income, loss of employment, unrealized production, and business disruption—were impossible to assess comprehensively and, for this reason alone, stand a lesser chance of being addressed through government compensation. The impact of the Mpila explosions was felt nationwide: emergency funding voted in April 2012 was aimed at reconstruction, but it did little more than fuel inflation because the domestic economy lacked the capacity to respond to the stimuli of additional government funds.

The Brazzaville case study shows that long-term efforts for improved ammunition management are time-sensitive; they require immediate and simultaneous buy-in from implementing organizations, donors, and, most critically, the host government. Risk awareness, national ownership, government resolve to prioritize the issue, and medium- to long-term donor commitment are all critical.

As of late-2013, progress on ammunition management in the RoC was slow, indicating timid buy-in from Congolese authorities, as well as donor fatigue and wariness from potential sponsors. Partners and observers agree that since the end of civil war (1997–2003) the country's security situation has gradually improved and is now quite stable. This stability offers the RoC an opportunity to address an often overlooked, yet no less critical, threat: poor ammunition management. ◾

LIST OF ABBREVIATIONS

ANFO	Ammonium nitrate/fuel oil
DaLA	Damage and loss assessment
DDR	Disarmament, demobilization, and reintegration
DGE	Direction générale de l'équipement (General Directorate of Logistics and Equipment)
DRC	Democratic Republic of the Congo
DTRA	Defense Threat Reduction Agency
ECLAC	United Nations Economic Commission for Latin America and the Caribbean
ECRRRAMU	Etablissement central de réparation, de rechange et de réserve en armement et munitions (Central Office for Weapons and Ammunition Repair, Replacement, and Reserves)
EOD	Explosive ordnance disposal
EU	European Union
FAC	Forces Armées Congolaises (Congolese Armed Forces)
GDP	Gross domestic product
GICHD	Geneva International Centre for Humanitarian Demining
IATG	International Ammunition Technical Guidelines
IMF	International Monetary Fund
IMSMA	Information Management System for Mine Action
MAG	Mines Advisory Group
MASAHS	Ministère des affaires sociales, de l'action humanitaire et de la solidarité (Ministry of Social Affairs, Humanitarian Action, and Solidarity)
MoD	Ministry of Defence
NGO	Non-governmental organization
NISAT	Norwegian Initiative on Small Arms Transfers
OCHA	United Nations Office for the Coordination of Humanitarian Affairs
PCT	Parti Congolais du Travail (Congolese Labour Party)
PoA	United Nations Programme of Action to Prevent, Combat and Eradicate the Illicit Trade in Small Arms and Light Weapons in All Its Aspects
PSSM	Physical security and stockpile management
RoC	Republic of the Congo
UEMS	Unplanned explosions at munitions sites
UN Comtrade	United Nations Commodity Trade Statistics Database
UNITA	União Nacional para a Independência Total de Angola
UNMAS	United Nations Mine Action Service
UNMAT	United Nations Mine Action Team
UNREC	United Nations Regional Centre for Peace and Disarmament in Africa
UXO	Unexploded ordnance
XAF	Central African franc

ANNEXES

Online annexe at <http://www.smallarmssurvey.org/publications/by-type/yearbook/small-arms-survey-2014.html>

Annexe 5.1. Summary of ammunition destruction in Brazzaville

Table 1 lists the categories, types, descriptions, and quantities of ammunition recovered and destroyed during the clearance activities undertaken from March 2012 to April 2013. Table 2 lists additional ammunition types that were destroyed by the EOD teams but not inventoried in the monthly destruction reports.

Annexe 5.2. Methodology

This annexe provides details on the methodology used to process the ammunition import and export data featured in this chapter's section entitled 'External procurement before the blasts'.

ENDNOTES

1   Data provided by the Norwegian Initiative on Small Arms Transfers (NISAT) of the Peace Research Institute Oslo (PRIO).

2   Photos obtained in Brazzaville by the assessment team during the EU-funded evaluation in January 2013.

3   In a deflagration, the surface of an explosive burns extremely fast, but not fast enough to become a detonation (Rawson, 2013a).

4   ANFO is a quarrying/blasting explosive used by commercial companies to remove rocks and to assist in the excavation of routes, among other uses. It comes as two separate constituents—ammonium nitrate, AN, a strong, commonly used agricultural fertilizer, and fuel oil, normal vehicle fuel. It can be stored safely when unmixed, but when mixed in the appropriate ratio it becomes a very powerful explosive; in most countries it is illegal to store it mixed, any excess having to be destroyed rather than saved or moved to another area. ANFO has more of a 'pushing' effect than a shattering one, which makes it better suited for quarrying, soil removal, and the like. Unfortunately, its composition renders it easily ignitable and, when its volume is large, it burns to detonation with ease (Rawson, 2013a).

5   Lazarevic (2012) reports that there were three containers.

6   MAG kindly provided the monthly reports during the EU-funded evaluation in January 2013.

7   During clearance operations, UXOs were collected by EOD teams from Angola, Demeter, the FAC, France, Handicap International, the International Committee of the Red Cross, MAG, the Swedish Civil Contingencies Agency (Myndigheten för samhällsskydd och beredskap), and the US Office of Weapons Removal and Abatement. A limited amount of items could not be moved and was thus destroyed on site. For the overwhelming majority of items, MAG administered a temporary ammunition storage area on site to keep the enormous amount of UXO and ammunition found in the area in secure conditions. When the temporary stock reached full capacity, items were systematically transported to an external location 60 km north of Brazzaville (the Bambou site), where MAG and the FAC carried out bulk demolitions on behalf of all the clearance actors (MAG, 2012e, p. 6).

8   The photos and videos were obtained by the assessment team during the EU-funded evaluation in January 2013.

9   Galloy and Gruénais (1997); IRIN (1997); *Africa Confidential* (2002); Lallemand (2002).

10   Author correspondence with Cédric Poitevin, Groupe de recherche et d'information sur la paix et la sécurité (GRIP), 4 November 2013.

11   Nic Marsh of NISAT provided the data; David Gertiser of the Small Arms Survey carried out the analysis.

12   The categories included (per source): **UN Comtrade 89129**: munitions of war; 930111: self-propelled artillery; 930690: bombs, grenades, ammunition, mines, and others; 95106: bombs, missiles, and ammunition; **UN Register of Conventional Arms**: 82 mm mortar; **Eurostat 93069090**: ammunition and projectiles and parts excluding for military purposes; 93SSS891: confidential trade in arms and ammunition; **EU annual reports**: Military List 3: ammunition, fuze setting devices, and specially designed components; Military List 4: bombs, torpedoes, rockets, missiles, other explosive devices and charges, related equipment, and accessories, specially designed for military use; **national reports**: explosives, unguided missiles; and the **media**: surface-to-air missiles.

13   Table 1 in Annexe 5.1 mentions the (unusual) presence of Iranian design PG-7 target practice rounds. This is confirmed by visual identification on field photos (author correspondence with Alex Diehl, 16 June 2013 and 10 January 2014).

14   In the mid-1970s ECLAC developed the DaLA methodology to assess the impact of natural disasters and to quantify their economic costs. The methodology can be used for non-natural disaster assessments as well (Zapata-Marti, 2013). It distinguishes the concepts of (i) direct damage ('complete or partial destruction' of assets), (ii) indirect loss ('the flows of goods and services that will not be produced or rendered over a time span that begins after the disaster and may extend throughout the rehabilitation and reconstruction periods'), and (iii) macroeconomic effects (impact on the main macroeconomic aggregates of the affected country) (ECLAC, 2003, pp. 9–15). This chapter uses the term 'damage' to refer to concept (i), and 'loss' to refer to concept (ii).

15   The camps included Armée du Salut, la Cathédrale Sacré Coeur, Cité des 17, Kimbaguiste, Nkombo, Notre Dame de Rosaire, Saint Grégoire de Massengo, Stade Annexe, and Stade Marchand (Croix rouge congolaise, 2012).

16   According to the director of MASAHS interviewed by the evaluation team, as of 7 January 2013 the camps still held 572 families, representing 2,618 individuals (EU, 2013, p. 14).

17   It is difficult to estimate the total value of international contributions to the emergency response, and space limitations preclude a comprehensive list of contributors. Among them were the EU, the United Nations (the Food and Agriculture Organization, OCHA, the UN Development Programme, UNESCO, UNICEF, UN Population Fund, the UN Refugee Agency, UNMAS, the World Food Programme, and the World Health Organization), NGOs (including ACTED, Caritas RoC, the Congolese and French Red Cross, Demeter, Handicap International, ICRC, and MAG), and a host of countries (including Angola, Benin, Central African Republic, Chad, China, the DRC, France, Gabon, Germany, Israel, Italy, Japan, Morocco, the Netherlands, Russia, São Tomé and Príncipe, South Africa, the UK, the United States—the US Agency for International Development's Office of US Foreign Disaster Assistance—and Zambia) (EU, 2013, p. 15; World Bank, 2012b, pp. 2–3).

18   In Brazzaville, risk education actors coordinated the development and publication of joint guidelines and educational material (EU, 2013, p. 34). These activities were subsequently extended through an education campaign at the institutional level, notably to introduce risk education into the school curriculum (author interview with Hugues Laurenge, UNICEF, Geneva, 9 December 2013).

19   For instance, in 2007 the UN Development Programme's Bureau for Crisis Prevention and Recovery conducted a one-week stockpile management training workshop, as well as a review of three small arms and light weapons armouries. The on-site visits included the main depot of the ECRRRAMU (BCPR, 2007).

20   Author correspondence with Chris Loughran, MAG, 11 November 2013.

21   Author correspondence and telephone interview with Karl Wagner and Leonardo Lara, UNREC, 7 June 2013.

BIBLIOGRAPHY

Africa Confidential. 2002. 'By Other Means.' Vol. 43, No. 12. 14 June.

—. 2004. 'Brazzaville Breakdown.' Vol. 45, No. 9. 30 April.

—. 2012a. 'Dying by the Sword.' Vol. 53, No. 7. 30 March.

—. 2012b. 'A Poverty of Strategy.' Vol. 53, No. 21. 19 October.

AOAV (Action on Armed Violence). 2012. *Case Studies of Explosive Violence: Republic of Congo*. June.
    <http://aoav.org.uk/wp-content/uploads/2013/06/2012_06_case_study_of_explosive_violence_republic_of_congo1.pdf>

Batchelor, Peter. 2010. *South Africa's Arms Trade and the Commonwealth: A Cause for Concern?* 21 December.
    <http://carecon.org.uk/Leverhulme/P12.pdf>

BBC News. n.d. 'Republic of Congo Profile.' <http://www.bbc.co.uk/news/world-africa-14121195>

BCPR (Bureau for Crisis Prevention and Recovery). 2007. 'One-page Mission Report Summary: Capacity Building (CB) regarding SALW Stockpile Management.' 29 January.

Berman, Eric G. and Pilar Reina, eds. 2014. *Unplanned Explosions at Munitions Sites (UEMS): Excess Stockpiles as Liabilities Rather than Assets*. Handbook No. 3. Geneva: Small Arms Survey.

Bevan, James, Glenn McDonald, and Sarah Parker. 2009. 'Two Steps Forward: UN Measures Update.' In Small Arms Survey. *Small Arms Survey 2009: Shadows of War*. Cambridge: Cambridge University Press.
    <http://www.smallarmssurvey.org/fileadmin/docs/A-Yearbook/2009/en/Small-Arms-Survey-2009-Chapter-04-EN.pdf>

Biddle, Ian, et al. 2003. 'Making the Difference? Weapon Collection and Small Arms Availability in the Republic of Congo.' In Small Arms Survey. *Small Arms Survey 2003: Development Denied*. Oxford: Oxford University Press, pp. 254–75.
    <http://www.smallarmssurvey.org/fileadmin/docs/A-Yearbook/2003/en/Small-Arms-Survey-2003-Chapter-08-EN.pdf>

Bowao, Charles Zacharie. 2012. 'Congo-Brazzaville : "Si je me suis trompé, c'est de bonne foi!".' *Jeune Afrique*, No. 2705. 11–17 November.

Croix rouge congolaise. 2012. *Rapport définitif sur l'opération assistance aux populations sinistrées de l'explosion du 04 mars 2012 du 06 mars au 27 octobre 2012*.

Demeter. 2012. 'Aide mémoire des masses par munition.'

Demetriou, Spyros, Robert Muggah, and Ian Biddle. 2002. *Small Arms Availability, Trade, and Impacts in the Republic of Congo*. Special Report No. 2. Geneva: Small Arms Survey. April. <http://www.smallarmssurvey.org/fileadmin/docs/C-Special-reports/SAS-SR02-Congo.pdf>

Doko, Pascal Azad. 2012. 'Commission d'évaluation des dégâts du drame de Mpila: Les maisons détruites ou endommagées seront reconstruites et réhabilitées.' *La Semaine Africaine*, No. 3181, p. 3. 3 April.

— and Aybienevie N'Kouka-Koudissa. 2012. 'Gilbert Odongo, à propos de l'allocation de soutien aux familles sinistrées: "Il y a autant d'argent disponible qu'il y a des ayants droit".' *La Semaine Africaine*, No. 3181, p. 3. 3 April.

Dombe Bemba, Ghys Fortune. 2012. 'Le drame du Congo: Une population sacrifiée à Mpila.' 16 March.
    <http://www.mampouya.com/article-le-drame-du-congo-une-population-sacrifiee-a-mpila-101711433.html>

EC–ECHO (European Commission–Directorate-General for Humanitarian Aid and Civil Protection). 2012. 'Single Form for Humanitarian Aid Actions: Intermediate Report—Emergency Response to Munitions Depot Explosion in Brazzaville.' Reference No. 2012/00397/IR/01/01. 29 June.

ECLAC (Economic Commission for Latin America and the Caribbean). 2003. 'Methodological and Conceptual Aspects.' In ECLAC. *Handbook for Estimating the Socio-economic and Environmental Effects of Disasters*, Vol. I. <http://www.cepal.org/cgi-bin/getProd.asp?xml=/publicaciones/xml/4/12774/P12774.xml&xsl=/mexico/tpl-i/p9f.xsl&base=/desastres/tpl/top-bottom.xsl>

EU (European Union). 2013. *Evaluation de l'action de déblaiement et de dépollution des quartiers affectés par l'explosion du dépôt de munitions de Mpila à Brazzaville, en République du Congo: Rapport final.* March.

<http://www.gichd.org/fileadmin/pdf/evaluations/database/Congo/EvaluationUE-Brazzaville-GICHD-Mars2013-fr.pdf>

Gac, Stéphane. 2012. *Mission d'évaluation des risques bâtimentaires faisant suite à la catastrophe du 4 mars 2012 au camp militaire de MPILA à Brazzaville.* Paris: Brigade des sapeurs pompiers de Paris. March.

Galloy, Martine-Renée and Marc-Éric Gruénais. 1997. 'Fighting for Power in the Congo.' *Le Monde diplomatique.* November.

<http://mondediplo.com/1997/11/africa2>

GICHD (Geneva International Centre for Humanitarian Demining). 2012. *UNMAS Rapid Response Project: Congo Brazzaville Case Study.* September.

HC (Haut Commissariat pour la Démobilisation et Réinsertion des ex-Combattants). 2013. 'Tableau récapitulatif du processus de désarmement au Congo.'

HI (Handicap International). 2012. *Amélioration de la sécurité des stocks de munitions et armes légères en République du Congo.* Brazzaville: HI. April.

IFRC (International Federation of the Red Cross and Red Crescent Societies). 2012. 'Emergency Appeal Operation Update: Republic of Congo—Explosion.' Emergency appeal No. MDRCG011. Update No. 1. 30 May.

IMF (International Monetary Fund). 2011. *République du Congo: Cinquième et sixième revues de l'accord triennal au titre de la facilité élargie de crédit et revue des assurances de financement—Rapport des services du FMI.* No. 11/255. August.

—. 2012a. 'Déclaration de la mission du FMI à l'issue des consultations de 2012 au titre de l'article IV.' 23 May.

—. 2012b. *Republic of Congo: 2012 Article IV Consultation—Staff Report; Public Information. Notice on the Executive Board Discussion; and Statement by the Executive Director for the Republic of Congo.* IMF Country Report No. 12/283. October.

—. 2013a. 'Déclaration à l'issue d'une visite des services du FMI en République du Congo.' 16 March.

—. 2013b. 'Une mission du FMI achève les entretiens relatifs aux consultations au titre de l'article IV avec la République du Congo.' Press release No. 13/167. 13 May.

IRIN (Integrated Regional Information Network for the Great Lakes). 1997. 'Background Brief on Congo-Brazzaville.' 22 October.

<http://reliefweb.int/report/congo/background-brief-congo-brazzaville>

Jeune Afrique. 2013a. 'Congo-Brazzaville: 6 condamnés et 26 acquittés dans l'affaire des explosions.' 10 September.

<http://www.jeuneafrique.com/Article/ARTJAWEB20130910151122/congo-brazzaville-mpila-armee-congolaisecongo-brazzaville-6-condamnes-et-26-acquittes-dans-l-affaire-des-explosions.html>

—. 2013b. 'Le marocain Alliances construit 3 000 logements à Brazzaville.' 22 November.

<http://economie.jeuneafrique.com/regions/afrique-subsaharienne/20749-le-marocain-alliances-construit-3000-logements-a-brazzaville.html>

—. 2013c. 'Congo-Brazzaville: arrestation du colonel Ntsourou, une quarantaine de morts dans les affrontements.' 16 December.

<http://www.jeuneafrique.com/Article/ARTJAWEB20131216124357/denis-sassou-nguesso-brazzaville-congo-brazzaville-jean-dominique-okemba-securite-congo-brazzaville-arrestation-du-colonel-ntsourou-une-quarantaine-de-morts-dans-les-affrontements.html>

—. 2013d. 'Marcel Ntsourou, le desperado de Brazza.' 26 December. <http://www.jeuneafrique.com/Article/JA2763p016.xml0/>

Lallemand, Alain. 2002. 'The Field Marshall.' Washington, DC: Center for Public Integrity. 15 November.

<http://www.publicintegrity.org/2002/11/15/5694/field-marshal>

La Semaine Africaine. 2012a. 'Après le drame de Mpila: le manque d'information favorise les rumeurs qui créent la psychose.' No. 3174. 9 March.

—. 2012b. 'Les quartiers sinistrés de Brazzaville seront reconstruits.' No. 3182, p. 3. 6 April.

—. 2012c. 'Des familles divisées sur l'allocation d'urgence de trois millions octroyée aux sinistrés.' No. 3187, p. 6. 27 April.

Lazarevic, Jasna. 2012. 'Survey Researcher Field Interview Notes, Brazzaville.' Geneva: Small Arms Survey.

LCMM (Landmine & Cluster Munition Monitor). 2012. 'Congo, Republic of.' 11 October.

<http://www.the-monitor.org/custom/index.php/region_profiles/print_profile/453>

Le Pape, Marc and Pierre Salignon. 2001. *Une guerre contre les civils: Réflexions sur les pratiques humanitaires au Congo Brazzaville (1998–2000).* Paris: Karthala.

Loutoumba, Nancy France. 2012. 'Le 4 mars, un casse-tête pour la République.' *Les Dépêches de Brazzaville,* No. 1572, p. 7. 10 September.

MAG (Mines Advisory Group). 2012a. 'MAG Assessment of Arms Depot Explosion at Mpila, Brazzaville.' 7 March.

—. 2012b. 'Brazzaville Response: Situation Report 1.' 9 March.

—. 2012c. *Concept Paper: Sub-Clearance & Rubble Removal Response to Mpila Depots Explosion in Brazzaville.* 25 May.

—. 2012d. *Situation Report 7.* June.

—. 2012e. 'Services de dépollution d'urgence dans le quartier de Mpila.' September.

—. 2012f. *Situation Report 10.* September.

—. 2012g. *Rapport narratif final.*

Moss, Robert. 1977. 'Castro's Secret War Exposed: How Washington Lost Its Nerve and How the Cubans Subdued Angola.' *Sunday Telegraph*. 30 January.
<http://www.rhodesia.nl/moss1.htm>

Mouébara, Olivier. 2013. 'Le général Blaise Adoua est-il mort empoisonné?' 17 April. <http://congo-liberty.com/?p=6107>

Muggah, Robert, Philippe Maughan, and Christian Bugnion. 2003. *The Long Shadow of War: Prospects for Disarmament Demobilisation and Reintegration in the Republic of Congo*. A Joint Independent Evaluation for the European Commission, United Nations Development Programme, and the Multi-Country Demobilization and Reintegration Program Secretariat.
<http://www.oecd.org/countries/democraticrepublicofthecongo/35113279.pdf>

Muggah, Robert and Ryan Nichols. 2007. *Quoi de neuf sur le front congolais? Evaluation de base sur la circulation des armes légères et de petit calibre en République du Congo*. Special Report No. 8. Geneva: Small Arms Survey and United Nations Development Programme.
<http://www.smallarmssurvey.org/fileadmin/docs/C-Special-reports/SAS-SR08-Congo-Brazzaville.pdf>

Nsoni, Joël. 2012a. 'La commission d'enquête passe à la vitesse supérieure!' *La Semaine Africaine*, No. 3181, p. 3. 5 April.

—. 2012b. 'Enquête après le drame de Mpila: Des dizaines d'armes de guerre saisies chez un officier supérieur en garde à vue.' *La Semaine Africaine*, No. 3183, p. 3. 12 April.

—. 2012c. 'Ouverture de la procédure judiciaire au tribunal de grande instance de Brazzaville.' *La Semaine Africaine*, No. 3191, p. 3. 11 May.

—. 2012d. 'Après le drame du 04 mars 2012: L'arrestation du colonel Ntsourou doit-elle entraîner celle de son supérieur hiérarchique, le contre-amiral Jean-Dominique Okemba?' *La Semaine Africaine*, No. 3194, p. 6. 22 May.

— and Cyr Armel Yabbat-Ngo. 2012. 'Après les explosions au camp du regiment blindé de Mpila (Brazzaville): Apocalypse dans les quartiers de Ouenzé et Talangaï.' *La Semaine Africaine*, No. 3173, p. 3. 6 March.

N'Zobo, Rock Euloge and Jean-Gabriel Mavanga Balaka. 2012. 'Explosion du dépôt de munitions de Mpila: conséquence de la négligence des plus hautes autorités du pays.' *La Semaine Africaine*, No. 3174, p. 5. 9 March.

OCHA (United Nations Office for the Coordination of Humanitarian Affairs). 2012. 'CERF gives $7 Million to Republic of Congo Following Arms Depot Explosions.' 30 April. <http://reliefweb.int/report/congo/cerf-gives-7-million-republic-congo-following-arms-depot-explosions>

Rawson, John. 2013a. *Explosions in the Ammunition Storage Area in Brazzaville*. Unpublished background paper. 6 May. Geneva: Small Arms Survey.

—. 2013b. 'Notes on Interview with Colonel Oyobé.' 16 January.

—. 2013c. 'Notes on Interview with MAG.' 16 January.

—. 2013d. 'Notes on Interview with Michel Rathqueber (Demeter).' 16 January.

RFI (Radio France International). 2013. 'Congo-Brazzaville: fin du procès des explosions de Mpila.' 9 September.
<http://www.rfi.fr/afrique/20130909-explosion-mpila-le-proces-est-termine>

RoC (Republic of the Congo). 2010. *Report of the Republic of the Congo Concerning the Implementation of the International Instrument to Enable States to Identify and Trace, in a Timely and Reliable Manner, Illicit Small Arms and Light Weapons and of the Programme of Action to Prevent, Combat and Eradicate the Illicit Trade in Small Arms and Light Weapons in All Its Aspects.*
<http://www.poa-iss.org/CASACountryProfile/PoANationalReports/2010@45@PoA-ITI-RepublicOfTheCongo-2010-E.pdf>

—. 2012. *Journal officiel*. 54th year, special edn. No. 1. 14 May.

RoC MoD (Republic of the Congo Ministry of Defence). 2012a. 'Fiche d'information à l'attention du général de division, chef d'état-major adjoint des forces armées congolaises.' No. 00112 /MDN/MID/GAS/CD/SUP. 30 November.

—. 2012b. *Rapport: Deuxième phase de la dépollution de la zone sinistrée suite aux explosions du 04 mars 2012*. No. 00042 /MDN/MID/GAS/CD/SUP. Brazzaville: RoC MoD. 14 May.

—. 2012c. *Rapport sur les opérations de dépollution de la zone sinistrée de Mpila*. 3 September.

—. 2012d. *Rapport sur les opérations de dépollution de la zone sinistrée de Mpila*. 5 September.

—. 2012e. *Rapport d'étape de la phase 3*. No. 00111/MDN/MID/GAS/CD/SUP. 30 November.

Servenay, David. 2004. 'Confessions d'un marchand d'armes.' RFI. 6 December. <http://www.rfi.fr/actufr/articles/060/article_32274.asp>

Skilling, Louise. 2013. 'Emergency Response in RoC, Brazzaville, March 2012.' Powerpoint presentation. Mines Advisory Group.

Small Arms Survey. 2001. 'Fuelling the Flames: Brokers and Transport Agents in the Illicit Arms Trade.' In Small Arms Survey. *Small Arms Survey 2001: Profiling the Problem*. Oxford: Oxford University Press, pp. 94–139.
<http://www.smallarmssurvey.org/fileadmin/docs/A-Yearbook/2001/en/Small-Arms-Survey-2001-Chapter-03-EN.pdf>

—. n.d. 'Unplanned Explosions at Munitions Sites (UEMS) Database.' Accessed February 2014. Geneva: Small Arms Survey.

Small Arms Survey and GRIP (Groupe de recherche et d'information sur la paix et la sécurité). 2013a. *The Fight against the Illicit Accumulation and Trafficking of Firearms in Africa: Baseline Study for the African Union and European Union Project—Final Report*. 30 June.

—. 2013b. 'Republic of Congo Mission Report.' In Small Arms Survey and GRIP, pp. 19–31.

TI (Transparency International). 2013. 'Corruption Perceptions Index 2013.' <http://www.transparency.org/cpi2013/results>

UNDP (United Nations Development Programme). 2013. *Human Development Report 2013—The Rise of the South: Human Progress in a Diverse World.* <http://hdr.undp.org/en/reports/global/hdr2013/download/>

UNGA (United Nations General Assembly). 2008. *Report of the Third Biennial Meeting of States to Consider the Implementation of the Programme of Action to Prevent, Combat and Eradicate the Illicit Trade in Small Arms and Light Weapons in All Its Aspects.* A/CONF.192/BMS/2008/3 of 20 August. <http://www.un.org/disarmament/convarms/BMS/bms3/1BMS3Pages/1thirdBMS.html>

—. 2012. *United Nations Regional Centre for Peace and Disarmament in Africa: Report of the Secretary-General.* A/67/117 of 28 June. <http://www.un.org/ga/search/view_doc.asp?symbol=A/67/117>

UNMAS (United Nations Mine Action Service). 2012a. 'Briefing Note: UNMAT RoC.' 27 November.

—. 2012b. *Evaluation of the Emergency Mine Action Response to the Ammunition Depot Explosion in Brazzaville, Republic of Congo.*

—. 2012c. 'Weekly Brief: Republic of Congo.' 2–7 April.

—. 2012d. 'Weekly Brief: Republic of Congo.' 9–14 April.

—. 2012e. 'Update Regarding the Mine Action Response in the Republic of Congo.' 7 July.

—. 2013. *IMAS 09.30: Explosive Ordnance Disposal.* Amendment 4. June. <http://www.mineactionstandards.org/fileadmin/user_upload/MAS/documents/imas-international-standards/english/series-09/IMAS-09-30-Ed2-Am4.pdf>

UNMAT RoC (United Nations Mine Action Team–Republic of the Congo). 2012a. 'Capacity Building Implementation.' 5 November.

—. 2012b. 'Monthly Field Report.' 5 October.

—. 2012c. 'Monthly Field Report.' 3 December.

—. 2013. 'Monthly Field Report.' 4 January.

UNODA (United Nations Office for Disarmament Affairs). 2011a. *International Ammunition Technical Guidelines (IATG): IATG 01.50 UN Explosive Hazard Classification System and Codes.* <http://www.un.org/disarmament/convarms/Ammunition/IATG/docs/IATG01.50.pdf>

—. 2011b. *International Ammunition Technical Guidelines (IATG): IATG 02.20 Quantity and Separation Distances.* <http://www.un.org/disarmament/convarms/Ammunition/IATG/docs/IATG02.20.pdf>

—. 2011c. *International Ammunition Technical Guidelines (IATG): IATG 03.10 Inventory Management.* <http://www.un.org/disarmament/convarms/Ammunition/IATG/docs/IATG03.10.pdf>

—. 2011d. *International Ammunition Technical Guidelines (IATG): IATG 05.30 Traverses and Barricades.* <http://www.un.org/disarmament/convarms/Ammunition/IATG/docs/IATG05.30.pdf>

—. 2011e. International Ammunition Technical Guidelines (IATG): IATG 07.20 Surveillance and In-service Proof. <http://www.un.org/disarmament/convarms/Ammunition/IATG/docs/IATG07.20.pdf>

—. 2012. *Matching Needs and Resources 2012–2014 : Assistance Proposals from Member States Submitted through Their 2012 National Reports under the Programme of Action on the Illicit Trade in Small Arms and Light Weapons.* <http://www.poa-iss.org/poa/2012-Matching-Needs-and-Reources.pdf>

UNSC (United Nations Security Council). 2000. 'Letter Dated 10 March 2000 from the Chairman of the Security Council Committee Established Pursuant to Resolution 864 (1993) Concerning the Situation in Angola Addressed to the President of the Security Council.' S/2000/203 of 10 March 2000. <http://www.un.org/News/dh/latest/angolareport_eng.htm>

Untitled. 2013. 'Explosions du 4 mars, un an après.'

Wezeman, Pieter, Siemon Wezeman, and Lucie Béraud-Sudreau. 2011. *Arms Flows to Sub-Saharan Africa.* SIPRI Policy Paper No. 30. Stockholm: Stockholm International Peace Research Institute. <http://books.sipri.org/files/PP/SIPRIPP30.pdf>

Wezeman, Siemon and Pieter Wezeman. 1998. 'Transfers of Major Conventional Weapons.' In Stockholm International Peace Research Institute (SIPRI). *SIPRI Yearbook 1998: Armaments, Disarmament and International Security.* Oxford: Oxford University Press, ch. 8. <http://www.sipri.org/research/armaments/transfers/publications/yearbook/CH8YB98>

World Bank. 2012a. 'Atelier de formation sur la méthodologie DaLA d'évaluation de catastrophes.' Brazzaville, Congo, 23–27 July 2012.

—. 2012b. 'République du Congo: Aide-mémoire—Mission d'appui à la planification de la reconstruction et à l'amélioration de la prévention.' 9–17 April.

—. 2012c. 'Transmission de l'aide-memoire de la mission de formation sur la méthode d'évaluation des dommages et des pertes et d'appui à la préparation du document d'evaluation des dommages, des pertes et des besoins de reconstruction de la catastrophe de Mpila.' 10 October.

—. 2014. 'Economy Rankings.' Accessed January 2014. <http://www.doingbusiness.org/rankings>

—. n.d. 'Data: Congo, Rep.' Accessed January 2014. <http://data.worldbank.org/country/congo-republic>

Yabbat-Ngo, Cyr Armel. 2012a. 'Obsèques des victimes du drame de Mpila: La République a rendu hommage aux martyrs des explosions du camp du régiment blindé.' *La Semaine Africaine*, No. 3175, p. 3. 13 March.

—. 2012b. 'Aide humanitaire: Mettre un terme à la pagaille dans la gestion des sites des sinistrés.' *La Semaine Africaine*, No. 3176, p. 3. 16 March.

—. 2012c. 'Assemblée nationale: Gilbert Ondongo a présenté le projet de budget rectificatif de l'Etat exercice 2012.' *La Semaine Africaine*, No. 3183, p. 3. 12 April.

—. 2012d. 'Assemblée nationale: Pascal Tsaty-Mabiala en faveur du traitement de l'ensemble des sinistres par l'Etat.' *La Semaine Africaine*, No. 3185, p. 3. 20 April.

Zapata-Marti, Ricardo. 2013. *Estimation of the Costs, Impact, and Consequences (Direct and Indirect) of the Mpila Explosions*. Unpublished background paper. Geneva: Small Arms Survey.

ACKNOWLEDGEMENTS

Principal author

Pierre Gobinet

Empty cartridges litter the ground next to government soldiers convening near Ajdabiya, Libya, March 2011. © Ahmed Jadallah/Reuters

Across Conflict Zones

AMMUNITION PROFILING

6

INTRODUCTION

In early 2012, the Small Arms Survey documented the presence in Libya of crates of 7.62 × 51 mm ammunition produced in Pakistan in 1981 (Jenzen-Jones, 2013a, pp. 22–23). While materiel produced more than 30 years ago would not normally raise questions about possible arms embargo violations, the Pakistani cartridges stood out in Libya, where most of the ammunition of this calibre was produced in Belgium (pp. 40–41). Furthermore, the packaging indicated that the Qatar Armed Forces were the intended recipient. The UN Panel of Experts monitoring the arms embargo on Libya found additional samples of this ammunition and approached Pakistani authorities, who confirmed that the Pakistan Ordnance Factories had shipped several million rounds of 7.62 × 51 mm ammunition to Qatar from 1981 to 1982 and concluded that 'some of that materiel must have been re-exported to Libya in violation of obligations contained in the end-user certificate signed by Qatar' (UN, 2013a, para. 69). This example demonstrates how profiling ammunition in circulation in particular countries can help distinguish what is common from what is unusual, and thus worthy of further examination. In this case, such data collection assisted in the investigation of possible arms embargo violations.

Investigators, researchers, war reporters, and activists are increasingly documenting ammunition found in or transferred to areas that are experiencing armed conflict. Photographs of ammunition markings and packaging taken on location, as well as shipping documents retrieved from various sources, provide a wealth of information on the countries and dates of manufacture of war materiel. In some cases, these efforts also allow ammunition to be traced back to the initial recipient as well as to subsequent intermediaries.

Highlighting the important contribution such efforts make to arms trafficking research, this chapter undertakes a meta-analysis of the characteristics of small-calibre ammunition—that is, of calibres of less than 20 mm—documented since 2010 in seven countries and territories: Côte d'Ivoire, Libya, Somalia, Somaliland, South Sudan, Sudan, and Syria. The study draws on samples of ammunition documented during past and ongoing field research by the Small Arms Survey, reports by UN panels of experts and peacekeeping missions, photographs taken by war journalists, and data shared by other partners and researchers. Pulling together this information into a single data set of 560 samples, the chapter analyses the diverse types of ammunition circulating across the seven case studies. In doing so, it aims to:

- establish a general profile of the types of ammunition in circulation in areas affected by conflict, with a particular focus on the calibre, as well as the country and date of manufacture, of the documented cartridges; and
- explore what these profiles can reveal about the production, procurement, and transfer of ammunition.

The chapter's key findings include:

- Facilities located in 39 countries produced the surveyed ammunition. Production plants located in China and the Soviet Union (now the Russian Federation) account for the greatest share—a combined 37 per cent—of the ammunition samples. The prevalence of cartridges of Sudanese and Iranian manufacture is also noteworthy.

- More than three-quarters of the ammunition samples were Eastern Bloc-calibre cartridges, and more than half were produced during the cold war—highlighting the role of old ammunition in fuelling armed conflict and underlining the importance of reducing stockpile surpluses.

- The presence of newly produced ammunition in several countries illustrates how quickly this materiel can be diverted or retransferred to situations of armed conflict. A total of 29 samples of ammunition observed in Côte d'Ivoire, Somalia, South Sudan, Sudan, and Syria were produced since 2010, for the most part in facilities located in China and Sudan.

- The presence of different types of unmarked cartridges in all but one of the countries and territories under review raises new hurdles for arms monitoring efforts. Markings on certain packaging points to Ethiopia as the manufacturer of some of this ammunition, but in the other cases it is difficult to identify producers conclusively.

- By revealing the presence of specific types of ammunition, several country profiles in this study provide the first evidence of clandestine or destabilizing transfers.

It is important to note that the producing countries identified in this chapter are not necessarily responsible for transferring the ammunition to the conflict environments and actors under study. Indeed, producers may have exported the ammunition legally to these or other countries before it was retransferred without their knowledge and used in conflict, or diverted to non-state armed groups or illicit markets. Information on producers is nevertheless important in generating a baseline of the ammunition in circulation, which in turn may facilitate the identification of unusual or new ammunition flows over time and across borders. Moreover, identifying producers is often a necessary first step in establishing the full chain of custody of ammunition transfers to areas affected by conflict.

This chapter has three sections. The first section presents the data sources and methodology for compiling information on small-calibre ammunition for this study. The second section establishes generic ammunition profiles for the whole data set and for the seven countries and territories under review, focusing on calibre, date, and country of manufacture. The last section provides in-depth information and analysis of instances where the same types of ammunition—some of which bear no markings—were found in multiple locations.

DATA COLLECTION AND METHODOLOGY

This section explains the data sources and methods used to identify, record, and analyse ammunition in the seven countries and territories under review. After providing a general overview of the complementary sources used by researchers to document small-calibre ammunition in conflict and post-conflict areas, it presents the data and methodology used for this chapter.

Documenting ammunition in conflict environments

In situations of armed conflict, it is as important to document ammunition as it is to record weapons. In places where weapons proliferation is widespread, armed actors are often especially concerned about securing their supplies of ammunition. Furthermore, weapons and ammunition are often transferred together. Ammunition identification can also provide information on the types of weapons in circulation (Leff and LeBrun, 2014, p. 13). Lastly, newly manufactured ammunition can also point to recent supply, even when the relevant weapons have been in circulation for decades.

Following an attack in the southwest of Côte d'Ivoire, a soldier stands next to a pile of ammunition, Saho, June 2012. © Issouf Sanogo/AFP Photo

Researchers, investigators, and war reporters have produced a growing body of information on the characteristics of ammunition circulating in conflict situations. This trend has become especially discernible in the last ten years, as toolkits have been developed to promote and guide the precise recording of and reporting on ammunition observed in the field.[1] By combining photographic evidence and contextual information on ammunition retrieved in conflict zones, this type of data collection has made it possible to compare the years and countries of manufacture as well as the physical characteristics of cartridges held by different armed actors. Developing and comparing 'profiles' of ammunition in the hands of various actors helps illustrate possible flows of ammunition between these actors—be they the result of trade, theft, or capture. One of the early studies uses ammunition profiles to expose the transfer of materiel between state security forces and Turkana pastoralist communities in Kenya (Bevan, 2008b, p. 18). A study in Rio de Janeiro, Brazil, shows that gangs were able to access restricted-use assault rifle ammunition held primarily by the police (Bevan and Dreyfus, 2007, p. 310).

The study of ammunition has progressively been integrated into important arms monitoring processes, including the work of panels of experts investigating compliance with UN Security Council arms embargoes, as well as multi-year research projects, such as the Survey's Human Security Baseline Assessment for Sudan and South Sudan (HSBA). Former members of UN panels of experts have also worked together to document the presence of Iranian-manufactured ammunition in several African countries (Conflict Armament Research, 2012). A handful of journalists covering conflict zones are also reporting on ammunition with increased precision and frequency. Most prominently, C. J. Chivers, a senior writer at *The New York Times*, documents, reports, and shares information on cartridges held by or seized from armed groups in locations such as Afghanistan, Libya, and Syria (Chivers, n.d.).

Researchers and journalists reporting on ammunition rely primarily on field-based investigation, interviews, and physical examination of ammunition in conflict environments. Yet the emergence of online networks of researchers, journalists, and activists covering particular conflicts, or tracking weapons and ammunition generally, has helped to increase the speed at which photographic evidence is shared and analysed, and to raise awareness among a wider group of journalists and activists about the value and importance of recording and documenting ammunition in the field. These trends have resulted in a more diverse set of sources on which analysts can rely, with social networking platforms facilitating information exchange and verification between a broader range of actors.

Data sources

Journalists report on ammunition found in conflict zones with increased precision.

This chapter draws on the diverse set of sources described above to compare small-calibre ammunition samples documented since 2010 in seven countries and territories: Côte d'Ivoire, Libya, Somalia, Somaliland, South Sudan, Sudan, and Syria (see Map 6.1). While data collection methods varied slightly depending on the case study, as described below, each ammunition sample is documented by primary evidence—in most cases photographic records of cartridges, photos of packaging, field observation, and, in a handful of cases, shipping documentation. Overall, 560 ammunition samples totalling millions of cartridges are reviewed across the seven case studies (see Table 6.1).

In this chapter, a 'sample' refers to a specific type of ammunition, characterized in most cases by a unique combination of calibre, year of manufacture, and production facility. As such, this unit of analysis does not infer quantities, although the dataset contains available information about the size of each sample of a specific type of ammunition. Samples range from a handful of cartridges documented from a combatant's magazine and larger stockpiles stored in crates, to spent cartridges collected on the battlefield. If the same variety of ammunition was documented several times in the same country or territory, it is considered part of a single sample within that case study. The same type of ammunition may appear in more than one of the countries or territories under study, however, as discussed below.[2]

Côte d'Ivoire

This case study includes 246 different samples of ammunition that the Integrated Embargo Monitoring Unit of the UN Operation in Côte d'Ivoire (UNOCI) documented between November 2011 and May 2013 (Anders, 2014, p. 5).[3] This period follows the disputed 2010 presidential election, after which forces loyal to opposition leader Alassane Ouattara launched a military offensive and dislodged incumbent Laurent Gbagbo in April 2011. As part of its Security Council mandate, UNOCI examined equipment and took photographs of ammunition and of its packaging during inspections of national defence and security installations, of the disarmament of former combatants and civilians, and of the recovery of ammunition from arms caches and sites of armed attacks. Sample sizes vary greatly, ranging from a few cartridges held by fighters to crates of thousands of units of the same ammunition.

Libya

Data for Libya includes 81 different ammunition samples compiled as part of the Survey's Security Assessment in North Africa project in Jenzen-Jones (2013a; 2013c). Sources for this case study include information and photographs that have been gathered by Survey staff and consultants, journalists—notably Damien Spleeters—other researchers, and organizations working in Libya during and in the aftermath of the 2011 armed conflict. Source material includes photos—of cartridge headstamps, cartridges, and ammunition packaging—as well as shipping documents pertaining to small-calibre ammunition transfers. Most photographs were taken in Tripoli during the first five months of 2012, with additional photos from Ajdabiya, Bani Walid, Benghazi, Misrata, Mizdah, Sebha, Zawiya, and western Libya between 2011 and 2013 (Jenzen-Jones, 2013a, p. 12; 2013c, p. 1). The ammunition samples were primarily sourced from armed group members and civilians, or found on the battlefield and in looted state storage facilities. The documented samples ranged in size from a few cartridges to transfer records concerning more than a million units.

Somalia and Somaliland

Data for Somalia and Somaliland includes 39 and 29 different ammunition samples, respectively. Data collectors took photographs of and recorded information on ammunition sold by arms dealers and in possession of civilians in Mogadishu, Somalia, and Burao, Somaliland, between April and November 2013. As a result of more than two decades of war and relative statelessness in Somalia, arms and ammunition have moved freely into and within the country. Until recently, arms and ammunition could be purchased without restriction at the Bakaara market, an open-air arms market in the centre of Mogadishu. In contrast, the semi-autonomous state of Somaliland has been relatively peaceful since it declared independence in 1991. However, Somaliland remains a crucial region for the delivery, transhipment, and sale of weapons. The town of Burao, in particular, has one of the most thriving arms markets in Somaliland. The information was gathered as part of the Survey's ongoing monitoring of these illicit arms markets.[4] Samples were typically small, ranging from a handful to a few hundred cartridges.

South Sudan and Sudan

The chapter reviews 36 ammunition samples from South Sudan and 61 from Sudan, as documented by the Survey's HSBA project between 2010 and 2013. HSBA personnel and consultants with specific expertise in weapons and ammunition identification and tracing undertook the data gathering (Leff and LeBrun, 2014; WEAPONS TRACING); published and unpublished findings from the UN Panel of Experts monitoring the arms embargo on Darfur supplemented the data collection.[5] In South Sudan, the documented ammunition was found in the hands of non-state armed groups operating in Jonglei, Unity, and Upper Nile states. In Sudan, the samples were observed mainly in the hands of armed groups in the Darfur region, and in Blue Nile and South Kordofan states. In both countries, sample size varied from a handful to several thousand cartridges.

Rebel groups in Sudan procure most of their ammunition through battlefield capture.

Most of the ammunition documented in South Sudan and Sudan derives from diversion from Sudan Armed Forces (SAF) stockpiles. Sudan supplies insurgent groups in South Sudan with ammunition, apparently in order to fuel opposition to the Juba government. Rebel groups operating in Sudan now procure most of their ammunition through battlefield capture from SAF (Leff and LeBrun, 2014, pp. 59–60).

Syria

Data for Syria includes 68 different samples of ammunition compiled as part of the Survey's Security Assessment in North Africa project in Jenzen-Jones (2014, p. 3). The sources include information and photographs gathered by journalists—in particular C. J. Chivers and Damien Spleeters—researchers, and organizations, as well as some open-source material. The photographs were taken primarily in the Idlib and Aleppo governorates, with images from ad-Dana, al-Bab, Aleppo, Atimah, Bab al-Hawa, Deir Sonbul, Ibleen, Idlib, Jabal al-Zawiya, Kafr Nabl, and Taftanaz. Most of the photographs were taken from March 2012 to May 2013, in the midst of the Syrian armed conflict. Ammunition samples were recovered from both non-state armed groups and government forces, as well as from battlefields, where

Free Syrian Army fighters clean their weapons and check ammunition at their base on the outskirts of Aleppo, November 2012. © Khalil Hamra/AP Photo

it may not be possible to determine the affiliation of the shooters.

In all seven case studies, sample ammunition was found in situations of active armed conflict or enduring post-conflict insecurity, either on the battlefield, in both secured and unsecured stockpiles, or in the hands of gunmen and local dealers. While regular government forces held some of the documented samples, the research shows that non-state armed groups in many conflict zones relied on the capture of government materiel for much of their small-calibre ammunition.

Methodology and caveats

International experts in ammunition identification analysed all the photographs and documentation assembled as part of the case studies for the specific purpose of identifying three main features of the ammunition, namely its calibre, production facility (from which the country of production is determined), and year of manufacture. In order to do so, the analysts reviewed a number of characteristics visible on the cartridges, including the markings applied on the ammunition headstamp or its packaging, as well as other physical characteristics of the cartridges (see Jorian and Regenstreif, 1995; Box 6.1). This information was then entered in a single data set, which served as the basis for producing the profiles presented below.

In total, 560 samples of ammunition were included in the data set (see Table 6.1). To ensure consistency between the case studies while enhancing the level of accuracy, recognized ammunition experts cross-checked the entire data set and standardized associated terminology. Although experts made every effort to identify countries of manufacture,

Box 6.1 Identification of small-calibre ammunition

The identification of small-calibre ammunition relies on a variety of components and characteristics (see Figure 6.1). These include:

General characteristics. Different types of cartridges are produced to fulfil different functions. They include ball, soft-point, hollow-point, tracer, incendiary, armour-piercing, and grenade-propelling cartridges, as well as training blanks.

Calibre. Although there are exceptions, the calibre designation of a cartridge is typically determined by measuring the projectile's diameter and the length of the cartridge case–measured from the case head to the case mouth for small-calibre ammunition.

Case type. Cartridges have distinct case types, including rimmed, semi-rimmed, rimless, and belted cases. Most of these can be identified visually, although it can be difficult to differentiate among some varieties.

Case composition. The type of material used in a cartridge case can provide an indication of the factory or country of production. Case materials include brass, copper-clad steel, coated or lacquered steel, aluminium, plastic, and nickeled brass. Brass and copper-clad steel are the most common cartridge case materials.

Headstamp. Cartridges typically feature alphanumeric characters and/or symbols on the case head, which are known as headstamps. These headstamps can provide valuable information about the country of origin, producer, year of production, calibre, and type of cartridge. Exceptionally, they may contain additional information, such as a lot or batch number.

Coloration and markings. Cartridges are marked and coloured in a variety of ways, generally to indicate type or purpose. Occasionally, markings denote a particular brand of ammunition.

Packaging and documentation. Packaging generally consists of outer packaging, such as wooden shipping crates, and inner packaging such as metal tins. Occasionally, smaller units of ammunition may be enclosed in cardboard or plastic packaging. Packaging can provide valuable clues as to the origin, place of production, type, and destination of the ammunition. It may also feature contract numbers, and provide clues as to ports of transit, dates of transfer, and other important information. Documentation, where present, can also provide a wealth of valuable information on the origin, quantities, dates, and ports of shipment involved in an ammunition transfer. In some cases, these documents reference intermediary parties or countries of origin other than the country of original manufacture.

Figure 6.1 **Components of a small-calibre cartridge**

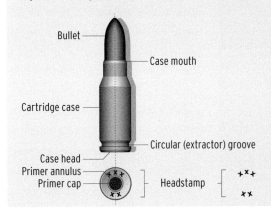

Bullet
Case mouth
Cartridge case
Circular (extractor) groove
Case head
Primer annulus
Primer cap
Headstamp

Sources: figure: Bevan (2008a, p. 3 of the 'Ammunition Tracing Manual' section); text: Jenzen-Jones (2013b, pp. 44–50)

they were unable to interpret the markings on a small number of cartridge cases and, in some cases, faced the complete absence of markings, as discussed below. It is also worth noting that cartridges marked with a specific country code and date of production may in fact have been assembled in a country and at a date distinct from those indicated on the headstamp. This is because headstamp markings may refer to the cartridge case and not necessarily the fully assembled cartridge.

The difficulties inherent in documenting conflict ammunition translate into a number of analytical limitations and potential biases in the data set under review. As previously noted, the unit of analysis—samples—refers to specific types of ammunition and not quantities. Sample size ranges from a single cartridge to several hundreds of thousands. As a result, while one country may have produced a large number of the observed samples of ammunition, these may be small in size and add up to relatively few cartridges. In contrast, one country may have manufactured a single sample of ammunition comprising tens of thousands of identical rounds contained in several crates. Quantifying conflict ammunition is nearly impossible, however, as conflict actors may quickly consume it and constantly need to replenish their stock. The chapter does not pretend to measure quantities of ammunition but seeks to advance knowledge on the main types of ammunition circulating in these areas, supplemented with available information on the quantities involved in relative terms, as available.

The focus of the research was not fully homogenous across the seven countries and territories. Research in South Sudan and Sudan, for instance, focused exclusively on materiel in the hands of non-state armed groups, while data collection in Somalia was centred on ammunition sold at illicit arms markets and in the hands of civilians. In Libya, one data collector homed in on materiel manufactured in Belgium, which allowed for particularly extensive coverage of ammunition produced in that country. Despite these differences, all the encountered types of ammunition were included in the data set. As a result, this chapter offers a strong—and so far unique—basis for analysing ammunition circulating in conflict and post-conflict environments.

AMMUNITION IN CONFLICT: A GENERAL PROFILE

This section presents and compares the general ammunition profiles for the seven countries and territories under review, using calibre, date, and country of manufacture as the key elements of each profile. The section then focuses on the most recently manufactured cartridges, illustrating how the profile of this new ammunition tends to differ from that of the whole data set.

Most of the ammunition samples under review are of Eastern Bloc calibres.

Calibre

Ammunition documented in the seven case studies has 23 different calibres, the distribution of which is presented in Table 6.1. More than three-quarters of the ammunition samples are of Eastern Bloc calibres. In all seven case studies, 7.62 × 39 mm ammunition is the most prominent calibre, accounting for almost half of all the identified samples. The abundance of 7.62 × 39 mm samples is not surprising as these cartridges are used with several weapons common to the countries and territories under study, including a variety of Kalashnikov-pattern assault rifles, as well as RPD- and RPK-pattern light machine guns. Other prominent Eastern Bloc calibres include 7.62 × 54R mm ammunition for use in general-purpose machine guns (such as the PK and PKM and their variants) or rifles (such as the Dragunov or Mosin-Nagant), and 12.7 × 108 mm ammunition for heavy machine guns (such as the DShK and its variants) and anti-materiel rifles (such as the OSV-96).

The most common NATO calibres in the data set are 7.62 × 51 mm, for use with automatic rifles such as the FAL or G3, and 5.56 × 45 mm, compatible with AR-15-pattern and FAMAS assault rifles. While Eastern Bloc calibres feature prominently in all seven case studies, NATO calibres were mainly seen in Côte d'Ivoire and Libya, two countries with a history of ammunition imports from Western countries. France was the main provider of ammunition for Côte d'Ivoire until the 1990s (Anders, 2014, p. 6); Belgium was an important supplier of arms and ammunition for Libya in the 1970s and 1980s as well as in 2008–09 (Jenzen-Jones, 2013a, p. 30; annexe 2; Spleeters, 2013, p. 1; annexes 1–2).

While a large variety of Soviet and NATO calibres are available in Côte d'Ivoire and Libya, the other case studies showed less diversity. The data set includes only four different calibres (Eastern Bloc or NATO standard) in South Sudan and five in Sudan, most likely because, as previously explained, the research there focused on cartridges held by non-state actors who obtain most of their ammunition from a single source—SAF—through battlefield capture or diversion. Only a few calibres were documented in Somalia and Somaliland, primarily because Somalia has been subject to an arms embargo for more than 20 years and its suppliers have tended to deal in a limited range of weapons, mostly of Eastern Bloc standard.

Table 6.1 Number of ammunition samples, by case study and calibre

	Côte d'Ivoire	Libya	Somalia	Somaliland	South Sudan	Sudan	Syria	Total
7.62 x 39 mm	109	17	27	15	18	26	46	258
7.62 x 54R mm	22	9	6	3	14	17	7	78
12.7 x 108 mm	11	6	0	0	3	14	4	38
7.62 x 51 mm	10	16	1	4	0	3	3	37
5.56 x 45 mm	25	3	0	0	1	1	0	30
14.5 x 114 mm	18	9	0	0	0	0	1	28
9 x 19 mm	18	6	0	0	0	0	0	24
7.62 x 25 mm	7	0	4	7	0	0	1	19
7.5 x 54 mm	14	0	0	0	0	0	0	14
12.7 x 99 mm	9	2	0	0	0	0	0	11
12-gauge	0	4	0	0	0	0	2	6
5.45 x 39 mm	3	0	0	0	0	0	1	4
5.7 x 28 mm	0	2	0	0	0	0	0	2
9 x 18 mm	0	1	1	0	0	0	0	2
Other	0	6	0	0	0	0	3	9
Total	**246**	**81**	**39**	**29**	**36**	**61**	**68**	**560**

Note: Samples in this chapter refer to specific types of ammunition–generally characterized by a unique combination of calibre, year of manufacture, and production facility–and do not infer actual quantities.

Table 6.2 Ammunition samples, by year of manufacture (as percentages)

	Côte d'Ivoire	Libya	Somalia	Somaliland	South Sudan	Sudan	Syria	Total
Before 1950	2	1	3	10	0	0	0	2
1950-59	15	0	8	10	0	5	1	8
1960-69	14	5	8	7	0	0	1	8
1970-79	18	35	23	48	31	15	6	21
1980-89	16	26	5	10	6	5	19	15
1990-99	15	2	10	3	3	10	18	11
Since 2000	16	14	38	0	56	64	46	28
n/a	4	17	5	10	6	2	9	7
Total	**100**	**100**	**100**	**100**	**100**	**100**	**100**	**100**

Notes: Totals do not always add up to 100 due to rounding. Samples in this chapter refer to specific types of ammunition–generally characterized by a unique combination of calibre, year of manufacture, and production facility–and do not infer actual quantities.

Year of manufacture

With the exception of a 6.5 × 52 mm Carcano cartridge produced in 1936 and found in Libya, all ammunition samples were manufactured after World War II, between 1946 and 2012. Significantly, more than half (54 per cent) of the identified ammunition samples were produced before 1990 (see Table 6.2). The presence of such a variety of older ammunition demonstrates the extended lifetime of small-calibre ammunition, its potential use in conflicts decades after its date of manufacture, and the possibility of a long chain of custody involving several transfers. Ammunition produced during the cold war features more prominently in some of the countries and territories under review, accounting for all but three of the samples documented in Somaliland and about two-thirds of those seen in Côte d'Ivoire and Libya.

Almost 30 per cent of the ammunition samples in all countries were produced after 2000, pointing to recent supply. This ammunition appears to be particularly prominent in Sudan, accounting for almost two-thirds of the documented samples, as well as—to a lesser extent—in South Sudan, Syria, and Somalia (56, 46, and 38 per cent of cases, respectively).

Country of manufacture

The ammunition samples originated in facilities located in 39 countries. Table 6.3 shows the main producing countries for each case study as well as for the entire data set. Overall, factories located in China and the former Soviet Union (in territory that is now the Russian Federation) manufactured the largest share of the samples under review (19 and 18 per cent, respectively). These two countries were the producers of the largest proportion of samples in all of the case studies under review, with the exception of Libya, where the greatest share of documented ammunition samples originated in Belgium.

Iranian- and Sudanese-produced ammunition circulates in multiple countries in Africa.

While this list of producers comprises mainly countries of the former Eastern Bloc, China, as well as several NATO members, a handful of countries from Africa, and some Middle Eastern states, are also identified. These include Algeria, Egypt, Iran, Israel, Sudan, Syria, Turkey, Uganda, and Zimbabwe. Among the samples, Iranian- and Sudanese-produced ammunition seem most widespread geographically, as they are found in four and five of the seven case studies, respectively. Iranian- and Sudanese-produced cartridges were found in Côte d'Ivoire, South Sudan, Sudan, and Syria—and Sudanese ammunition was also found in Somalia.[6] This finding is consistent with a growing body of evidence showing the presence of Iranian and Sudanese arms and ammunition in multiple countries in Africa (Conflict Armament Research, 2012; Leff and LeBrun, 2014, pp. 44–55). It is also important to note that Sudan and Syria produce their own ammunition, samples of which are documented in the data set. Syrian ammunition was not found outside of Syria, however.

As noted above, the producing countries reported in Table 6.3 did not necessarily transfer ammunition directly to the seven countries and territories under study. A careful examination of authorized ammunition transfers data can reveal instructive correspondences between documented producers and reported exporters, however. France, for instance, reported regular transfers of ammunition to Côte d'Ivoire between 1978 and 1990, in which some of the ammunition samples documented in this chapter and dating from the same time period might have originated. Similarly, some of the recently produced Chinese ammunition found in Sudan may have been transferred as part of China's export of USD 535,500 worth of small arms ammunition that Sudan reported in 2007 (NISAT, n.d.). Iran reported transfers of small arms ammunition to Syria amounting to more than USD 2 million in 1999 and 2000, which may explain the presence of Iranian ammunition produced in 1999 in the Syria case study.

That said, the overlap between producer and exporter data is of little utility for determining the source of the ammunition documented in this chapter. States are under no obligation to report to existing arms transfer databases. Some countries do so on a voluntary basis, while others fail to report part or all of the transfers they authorize.[7] Moreover, states that report their exports may be exporting ammunition produced in other countries. As a result, the correspondence

Table 6.3 Ammunition samples, by country of manufacture (as percentages)

Côte d'Ivoire		Libya		Somalia		Somaliland	
Soviet Union (now Russian Federation)	27	Belgium	26	China	31	Soviet Union (now Russian Federation)	31
France	15	Soviet Union (now Russian Federation)	15	Soviet Union (now Russian Federation)	13	Bulgaria	14
China	7	China	11	Soviet Union (now Ukraine)	13	Hungary	7
Soviet Union (now Kyrgyzstan)	6	Romania	9	Bulgaria	8	Russian Federation	7
Soviet Union (now Ukraine)	6	Russian Federation	5	Sudan	8	Albania	3
Bulgaria	4	Czechoslovakia (now Czech Republic)	4	Uganda	8	China	3
South Africa	4	Bulgaria	2	Russian Federation	5	Czechoslovakia (now Czech Republic)	3
Sudan	4	Italy	2	Algeria	3	Egypt	3
Iran	3	Hungary	2	Poland	3	German Democratic Republic (now Germany)	3
Israel	3	Portugal	2	Federal Republic of Yugoslavia	3	North Korea (presumed)	3
Other	18	Other	15	Other	3	Other	14
n/a	2	n/a	6	n/a	5	n/a	7
Total	**100**	**Total**	**100**	**Total**	**100**	**Total**	**100**

Notes: Totals do not always add up to 100 due to rounding. Samples in this chapter refer to specific types of ammunition–generally characterized by a unique combination of calibre, year of manufacture, and production facility–and do not infer actual quantities.

Open-source databases of authorized small arms transfers indicate that the producing countries in darker grey cells exported ammunition to the countries under consideration at some point between 1962 and 2012 (NISAT, n.d.). Only transfers of a value exceeding USD 10,000, and for which NISAT ranked the sources as highly reliable, were retained in the analysis. The reviewed data includes UN Comtrade

between a reported transfer and a documented ammunition sample, highlighted in a darker grey in Table 6.3, does not necessarily show the direct supply of the case study country by the producing country. In fact, the many ammunition samples that bear no correspondence with authorized trade data underline the lack of such a correlation, emphasizing the need for in-depth research to determine the origins of ammunition found in conflict environments (WEAPONS TRACING).

South Sudan		Sudan		Syria		Total	
China	44	China	56	China	24	China	19
Sudan	22	Sudan	23	Iran or Syria	12	Soviet Union (now Russian Federation)	18
Soviet Union (now Kyrgyzstan)	8	Iran	10	Soviet Union (now Russian Federation)	9	Sudan	7
Bulgaria	6	Israel	3	Syria	9	France	7
Soviet Union (now Ukraine)	6	Soviet Union (now Kyrgyzstan)	3	Sudan	7	Belgium	4
Czechoslovakia (now Czech Republic)	3	Soviet Union (now Russian Federation)	2	Syria (presumed)	6	Bulgaria	4
Iran	3	Soviet Union (now Ukraine)	2	Iran	4	Soviet Union (now Kyrgyzstan)	4
Soviet Union (now Russian Federation)	3	.		Romania	4	Soviet Union (now Ukraine)	4
.		.		Russian Federation	4	Iran	3
.		.		Czechoslovakia (now Czech Republic)	3	Romania	3
Other	0	Other	0	Other	15	Other	24
n/a	6	n/a	2	n/a	3	n/a	3
Total	100	Total	100	Total	100	Total	100

categories 930630 (small arms ammunition) and 930621 (shotgun cartridges), EU category ML3 (ammunition and fuze setting devices, and specially designed components), and small arms ammunition transfers as reported in states' national reports.

The lighter grey cell indicates that, although Belgium did not report these transfers to the above databases, Belgian government and FN Herstal documents published by the Survey show that Belgium exported small arms ammunition to Libya in the 1970s, 1980s, as well as in 2008 and 2009 (Jenzen-Jones, 2013a, annexe 2; Spleeters, 2013, annexe 1).

Box 6.2   Unpacking ammunition supplies: a case study of ammunition packaging in South Sudan and Sudan

Ammunition packaging is powerful evidence that can provide clues as to the origin, factory of production, type, and destination of the enclosed ammunition. It may also reveal information pertaining to the date of transfer and the total quantity of a certain consignment, which helps arms monitors to extrapolate the size of national ammunition stockpiles.[8] This information is often marked on the exterior of the packaging, which generally consists of outer packaging, most often wooden shipping crates, and inner packaging, such as metal tins. In some instances, smaller units of ammunition may be contained in cardboard or plastic packaging inside the shipping crate.

Since ammunition headstamps found in conflict zones often reveal little more than the production facility and year of manufacture, extensive research must be carried out and large data sets created to draw definite conclusions about the chain of custody of any single item or combination of ammunition types. Packaging, on the other hand, may include information on the intended recipient. If this information is missing, arms monitors can sometimes use alternative details, such as unique lot numbers on the packaging, to identify the recipient. If manufacturing states refuse to divulge information on their arms exports, the cross-referencing of similar or identical packaging may prove informative–as illustrated by the following case from Sudan and South Sudan.

In May 2012, the Small Arms Survey documented weapons in South Kordofan state, Sudan. The rebel group Sudan People's Liberation Movement-North (SPLM-N) had captured them from the Sudan Armed Forces during battle earlier that year. Among the cache of weapons were five crates of Chinese-manufactured 7.62 x 54R mm ammunition (see Figure 6.2). Although it was not possible to inspect the contents of the boxes, which were sealed, the construction

of the box and markings on the exterior of the packaging, in particular the contract number ('10XSD14E0128STC/SD'), appeared to indicate that in 2010 ('10') the Xinshidai ('XSD')[9] company of China had signed a contract for the delivery of the ammunition to the Sudan Technical Center ('STC') in Sudan ('SD'). This shipment appears to have been part of a consignment of 6,998 cases–each containing 1,000 rounds and totalling nearly 7 million rounds–of 7.62 x 54R mm ammunition that China supplied to Sudan after 2010.[10]

On a weapons tracing mission in September 2012, the Small Arms Survey documented weapons that the South Sudan Democratic Movement/Army (SSDM/A), a Khartoum-backed rebel group, had handed over to the Sudan People's Liberation Army (SPLA), South Sudan's military, following a peace deal with the Juba government. Among the weapons was one box of 7.62 x 54R mm ammunition with the same contract and total case numbers (see Figure 6.3). This time, the Survey was able to open the crate to inspect the contents. Inside the wooden box were two metal tins, each containing 500 rounds of a commonly observed variety of Chinese-manufactured factory 945 7.62 x 54R mm ammunition, produced in 2010.

Whereas the documentation of one or even 1,000 headstamps of a single type of ammunition can reveal something about the types of ammunition being supplied to a particular country or armed actor, a single crate of ammunition can bring to light something about much larger-scale consignments. When ammunition is delivered to illegal arms markets, brokers and dealers often transport the ammunition in sacks or other types of discreet packaging to conceal it. As a result, original ammunition packaging is unusual to come by in arms bazaars. As noted here, in cases of deliberate supply from state to non-state armed groups, packaging can serve as an important source of information.

Figure 6.2   Ammunition crates held by the SPLM-N, South Kordofan, Sudan, May 2012

© Claudio Gramizzi/Small Arms Survey

Figure 6.3   Ammunition crate and headstamp of the 7.62 x 54R mm cartridges it contained, handed over by the SSDM/A to the SPLA in early 2012, South Sudan, September 2012

© Jonah Leff/Small Arms Survey

Ammunition produced since 2000

The data set includes 156 samples of ammunition identified as having been manufactured since 2000. Examining ammunition of recent manufacture is valuable in that the time between production and the moment the ammunition was found in a conflict environment is relatively short. As a result, it is generally easier, with additional research and documentation, such as packaging information (see Box 6.2), to determine proximate sources and chains of custody than it is for older ammunition, whose ownership may have changed a number of times before finding its way to an armed conflict.

Comparing the profile of the whole data set with that of ammunition produced since 2000 yields some interesting insights. The post-1999 subset comprises only eight types of calibres, compared with 23 for the whole data set. Eastern Bloc calibres dominate the post-1999 subset even more than the overall sample, with 7.62 × 39 mm, 7.62 × 54R mm, and 12.7 × 108 mm samples representing 90 per cent of the subset (see Table 6.4). NATO calibre ammunition represents only 7 per cent of the samples identified as having been manufactured after 1999. This finding suggests a growing demand for Eastern Bloc calibres in recent years; it also accords with increasing proportions of Eastern Bloc weapons in the countries and territories under study.[11]

China dominates the list of producing countries for ammunition manufactured since 2000, with Chinese factories identified as the producers for 37 per cent of these samples (see Table 6.5). In fact, recently manufactured Chinese ammunition was documented in all of the countries and territories under review, barring Somaliland. Sudanese ammunition was also widespread, accounting for 24 per cent of the samples of recent ammunition and found in all of the countries and territories save Libya and Somaliland. Iranian ammunition accounted for about 9 per cent of these samples and was found in four of the seven case studies.[12] Another 14 countries produced the remaining samples, but, overall, China and Sudan stand out as having produced the great majority of the recently manufactured samples of ammunition documented here. As discussed below, Chinese samples tend to involve larger quantities of cartridges than the Sudanese samples.

Table 6.4 **Number of ammunition samples manufactured since 2000, by calibre**							
	Côte d'Ivoire	Libya	Somalia	South Sudan	Sudan	Syria	Total
7.62 x 39 mm	22	6	11	7	14	27	87
7.62 x 54R mm	10	0	3	9	10	3	35
12.7 x 108 mm	3	0	0	3	11	1	18
5.56 x 45 mm	4	2	0	1	1	0	8
7.62 x 51 mm	0	0	0	0	3	0	3
5.7 x 28 mm	0	2	0	0	0	0	2
14.5 x 114 mm	1	1	0	0	0	0	2
9 x 18 mm	0	0	1	0	0	0	1
Total	**40**	**11**	**15**	**20**	**39**	**31**	**156**

Notes: No cartridges with an identified production date in or after 2000 were documented in Somaliland. Samples in this chapter refer to specific types of ammunition–generally characterized by a unique combination of calibre, year of manufacture, and production facility–and do not infer actual quantities.

Table 6.5 Number of samples of ammunition manufactured since 2000, by country of manufacture

	Côte d'Ivoire	Libya	Somalia	South Sudan	Sudan	Syria	Total
China	7	3	7	11	21	8	57
Sudan	10	0	3	8	12	5	38
Iran	7	0	0	1	4	2	14
Iran or Syria	0	0	0	0	0	8	8
Israel	3	0	0	0	2	0	5
Russian Federation	0	4	1	0	0	0	5
Romania	3	0	0	0	0	1	4
Belgium	0	3	0	0	0	0	3
Bulgaria	3	0	0	0	0	0	3
Serbia	3	0	0	0	0	0	3
Syria (presumed)	0	0	0	0	0	3	3
Uganda	0	0	3	0	0	0	3
Czech Republic	2	0	0	0	0	0	2
Algeria	0	0	1	0	0	0	1
Bangladesh	1	0	0	0	0	0	1
Iran (presumed)	0	0	0	0	0	1	1
Kyrgyzstan	0	0	0	0	0	1	1
Spain	0	1	0	0	0	0	1
Syria	0	0	0	0	0	1	1
Ukraine	0	0	0	0	0	1	1
n/a	1	0	0	0	0	0	1
Total	**40**	**11**	**15**	**20**	**39**	**31**	**156**

Notes: No cartridges with an identified production date in or after 2000 were documented in Somaliland. Samples in this chapter refer to specific types of ammunition–generally characterized by a unique combination of calibre, year of manufacture, and production facility–and do not infer actual quantities.

A closer look at the 29 ammunition samples produced in 2010, 2011, and 2012—meaning at most two years before they were found in the conflict environments under review—suggests the growing presence of Sudanese- and Chinese-manufactured ammunition (see Table 6.6).[13] The Military Industry Corporation (MIC) in Khartoum produced 12 of these samples. Chinese-produced cartridges also make up 12 samples, with Iranian, Romanian, Russian, and Ukrainian samples—as well as one attributed to either Iran or Syria—completing the list. Most ammunition samples produced during this period were of 7.62 × 39 mm, 7.62 × 54R mm, and 12.7 × 108 mm calibre. This data shows how little time need pass between the production of ammunition and its entry into conflict zones.

Table 6.6 Spotlight on ammunition samples produced since 2010

Calibre	Country where documented	Headstamp information	Year of production	Country of manufacture	Production facility	Headstamp photo
7.62 x 39 mm	Syria	1_39_012	2012	Sudan	Military Industry Corporation (MIC), Khartoum	© C.J. Chivers (The New York Times)
7.62 x 39 mm	Syria	1_39_12	2012	Sudan	MIC, Khartoum	© C.J. Chivers (The New York Times)
7.62 x 39 mm	Syria	7.62 x 39_12	2012	Romania	Unidentified	© C.J. Chivers (The New York Times)
7.62 x 39 mm	Côte d'Ivoire	1_39_011	2011	Sudan	MIC, Khartoum	© Holger Anders/UNOCI
7.62 x 54R mm	Côte d'Ivoire	1_54_011	2011	Sudan	MIC, Khartoum	© Holger Anders/UNOCI
7.62 x 54R mm	South Sudan	2_54_011	2011	Sudan	MIC, Khartoum	© Small Arms Survey
7.62 x 54R mm	South Sudan	3_54_011	2011	Sudan	MIC, Khartoum	© Small Arms Survey
7.62 x 39 mm	South Sudan	61_11	2011	China	Unidentified	© Small Arms Survey
7.62 x 54R mm	South Sudan	945_11	2011	China	Unidentified	© Small Arms Survey
7.62 x 39 mm	Sudan	2_39_011	2011	Sudan	MIC, Khartoum	© Small Arms Survey
7.62 x 39 mm	Syria	2_39_011	2011	Sudan	MIC, Khartoum	© C.J. Chivers (The New York Times)
7.62 x 39 mm	Syria	7.62 x 39_7_11	2011	Iran	Defense Industries Organization	© C.J. Chivers (The New York Times)
7.62 x 39 mm	Syria	811_11	2011	China	Unidentified	© C.J. Chivers (The New York Times)
7.62 x 54R mm	Syria	945_11	2011	China	Unidentified	© C.J. Chivers (The New York Times)
7.62 x 39 mm	Côte d'Ivoire	1_39_10	2010	Sudan	MIC, Khartoum	© Holger Anders/UNOCI

▶

Calibre	Country where documented	Headstamp information	Year of production	Country of manufacture	Production facility	Headstamp photo
12.7 x 108 mm	Côte d'Ivoire	41_10	2010	China	Unidentified	© Holger Anders/UNOCI
7.62 x 39 mm	Somalia	1_39_10	2010	Sudan	MIC, Khartoum	© Small Arms Survey
9 x 18 mm	Somalia	LVE_10_9mm Makarov	2010	Russian Federation	Novosibirsk Cartridge Plant, Novosibirsk	© Small Arms Survey
7.62 x 39 mm	South Sudan	1_39_10	2010	Sudan	MIC, Khartoum	© Small Arms Survey
12.7 x 108 mm	South Sudan	11_10	2010	China	Mudanjiang North Alloy Tool, Mudanjiang	© Small Arms Survey
12.7 x 108 mm	South Sudan	41_10	2010	China	Unidentified	© Small Arms Survey
7.62 x 54R mm	South Sudan	945_10	2010	China	Unidentified	© Small Arms Survey
12.7 x 108 mm	Sudan	11_10	2010	China	Mudanjiang North Alloy Tool, Mudanjiang	© Small Arms Survey
12.7 x 108 mm	Sudan	41_10	2010	China	Unidentified	© Small Arms Survey
7.62 x 54R mm	Sudan	945_10	2010	China	Unidentified	© Small Arms Survey
7.62 x 39 mm	Syria	1_39_10	2010	Sudan	MIC, Khartoum	© C. J. Chivers (The New York Times)
12.7 x 108 mm	Syria	41_10	2010	China	Unidentified	© C. J. Chivers (The New York Times)
7.62 x 39 mm	Syria	7.62 x 39_7_2010_7	2010	Iran or Syria	Unidentified	© C. J. Chivers (The New York Times)
7.62 x 39 mm	Syria	LCW_10_7.62 x 39	2010	Ukraine	Lugansk Cartridge Works, Lugansk	© Damien Spleeters

Notes: Samples in this chapter refer to specific types of ammunition–generally characterized by a unique combination of calibre, year of manufacture, and production facility–and do not infer actual quantities.

AMMUNITION WITHOUT BORDERS

This section reviews available information on types of ammunition documented in multiple locations, relying on the reporting of data collectors as well as background information shared by a network of arms monitors (see Map 6.1). Overall, there was relatively little overlap in the types of ammunition headstamps found across the case studies, with only six cartridge types found in three or more of the countries and territories under review (see Table 6.7). While more field research is needed to fully interpret this finding, it may indicate limited circulation of ammunition between the conflict zones under review.

Map 6.1 **Selected ammunition found in case study countries and territories**

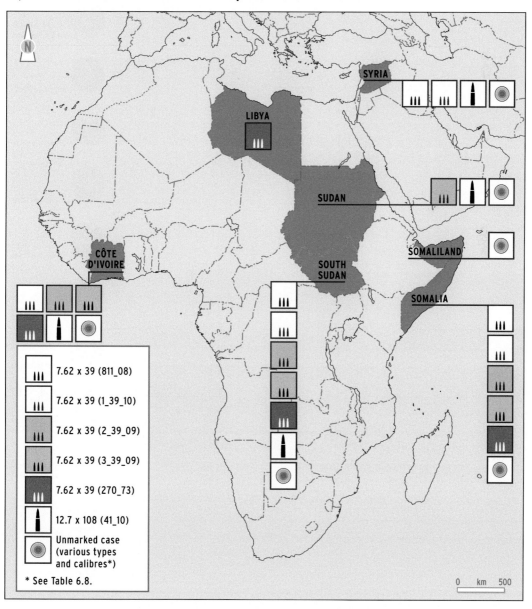

Table 6.7 Specific ammunition headstamps found in three or more countries in the study

Country of manufacture	Headstamp information	Year of production	Production facility	Calibre	Countries where documented	Headstamp photos
China	811_08	2008	Unidentified Chinese manufacturer	7.62 x 39 mm	Somalia	© Small Arms Survey
					South Sudan	© Small Arms Survey
					Syria	© C. J. Chivers (The New York Times)
	41_10	2010	Unidentified Chinese manufacturer	12.7 x 108 mm	Côte d'Ivoire	© Holger Anders/UNOCI
					South Sudan	© Small Arms Survey
					Sudan	© Small Arms Survey
					Syria	© C. J. Chivers (The New York Times)
Sudan	1_39_10	2010	Military Industry Corporation (MIC), Khartoum	7.62 x 39 mm	Côte d'Ivoire	© Holger Anders/UNOCI
					Somalia	© Small Arms Survey
					South Sudan	© Small Arms Survey
					Syria	© C. J. Chivers (The New York Times)
	2_39_09	2009	MIC, Khartoum	7.62 x 39 mm	Côte d'Ivoire	© Holger Anders/UNOCI
					Somalia	© Small Arms Survey

Country of manufacture	Headstamp information	Year of production	Production facility	Calibre	Countries where documented	Headstamp photos
					South Sudan	© Small Arms Survey
					Sudan	© Small Arms Survey
	3_39_09	2009	MIC, Khartoum	7.62 x 39 mm	Côte d'Ivoire	© Holger Anders/UNOCI
					Somalia	© Small Arms Survey
					South Sudan	© Small Arms Survey
Soviet Union (now Ukraine)	270_73	1973	Lugansk Cartridge Works, Lugansk	7.62 x 39 mm	Côte d'Ivoire	© Holger Anders/UNOCI
					Libya	© Damien Spleeters
					Somalia	© Small Arms Survey
					South Sudan	© Small Arms Survey

The overlap that does exist across the seven countries and territories is nevertheless revealing and confirms some of the major patterns discussed above. Four types of cartridge—two of Sudanese manufacture, one Chinese, and one Ukrainian—were found in four of the seven countries and territories under review. Another two types of ammunition produced in China and Sudan appeared in three of the case studies. Interestingly, five of these six types of ammunition were produced in 2008 or later, illustrating the proliferation of some varieties of recently manufactured ammunition across conflict areas. In addition, several types of unmarked cartridges of 7.62 × 39 mm, 7.62 × 54R mm, and 7.62 × 51 mm calibre were found in six of the seven countries and territories (see Table 6.8). While some packaging suggests that certain types of unmarked ammunition were manufactured in Ethiopia, little information is available on the origins of the other unmarked ammunition. The rest of this section analyses the circumstances surrounding some of these samples, revealing a number of ammunition transfer and diversion patterns.

Chinese ammunition

China is one of the world's most significant exporters of small arms, and data for the period 2006–10 suggests that African states account for the largest share of reported imports of Chinese military small arms (Bromley, Duchâtel, and Holtom, 2013, pp. vi, vii, 43). While African states are the recipients of these reported transfers, Chinese small arms ammunition has also been observed with various non-state armed groups on the continent, presumably as a result of diversion, theft, or capture from the recipient states' arsenals.[14] As noted above, Chinese ammunition represents the largest share (37 per cent) of all recently manufactured samples of ammunition in the data set and was documented in all the countries and territories under review.

African states are the main importers of Chinese military small arms.

The most common Chinese sample in the data set is 12.7 × 108 mm ammunition marked '41_10' and produced in 2010. This variety was documented in four states: Côte d'Ivoire, South Sudan, Sudan, and Syria. The largest quantity of '41_10' ammunition was observed with the rebel group Sudan People's Liberation Movement–North (SPLM–N) in South Kordofan and Blue Nile states, Sudan. The SPLM–N acquires the bulk of its weapons from SAF through battlefield capture. Small Arms Survey researchers documented about 2,000 rounds of '41_10' ammunition with fighters in South Kordofan and about 500 rounds with the SPLM–N in Blue Nile in May and December 2012, respectively.[15] In both cases, the ammunition was contained in Sudanese packaging similar to that described below, probably indicating that it had been repackaged after import (Leff and LeBrun, 2014, p. 32). Prior to this research, in May 2011, investigators had documented 50 rounds of the same ammunition alongside matching Sudanese crates at a SAF military camp in East Darfur, Sudan.[16]

Identical ammunition is also present in South Sudan. When the Khartoum-backed South Sudan Liberation Movement/ Army (SSLM/A) accepted an amnesty in April 2013, they crossed from South Kordofan, Sudan, into Unity state, South Sudan, where, in May, the Small Arms Survey viewed their weapons. Among vast quantities of military equipment were about 500 cartridges of '41_10' ammunition. Unlike the samples in Sudan, however, these were contained in Chinese packaging (Leff and LeBrun, 2014, p. 32). In addition, in South Sudan's Unity state in May 2012, the Survey documented dozens of Chinese '41_10' cartridges with the Justice and Equality Movement, which had captured the supply from SAF in February 2012.[17]

Chinese '41_10' 12.7 × 108 mm ammunition was also documented in Côte d'Ivoire in 2011–13 and in Aleppo, Syria, in December 2012. In both cases the sample sizes and users are unclear.

Although not included in the chapter data set, '41_10' ammunition was also previously documented in Somalia. In 2010 and 2011, peacekeepers of the African Union Mission in Somalia (AMISOM) were the sole supplier of ammunition to the beleaguered Somali Transitional Federal Government (TFG). A 2011 report by the UN Somalia and Eritrea Monitoring Group (UN SEMG) states that several sources, including members of the Somali military itself, held that the Somali army sold off one-third to one-half of its ammunition stockpiles. The UN SEMG likewise found 'a strong correlation between the ammunition issued to TFG and pro-TFG militia, ammunition sold in Bakaara market, and ammunition confiscated from Al-Shabaab' (UN, 2011b, p. 231). AMISOM supplied large quantities of '41_10' ammunition to the TFG in 2010 and 2011.

According to the UN SEMG, 41_10 ammunition constituted about 90 per cent of all 12.7 × 108 mm ammunition being sold at the Bakaara market at that time (UN, 2011b, pp. 232–33). Since this ammunition was produced in 2010, only a number of months before it was documented, it is improbable that it would have reached Mogadishu through traditional trafficking channels in such a short period of time. Interviews with several current and former arms dealers in Mogadishu further indicated that the majority of their ammunition, in particular that which was recently manufactured, had been sold to them by Somali forces.[18] Although it is difficult to verify the exact chain of custody of this ammunition, particularly that in the hands of Al Shabaab,[19] it appears plausible that it is, at least in part, the same ammunition that AMISOM transferred to the Somali armed forces.

Chinese-produced Factory 811 7.62 × 39 mm ammunition dated 2008 ('811_08') appeared in Somalia, South Sudan, and Syria. It was the most common ammunition among the 15 types that the UN SEMG documented in Mogadishu between January and April 2011. Not only were tens of thousands of rounds observed at the Bakaara market, but the type was also identified in four separate seizures of ammunition from Al Shabaab, totalling around 1,000 cartridges (UN, 2011b, p. 231). Between May and November 2013, the Small Arms Survey documented '811_08' ammunition with arms dealers in Mogadishu, Somalia, on five separate occasions, totalling more than 1,500 cartridges.

The same type of ammunition was also observed with the South Sudan Democratic Movement/Army (SSDM/A), a Khartoum-backed armed insurgent group led by George Athor in Jonglei state, South Sudan. In early 2011, his forces repeatedly clashed with the Sudan People's Liberation Army (SPLA) in the aftermath of elections in which he was defeated while running for governor of Jonglei state. Among the large quantities of weapons that the SPLA captured from the SSDM/A were several rounds of '811_08' ammunition.[20] In May 2013, war journalist C. J. Chivers documented one '811_08' cartridge that was with an opposition commander in Idlib, Syria.[21]

An Ethiopian police officer in plain clothes overlooks weapons and ammunition seized from Bakaara market as part of a security crackdown, Mogadishu, July 2007. © Mohamed Sheikh Nor/AP Photo

Although these '811_08' cartridges are not included in the data set, investigators also claim to have observed this ammunition in the following contexts:

- with government forces in the Democratic Republic of the Congo (DRC) in 2013;[22]
- used by a non-state armed group in an attack against UN peacekeepers in East Darfur in July 2013;[23]
- in various locations in Niger and Mali in 2013 (UN, 2014, p. 88);[24] and
- at the site of a gun battle between Seleka and anti-balaka combatants in Bossangoa, Central African Republic, where Peter Bouckaert of Human Rights Watch retrieved 17 cartridges on 5 December 2013.[25]

Figure 6.4 **Sudanese packaging for 7.62 x 39 mm ammunition, Côte d'Ivoire, 2013**

© Holger Anders/UNOCI

Sudanese ammunition

Sudan has manufactured small arms ammunition at least since the 1950s (HSBA, 2011, p. 1). Although Sudan's Military Industry Corporation says it produces a full range of small arms ammunition,[26] the Small Arms Survey has documented only Sudanese-manufactured 7.62 × 39 mm, 7.62 × 51 mm, and 7.62 × 54R mm in the countries and territories under review.[27] Sudanese ammunition characteristically bears three- and four-entry headstamp codes, though the Survey's data set primarily includes three-entry cartridges, which are of more recent manufacture than four-entry varieties. Sudan's three-entry headstamp codes are unique in that it appears that the first digit—ordinarily a '1', '2', or '3'—indicates the batch number of the cartridge case production run, the second number the case length, and the third the year of manufacture (Bevan, 2012; HSBA, 2011).

The most common Sudanese-manufactured ammunition recorded in the countries and territories under review was a 7.62 × 39 mm round with the headstamp '1_39_10' with '1' probably denoting the batch, '39' the case length, and '10' the year of manufacture (2010). This type of ammunition was documented, in varying quantities, in Côte d'Ivoire, Somalia, South Sudan, and Syria. The case of Côte d'Ivoire is particularly striking. Sudan reportedly supplied these rounds to the Gbagbo government, with large quantities later diverted to rebels and ultimately civilians in early 2011 (Anders, 2014, pp. 8–9).[28] Tens of thousands of rounds of this ammunition were observed in their original Sudanese packaging, which is distinguishable by its rudimentary construction; a small white label featuring the boxes' contents, dimensions, and date of packaging; and 15 black polyethylene bags, each holding 100 rounds contained inside the box (see Figure 6.4).

Between 2011 and 2013, the Survey also observed large quantities of this ammunition with Khartoum-backed South Sudanese insurgent groups. For example, South Sudan's military, the SPLA, captured more than 150 Chinese-manufactured Type 56-1 assault rifles (similar in construction to various Kalashnikov assault rifles with a folding metal stock) from forces of the SSLM/A in Unity state, South Sudan, in early 2011. The rifles were loaded with a single variety of '1_39_10' 7.62 × 39 mm ammunition, totalling about 4,000 rounds. Subsequently, the Survey documented the same type of ammunition, but in much smaller quantities, with the Khartoum-backed SSDM/A and the South Sudan Defence Forces (SSDF) in Jonglei state, South Sudan, in February 2011 and September 2012, respectively (Leff and LeBrun, 2014, p. 46–47).

Identical cartridges have also appeared in conflicts in Somalia and Syria. In May 2013, for instance, C.J. Chivers documented a handful of '1_39_10' rounds with the Soqour al-Sham rebel group in Idlib, Syria.[29] In August 2013, *The New York Times* reported that Sudan had supplied weapons to rebels in Syria via Turkey with Qatari support (Chivers and Schmitt, 2013). The Survey has been unable to verify whether this ammunition was delivered as part of the consignment of weapons. Only one month later, the Survey documented eight rounds of '1_39_10' ammunition with an arms dealer in Mogadishu, where it was being sold for USD 0.90 per unit. While the UN reported that Sudan supplied a consignment of medium-calibre arms and ammunition to the then Somali TFG in 2010, it remains unclear whether the Sudanese '1_39_10' ammunition seen in Somalia was part of such a direct transfer (Leff and LeBrun, 2014, p. 46; UN, 2013b, p. 289).

A similar type of Sudanese ammunition bearing the headstamp code '2_39_09' has also appeared in Côte d'Ivoire, Somalia, South Sudan, and Sudan. Unlike the '1_39_10' variety, all of the documented '2_39_09' headstamps were poorly marked (see Figure 6.5).[30] In late 2013, large quantities of '2_39_09' began appearing in arms markets in Mogadishu. In July–November, the Survey recorded it with arms dealers on multiple occasions, and in one instance, as described above, documented it with its original Sudanese packaging. Likewise, in 2011, the Survey observed this ammunition among equipment that the SPLA captured from the SSLM/A in Unity state, South Sudan, where it was not possible to photograph it. The Survey also documented a number of '2_39_09' rounds with the SSDF in September 2012 and once with the SSLM/A in May 2013.

A third type of ammunition of the same variety—'3_39_09'—was observed in Côte d'Ivoire, Somalia, and South Sudan. The UN first identified it with pro-Gbagbo forces in Côte d'Ivoire in November 2011. Nearly one year later, the Survey documented a handful of identical rounds with the SSDF in South Sudan. Most recently, in September–November 2013, the Survey recorded more than 400 rounds of '3_39_09' ammunition with arms dealers in Mogadishu (Leff and LeBrun, 2014, p. 47).[31]

Although three-entry Sudanese headstamps are most common in the data set, researchers identified 7.62 × 39 mm rounds with a four-entry headstamp ('SU_1_39_01') in several countries. In this case, 'SU' denotes the country of manufacture (Sudan), '1' possibly the lot number, '39' the case length, and '01' the year of manufacture (HSBA, 2011, p. 5). One sample of this type was collected at the site of an attack on a UN peacekeeping convoy in South Darfur in February 2010. The identity of the perpetrators is unclear.[32] UN monitors documented hundreds of the same type of ammunition in the framework of voluntary weapons and ammunition collection programmes in Côte d'Ivoire (Anders, 2014, p. 9).[33] The rounds were recovered without any packaging. According to another weapons researcher, the same ammunition

Figure 6.5 Sudanese-manufactured 7.62 x 39 mm ammunition that the SPLA seized from the SSLM/A, South Sudan, 2011

© Jonah Leff/Small Arms Survey

was observed in 2009 with Mai Mai armed groups and the Forces Républicaines Fédéralistes in the DRC, yet it is not included in the data set.[34]

Ukrainian ammunition

Ukraine is one of several former Eastern Bloc states that sold off large quantities of surplus weapons and ammunition, largely as a result of military downsizing (Gobinet and Gramizzi, 2011, p. 2; Griffiths and Karp, 2010, p. 213).[35] Among the older varieties in the data set, former Soviet/Ukrainian 7.62 × 39 mm ammunition from the Lugansk Cartridge Works with factory code 270 and produced in 1973 ('270_73') appears particularly common.[36] This ammunition can be distinguished from other types not only because of its production date, but also because it circulates in four of the conflict areas under review: Côte d'Ivoire, Libya, Somalia, and South Sudan.

Ammunition marked '270_73' is readily available in Mogadishu. In June 2013, the Survey documented 200 cartridges of '270_73' ammunition with an arms dealer who was charging USD 0.90 per round. The following month, two separate civilians showed the Survey 170 and 15 '270_73' cartridges, respectively, that they had purchased in Mogadishu. In 2011, the UN SEMG documented large quantities of '270_73' ammunition at the Bakaara market as well as with Al Shabaab, although it did not see any with AMISOM forces (UN, 2011b, p. 231).[37]

In addition to the thousands of rounds of Sudanese-manufactured 7.62 × 39 ammunition that the SPLA captured from the SSLM/A in Unity state, South Sudan, in 2011, the SPLA seized at least one dozen Ukrainian rounds with headstamp '270_73'. It is not clear whether this ammunition was supplied by an external source or whether it belonged to SPLA stockpiles that SSLM/A forces took with them when they defected from the SPLA.[38]

In February 2012 war journalist Damien Spleeters documented a '270_73' cartridge in Tripoli, Libya. It was observed at the site where the loyalist Khamis brigade orchestrated a massacre in August 2011, yet it is not clear who the user was.[39] UNOCI documented about 100 '270_73' cartridges in several locations in Côte d'Ivoire in 2012–13, mainly in the context of arms collection programmes for civilians and former combatants, as well as with government forces.[40]

In 2006–08, the Survey recorded '270_73' ammunition with pastoralists in Kenya, Sudan, and Uganda, yet this type is not included in the data set. In 2013, an investigator observed the same ammunition in Tunisia.[41]

Unmarked ammunition

While the vast majority of ammunition bears markings that provide some information on its origins, Survey research has uncovered several examples of unmarked ammunition—meaning that no information was stamped onto the head of the cartridge, where a headstamp would normally appear—in six of the seven countries and territories under review (see Table 6.8). It is not immediately clear if manufacturers produce unmarked ammunition to conceal its origin or because of a lack of oversight or interest. In any case, the resulting lack of information makes arms monitoring more difficult. Although the Small Arms Survey and associated experts have not been able to identify the origin of several types of unmarked ammunition in the data set, information inscribed on packing slips points to Ethiopia as one of the producers.

Unmarked 7.62 x 39 mm ammunition

The data set includes similar samples of unmarked 7.62 × 39 mm ammunition that were observed in Somalia, South Sudan, and Sudan. Common characteristics include a brass case and red sealant at the primer annulus, which appear to be from the same factory. The ammunition has a flat-bottom bullet rather than a more common boat-tail bullet, and

Unmarked ammunition was uncovered in six of the seven countries and territories under review.

Table 6.8 Headstamp photos and key characteristics of samples of unmarked ammunition

Ammunition characteristics	Calibre	Country or territory where documented	Headstamp photos
Brass cartridge case and red primer sealant	7.62 x 39 mm	Somalia	© Small Arms Survey
		South Sudan	© Small Arms Survey
		Sudan	© Small Arms Survey
Copper-clad steel cartridge case with unevenly applied red primer sealant and yellow neck sealant	7.62 x 54R mm	Côte d'Ivoire	© Holger Anders/UNOCI
		South Sudan	© Small Arms Survey
Brass cartridge case and red primer sealant	7.62 x 54R mm	Somalia	© Small Arms Survey
		South Sudan	© Small Arms Survey
Brass cartridge case and red primer sealant	7.62 x 51 mm	Somaliland	© Small Arms Survey
Brass cartridge case with green primer sealant and three-square-stake primer crimp	7.62 x 51 mm	Syria	© C.J. Chivers (The New York Times)

is Berdan-primed brass.[42] Twenty cartridges are contained in white cardboard inner packaging with blue/purple ink marks. Similar outer packaging—dark green crates (see Figure 6.6)—was found in both South Sudan and Sudan.[43] The outer packaging found in Sudan appears identical to that found with unmarked 7.62 × 54R mm ammunition in Somalia, which also featured packing slips from the Homicho Ammunition Engineering Industry (HAEI) company in Ethiopia (see Figure 6.7).[44] As of January 2014, the HAEI website listed South Sudan and Sudan among its foreign clients (HAEI, n.d.). For these reasons, it appears likely that HAEI also manufactured the unmarked 7.62 × 39 mm ammunition documented in South Sudan and Sudan.

The Survey first documented about 100 rounds of this unmarked 7.62 × 39 mm ammunition in April 2011 among a cache of weapons that the SPLA had seized from the rebel group SSDM/A, which operated under the leadership of George Athor in Jonglei state, South Sudan. One year later in South Kordofan, Sudan, the Survey recorded 1,300 similar rounds in their original packaging, dated 2003, with the SPLM-N, which claimed to have captured the ammunition

Figure 6.6 **Box of unmarked 7.62 x 39 mm ammunition in South Kordofan, Sudan, May 2012**

© Claudio Gramizzi/Small Arms Survey

from SAF. Then, in September 2012, the Survey observed 1,300 rounds of the same ammunition in identical packaging dated 2001 that the SPLA had collected from the SSDM/A in Jonglei state, South Sudan. Two months later, the same ammunition, though in loose form, was observed in Blue Nile, Sudan, once again with SPLM-N troops, who, like their comrades in South Kordofan, claimed to have seized it from SAF. The SPLM-N in Blue Nile also had several boxes identical to those documented in South Kordofan and Jonglei in their possession, but claimed that they were part of their ammunition stockpile, rather than materiel captured from SAF. In July 2013, the Survey documented hundreds of rounds among weapons that the SPLA had seized from the SSDM/A under the leadership of David Yau Yau in Jonglei state, South Sudan. Lastly, the Survey documented four similar unmarked 7.62 × 39 mm cartridges in May 2013 with an arms dealer in Mogadishu, Somalia; in July of the same year, the Survey recorded 50 cartridges with a civilian residing in Mogadishu (Leff and LeBrun, 2014, pp. 65–66).[45]

Unmarked 7.62 x 54R mm ammunition

The data set includes three types of unmarked 7.62 × 54R mm ammunition. The Survey documented 45 rounds of 7.62 × 54R mm ammunition with brass cartridge cases and red primer sealant in the possession of an arms dealer in Mogadishu, Somalia, in May 2013. The same ammunition was again observed in Mogadishu in early 2014; this time researchers documented dozens of green boxes with the unmarked ammunition inside white cardboard boxes (20 cartridges per box) that appear identical to those containing the abovementioned unmarked 7.62 × 39 mm ammunition in South Sudan and Sudan.[46] On the boxes were packing slips identifying the manufacturer as HAEI in Ethiopia (see Figure 6.7).

In July 2013, the Survey observed hundreds of rounds of 7.62 × 54R mm ammunition that the SPLA had captured from Yau Yau's SSDM/A forces in Jonglei, South Sudan. The brass case and red primer sealant of these cartridges appear slightly different from the cartridges found in Somalia, and this ammunition's origin remains unknown.

A third type of unmarked 7.62 × 54R mm ammunition is composed of a copper-clad steel case with unevenly applied red primer sealant and yellow neck sealant.[47] It was observed in both Côte d'Ivoire and South Sudan. Survey researchers saw about 200 rounds of this unmarked ammunition in a box of Sudanese manufacture contained in black polyethylene bags (similar to the Sudanese 7.62 × 39 mm packaging seen in Figure 6.4) during the same April 2011 inspection of weapons that the SPLA had seized from the SSDM/A in Jonglei state, South Sudan, described above.[48] Between May and September 2013, UN monitors documented hundreds of these unmarked 7.62 × 54R mm cartridges in Côte d'Ivoire, alongside Sudanese ammunition, and some inside Sudanese packaging (Anders, 2014, p. 36).[49] Due to the circumstances in which this ammunition has appeared in both Côte d'Ivoire and South Sudan, as well as technical considerations, including their Sudanese packaging and distinctive neck and primer sealants, it appears possible that this type of unmarked 7.62 × 54R mm ammunition is Sudanese-manufactured (Anders, 2014; Leff and LeBrun, 2014).[50]

Unmarked 7.62 x 51 mm ammunition

Although NATO-standard unmarked 7.62 × 51 mm ammunition is not as common as 7.62 × 39 or 7.62 × 54R mm unmarked ammunition, the Survey has documented it in Somaliland, with brass cases and red primer sealant similar to those of the 7.62 × 39 rounds described above. In November 2013, the Survey documented several rounds of this ammunition with an arms dealer in Burao. Further, a 7.62 × 51 mm unmarked headstamp was documented in Idlib, Syria, in September 2012, along with its packaging, which indicated that it originally contained 1,000 cartridges. The cartridge appeared to be of brass alloy, with green sealant at the primer annulus and a three-square-stake primer crimp (Jenzen-Jones, 2014, p.13).

Figure 6.7 **Outer packaging, packing slip, and headstamp of unmarked 7.62 x 54R mm ammunition, Mogadishu, 2014**

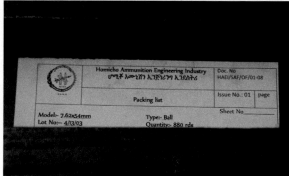

© Confidential source

CONCLUSION

This chapter draws from seven country/territory ammunition profiles to generate a deeper understanding of the types of ammunition circulating in recent conflict and post-conflict areas in sub-Saharan Africa, North Africa, and the Middle

East. Of the ammunition samples under review, more than three-quarters were Eastern Bloc-calibre cartridges, and more than half were produced during the cold war. This highlights the role old stockpiles of small-calibre ammunition continue to play in armed conflict and underlines the relevance of efforts to reduce aging surpluses.

Yet this pattern is shifting markedly, as various other types of ammunition now also circulate in conflict-affected environments. Cartridges manufactured since 2000 were available in all the countries and territories under review barring Somaliland.

As many as 29 samples of ammunition were produced after 2009—meaning at most two years before they were found in the surveyed conflict environments. Chinese and Sudanese ammunition constitute the bulk of the samples of this new ammunition. Domestically produced ammunition is also in use in the battlefields of Sudan and Syria. Overall, the data suggests a more diverse profile for conflict ammunition than was previously assumed.

The country/territory profiles also make it possible to identify single types of ammunition that are circulating in multiple locations. While the data set contains only few such cases, they reaffirmed some of the above findings—such as the seemingly increased importance of Chinese and Sudanese ammunition in conflict-affected situations. They also point to broader patterns of ammunition transfer.

The reported involvement of Sudan in transferring arms and ammunition to several of the case study countries—including Côte d'Ivoire, Somalia, South Sudan, and Syria—is an example that highlights the utility of establishing profiles of conflict ammunition. In fact, in several cases, efforts to map and monitor ammunition over time provided the first evidence of clandestine or destabilizing transfers of specific types of cartridges.

While arms monitors have accorded increasing importance to ammunition in recent years, the presence of unmarked cartridges, in several cases of unknown origin, in most of the conflict zones under review raises new hurdles for monitoring work. As the chapter also points out, patchy reporting by states on their authorized transfers severely limits the utility of existing databases and complicates research on the possible provenance of conflict ammunition. More systematic reporting, data collection, and information sharing, as well as the use of more sophisticated ammunition recognition and tracing techniques, will be critical to improving our understanding—and our ability to track—conflict ammunition in the years to come. ◾

LIST OF ABBREVIATIONS

AMISOM	African Union Mission in Somalia
DRC	Democratic Republic of the Congo
HAEI	Homicho Ammunition Engineering Industry
HSBA	Human Security Baseline Assessment for Sudan and South Sudan
MIC	Military Industry Corporation
SAF	Sudan Armed Forces
SPLA	Sudan People's Liberation Army
SPLM–N	Sudan People's Liberation Movement–North
SSDF	South Sudan Defence Force
SSDM/A	South Sudan Democratic Movement/Army
SSLM/A	South Sudan Liberation Movement/Army
TFG	Transitional Federal Government
UNOCI	United Nations Operation in Côte d'Ivoire
UN SEMG	United Nations Somalia and Eritrea Monitoring Group

ENDNOTES

1   See Bevan (2008a).

2   As a result, the totals in the following tables reflect a limited amount of double counting of specific types of ammunition that are found in more than one country.

3   Information was supplemented by the findings of the UN Groups of Experts concerning Côte d'Ivoire; see UN (n.d.a).

4   In 2013, the Small Arms Survey published a detailed analysis of the prices of arms and ammunition sold at several illicit markets, including in Somalia and Somaliland. See Florquin (2013).

5   To view the reports of the Panel of Experts, see UN (n.d.b).

6   Although this information was not published in time for inclusion in the chapter data set, the UN Panel of Experts on Libya also documented Sudanese-produced ammunition in Libya 'following armed clashes that took place in November 2013 in Tripoli between Tripoli and Misrata brigades' (UN, 2014, para. 82). The cartridges were marked with '2_39_011' and '1_39_12' headstamps, indicating production in 2011 and 2012 (Figures IV and V).

7   For an example of unreported Belgian exports to Libya, see Table 6.3 and the associated note.

8   As portions of any one consignment can be retransferred, reliable estimates remain difficult to establish, however.

9   In a 2013 report, the UN Group of Experts on Côte d'Ivoire notes that the abbreviation 'XSD' refers to the Xinshidai Company (UN, 2013c, para. 48). See also Bevan (2012, p. 13).

10 The contract number on the crate bears the date 2010, which is the year the contract was signed, not necessarily the year that the items were delivered.

11 Author correspondence with two weapons researchers, October 2013.

12 The proportion of Iranian-manufactured ammunition in the data set is probably higher, as experts were not able to determine conclusively whether eight samples of recently manufactured ammunition were of Iranian or Syrian origin, given the similarities in the characteristics of these two countries' ammunition. See Jenzen-Jones (2014, pp. 6–9).

13 A headstamp year indicates the earliest possible date for the assembling of the cartridge. Yet assembly occurs after the case was made and may involve components produced elsewhere, or produced prior to assembly.

14 See Leff and LeBrun (2014, pp. 30–35) and UN (2011a, pp. 20–25; 2011b, para. 103, annexe 5.1) for examples of Chinese ammunition in the possession of non-state actors in Africa.

15 During the same visit, investigators also documented the possession by the SPLM–N of Factory 41 12.7 × 108 mm ammunition produced in 1991, 2006, and 2007.

16 Author correspondence with a weapons researcher, 23 September 2013.

17 HSBA inspection of materiel in South Kordofan, Sudan, and Unity state, South Sudan, in May 2012, and in Blue Nile state, Sudan, in December 2012.

18 The bulk of other ammunition supplies tends to be shipped from Yemen and usually comprises older varieties. Small Arms Survey interviews with Somali arms dealers, Mogadishu, 2011–13.

19 Although Al Shabaab may have relied on several channels for its supply of ammunition, in 2011 it took advantage of the convenience and affordability of the Al Shabaab-controlled Bakaara market. Small Arms Survey interviews with Somali shopkeepers and arms dealers, Mogadishu, 2011–13.

20 HSBA inspection of materiel in Jonglei state, South Sudan, 2011.

21 Author correspondence with N. R. Jenzen-Jones, September 2013.

22 Investigators also documented Factory 811 ammunition produced in 2001, 2006, and 2007. Author correspondence with a former embargo monitor, 23 September 2013.

23 Author correspondence with a weapons researcher, 24 September 2013.

24 Author correspondence with a weapons researcher, 21 September 2013.

25 Author correspondence with Peter Bouckaert, Human Rights Watch, 14 January 2014.

26 See MIC (2014).

27 MIC's website features 7.62 × 39 mm (Maz) and 7.62 × 54R mm (Mokhtar), but not 7.62 × 51 mm ammunition (MIC, 2014).

28 Author correspondence with a weapons researcher, September 2013.

29 Author correspondence with C. J. Chivers, September 2013.

30 Sudanese-manufactured ammunition is known for the poor quality of its headstamps. Headstamps on ammunition produced in 2009 are especially difficult to decipher.

31 HSBA and Small Arms Survey inspections in South Sudan and Mogadishu, September 2012 and September–November 2013, respectively. Although not in the data set, similar varieties of Sudanese ammunition with headstamps '1_39_08', '1_39_07', '2_39_07', and '2_39_06' were documented with M23 rebels in North Kivu, DRC, in late 2013. Author correspondence with a researcher in the DRC, December 2013.

32   HSBA interview with a former member of UN Panel of Experts on Sudan, 25 September 2013.

33   The UN Group of Experts on Côte d'Ivoire also documented this type of ammunition in its 2009 final report (UN, 2009, p. 33).

34   Author correspondence with a weapons researcher, 23 September 2013.

35   An estimated 85 per cent of Ukraine's arsenal became obsolete due to these changes (Gobinet and Gramizzi, 2011, p. 2).

36   In some cases in Mogadishu, headstamps with '270_73' have included a full stop after the '/3 ('/3.').

37   Author interview with a former member of the UN SEMG, 25 September 2013.

38   HSBA inspection of materiel in Unity state, South Sudan, April 2011.

39   Author correspondence with Damien Spleeters, 25 September 2013.

40   Author correspondence with a weapons researcher, 17 December 2013.

41   Author correspondence with a weapons researcher, 21 September 2013.

42   The heads of brass cartridges are manufactured with either berdan or boxed primers.

43   While the colour of the markings differed—yellow on the crates in Sudan, white in South Sudan—experts believe they originate from the same factory. Given the similar construction and colour of the crates, their contents, and the nature of the information provided by the markings, it appears plausible that the boxes with white markings were simply earlier versions of those with yellow markings. Author correspondence with weapons researchers, February 2014.

44   As stated on the HAEI website: 'Established in 1987 as Project 130, the company was designed to build the local manufacturing capacity of ammunition products. In 2010, the company was restructured under the Metals and Engineering Corporation (METEC)' (HAEI, n.d.).

45   The 2012 report of the UN SEMG describes a delivery in October 2010 of 7.62 × 39 mm ammunition dated 2001 to the private security company Saracen International Ltd. in Puntland, Somalia. Although not recorded in the chapter data set, this ammunition was observed in packaging that matched that found with the unmarked 7.62 × 39 mm cartridges retrieved in South Sudan—dark green crates with white markings (UN, 2012, p. 257). A weapons researcher also spotted similar types of unmarked 7.62 × 39 mm ammunition in Tunisia, but without its packaging. Author correspondence with a weapons researcher, 21 September 2013.

46   Author correspondence with weapons researchers, March 2014.

47   Sealant is used to attach the neck of the cartridge to the base side of the bullet.

48   HSBA inspection of materiel in Jonglei state, South Sudan, April 2011.

49   Author correspondence with a weapons researcher in Côte d'Ivoire, September 2013.

50   Author correspondence with a weapons researcher in Côte d'Ivoire, September 2013.

BIBLIOGRAPHY

Anders, Holger. 2014. *Identifying Sources: Small-calibre Ammunition in Côte d'Ivoire*. Special Report. Abidjan and Geneva: United Nations Operation in Côte d'Ivoire and Small Arms Survey.

Bevan, James. 2008a. *Ammunition Tracing Kit: Protocols and Procedures for Recording Small-calibre Ammunition*. Geneva: Small Arms Survey. June.

—. 2008b. *Blowback: Kenya's Illicit Ammunition Problem in Turkana North District*. Occasional Paper 22. Geneva: Small Arms Survey. June.

—. 2012. 'Sudan Ammunition.' Unpublished technical paper. London: Conflict Armament Research. 27 September.

— and Pablo Dreyfus. 2007. 'Enemy Within: Ammunition Diversion in Uganda and Brazil.' In Small Arms Survey. *Small Arms Survey 2007: Guns and the City*. Cambridge: Cambridge University Press, pp. 289–315.

Bromley, Mark, Mathieu Duchâtel, and Paul Holtom. 2013. *China's Exports of Small Arms and Light Weapons*. Policy Paper No. 38. Stockholm: Stockholm Peace Research Institute. October.

Chivers, C. J. n.d. 'The Gun.' Blog. Accessed December 2013. <http://cjchivers.com/>

— and Eric Schmitt. 2013. 'Arms Shipments Seen from Sudan to Syria Rebels.' *The New York Times*. 12 August. <http://www.nytimes.com/2013/08/13/world/africa/arms-shipments-seen-from-sudan-to-syria-rebels.html?pagewanted=all&_r=1&>

Conflict Armament Research. 2012. *The Distribution of Iranian Ammunition in Africa: Evidence from a Nine-country Investigation*. London: Conflict Armament Research. December. <http://www.conflictarm.com/images/Iranian_Ammunition.pdf>

Florquin, Nicolas. 2013. 'Price Watch: Arms and Ammunition at Illicit Markets.' In Small Arms Survey. *Small Arms Survey 2013: Everyday Dangers*. Cambridge: Cambridge University Press, pp. 250–81.

Gobinet, Pierre and Claudio Gramizzi. 2011. *Scraping the Barrel: The Trade in Surplus Ammunition*. Issue Brief No. 2. Geneva: Small Arms Survey.

Griffiths, Hugh and Aaron Karp. 2010. 'Ukraine: Coping with Post-Soviet Legacies.' In Aaron Karp, ed. *The Politics of Destroying Surplus Small Arms: Inconspicuous Disarmament.* New York: Routledge, pp. 208–33.

HAEI (Homicho Ammunition Engineering Industry). n.d. Company website. Accessed 23 January 2014.

<http://www.metec.gov.et/index.php/en/metec-industries/homicho-ammunition-industry>

HSBA (Human Security Baseline Assessment). 2011. 'A Guide to Sudanese Ammunition (1954–Present).' Tracing Desk Report. Geneva: Small Arms Survey. 11 November. <http://www.smallarmssurveysudan.org/fileadmin/docs/facts-figures/arms-ammunition-tracing-desk/HSBA-Sudanese-ammunition.pdf>

Jenzen-Jones, N. R. 2013a. *Following the Headstamp Trail: An Assessment of Small-calibre Ammunition Found in Libya.* Working Paper No. 16. Geneva: Small Arms Survey.

—. 2013b. *The Identification of Small Arms, Light Weapons, and Associated Ammunition: An Introductory Guide.* Unpublished HSBA Training Manual. Geneva: Small Arms Survey.

—. 2013c. *Small-calibre Ammunition in Libya: An Update.* Security Assessment in North Africa Dispatch No. 2. Geneva: Small Arms Survey.

—. 2014. *Known Small-calibre Ammunition in Syria: An Overview.* Geneva: Small Arms Survey.

Jorian, Serge and Philippe Regenstreif. 1995. *Culots de Munitions Atlas,* Vol. II. Toulouse: Cépaduès-Editions.

Leff, Jonah and Emile LeBrun. 2014. *Following the Thread: Tracing Arms and Ammunition in Sudan and South Sudan.* HSBA Working Paper No. 32. Geneva: Small Arms Survey.

MIC (Military Industry Corporation). 2014. 'Ammunitions.' Company website. Accessed 13 January 2014.

<http://www.mic.sd/idex/en/products/ammunitions>

NISAT (Norwegian Initiative on Small Arms Transfers). n.d. 'Small Arms Trade Database' Oslo: NISAT. Accessed 12 February 2014.

<http://legacy.prio.no/pd/GenericPage.aspx?id=134>

Spleeters, Damien. 2013. *FAL Rifles in Libya: A Guide to Data Gathering.* Security Assessment in North Africa Dispatch No. 1. Geneva: Small Arms Survey.

UN (United Nations). 2009. *Final Report of the Group of Experts on Côte d'Ivoire Pursuant to Paragraph 11 of Security Council Resolution 1842 (2008).* S/2009/521 of 9 October 2009.

—. 2011a. *Report of the Panel of Experts on the Sudan Established Pursuant to Resolution 1591 (2005).* S/2011/111 of 8 March 2011.

—. 2011b. *Report of the Monitoring Group on Somalia and Eritrea Submitted in Accordance with Resolution 1916 (2010).* S/2011/433 of 18 July.

—. 2012. *Report of the Monitoring Group on Somalia and Eritrea Pursuant to Security Council Resolution 2002 (2011).* S/2012/544 of 13 July.

—. 2013a. *Final Report of the Panel of Experts in Accordance with Paragraph 10(d) of Resolution 2040 (2012).* S/2013/99 of 15 February.

—. 2013b. *Report of the Monitoring Group on Somalia and Eritrea Pursuant to Security Council Resolution 2060 (2012): Somalia.* S/2013/413 of 12 July.

—. 2013c. *Midterm Report of the Group of Experts Submitted in Accordance with Paragraph 19 of Security Council Resolution 2101 (2013).* S/2013/605 of 14 October.

—. 2014. *Final Report of the Panel of Experts Established Pursuant to Resolution 1973 (2011) Concerning Libya.* S/2014/106 of 15 February.

—. n.d.a. 'Reports of the Group of Experts Submitted through the Security Council Committee Established Pursuant to Resolution 1572 (2004) Concerning Côte d'Ivoire.' <http://www.un.org/sc/committees/1572/CI_poe_ENG.shtml>

—. n.d.b. 'Reports of the Panel of Experts Submitted through the Security Council Committee Established Pursuant to Resolution 1591 (2005) Concerning the Sudan.' <http://www.un.org/sc/committees/1591/reports.shtml>

ACKNOWLEDGEMENTS

Principal authors

Nicolas Florquin and Jonah Leff

Contributors

Holger Anders, Alex Diehl, N. R. Jenzen-Jones, and Phoebe Brundle

Red Arrow 8 anti-tank guided missiles captured by the
Sudan People's Liberation Movement-North (SPLM-N)
from the Sudan Armed Forces, South Kordofan, Sudan,
December 2012. © Alan Boswell

Signs of Supply

WEAPONS TRACING IN SUDAN AND SOUTH SUDAN

7

INTRODUCTION

The second civil war (1983–2005) between the Government of Sudan (GoS) and the Sudan People's Liberation Movement/Army (SPLM/A) led to the secession of South Sudan, in July 2011, but not to an end to armed conflict within or between the two countries. From 2010 to late 2013, a number of anti-government militias were engaged in vigorous insurgencies in South Sudan, while separate branches of the SPLM–North (SPLM–N) were fighting a rebellion on two fronts in the Sudanese states of South Kordofan and Blue Nile. The SPLM–N also established an alliance with armed opposition groups in Darfur, which continue their campaigns despite peace agreements signed in 2006 and 2011.[1]

None of these opposition forces could pose a threat without access to small arms and light weapons and ammunition. Yet, while the Small Arms Survey and others have documented the role of weapons in the multiple conflicts involving Sudan and South Sudan over the past ten years, details related to the specific types of materiel, their sources, and possible pathways into the hands of non-state armed actors have been slow to emerge.

To address this information gap, the Small Arms Survey's Human Security Baseline Assessment (HSBA) for Sudan and South Sudan launched the Arms and Ammunition Tracing Desk in 2011. The project's goals are to (a) refine previous estimates of the numbers and types of weapons held by various actors through focused field research; (b) apply tracing techniques employed by UN expert panels and other official bodies to investigate the origins and possible sourcing routes of weapons and ammunition; and (c) promote best practices for the identification and tracing of arms and ammunition in Sudan and South Sudan among all interested stakeholders.

This chapter provides an overview of the project's findings with regard to the types of weapons observed among non-state armed actors—including rebels and tribal groups—their origins, and proximate sources. It synthesizes the findings of more than two years of fieldwork and follow-up investigations initially published in periodic web-based reports. Key findings include the following:

- The systematic identification and tracing of small arms, light weapons, and their associated ammunition have uncovered patterns of illicit arms supply to non-state groups in Sudan and South Sudan.
- Non-state armed groups in Sudan and South Sudan have access to a variety of types and quantities of arms and ammunition, including civil war-era weapons, as well as newer Chinese and Sudanese weapons and ammunition.
- Investigators have documented newer (post-2000) Sudanese-manufactured small- and medium-calibre ammunition in large quantities among non-state armed groups in Sudan and South Sudan.
- GoS stockpiles are the primary source of weapons to non-state armed groups of all allegiances in Sudan and South Sudan, through deliberate arming and battlefield capture.
- Direct military contributions from Sudanese security forces represent the majority of weapons and ammunition documented among South Sudanese insurgent groups.

- Investigations reveal that South Sudanese armed groups are in possession of an increasing number of weapons whose factory marks and serial numbers have been removed, a tactic designed to undermine identification and tracing.
- By responding to information requests from investigators, exporting states have shown a willingness to cooperate in the process of weapons and ammunition tracing in conflict zones.

This chapter begins by describing the context and need for arms tracing in Sudan and South Sudan and the working methods of the HSBA tracing project. It then presents the project's overall findings on the sources of arms documented in the hands of non-state actors, their commonalities across groups, and likely patterns of supply.

'POST-CONFLICT' SUDAN AND SOUTH SUDAN

Civil war and its aftermath

In 2013, the GoS was fighting two conflicts within its territory.

In December 2009 the Small Arms Survey estimated that Sudan and South Sudan contained some 2.7 million small arms and light weapons, more than two-thirds of which were in the hands of non-state actors, including civilians, rebel groups, and tribal militias (Small Arms Survey, 2009, p. 8). Widespread arms proliferation among non-state actors has long been identified as a critical factor leading to the outbreak and escalation of armed violence and conflict in Sudan and South Sudan.

During the second civil war (1983–2005) and during the six-year interim period following the Comprehensive Peace Agreement (2005), older weapons continued to circulate, but new inflows clearly persisted. In most cases, arms appeared to arrive in Sudan as the result of transfers approved by countries of export.[2] But some of those weapons were eventually retransferred illicitly within the country (to Darfur, in violation of the UN arms embargo) or across the Southern border to non-state armed groups, such as tribal militias and insurgent forces, to further the Sudanese government's political and military goals (Lewis, 2009; Small Arms Survey, 2009; 2012a). Meanwhile, the SPLA and other insurgent forces obtained weapons from both battlefield capture and external supply, occasionally passing some on to tribal militias. Yet, on these points and others concerning overall arms acquisitions by state and non-state forces, there was much speculation and little evidence.

Since South Sudan's independence in 2011, renewed armed conflict has erupted on both sides of the Sudan–South Sudan border. In 2013, the GoS was fighting two conflicts within its territory. The first pitted the GoS against a coalition of armed opposition groups in Darfur; the second erupted in the border states of South Kordofan and Blue Nile, where Khartoum took on indigenous rebels who maintain some ties with South Sudan and who recently allied themselves with Darfur's main rebel groups (see Table 7.1). The current conflicts in South Kordofan and Blue Nile have been described as new phases of a 'previous, partially unresolved conflict' of the second civil war (Gramizzi, 2013, p. 11).

After more than a decade of rebellion, proxy arming, and shifting alignments between the GoS and both Arab and non-Arab populations in the region, the Darfur conflict continues despite two peace agreements—the Darfur Peace Agreement of 2006 and the Doha Document for Peace in Darfur of 2011. While the conflict has evolved since 2003, widespread violence, massive displacement, and aerial bombardment remain dominant themes. From January to August 2013, new violence displaced nearly 300,000 people, more than in the two previous years combined (OCHA, 2013).

During Sudan's civil war, much of the fighting took place in the South, with both sides arming Southern militias. The rebellion split numerous times, with some factions returning to the government only to rebel once again. In the latter phases of the war, much of the conflict was intra-Southern, with pro-government fighting conducted by a patchwork of Khartoum-supported Southern commanders and militias.

Table 7.1 Selected non-state armed groups in Sudan and South Sudan, as of late 2013

Region or state	Armed group	Location	Strength	Status as of November 2013
Darfur, Sudan	Justice and Equality Movement (JEM)-Darfur	North-western to south-eastern Darfur	100 vehicles	Active
	Sudan Liberation Army-Minni Minawi (SLA-MM)	South Darfur (including east Jebel Marra and Nyala area), East Darfur, North Darfur	250 vehicles	Active
	Sudan Liberation Army-Abdul Wahid (SLA-AW)	Jebel Marra, North Darfur	50 vehicles, ability to mobilize foot soldiers	Active
South Kordofan, Sudan	SPLM-N 1st Division	Southern Nuba Mountains, South Kordofan	<20,000 troops	Active
	JEM-South Kordofan	Moving between SPLM-N-controlled areas in the Nuba Mountains and Missiriya areas in West Kordofan, as well as northern Abyei	150 vehicles	Active
Blue Nile, Sudan	SPLM-N 2nd Division	The SPLM-N controls the southern part of Blue Nile from Deim Monsour in the east to the Upper Nile border west of Kubra	<10,000 troops	Active
Greater Upper Nile, South Sudan*	South Sudan Democratic Movement/Army (SSDM/A)-Athor**	Jonglei	No active troops	Athor killed in December 2011; his troops were integrating into the SPLA as of late 2013
	SSDM/A-Yau Yau	Pibor county, Jonglei	500–1,000 core troops; can mobilize 3,000–6,000 Murle youths	Active
	SSDM/A-Olony***	Fashoda county, Upper Nile, with affiliates in South Kordofan, Sudan	<3,000 troops	Negotiating integration
	South Sudan Defence Forces (SSDF)	Multiple factions co-located in rear bases in Bwat, Blue Nile, Sudan	<1,000 troops	Active
	South Sudan Liberation Movement/Army (SSLM/A)	In Mayom, Unity, awaiting integration	<3,000 troops	Accepted amnesty; negotiating integration
	Lou Nuer (White Army)	Jonglei	Can mobilize up to 8,000 troops	Active
	Murle militia	Jonglei	Usually attack in small groups	Active

Notes:

* The Greater Upper Nile region of South Sudan includes Jonglei, Unity, and Upper Nile states.

** Although Athor's faction is no longer active, it is included here because of its importance in the development of the more recent branches of the SSDM/A (Yau Yau and Olony).

*** Also known as the SSDM/A-Upper Nile faction.

Sources: Gramizzi (2013, pp. 40-44); Gramizzi and Tubiana (2013, pp. 27-32); Small Arms Survey (2013b, p. 2)

Map 7.1 **Non-state armed groups and conflict zones, Sudan and South Sudan, 2013**

Armed groups		
SLA-AW/MM	SSDM/A-Olony	Conflict zone
JEM	SSDM/A-Athor	African Union-proposed border
SPLM-N	SSDM/A-Yau Yau	International boundary
SSLM/A	Lou Nuer (White Army)	Abyei
SSDF	Murle militia	National capital
		State boundary

Icons are not intended to specify precise locations of armed groups

Following the Comprehensive Peace Agreement, President Salva Kiir of South Sudan attempted to persuade rival militia commanders and their forces to integrate into the Southern army. Many commanders took advantage of the generous packages offered during the Agreement's six-year interim period. But following national and state-level elections in 2010, and in the lead-up to official Southern independence, a new generation of militia leaders emerged (see Table 7.1).

In September 2013, the SPLA was attempting to contain insurgencies in Greater Upper Nile while simultaneously working to integrate the forces of other commanders who had accepted amnesty, surrendered, or died. In December 2013 and January 2014, however, dynamics among Southern militias appeared to shift after widespread civil conflict erupted between President Kiir of South Sudan and political opposition leader Riek Machar, with the latter drawing a number of dissident commanders, as well as thousands of SPLA soldiers, to his side. This chapter does not reflect the evolution of this conflict beyond late 2013.

Map 7.1 shows conflict zones in Sudan and South Sudan as well as the non-state actors involved in the conflicts as of September 2013.

SPLA-N fighters watch over ammunition and weapons captured from the Sudan Armed Forces, near Gos village in the Nuba Mountains, South Kordofan, Sudan, May 2012.
© Goran Tomasevic/Reuters

The legal context for arms imports[3]

The Darfur region of Sudan is subject to a United Nations arms embargo, first established in July 2004 in response to an international outcry over the humanitarian impact of the conflict there (UNSC, 2004). The resolution demanded that the GoS 'fulfil its commitments to disarm the Janjaweed militias' (para. 3) and established a ban on supplies of arms and related materiel to 'non-governmental entities and individuals, including the Janjaweed' (para. 7) operating in North, South, and West Darfur. By referring to 'janjaweed', the Security Council intended to include GoS-supported groups, but the vague phrasing allowed the GoS to argue that the embargo did not cover state-backed militias. A March 2005 resolution established mechanisms for monitoring compliance with the embargo (UNSC, 2005).

Nevertheless, as the Small Arms Survey reported in 2012, 'all sides in the Darfur conflict have continued to gain access to military resources' and the embargo was violated 'openly, consistently, and without consequence' (Small Arms Survey, 2012b, p. 10). The Survey found that the embargo's 'limited geographical scope, covering only the Darfur states, has for the last seven years allowed international suppliers (state and commercial) to furnish arms and assistance to the GoS entirely legally, despite clear evidence that the GoS is moving the arms rapidly and continually into Darfur' (Small Arms Survey, 2012b, p. 10).

The Council of the European Union (EU) integrated the UN sanctions into its existing regime of restrictive measures on Sudan, which had first been imposed in March 1994 (CEU, 1994; 2004; 2005). The EU embargo covers the entirety of Sudanese territory rather than just the Darfur states. Following the independence of South Sudan, the EU embargo was extended to the new state, such that it could maintain its original geographic coverage (CEU, 2011).

Figure 7.1 **Annual imports of small arms and light weapons, their ammunition, and 'conventional weapons' reported by Khartoum to UN Comtrade, 2001–12 (USD millions)**

■ Small arms and light weapons and their parts   ■ Small arms and light weapons ammunition
■ Conventional weapons   ■ Annual totals

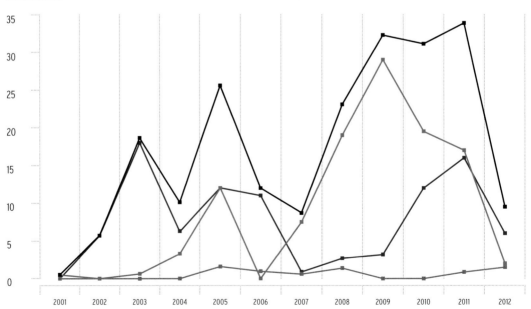

USD MILLIONS

Sources: El Jamali (2013); UN Comtrade data provided by the Peace Research Institute Oslo

In contrast, in January 2012, US President Barack Obama lifted restrictions on the supply of defence materiel to South Sudan, stating that this would 'strengthen the security of the United States and promote world peace' (White House, 2012). US State Department officials indicated that the government was in discussions with the South Sudanese about how to 'secure their borders' and 'defend themselves', but that the United States had no immediate plans to approve the transfer of lethal equipment (Reuters, 2012). As of late 2013, this remained US policy.[4]

Reported Sudanese arms imports

For the period 2001–12, Khartoum's reports to the United Nations Commodity Trade Statistics Database (UN Comtrade) reveal significant fluctuation in annual conventional arms imports (see Figure 7.1). The aggregate total values increased steeply—from less than USD 1 million in 2001 to almost USD 34 million in 2011, with a drop to less than USD 10 million in 2012. 'Conventional weapons'[5] represented more than half of the total value imported over the entire period (52 per cent). Small arms and light weapons and their parts represented 44 per cent of the total, and small arms and light weapons ammunition were 3 per cent of the total over the period.

The majority of the Sudanese government's total self-reported imports of small arms and light weapons, their ammunition, and 'conventional weapons' over the period originated in China (58 per cent), followed by Iran (13 per cent), St. Vincent and the Grenadines[6] (9 per cent), and Ukraine (8 per cent).

As of late 2013, South Sudan had not reported any arms imports to UN Comtrade.

> Sudan's reported conventional arms imports fluctuated significantly from 2001 to 2012.

WEAPONS TRACING IN SUDAN AND SOUTH SUDAN

The HSBA Tracing Desk

The tracing of weapons in conflict and post-conflict settings serves to 'monitor potentially escalatory influxes of weapons and to investigate particular cases of concern' (Bevan, 2009, p. 109). As noted above, the HSBA Arms and Ammunition Tracing Desk launched in September 2011. During its first year, the Tracing Desk produced an *Issue Brief* on weapons documented in the hands of Southern insurgent groups (Small Arms Survey, 2012a); it also established regular web-based reporting on arms and ammunition tracing fieldwork conducted in South Sudan and the Sudanese border areas. Eighteen such reports were released through September 2013.[7]

In its tracing work, the HSBA applies a multi-step process of *identification*, *mapping*, and *verification* of arms and ammunition, as described below.

The HSBA tracing process
Identification

Identification involves recording the make, model, and unique identifying characteristics and markings of each weapon, round of ammunition, and weapons- or ammunition-bearing container or vessel (such as ammunition crates). Models in widespread circulation, such as AK-pattern assault rifles, can often be distinguished from one another only after close physical inspection and with particular attention to one or two specific features, such as the type of buttstock and muzzle attachment (see Figure 7.2) and marking position (see Figure 7.3). Essential information for investigators includes the model, marks designating the manufacturer, the serial number, import marks, and proof house marks—some or all of which suppliers or users may attempt to remove or obscure (see Box 7.1). When feasible, field investigators photograph weapons and ammunition markings for entry in the databases used for mapping.

Figure 7.2 **Identifying features of a modern military rifle**

Source: reproduced from Jenzen-Jones (2013, p. 9)

Figure 7.3 **Positions of identifying marks on AK-pattern weapons**

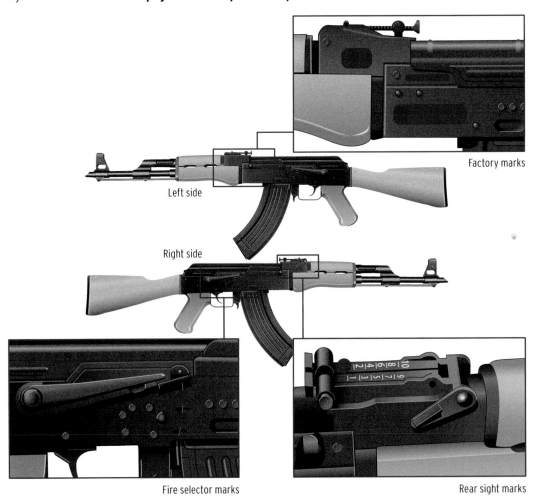

Source: reproduced from Conflict Armament Research (2012a, p. 6)

Mapping

Arms and ammunition mapping is a powerful tool that the HSBA uses to illuminate patterns in holdings and procurement across different actors in Sudan and South Sudan. It relies on custom-built data sets of arms and ammunition, which incorporate the identifying markings, quantities, locations, and circumstances of documented arms and ammunition, linked to photographs taken by field researchers. The HSBA data sets now include information from dozens of arms caches observed by researchers, representing many thousands of weapons and significant quantities of ammunition.

Mapping involves, therefore, the cross-referencing and analysis of separate samples of arms and ammunition. It allows researchers to identify trends and patterns as data sets grow, and ultimately leads to a better understanding of the types of arms and ammunition that armed groups have in their stockpiles. Over time, it becomes possible to draw conclusions about the chain of custody of particular materiel. For instance, matching lot numbers of ammunition found in the stockpiles of several armed groups may indicate the same source-to-recipient pattern of supply. Likewise, a new variety of rifle never before observed in Sudan or South Sudan in the hands of two geographically distinct rebel groups may point to a single source.

Verification

In verifying its weapons and ammunition data, the HSBA confirms its initial findings by using, first, a number of official, published sources of information, including:

- national arms export reports, provided by a government on its initiative or pursuant to multilateral arms control agreements;

Box 7.1 Serial number and factory mark removal in Sudan and South Sudan: a new trend?

In 2009, arms investigator James Bevan wrote:

> [I have] viewed many thousands of military weapons, held by numerous parties to armed conflict, and have found few weapons that were not marked with a serial number (however faded or damaged). Reviews of thousands of weapons collection records also suggest that the intentional removal of serial numbers is uncommon in the context of armed conflict. The probable reason is that, in contrast to crime situations in which criminals (notably illegal sellers) may fear discovery by law enforcement officials, most combatants have little reason to believe that their weapons will be subject to investigation (Bevan, 2009, p. 131, n. 12).

When the HSBA began tracing arms and ammunition in 2011, its investigators also noted that very few of the encountered weapons had intentionally removed markings. Yet, in 2013, by which time the HSBA had gathered compelling evidence that the GoS was arming Southern rebels, investigators were observing an increasing number of rebel-held weapons whose markings (serial numbers and factory markings) had been removed. Most obliterated markings had been ground out manually, probably with a grinder or a mill, which are typically used in criminal contexts. The obviously visible markings were removed, while marks that were harder to observe or reach were untouched. According to several rebel defectors, markings on their weapons had already been removed when they received them from Sudanese security officers.

Without a serial number or factory mark, investigators cannot uniquely identify a weapon.[8] But other clues–such as remaining markings and possibly unique model characteristics, as well as the location of the weapon and the other weapons and ammunition with which it was seen–may provide important contextual information. The fact that a weapon's markings have been intentionally removed is also itself an important detail; it is a clear red flag–evidence that at least one party found it necessary to obscure the weapon's indentifying features. For this reason alone, the HSBA has made it a point to document all weapons with intentionally removed markings. Over time, documentation of these weapons will almost certainly reveal patterns of interest to investigators.

A CQ rifle, with its markings removed, handed over by SSDM/A-Yau Yau defectors to the SPLA, Jonglei, South Sudan, February 2013. © Judith McCallum

- publicly available trade databases such as UN Comtrade, the UN Register of Conventional Arms, and the Stockholm International Peace Research Institute's Arms Transfers Database; and

- qualitative data, including media and research reports.

Second, the verification process relies on information culled from interviews with respondents in the field and beyond—such as military commanders, rebel representatives, local community members with specific knowledge, government officials, and arms show representatives. Testimony from such key informants can provide essential contextual information to help corroborate or discount other interpretations of the data. Given the possibility of receiving false, misleading, or incomplete information, project investigators independently corroborate and cross-check testimony.

The third source of information used in data verification involves responses to written inquiries and information requests to exporting governments, manufacturers, and transport companies. The requests detail the type of weapon(s) observed, identifying markings, and the circumstances under which the weapon was observed. They typically seek information such as:

Box 7.2 Tracing cooperation

Since the HSBA tracing project began, it has received positive cooperation from many government agencies and companies, although responses have varied in usefulness (see Table 7.2). For example, exporters can rightfully or wrongfully deny that they produced an item, state that they no longer have records for its sale, or, in contrast, confirm that they manufactured an item and supplied it to a specific country. In some instances, particularly with companies that have been involved in the supply of dual-use items such as 4x4 vehicles,[9] information may be provided about a third party that is in some way involved in the transaction.

Government agencies responded to initial information requests in 12 of 18 cases. In 9 of 12 responses, governments provided 'useful' information that either helped to confirm that an item was supplied to a specific destination or provided information that required sending a new request to another government or company. Three other 'somewhat useful' responses included partial answers or referrals to other parties.

The relatively positive picture presented here hides an important caveat. According to UN panel reports, most major arms exporters that supply Sudan have failed to respond to information requests of this type (UNSC, 2009, p. 80; 2011a, pp. 26-28; Gramizzi, Lewis, and Tubiana, 2012, pp. 22-23). There are indications, however, that China–one of Sudan's top suppliers–recently began to cooperate more closely with UN panels.[10]

The HSBA has also sent 23 inquiries to companies–including manufacturers, shipping agencies, maintenance companies–often focusing on military vehicles or commercial 4x4 vehicles that have been converted into 'technicals' by military forces or armed groups. In some cases, potential embargo violations were investigated. Of the 11 responses received from companies to date, nine helped to confirm the export of equipment or services to a specific party. The presence of 4x4 technicals equipped with heavy machine guns in the possession of the SPLM-N in South Kordofan prompted the HSBA to improve its understanding of the supply routes of these vehicles to Sudan, including the place of their conversion from civilian to military use.

- confirmation that a weapon was manufactured in the country of export;
- date of manufacture;
- date of export;
- information on the intended end users;
- transporter/shipper;
- broker information, if applicable;
- confirmation that an export licence was required and obtained for the export to proceed; and
- information on possible resale or retransfer of the weapon(s).

Table 7.2 **HSBA inquiries sent to exporting states**				
State	**Number of inquiries submitted**	**Number of responses, by type**	**Unanswered inquiries**	**Comments**
Belgium	1	1 somewhat useful	0	Referred to the Dutch Ministry of Economic Affairs.
Bosnia and Herzegovina	1	0	1	
Bulgaria	5	4 useful 1 somewhat useful	0	Confirmed that 82 mm mortars were supplied to Ethiopia in 1999; 23 mm ammunition was supplied to Uganda in 2010; weapons and technology were transferred to Sudan in the late 1990s.
Croatia	1	0	1	
Czech Republic	1	1 useful	0	Noted that ammunition was produced in present-day Slovakia.
Germany	3	2 useful	1	Provided information on the supply of vehicles to Sudan and the production of Heckler & Koch G3 rifles.
Netherlands	1	1 useful	0	Provided information on the export of 4x4 vehicles to Port Sudan.
Serbia	1	0	1	
Slovakia	1	1 somewhat useful	0	Confirmed manufacture of 100 mm ammunition, but provided no records on the item in question because it was more than 30 years old.
South Korea	1	0	1	
Ukraine	1	0	1	
United States	1	1 useful	0	Confirmed supply of 106 mm ammunition to Sudan in 1980.
TOTALS	**18**	**12** (9 useful, 3 somewhat useful)	**6**	

HSBA information requests do not assert any wrongdoing or impropriety on the part of the exporting state, company, or individual. Nor are exporting agencies or private companies under any legal obligation to provide this information to investigators. In many cases, however, respondents do so willingly as a matter of cooperation and transparency (see Box 7.2).

The HSBA employs tools and techniques that emerged from UN panel investigations of embargo violations and illicit transfers. The recent 'privatization' of arms and ammunition tracing, conducted by experts and supported by donors, also shows strong potential in this field. A number of conditions are probably necessary for the successful replication of this work, however, including: the independence and reliability of the field researchers; strong relationships with official forces; and the willingness of governments to open up to scrutiny activities that are sometimes deliberately obscured.

Working methods

Tracing requires, first and foremost, field-based observations of weapons and ammunition. The HSBA personnel and consultants who conduct these field investigations have expertise in weapons and ammunition identification and tracing and have served on UN panels of experts in Côte d'Ivoire, Darfur, the Democratic Republic of the Congo, Somalia, and elsewhere.[11]

The decision about *where* to conduct tracing fieldwork is based on a range of factors, including:

- Relevance: Are the suspected weapons associated with a particular conflict or are or were they held by actors who are strongly linked to armed violence or insecurity?
- Authorization: Can permission be obtained to view the weapons and speak to key informants?
- New research area: Is the weapons cache associated with an actor or conflict that the HSBA has not yet investigated?
- Staffing: Is a qualified arms and ammunition investigator available to conduct the fieldwork?
- Accessibility: Can the site be reached by commercial flights, private vehicle hire, or UN escort?
- Safety: Will investigators be protected from insecurity?

Since 2011, the HSBA Tracing Desk has conducted 14 tracing missions in the South Sudanese states of Jonglei, Unity, Upper Nile, and Western Bahr al Ghazal, as well as in Blue Nile and South Kordofan, Sudan. Fieldwork investigations would not be possible without considerable trust and cooperation offered by numerous actors in the chain of command of the SPLA and the Government of South Sudan. Over the eight years of its work, the HSBA has built positive relationships with key South Sudanese lawmakers and military personnel, while continuing to maintain independence and editorial control over its publications.[12]

An SSLM/A fighter with mounted DShKM-type machine gun after accepting amnesty in Unity state, South Sudan, May 2013. © Jonah Leff

WEAPONS DOCUMENTED AMONG ARMED ACTORS

This section reviews the results of the Small Arms Survey's tracing missions in Sudan and South Sudan as well as documentation received from independent experts, focusing on significant weapon types (makes and models) and country of manufacture. It pays special attention to weapons and ammunition that were produced from the late 1990s onward, as opposed to older Warsaw Pact equipment that is ubiquitous throughout East Africa and the Horn and that is particularly difficult to trace. The section examines the countries of manufacture of weapons observed in Sudan and South Sudan, identifying several specific weapon models and ammunition production lots that proliferate across the conflict areas of the two countries.[13] Ammunition-specific findings from the Survey's work in the two countries are also presented in Chapter 6 of this volume (AMMUNITION PROFILING).

Chinese weapons

Throughout the past decade, Chinese military equipment has become increasingly common in Sudan and South Sudan, especially among the Sudan Armed Forces (SAF) and its allied militias. While customs data does not reflect the full extent of transfers between importing and exporting states, it indicates that in 2001–12 China accounted for 58 per cent of reported transfers to Sudan of small arms and light weapons, their ammunition, and 'conventional weapons'. New varieties of Chinese weapons and ammunition are far less common in SPLA stockpiles but, as transfers to South Sudan have not yet been captured by UN Comtrade, it is difficult to quantify the new state's acquisition of Chinese-made weapons.

Field inspections in Sudan and South Sudan have noted a large variety of Chinese equipment, including assault rifles, general-purpose and heavy machine guns, RPG-7-pattern rocket launchers, automatic grenade launchers, anti-tank missiles, various types of rockets, and small-calibre ammunition (see Table 7.3 and Map 7.2).

Weapons seized by the SPLA from SSLM/A forces, Unity state, South Sudan, April 2011. © Jonah Leff

Table 7.3 Selected Chinese military equipment documented among armed actors, 2011–13

Equipment	Armed actor	Location and date	Notes
Type 56-1 assault rifle (copy of Kalashnikov with folding buttstock)	SSLM/A	Rubkhona, Unity, South Sudan, April 2011	150 viewed. Seized by the SPLA. Also seen in videos of SSLM/A posted to the Web in 2011.[14] Loaded with identical Sudanese-manufactured 7.62 x 39 mm ammunition.
	SSDM/A-Athor	Jonglei, South Sudan, April 2011	Captured by the SPLA.
	Lou Nuer	Pieri, Jonglei, South Sudan, August 2011	Youths armed by George Athor. Documented by a UN mission observer (Small Arms Survey, 2012a, p. 9).
	Lou Nuer	Akobo, Jonglei, South Sudan, January 2012	Seen returning from Pibor county, where an attack took place in December 2011.[15]
CQ assault rifle (copy of M16)	SSDM/A-Yau Yau	Jonglei, South Sudan, Feburary and July 2013	Markings and serial numbers systematically removed.
	SSLM/A	Mayom, Unity, South Sudan, May 2013	Hundreds held by forces that accepted amnesty. Markings and serial numbers removed.
	SSDM/A-Olony	Lul, Upper Nile, South Sudan, July 2013	Markings and serial numbers removed.
	Lou Nuer	Jonglei, South Sudan, July 2013	Among Lou Nuer forces that attacked Murle villages in Pibor in April and July 2013. Loaded with Chinese Factory 71 5.56 x 45 mm ammunition. May have originated with Yau Yau or the SPLA troops, who captured some CQs during counter-insurgency operations in Murle areas.[16]
	Murle	Walgak, Jonglei, South Sudan, July 2013	Observed during their attack on Lou Nuer, possibly associated with SSDM/A-Yau Yau.
Type 80 machine gun (copy of Soviet/ Russian PKM)[17]	SLA	North Darfur, Sudan, 2009	Captured from SAF during battle.[18]
	SSDF	Paryak, Jonglei, South Sudan, September 2012	Including two with close serial numbers, suggesting that they were part of the same consignment.
	SSDM/A-Yau Yau	Paryak, Jonglei, South Sudan, February and July 2013	Markings removed.
QLZ 87 automatic grenade launchers and ammunition[19]	Khartoum-backed Chadian forces	Darfur, Sudan, February 2006	QLZ 87 launcher documented by Amnesty International (AI, 2006, p. 12).
	Chadian armed opposition group	Darfur, Sudan, May 2009	QLZ 87 launcher documented by UN Panel of Experts (UNSC, 2009, p. 34).
	Unknown[20]	Tukumare village, North Darfur, Sudan, May 2011	QLZ 87 ammunition documented by the UN Panel of Experts, manufactured in 2007, suggesting recent supply (Gramizzi, Lewis, and Tubiana, 2012).
	SPLM-N	South Kordofan, Sudan, May 2012, and Blue Nile, Sudan, December 2012	Three launchers captured from SAF documented in the two states, same producer ('9656') with close serial numbers, suggesting part of a single consignment from China. The Small Arms Survey later documented a QLZ 87 crate that the SPLM-N had seized during the battle of al Hamra; it contained markings indicating

Equipment	Armed actor	Location and date	Notes
			that China's Xinshidai Company sold a total of 500 QLZ 87 sets to Sudan's Yarmouk Industrial Complex in 2008. Ammunition was only observed in South Kordofan.
Type 69 40 mm HEAT (RPG) ammunition	SSDM/A-Athor	Fangak county, Jonglei, South Sudan, February 2011	Captured by the SPLA and documented by the UN Somalia and Eritrea Monitoring Group (UNSC, 2011b, p. 89).[21] Matched lot numbers observed with Ogaden National Liberation Front (ONLF) forces in their attack on Ethiopia in 2010.
	SSDM/A-Athor	Paryak, Jonglei, South Sudan, September 2012	Seen among the weapons of Peter Kuol Chol Awan, an Athor commander who surrendered with his men in February 2012. Matched lot numbers observed with ONLF forces in their attack on Ethiopia in 2010 (UNSC, 2011b, p. 358).[22]
Red Arrow 8 anti-tank guided missile	SPLM-N	Daldoko, South Kordofan, Sudan, December 2012	Two captured from SAF. First time this advanced and expensive weapon is documented in Sudan. One manufactured in 2009, shipped as part of a total order of 100; the other manufactured in 2011 and shipped as part of a total order of 350.[23]
Factory 71 5.56 x 45 mm ammunition	SSDM/A-Yau Yau	Pariak, Unity, South Sudan, February and July 2013	Hundreds of rounds viewed with Yau Yau defectors and with stockpiles that the SPLA captured from Yau Yau's forces in 2013.
	SSLM/A	Mayom, Unity, South Sudan, May 2013	Hundreds of rounds with SSLM/A forces that accepted amnesty.
	SSDM/A-Olony	Lul, Upper Nile, South Sudan, July 2013	Present with Olony's forces, which accepted amnesty.
	Murle militia	Jonglei, South Sudan, July 2013	Present with Murle militia during attacks on Lou Nuer.
	Lou Nuer (White Army)	Jonglei, South Sudan, July 2013	Present with Lou Nuer militia during attacks on Murle.
Factory 945 7.62 x 54R mm ammunition	SAF	Darfur, Sudan, 2010	Observed on the battlefield after SAF attacks in various locations throughout Darfur.[24]
	SSDM/A-Athor	Jonglei, South Sudan, April 2011	Hundreds of rounds observed in Sudanese packaging.
	Lou Nuer (White Army)	Pibor, Jonglei, South Sudan, February 2012	Dozens of rounds observed after White Army attack on Pibor county.
	SPLM-N	South Kordofan, Sudan, May 2012	Thousands of rounds that the SPLM-N captured from SAF. Five boxes with the same contract number as documented with SSDM/A in Jonglei, South Sudan.
	SSDM/A-Athor	Jonglei, South Sudan, September 2012	One box observed with a contract number identifying Sudan as the consignee. Same contract number as the five boxes observed with SPLM-N in South Kordofan, Sudan.
	SPLM-N	Blue Nile, Sudan, December 2012	Hundreds of rounds that the SPLM-N captured from SAF.

▶

Equipment	Armed actor	Location and date	Notes
	SSDM/A-Yau Yau	Pariak, Jonglei, South Sudan, February 2013	Dozens of rounds with a group of Yau Yau defectors.
	SSLM/A	Mayom, Unity, South Sudan, May 2013	Hundreds of rounds observed with SSLM/A forces, which accepted amnesty.
Factory 11 and 41 12.7 x 108 mm ammunition	SAF	Darfur, Sudan, 2010	Observed on the battlefield after SAF attacks in various locations throughout Darfur.[25]
	SPLM-N	South Kordofan, Sudan, May 2012	Thousands of rounds that the SPLM-N seized from SAF.
	SSDF	Paryak, Jonglei, South Sudan, September 2012	Hundreds of rounds observed with SSDF defectors under the command of John Duit.
	SPLM-N	Blue Nile, Sudan, December 2012	Hundreds of rounds that the SPLM-N seized from SAF.
	SSLM/A	Mayom, Unity, South Sudan, May 2013	Hundreds of rounds observed with SSLM/A troops, which accepted amnesty.

Map 7.2   **Chinese weapons among armed actors, Sudan and South Sudan, 2011-13**

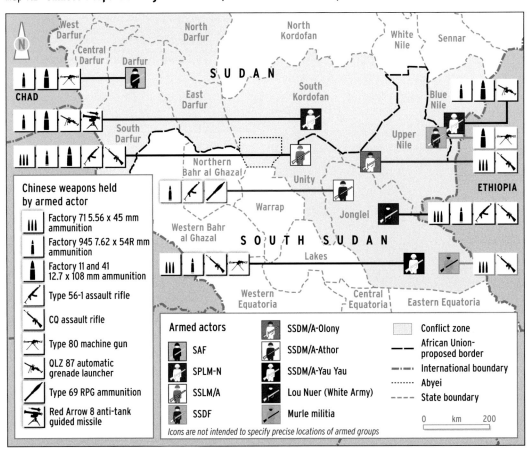

Iranian weapons

Iran has been a significant exporter of weapons to Sudan since at least the 1990s.[26] Whereas China's military relationship with Sudan centres on oil and other economic interests, Iran's role in Sudan's defence industry is primarily ideological. Military ties between Iran and Sudan have grown strong over the years. According to UN Comtrade, Iran was the source of 13 per cent of Khartoum's self-reported arms imports in 2001–12. In January 2007, the two countries signed a mutual defence agreement, which reportedly accelerated the sale of weapons, including Iranian missiles, rocket-propelled grenades, unmanned aerial vehicles, and 'other equipment' (*Sudan Tribune*, 2007a; 2007b). There is also emerging evidence that Iran has played a significant role in supporting Sudan's weapons manufacturing sector and uses the Yarmouk Industrial Complex as a production and onward supply hub for Iranian and Iranian-designed weapons (Conflict Armament Research, 2012b, p. 26). Table 7.4 and Map 7.3 summarize the types of Iranian weapons observed among various armed actors in Sudan and South Sudan.

Table 7.4 **Selected Iranian military equipment among armed actors, 2011–13**			
Equipment	**Armed actor**	**Location and date documented**	**Notes**
Suspected Iranian RPG-7-pattern launchers[27]	SSLM/A	Rubkhona, Unity, South Sudan, April 2011	Eight captured by the SPLA. No markings visible.
	SSDM/A-Athor	Paryak, Jonglei, South Sudan, February 2012	Seen among the weapons of Peter Kuol Chol Awan, an Athor commander who surrendered with his men in February 2012. No markings visible.
	SSLM/A	Mayom, Unity, South Sudan, May 2013	Seen after forces accepted amnesty. No markings visible.
	SSDM/A-Yau Yau	Jonglei, South Sudan, July 2013	Seen with weapons captured by the SPLA. No markings visible.
	SSDM/A-Olony	Kodok, Upper Nile, South Sudan, July 2013[28]	Present with Olony's forces, which accepted amnesty. No markings visible.
No. 4 anti-personnel landmines	SPLM-N	Toroji town, South Kordofan, Sudan, February 2012	Captured from SAF. Have Farsi markings, suggesting Iranian production. The mines are contained in crates intended for M-6 fuzes with markings from the Yarmouk Industrial Complex, which indicates that the mines were most probably repackaged by Sudanese state forces.[29]
	SPLM-N	Belilia, Blue Nile, Sudan, December 2012	Identical landmines (roughly a dozen pieces) that the SPLM-N reportedly captured from SAF during the civil war.[30]
Mortar rounds and tubes	SPLM-N	South Kordofan, Sudan, May 2012	SPLM-N captured 60 mm and 81 mm mortar rounds with Farsi markings from SAF. The 60 mm rounds are hybrid systems fitted with Chinese-made MP-5B point-detonating fuzes.
	SPLM-N	Blue Nile, Sudan, December 2012	120 mm mortar tube reportedly captured from SAF in September 2011.

▶

Equipment	Armed actor	Location and date documented	Notes
7.62 x 39 mm ammunition	SAF	Darfur, Sudan, 2010	Observed on the battlefield after SAF attacks in various locations throughout Darfur.[31]
	SPLM-N	South Kordofan, Sudan, May 2012	Dozens of rounds that the SPLM-N seized from SAF.
	SPLM-N	Blue Nile, Sudan, December 2012	Dozens of rounds that the SPLM-N seized from SAF.
	SSLM/A	Mayom, Unity, South Sudan, May 2013	Dozens of rounds observed with SSLM/A, which accepted amnesty.
12.7 x 108 mm ammunition	SAF	Darfur, Sudan, 2010	Observed on the battlefield after SAF attack in East Darfur.[32]
	SPLM-N	South Kordofan, Sudan, May 2012	Dozens of rounds that the SPLM-N seized from SAF.
	SPLM-N	Blue Nile, Sudan, December 2012	Dozens of rounds that the SPLM-N seized from SAF.

Map 7.3 **Iranian weapons among armed actors, Sudan and South Sudan, 2011–13**

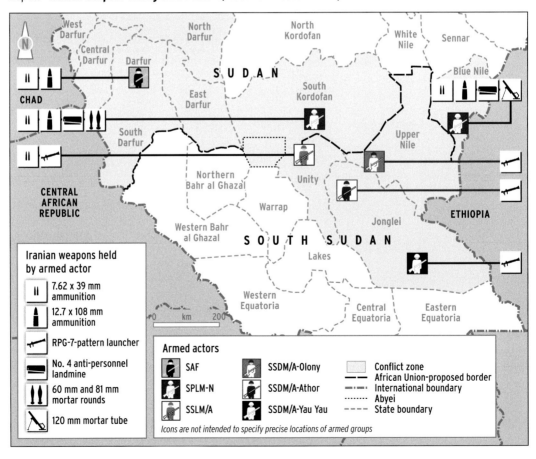

Sudanese weapons

Sudan has become a significant arms manufacturer in Africa. While the extent of Sudan's exports on the global market is unclear,[33] significant quantities of Sudanese-produced arms and ammunition have been observed with Sudanese forces, South Sudanese insurgents, and in several other conflict zones outside of Sudan and South Sudan (see Table 7.5 and Map 7.4).[34] According to Sudan's Military Industry Corporation (MIC) website as well as samples present at the MIC's booth at the 2013 IDEX weapons convention in Abu Dhabi, Sudan manufactures a broad range of small arms and ammunition, as well as armoured vehicles and main battle tanks (MIC, n.d.a). Most of these systems seem to be copies of products manufactured in other countries.

The HSBA has documented among Sudanese armed actors a small portion of the weapons that the MIC claims to manufacture, including machine guns, mortars, various rockets, and small arms ammunition. Due to limited information regarding the MIC's manufacturing capabilities, it is unclear whether Sudan fully manufactures these items, assembles them, simply re-marks foreign-made weapons, or a combination of the three (see Box 7.3).

Map 7.4 **Sudanese weapons among armed actors, Sudan and South Sudan, 2011–13**

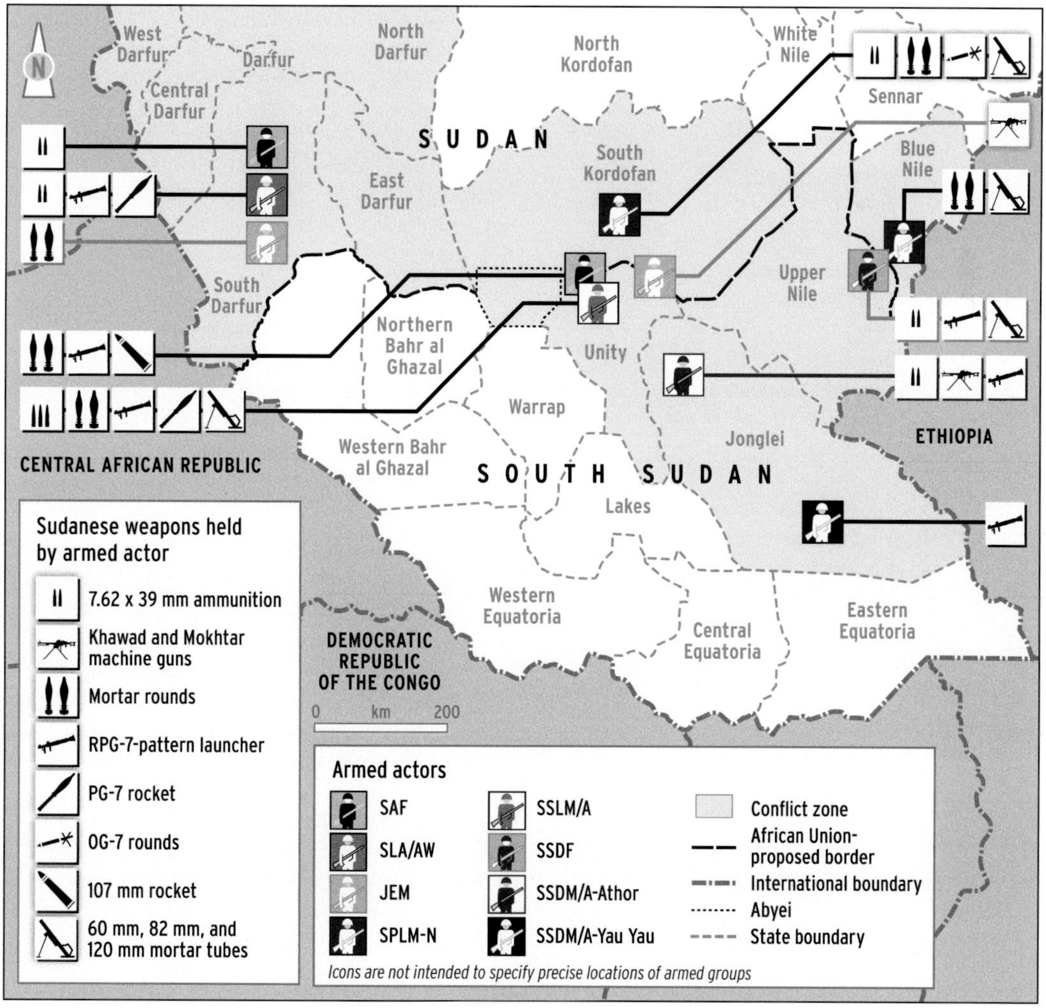

Box 7.3 Sudan's Military Industry Corporation

With increasing numbers of Sudanese-manufactured weapons appearing on the battlefields in Sudan and South Sudan, and in conflict arenas both in and out of the region, there has been a growing interest in Sudan's weapons manufacturing capabilities. This box briefly reviews what is currently known, based on open sources and some research in Khartoum. Further research is required to verify the full scope of manufacturing at Sudan's Military Industry Corporation (MIC).

Sudan's defence industry dates back to 1959, when the government of President Ibrahim Abboud established the Al Shaggara ammunition plant to produce small arms ammunition. Production was expanded in 1993, when President Omar al Bashir established the MIC (MIC, n.d.b; Raheel, 2012). Today, Sudan claims to be the third largest weapons manufacturer in Africa, after Egypt and South Africa (Bors, 2007).

The MIC uses 'technical expertise' from both China and Iran in the production of various weapons and ammunition and also for the maintenance of aircraft and ground vehicles used by the Sudanese army (Sirri, 2013; Ashour, 2013). A technical review of Sudanese-manufactured weapons reveals that they derive from Bulgarian, Chinese, Iranian, and Soviet designs. The MIC produces a variety of military products in at least seven distinct manufacturing plants. These include:

- Yarmouk Industrial Complex;
- Al Shaggara Ammunition Plant;
- Elshaheed Ibrahim Shams el Deen Complex for Heavy Industries;
- Safat Aviation Complex;
- Al Zarghaa Engineering Complex; and
- Saria Industrial Complex.

Each of these is briefly reviewed below.

The **Yarmouk Industrial Complex** was constructed in 1994 and began operations in 1996 at the site of an old fertilizer factory in the Soba section of Khartoum. Yarmouk manufactures conventional weapons, artillery, and ammunition at five main factories. Managed by the National Intelligence and Security Service, the complex is reportedly 35 per cent Iranian-owned, with some 300 Iranian technicians and members of the Iranian Revolutionary Guard Corps working there (*Africa Confidential*, 2012, p. 2).[35] According to Sudanese and Bulgarian officials, Yarmouk was built with assistance from Bulgaria (Barzashka, 2013; Collins, 2012).

The **Al Shaggara Ammunition Plant**, established on 17 November 1959, was the first weapons-manufacturing plant in Sudan. In 1994, it was incorporated into the MIC. At that time, the plant increased its production to include

mortar rounds,[36] 7.62 x 54R mm ammunition, 19 x 9 mm ammunition, 12.7 x 108 mm ammunition, and aircraft bombs. The plant also produces spare parts for these products under the supervision of a quality control department (Raheel, 2012).

The **Elshaheed Ibrahim Shams el Deen Complex for Heavy Industries** was established in September 2002 in Giad Industrial City for the production of heavy machinery. It reportedly produces tanks, armoured personnel carriers, and self-propelled guns, in addition to other products and services, such as earth-moving equipment, rehabilitation of railways, and river transport. The complex contains various industrial machines, a rehabilitation centre, and an assembly area (Raheel, 2012).

The **Safat Aviation Complex**, 20 km north of Khartoum in Karary, opened in 2005. It includes different centres and factories specialized in aircraft maintenance and the installation of various aircraft parts. The Safat plant is reportedly supported by several foreign companies, including a Sharjah-based aviation company, Al Amyal Aviation Services FZE, which is part of an investment group called VBA Incom registered in the United Arab Emirates and provides Safat with 'production management, repair, and maintenance engineering', according to the company. But Al Amyal publicly insists that it is only directly involved with overhauling civilian aircraft at Safat (Al Amyal, n.d.).

The **Al Zarghaa Engineering Complex** was created in 1999 in the Halfaya area of Khartoum. It specializes in communications, electronics, and research and development. The complex carries out the manufacture, assembly, programming, and testing of electronic devices. It also produces wireless communications devices and electro-optical devices used in defence (Raheel, 2012).

The **Saria Industrial Complex** was established in 1997 and reportedly includes nine factories that produce 60 different products. The complex provides Sudan's armed forces with military clothing and supplies, simple electronics, and appliances. According to Saria's website, its shoe factory was established to manufacture military and civilian shoes with support from a Lebanese investor, Mohamed Omar Rifa'i. According to its director, Mohamed Bushra Ibrahim, Saria produces military clothing for SAF in partnership with Turkey. The complex established the Sour Factory in 2004 to manufacture additional supplies for the armed forces. The Sour Factory is reportedly owned by the National Defence Ministry (10 per cent), the Saria Industrial Complex (30 per cent), and an unidentified Turkish company (60 per cent) (Al Toum, 2012; Saria Industrial Complex, n.d.).[37]

Table 7.5 Selected Sudanese military equipment among armed actors, 2011–13

Equipment	Armed actor	Location and date documented	Notes
'Khawad' (12.7 x 108 mm) and 'Mokhtar' (7.62 x 54 mm) machine guns[38]	SSDM/A-Athor	Jonglei, South Sudan, April 2011	Seized by the SPLA in March 2011. According to markings, the Khawad was manufactured in 2009; the Mokhtar's marks were partially scratched off but were identifiable as Sudanese.[39]
	JEM	Yida, Unity, South Sudan, May 2012	Khawad captured from SAF in battle over Jaw in February 2012. Appears to have been produced in 2010.
60 mm, 82 mm, and 120 mm mortar rounds[40]	JEM	Darfur, Sudan, 2009	120 mm mortar rounds captured from SAF in 2009. Manufactured in 2001, 2004, and 2006 in Workshop 116.[41]
	SSLM/A	Rubkhona, Unity, South Sudan, May 2011	Seized by the SPLA. Had similar markings to the 120 mm rounds observed in Darfur, and were produced in Workshop 116 in 2010.
	SPLM-N	South Kordofan and Blue Nile, Sudan, 2011–12	82 mm mortar rounds seized from SAF in battle. Identical to 82 mm rounds observed with the SSLM/A; ranged in manufacture date from 2006 to 2011.
	SPLA/JEM[42]	Hejlij, South Kordofan, Sudan, April 2012	JEM and the SPLA captured several boxes of Sudanese-produced 60 mm, 82 mm, and 120 mm mortar rounds from a SAF depot during battle at Hejlij.
	Somali Transitional Federal Government (TFG)	Mogadishu, Somalia, January 2011	Dozens of 82 mm mortar rounds supplied to the TFG in 2010 in violation of the UN arms embargo on Somalia. The casings were manufactured on 27 October 2008; they were filled in 2010 in Workshop 116 at Factory A10 of the Yarmouk Industrial Complex in Khartoum, according to the container's quality control certificate and markings on the rounds.[43]
	SSLM/A	Mayom, Unity, South Sudan, May 2013	Large quantities of Sudanese-produced 60 mm and 82 mm mortar rounds in their original packaging. The markings on the rounds and crates reveal that the 60 mm and 82 mm rounds were manufactured in 2008 and 2012, respectively. The 2012 production date indicates that the 82 mm rounds were probably supplied to the SSLM/A not long before they accepted amnesty in April 2013.[44]
60 mm, 82 mm, and 120 mm mortar tubes	SSLM/A	Unity, South Sudan, May 2011	The Small Arms Survey obtained photographic evidence of an 82 mm mortar tube seized by the SPLA.
	SPLM-N	South Kordofan, Sudan, May 2012	60 mm, 82 mm, and 120 mm mortar tubes among weapons that the SPLM-N seized from SAF.
	SSDF	Jonglei, South Sudan, September 2012	60 mm mortar tube among weapons that the SSDF handed over to the SPLA.
	SPLM-N	Blue Nile, Sudan, December 2012	60 mm, 82 mm, and 120 mm mortar tubes among weapons that the SPLM-N seized from SAF.
	SSLM/A	Unity, South Sudan, May 2013	60 mm, 82 mm, and 120 mm mortar tubes among weapons with the SSLM/A.

▶

Equipment	Armed actor	Location and date documented	Notes
RPG-7-pattern launchers ('Sinnar RPG-7 light anti-tank')[45]	SLA-AW	South Darfur, Sudan, 2009	The Small Arms Survey obtained photographic evidence of this weapon, which was seized by SAF.[46]
	SSDM/A-Athor	Jonglei, South Sudan, early 2011	The Small Arms Survey received documentation in March 2011. Later in 2011, investigators documented additional weapons that the SPLA captured from Athor's men. Another distinct RPG-7-pattern launcher had identical marks on the trigger assembly and matched the launcher featured on the MIC website.
	Defectors from SAF Joint Integrated Unit	Mapel, Western Bahr al Ghazal, South Sudan, November 2011	Among the weapons brought in by SAF Lt. Col. Peter Wol was an RPG-7-pattern launcher identical to the second one found with Athor and featured on the MIC website. The marks reveal that the launcher was produced at Factory A30 and that it has the serial number 'NY-12-35'.
	SSDF	Paryak, Jonglei, South Sudan, September 2012	The SSDF handed over Sudanese RPG-7-pattern launchers to the SPLA upon giving up its insurgency. They are identical to those captured from Athor, in possession of the SAF Joint Integrated Unit, and to those featured on the MIC website. Manufactured at Factory A30.
	Somali TFG	Mogadishu, Somalia, January 2011	The Small Arms Survey received documentation in late 2012 of a box of nine Sudanese-manufactured RPG-7-pattern launchers with the Somali TFG, as part of same consignment described above. They were manufactured at Factory A30 in October 2010, according to the quality control certificate.
	SSDM/A-Yau Yau	Jonglei, South Sudan, February and July 2013	The SPLA captured several RPG-7-pattern launchers. Markings deliberately removed by grinding.
	SSLM/A	Mayom, Unity, South Sudan, May 2013	Brought dozens across the border when they accepted amnesty. Markings deliberately removed by grinding.
PG-7 rockets ('Sinar PG-7V'[47])	SLA-AW	South Darfur, Sudan, 2009	Received documentation of PG-7s with the RPG-7-pattern launcher noted above. Appear to have been produced in 2008.
	SSLM/A	Mayom, Unity, South Sudan, May 2013	Brought hundreds with them to South Sudan upon surrender to the SPLA. Markings similar to those observed in Darfur in 2009. Appear to have been produced in 2009.
OG-7 HE fragmentation rounds ('Round Sinar OG-7')	SPLM-N	South Kordofan, Sudan, May 2012	Captured from SAF during battle. Manufactured in 2009.
	Somali TFG	Mogadishu, Somalia, January 2011	One box containing OG-7s produced in 2009 and supplied to the TFG in 2010.
107 mm rockets ('Taka 107 mm rocket')	SAF	Hejlij, South Kordofan, Sudan, April 2012	SPLA and JEM captured several boxes of Sudanese 107 mm rockets during an attack on Hejlij in April 2012.
	Somali TFG	Mogadishu, Somalia, January 2011	Found with consignment of Sudanese manufactured wagons noted above.

Equipment	Armed actor	Location and date documented	Notes
7.62 x 39 mm ammunition	SAF	Darfur, Sudan, 2010	Observed on the battlefield after SAF attacks in various locations throughout Darfur.[48]
	SSLM/A	Rubkona, Unity, South Sudan, April 2011	Thousands of the same lot number loaded into 150 Type 56-1 assault rifles that the SPLA seized from the SSLM/A.
	SLA-AW	North Darfur, Sudan, June 2011	A handful of rounds that an SLA-AW faction reportedly captured from SAF in battle.
	SPLM-N	South Kordofan, Sudan, May 2012	Hundreds of rounds that the SPLM-N seized from SAF.
	SSDF	Paryak, Jonglei, South Sudan, September 2012	Dozens of rounds observed with SSDF defectors under the command of John Duit.
	SSLM/A	Mayom, Unity, South Sudan, May 2013	Dozens of rounds observed with SSLM/A, which accepted amnesty.

SUPPLY TO NON-STATE ACTORS

Since the end of the Sudanese civil war, large volumes of small arms and light weapons have continued to flow into Sudan. While these authorized transfers do not necessarily violate existing embargoes or agreements on Sudan, investigations by the Survey and others indicate that some of these newer weapons have reached non-state armed groups on both sides of the Sudan–South Sudan border in the post-war period.

Non-state armed groups in Sudan and South Sudan rarely obtain their weapons directly from foreign states; instead, they tend to receive materiel from local sources. Some of the arming has been deliberate, as in the case of Khartoum's arming of Southern rebel commanders—who have in turn passed on weapons to tribal militias; battlefield capture and small-scale leakage have served as additional means to secure weapons. Non-state armed groups have also acted as suppliers to civilians.

The next sections examine the three most common types of sourcing to non-state actors in Sudan and South Sudan, namely:

1) direct supply from state to non-state armed groups;
2) capture of military equipment on the battlefield; and
3) supply from non-state armed groups to civilians.

State supply to non-state armed groups

To further political and ideological aims and to carry out counter-insurgency operations in its peripheral areas, the GoS has had a long-standing practice of arming both paramilitary and non-state forces. The most documented cases relate to Sudan's arming of the tribal militias and armed groups during its civil war with the South and the establishment of pro-government militias, made up of mostly Arab tribes, which were tasked with suppressing an uprising in Darfur.[49] More recently, the Small Arms Survey's tracing work repeatedly identified instances of Sudanese military support to Southern insurgent groups, whose publicly declared aim has been to overthrow the Juba government. Sudan has

Armed Nuer youths on the march with a number of weapon types, including an RPG (foreground), Upper Nile state, South Sudan, 12 February 2014.
© Goran Tomasevic/Reuters

supplied significant quantities of military equipment to these groups by land and by air, reportedly through the National Intelligence and Security Services.[50]

Former Southern insurgents have provided detailed information about truckloads of weapons arriving from Khartoum to their rear bases in South Kordofan and Blue Nile.[51] During interviews conducted in February 2013, for example, militiamen formerly under David Yau Yau in Jonglei, including senior-level commanders, claimed that air-drops orchestrated by the National Intelligence and Security Services were the primary source of the group's arms and ammunition. They gave accounts of drops between August 2012 and December 2012—with a further drop reported after the group's defection in January 2013. They also asserted that an airplane had flown directly from Khartoum on the night of each drop. According to the commanders, the militia groups on the ground were in direct contact with the aircraft via satellite phone and marked each drop zone with a line of fires immediately prior to the drop.

Ex-militiamen described the dropped materiel as packed in reinforced wooden boxes of uniform size and shape. Each box was said to be approximately the dimension of an ISO shipping container (1.5 m in height and about 2.4 m in width). The boxes were reportedly painted either green (containing weapons) or yellow (containing ammunition). Ex-militiamen said all of the boxes were delivered by parachute, falling roughly in a line, the length of the drop zone. Small Arms Survey investigators did not view such boxes and could not independently confirm the airdrop claims (Small Arms Survey, 2013a, p. 1).

China, which accounts for the largest percentage of Sudan's reported arms imports, is reportedly aware of the problem of retransfer in the context of the UN embargo on Darfur. In 2011, Beijing provided investigators with a model end-user certificate in which recipients were asked to 'guarantee that, without the written consent of the competent authority of the Chinese Government, we will not transfer the above-said items to any third party' (Gramizzi, Lewis, and Tubiana, 2012a, p. 22, annexe XVIII). But China declined to provide investigators with actual, signed certificates, and Chinese Factory 41 ammunition manufactured as late as 2010 was documented in Darfur in mid-2011, with the UN embargo still in force (p. 15). Communication with officials in Beijing in August 2013, reported to the Survey, indicates that the government knows of the problem of unauthorized retransfer to South Sudanese rebels, as well as to Darfur, and is increasingly frustrated with Khartoum's unauthorized supply to these groups.[52] Yet, as of September 2013, there were no indications of any change in Chinese export practices regarding Sudan.

The SPLM/A has a history of arming tribal youths to defend against insurgencies, especially in Jonglei state. In 2010 and 2011, the SPLA—under the leadership of the former Jonglei governor, Koul Manyang—supplied arms and ammunition to youths throughout the state to fight against George Athor's militia. During Yau Yau's first rebellion in 2011, the Jonglei government formed a paramilitary force called the 'SPLA Youth', comprising mostly Murle youths to take on Yau Yau's forces. Similarly, during inter-tribal conflict in Jonglei, SPLA soldiers provided weapons and ammunition to their fellow tribesmen to supplement their firepower (Small Arms Survey, 2012c, p. 4). Local communities have accused the SPLA of supplying firearms to Lou Nuer youths prior to their attack on Pibor county in July 2013, in an effort to stem Yau Yau's second rebellion.[53] Aside from initial assistance in the very early stages of the conflicts in South Kordofan and Blue Nile, the Small Arms Survey has not documented Southern military support for the SPLM–N in those states, although the GoS and several Western diplomatic sources accuse South Sudan of providing such backing.[54]

> The Chinese government is reportedly aware of the problem of unauthorized retransfer.

Although the Arms Trade Treaty has introduced new international standards for arms exports, it is still up to exporting states to apply these standards in specific cases (UNGA, 2013; ARMS TRADE TREATY). US and EU perspectives with respect to arms exports to South Sudan have diverged to date; following South Sudan's secession, the EU decided to maintain its embargo on the entire Sudan–South Sudan region, while the United States lifted a ban on defence exports to Juba. It is too soon to say whether the Arms Trade Treaty will lead to greater convergence on arms export practices concerning the region. In any case, the majority of weapons in the two countries are in the hands of non-state actors, whether through deliberate supply or accidental diversion. Lying outside state control and completely unregulated, these are the weapons that fuel insurgencies and inter-communal violence in Sudan and South Sudan.

Battlefield capture

Non-state armed groups also acquire weapons from state forces through battlefield capture. Some groups are more successful at this than others. With decreasing support from external actors, the Sudan Revolutionary Front has maintained a sizeable arsenal through its military victories against SAF. In South Kordofan, the SPLM–N captured hundreds of thousands of rounds of small- to medium-calibre ammunition as well as more than a dozen vehicles and tanks from SAF in 2012.[55] While the SPLM–N in Blue Nile has been somewhat less successful at capturing military equipment than their South Kordofan counterparts, they too have seized significant quantities of SAF weapons during battle (Gramizzi, 2013). In most instances, these weapons not only correlate with the materiel that the SPLM–N captured in South Kordofan, but also match the equipment captured from SAF in Darfur and that found in the hands of Southern militias in South Sudan.

In general, Sudanese government stockpiles have proved to be the main source of military hardware for insurgent groups and a crucial alternative to externally sourced supplies, which have dwindled. The rapprochement between Chad and Sudan in 2010, the regime change in Libya in 2011, and the necessity for South Sudan to normalize its bilateral relations with Sudan have all contributed to a reduction of arms supplies to non-state armed groups in Darfur, in particular. In the long term, the Khartoum government's inability to secure control over its own stockpiles could harm its relationship with some international suppliers, some of whom appear quite concerned about serving as an indirect source of weapons for non-state actors, sometimes in violation of UN sanctions.

Likewise, Southern insurgent groups have captured arms and ammunition from the SPLA. In 2012–13, Yau Yau's militia secured large numbers of weapons and their associated ammunition as a result of its battlefield successes against the SPLA in Jonglei. These weapons included heavy machine guns, mortars, and several vehicles.[56]

Supply from non-state armed groups to civilians

Non-state armed groups are a continuous source of arms and ammunition to civilians. Non-state armed groups operating on both sides of the Sudan–South Sudan border are a continuous source of arms and ammunition to civilian populations. In Sudan, for example, tribal militias such as those formed by Missiriya groups that receive weapons from SAF and its affiliate forces have occasionally armed local pastoralist communities to advance their quest for land and resources in competition with neighbours (Craze, 2013). In South Sudan, insurgent groups that receive regular supplies from Khartoum have used the weapons as recruitment tools in launching attacks against SPLA installations. During Yau Yau's second rebellion, he succeeded in luring thousands of Murle youths to his ranks by providing them with weapons after an SPLA disarmament programme in 2012 generated widespread grievances among these communities. Sometimes this practice has unintended consequences, however. When Athor armed Nuer youths in Jonglei to attack the SPLA in May 2011, for instance, the Nuer refused to obey Athor's orders, and instead used their newly acquired weapons to attack their Murle adversaries (Small Arms Survey, 2012a, p. 9).

CONCLUSION

Sudan and South Sudan are paradigmatic 'post-conflict' countries in the sense that they remain highly affected by armed violence as a result of unresolved territorial, economic, political, and ideological claims following peace agreements. The influx and diffusion of weapons—including newer models from China—among all armed groups has exacerbated the frequency and duration of armed conflicts in the post-war era. Sudanese-produced ammunition has also found its way into the hands of insurgents and tribal groups. In almost all documented cases, the arms and ammunition with non-state groups were traced back to Sudanese state stockpiles and were obtained through either deliberate transfer by Sudanese forces or battlefield capture.

Over the course of two years, the HSBA Arms and Ammunition Tracing Desk has generated a body of empirical evidence about the proliferation of arms and ammunition in Sudan and South Sudan. It has done so at relatively modest cost, with the assistance of official bodies within South Sudan, as well as the cooperation of other governments, arms manufacturers, and commercial bodies. Field-based research and analysis serve as a monitoring mechanism that can readily detect the arrival of new weapons systems and that can help to inform governments and exporting states about the actual end-users of some of the arms and ammunition they have exported. The project has relied on, but also catalysed, international cooperation for purposes of clarifying the illicit supply of arms to rebels and other non-state actors.

Much has already been learned in Sudan and South Sudan, but much remains unknown. The particulars of the supply chain—the specific actors involved, their motivations, and potential rewards—require further study. It is not only the large-scale supply of weapons and ammunition by airdrop, but also the dimensions of smaller-scale diversion from state stockpiles and the cross-border 'ant trade' that require investigation.

Tracing in Sudan and South Sudan also faces new challenges. Perhaps the most difficult is the increase in newer-model weapons documented with removed serial numbers and markings. Such mark removal may be a response to investigations into the custody chain of newly arrived weapons. While this practice makes tracing much more difficult—although not impossible—it is also a clear indicator of illicit supply.

The diffusion of Sudanese-manufactured weapons and ammunition in Sudan and South Sudan—as well as in several other conflict zones across Africa—presents additional challenges. Because of a general lack of transparency on the part of Sudan with regard to its arms manufacture and trade, and its lack of cooperation to date with weapons monitors, tracing the chain of custody of its domestically produced arms and ammunition has proven difficult.

The resumption of large-scale intra-Southern conflict in December 2013 may signal a new phase in insurgent operations in South Sudan. As of January 2014, the situation was still evolving, and ultimate outcomes were impossible to predict, but one thing was clear: all sides will continue to seek out and expand their supplies of arms and ammunition. Given the evidence presented here concerning the final destination of some of the weapons transferred to Sudan, exporting states may want to reconsider their arms export policies. In any case, weapons tracing will continue to be an important tool for understanding transfer patterns in a region where most weapons are beyond state control, armed groups are a primary source of insecurity, and state security provision is weak. ◾

LIST OF ABBREVIATIONS

EU	European Union
GoS	Government of Sudan
HSBA	Human Security Baseline Assessment for Sudan and South Sudan
JEM	Justice and Equality Movement
MIC	Military Industry Corporation
ONLF	Ogaden National Liberation Front
SAF	Sudan Armed Forces
SLA	Sudan Liberation Army
SLA–AW	Sudan Liberation Army–Abdul Wahid
SLA–MM	Sudan Liberation Army–Minni Minawi
SPLM/A	Sudan People's Liberation Movement/Army
SPLM–N	Sudan People's Liberation Movement–North
SSDF	South Sudan Defence Forces
SSDM/A	South Sudan Democratic Movement/Army
SSLM/A	South Sudan Liberation Movement/Army
TFG	Transitional Federal Government
UN Comtrade	United Nations Commodity Trade Statistics Database
UNMISS	United Nations Mission in South Sudan

ENDNOTES

1   For detailed reports on these conflicts, in both English and Arabic, see Small Arms Survey (n.d.a).

2   Although exceptions continue to occur, evidence suggests that few non-state groups in Sudan and South Sudan currently receive direct transfers of arms or ammunition from outside the two countries. In contrast, Ethiopia assisted the rebels during the civil war and, in earlier phases of the Darfur conflict, security service elements in Chad, Eritrea, and Libya supported some Darfur rebel groups. On Chadian military support to Darfur rebels, see Tubiana (2011).

3   This section draws on Small Arms Survey (2012a, p. 2).

4   Author correspondence with a representative of the US Department of Defense, 15 November 2013.

5   'Conventional weapons' is a UN Comtrade category that includes artillery, rocket launchers, and grenade launchers, among other weapons systems, as well as their projectiles. For a list of the Comtrade categories analysed in this section, see Small Arms Survey (2009, p. 10, n. 18).

6   All of the alleged transfers from St. Vincent and the Grenadines—a country that does not produce weapons or ammunition—reportedly occurred in 2009 and were categorized as 'parts and accessories for small arms and light weapons' (Comtrade code 930599). Whether the transfer(s) took place or represent a coding error is not known.

7   HSBA tracing reports are available at Small Arms Survey (n.d.b).

8   Some forensic labs have the ability to recover markings that are not visible to the human eye, but relatively few such labs exist in Africa.

9   Vehicles can be sold as civilian goods, but later converted into military vehicles. It is not always certain where in the chain of custody the conversion takes place.

10 Author correspondence with a UN official, 15 November 2013.

11 In some cases the HSBA received verifiable documentation from independent experts and journalists working in Sudan and South Sudan.

12 The Government of South Sudan and the SPLA have continued to provide HSBA investigators access to highly sensitive areas and materiel although the project's findings have not always been to their advantage.

13 For a fuller account of all the weapons systems and ammunition documented by the HSBA tracing project, see Leff and LeBrun (2014).

14 See the videos posted by BolKol1000 (n.d.).

15 See Small Arms Survey (2012d).

16 Author phone interviews with members of the Lou Nuer and Murle communities and UN Mission in South Sudan (UNMISS) officials, July 2013.

17 See Jane's (2002, p. 335).

18 Author correspondence with a former UN expert on Darfur, 15 November 2013.

19 The QLZ 87 is also known as the Type 87.

20 Ammunition was found at the site of a battle between SAF and an SLA–MM affiliate.

21 Although it is unclear how Athor obtained these rounds, he had a close relationship with President Isaias Afwerki of Eritrea over many years and reportedly visited Asmara at least three times in 2010–11 (UNSC, 2011b, pp. 328–35). Jonglei representatives also allege that Athor purchased weapons from the leader of the Asmara-backed Ethiopian United Patriotic Front in the Gambella region of Ethiopia, which borders Jonglei (Small Arms Survey, 2012a, p. 7).

22 Without knowing to which country or countries China supplied the rockets, it is extremely difficult to trace the precise chain of custody of the items. But considering that two identical lot numbers appeared in Eritrean-supplied ONLF stocks and with Athor's stocks at a time when he seemed to be in close contact with Asmara, the rounds most likely all trace back to Eritrea. Another possible scenario is that the rockets were originally supplied from China to Sudan, which transferred some of them across the border to Eritrea and others to Athor in Jonglei.

23 The timing of these two consignments, totalling 450 missiles combined, suggests that Sudan may have purchased the missiles from China for potential use against the South Sudanese military and its newly procured fleet of tanks, which arrived around the same time as the order, rather than for an internal counter-insurgency.

24 Author correspondence with a former UN expert on Darfur, 15 November 2013.

25 Author correspondence with a former UN expert on Darfur, 15 November 2013.

26 Human Rights Watch (1998) was one of the first observers to provide details of Iranian weapons in Sudan, documenting them among the stockpiles of SAF weapons captured by the SPLA during the civil war. The dates of manufacture of many of the weapons indicated that they had been produced in the early 1990s.

27 Unlike Iranian RPG launchers found in other conflict arenas, these launchers usually do not bear any markings, rendering the origin difficult to ascertain. Since these features are distinctly Iranian, however, the launchers are most likely Iranian-produced, fully produced in Khartoum based on Iranian design, or the parts are fabricated in Iran and shipped to Khartoum for assembly.

28   Olony's forces did not allow the Small Arms Survey to photograph their weapons, but the launchers were identified visually.

29   Sudan signed the Anti-Personnel Mine Ban Convention (Ottawa Treaty) in 1997 and ratified it in 2003, thereby banning the use, stockpiling, production, and transfer of landmines.

30   The SPLM–N did not allow the inspectors to photograph the landmines because they considered them SPLM–N stockpiles.

31   Author correspondence with a former UN expert on Darfur, 15 November 2013.

32   Author correspondence with a former UN expert on Darfur, 15 November 2013.

33   Sudan has not reported any exports to UN Comtrade, nor has any country reported imports from Sudan. Sudan's Military Industry Corporation (MIC), however, stated publicly that it had sold weapons to Ethiopia and Mozambique (Binnie, 2013; *Alkhaleej*, 2013). Sudan has also covertly supplied weapons to Côte d'Ivoire and Somalia (UNSC, 2013a; 2013b).

34   On the presence of Sudanese arms and ammunition in other conflict zones, see, for example, Anders (2013) on Côte d'Ivoire, Chivers and Schmitt (2013) on Syria, and UNSC (2013a, p. 289) on Somalia.

35   Small Arms Survey interview with a former Giad engineer, Khartoum, June 2011.

36   Survey investigators have observed that, in 2010 at least, the Yarmouk Industrial Complex was producing mortar rounds. It is possible that the production had moved over to Yarmouk or that Al Shaggara was absorbed into Yarmouk.

37   Author telephone interview with a Saria representative, 26 November 2013.

38   Sudan's MIC claims to produce general-purpose and heavy machine guns, which appear to be identical to those manufactured by China. According to the MIC website, the factory produces a 7.62 × 54 mm general-purpose machine gun called the Mokhtar and a 12.7 x 108 mm heavy machine gun called the Khawad, which are copies of the Chinese Type 80 (based on the Russian PKM) and Type 85 machine guns (based on the Russian DShKM machine gun), respectively. It is not clear whether Sudan manufactures these weapons under licence from China, or if it assembles them in Khartoum. The Sudanese factory markings are distinct from those applied by China.

39   The markings and construction of the weapons were identical to those on display at the 2013 IDEX convention.

40   These rounds closely resemble Bulgarian types. The Bulgarian manufacturer, Arsenal Joint Stock Company, manufactures the same 82 mm and 120 mm designations, but it does not manufacture the same type of 60 mm rounds. Bulgaria reports having authorized licences for the export of manufacturing equipment for the production of 82 mm and 120 mm mortar rounds to Sudan between 1996 and 1998. Sudan has assigned the following names to its mortar ammunition: 'Nimir 60 mm (HE)', 'Aboud 82 mm (HE)', and 'Ahmed 120 mm (HE)' (MIC, n.d.c). According to Yarmouk documents, which were viewed by Survey investigators and correspond to markings on the rounds and shipping boxes, MIC's mortar rounds are manufactured at Factory A10 in Workshop 116. Most Sudanese mortar rounds observed by the HSBA tend to be hybrids, often containing Chinese-manufactured fuzes and Bulgarian ignition charges.

41   Author correspondence with a former UN expert on Darfur, 15 November 2013.

42   It is not clear which group captured these specific items from SAF in the joint attack by the SPLA and JEM.

43   Mortar rounds are ordinarily manufactured in phases. The bomb casings are usually produced first and are engraved with a manufacture date. The bombs are later filled with explosives and given a lot number that, along with the year and workshop code, is painted on the final product. This number is important both for storage and identification purposes.

44   Further confirming the origin of the mortar ammunition, Sudanese-manufactured 60 mm, 82 mm, and 120 mm mortar rounds were on display at the 2013 IDEX weapons convention. Although painted in a colour distinct from those documented previously, the construction and marking configurations are identical to those observed in Sudan and South Sudan. According to the markings, the rounds were manufactured in 2012 in Workshop 116.

45   See MIC (n.d.d).

46   Most of the weapons in the SLA–AW's arsenal at the time were weapons captured from SAF during battle.

47   The 'V' denotes that it is a complete round, as opposed to the PG-7 warhead.

48   Author correspondence with a former UN expert on Darfur, 15 November 2013.

49   See, for example, de Waal and Flint (2005).

50   Small Arms Survey interviews with dozens of former Southern insurgents, South Sudan, 2011–13.

51   Small Arms Survey interviews with dozens of former Southern insurgents, South Sudan, 2011–13.

52   Author correspondence with an arms investigator with ties to China, August 2013.

53   Author phone interviews with Lou Nuer and Murle community members and UNMISS officials, July 2013.

54   Author interviews with Western diplomats, Juba, South Sudan, 2011–13.

55   HSBA fieldwork conducted throughout 2012.

56   Author correspondence with a UN official close to the conflict, 15 October 2013.

BIBLIOGRAPHY

Africa Confidential. 2012. 'Target Khartoum.' Vol. 53, No. 22. 2 November.

AI (Amnesty International). 2006. *Sustaining Conflict and Human Rights Abuses: The Flow of Arms Accelerates.* June.
<http://www.amnesty.org/en/library/asset/ASA17/030/2006/en/be25c03a-d42b-11dd-8743-d305bea2b2c7/asa170302006cn.pdf>

Al Amyal (Al Amyal Aviation Services). n.d. 'Safat.' <www.vba.ae/main/al-amyal/safat>

Alkhaleej. 2013. 'Sudan Tanks Made Locally [in Arabic].' 23 February. <http://www.alkhaleej.ae/alkhaleej/page/4fd728a0-ef61-4aa5-8585-01653aad5a95>

Al Toum, Rasha. 2012. 'Statement of Director General of Sariya Industrial Complex Mohamed Bushra.' *Alintibaha.* 14 October. <http://bit.ly/1cPmM5J>

Anders, Holger. 2013. 'Identifying Sources: Small-calibre Ammunition in Côte d'Ivoire.' Unpublished background paper. Geneva: Small Arms Survey. 28 July.

Ashour, Kareem, 2013. 'Iran Officially Intervenes in the Khartoum War against Its Rebels: The Sudanese Army Uses Iranian Weapons in Operations [in Arabic].' *Alwatanalarabi.* 11 May. <http://bit.ly/17d8RDI>

Barzashka, Ivanka. 2013. *Sudan's Weapons Production Capabilities: Investigating the Bulgarian Connection.* Unpublished background paper. Geneva: Small Arms Survey.

Bevan, James. 2009. 'Revealing Provenance: Weapons Tracing during and after Conflict.' In Small Arms Survey. *Small Arms Survey 2009: Shadows of War.* Cambridge: Cambridge University Press.

Binnie, Jeremy. 2013. 'IDEX 2013: Sudan Makes First Appearance at IDEX.' *Jane's Defence Weekly.* February.

BolKol1000. n.d. Uploaded videos. <http://www.youtube.com/user/BolKol1000#p/u/4/hC2RzJFs-2s>

Bors, Quds. 2007. 'Sudan Reveals Manufactured Drones and Its Intention to Produce Missiles: The Defense Minister Says Sudan Is the Third African Country in the Military Industry [in Arabic].' *Al Arabiya.* 3 September. <http://www.alarabiya.net/articles/2007/09/03/38638.html>

CEU (Council of the European Union). 1994. Council Decision 94/165/CFSP of 15 March 1994 on the Common Position Defined on the Basis of Article J.2 of the Treaty on European Union Concerning the Imposition of an Embargo on Arms, Munitions and Military Equipment on Sudan. 15 March.

—. 2004. Common Position 2004/31/CFSP of 9 January 2004 Concerning the Imposition of an Embargo on Arms, Munitions and Military Equipment on Sudan.

—. 2005. Common Position 2005/411/ CFSP of 30 May Concerning Restrictive Measures against Sudan and Repealing Common Position 2004/31/CFSP.

—. 2011. Council Decision 2011/423/CFSP of 18 July 2011 Concerning Restrictive Measures against Sudan and South Sudan and Repealing Common Position 2005/411/ CFSP. 18 July.

Chivers, C. J. and Eric Schmitt. 2013. 'Arms Shipments Seen from Sudan to Syria Rebels.' *New York Times.* 12 August.
<http://www.nytimes.com/2013/08/13/world/africa/arms-shipments-seen-from-sudan-to-syria-rebels.html?pagewanted=all&_r=0.>

Collins, Toby. 2012. 'Sudanese Ambassador to the UK: Israeli Lobby's Anti-Sudan Campaign.' *Sudan Tribune.* 26 November.
<http://www.sudantribune.com/spip.php?iframe&page=imprimable&id_article=44635>

Conflict Armament Research. 2012a. 'Identifying Marks on Kalashnikov-pattern Rifles.' Field Guide No. 4. London: Conflict Armament Research.
<http://www.conflictarm.com/images/FG4_Kalashnikov-pattern_marks_.pdf>

—. 2012b. 'The Distribution of Iranian Ammunition in Africa: Evidence from a Nine-country Investigation.' London: Conflict Armament Research. December.
<http://www.conflictarm.com/images/Iranian_Ammunition.pdf>

Craze, Joshua. 2013. *Dividing Lines: Grazing and Conflict along the Sudan–South Sudan Border.* HSBA Working Paper 30. Geneva: Small Arms Survey. July.

de Waal, Alex and Julie Flint. 2005. *Darfur: A Short History of a Long War.* New York: Zed Books.

El Jamali, Hasnaa. 2013. 'Khartoum-reported Imports of Small Arms and Light Weapons, Their Ammunition, and Conventional Weapons, 2001–12.' Unpublished background paper. Geneva: Small Arms Survey.

Gramizzi, Claudio. 2013. *At an Impasse: The Conflict in Blue Nile.* HSBA Working Paper No. 31. Geneva: Small Arms Survey. December.

—, Mike Lewis, and Jérôme Tubiana. 2012. 'Letter Dated 24 January 2011 from Former Members of the Panel of Experts on the Sudan Established Pursuant to Resolution 1591 (2005) and Renewed Pursuant to Resolution 1954 (2010) Addressed to the Chairman of the Security Council Committee Established Pursuant to Resolution 1591 (2005) Concerning the Sudan.' *Africa Confidential.* 13 April. <http://bit.ly/Ijpkqp>

— and Jérôme Tubiana. 2013. *New War, Old Enemies: Conflict Dynamics in South Kordofan.* HSBA Working Paper No. 29. Geneva: Small Arms Survey. March.

Human Rights Watch. 1998. *Global Trade, Local Impact: Arms Transfers to All Sides in the Civil War in Sudan.* August.
<http://www.hrw.org/legacy/reports/reports98/sudan/>

Jane's. 2002. *Jane's Infantry Weapons 2003–2004.* Coulsdon: Jane's Information Group.

Jenzen-Jones, Nic. 2013. *The Identification of Small Arms, Light Weapons, and Associated Ammunition: An Introductory Guide.* Unpublished HSBA Workshop Training Manual. Geneva: Small Arms Survey.

Leff, Jonah and Emile LeBrun. 2014. *Following the Thread: Tracing Arms and Ammunition in Sudan and South Sudan.* HSBA Working Paper No. 32. Geneva: Small Arms Survey.

Lewis, Mike. 2009. *Skirting the Law: Sudan's Post-CPA Arms Flows*. HSBA Working Paper No. 18. Geneva: Small Arms Survey. September.

MIC (Military Industry Corporation). n.d.a. 'Products.' <http://www.mic.sd/idex/en/products>

—. n.d.b. 'About.' <http://www.mic.sd/idex/en/about>

—. n.d.c. 'Ammunitions.' <http://www.mic.sd/idex/en/products/ammunitions>

—. n.d.d. 'Small Arms.' <http://www.mic.sd/idex/en/products/smallarms>

OCHA (United Nations Office for the Coordination of Humanitarian Affairs). 2013. 'United Nations Grants Sudan $10 Million from the Central Emergency
    Response Fund.' Press release. 28 August. <http://staging-01.unocha.org/cerf/node/1480>

Raheel, Ibrahim. 2012. 'MIC Profile [in Arabic].' *Alintibaha*. 25 October. <http://bit.ly/12uZqfM>

Reuters. 2012. 'Obama Lifts Ban on U.S. Defense Exports to South Sudan.' 6 January.

Saria Industrial Complex. n.d. 'Saria Industrial Complex [in Arabic].' <http://saria.sd/site/shoes/index.htm>

Sirri, Mustafa. 2013. 'Sudanese Forces Begin to Use Sophisticated Rocket and Technical Expertise from Iran and China [in Arabic].' *Asharq Al-Awsat*. 9 May.
    <http://www.aawsat.com/details.asp?section=4&article=727825&issueno=12581#.UgzC76zhfvA>

Small Arms Survey. 2009. *Supply and Demand: Arms Flows and Holdings in Sudan*. HSBA Issue Brief No. 15. Geneva: Small Arms Survey. December.

—. 2012a. *Reaching for the Gun: Arms Flows and Holdings in South Sudan*. HSBA Issue Brief No. 19. Geneva: Small Arms Survey. April.

—. 2012b. *Business as Usual: Arms Flows to Darfur, 2009–12*. HSBA Issue Brief No. 20. Geneva: Small Arms Survey. September.

—. 2012c. *My Neighbour, My Enemy: Inter-tribal Violence in Jonglei*. HSBA Issue Brief No. 19. Geneva: Small Arms Survey. October.

—. 2012d. 'White Army Arms and Ammunition.' HSBA Tracing Desk Report. 22 March.
    <http://www.smallarmssurveysudan.org/fileadmin/docs/facts-figures/arms-ammunition-tracing-desk/HSBA-white-army-arms-ammunition.pdf>

—. 2013a. 'Weapons in Service with David Yau Yau's Militia, Jonglei State, Feburary 2013.' HSBA Tracing Desk Report. April 2013.
    <http://www.smallarmssurveysudan.org/fileadmin/docs/facts-figures/arms-ammunition-tracing-desk/HSBA-Tracing-Desk-Yau-Yau-April-2013.pdf>

—. 2013b. *Pendulum Swings: The Rise and Fall of Insurgent Militias in South Sudan*. HSBA Issue Brief No. 22. Geneva: Small Arms Survey. November.

—. n.d.a. 'Human Security Baseline Assessment for Sudan and South Sudan.' <www.smallarmssurveysudan.org>

—. n.d.b. 'HSBA Arms and Ammunition Tracing Desk.' <http://www.smallarmssurveysudan.org/facts-figures/arms-and-ammunition-tracing-desk.html>

Sudan Tribune. 2007a. 'Sudanese Minister Visits Iranian Military Airplane Complex.' 17 January.

—. 2007b. 'Iran Offers to Train and Equip Sudan's Army.' 9 January.

Tubiana, Jérôme. 2011. *Renouncing the Rebels: Local and Regional Dimensions of Chad–Sudan Rapprochement*. HSBA Working Paper 25. Geneva:
    Small Arms Survey.

UNGA (United Nations General Assembly). 2013. Arms Trade Treaty. 'Certified true copy (XXVI-8).' May.
    <https://treaties.un.org/Pages/ViewDetails.aspx?src=TREATY&mtdsg_no=XXVI-8&chapter=26&lang=en>

UNSC (United Nations Security Council). 2004. Resolution 1556. S/RES/1556 of 30 July.

—. 2005. Resolution 1591. S/RES/1591 of 29 March.

—. 2009. *Report of the Panel of Experts Established Pursuant to Resolution 1591 (2005)*. S/2009/562 of 29 October 2009.

—. 2011a. *Report of the Panel of Experts Established Pursuant to Resolution 1591 (2005)*. S/2011/111 of 8 March 2011.

—. 2011b. *Report of the Monitoring Group on Somalia and Eritrea Submitted in Accordance with Resolution 1916 (2010)*. S/2011/433 of 18 July.

—. 2013a. *Report of the Monitoring Group on Somalia and Eritrea Pursuant to Security Council Resolution 2060 (2012): Somalia*. S/2013/413 of 12 July.

—. 2013b. *Midterm Report of the Group of Experts on Côte d'Ivoire Pursuant to Paragraph 19 of Security Council Resolution 2101 (2013)*. S/2013/605
    of 14 October.

White House. 2012. 'Presidential Memorandum—Presidential Determination on the Eligibility of South Sudan to Receive Defense Articles and Defense
    Services.' 6 January.

ACKNOWLEDGEMENTS

Principal authors

Emile LeBrun and Jonah Leff

Contributor

Hasnaa El Jamali

A gang member looks out of the window to check his
turf in Harlem, New York, July 2007.
© Scott Houston

On the Record

ILLICIT WEAPONS IN THE UNITED STATES

8

INTRODUCTION

During the crack epidemic in the United States in the 1980s and early 1990s, a steady stream of movies, television shows, and songs depicting gang life and drug violence in US cities captured the popular imagination.[1] Among the most startling of these images were drive-by shootings: teenaged gang members spraying blighted city neighbourhoods with bullets fired from automatic rifles and machine pistols. These scenes—and the assumptions that underpin them—continue to shape public perceptions of urban violence in the United States today.[2] But how accurate are these images? Are automatic rifles and machine pistols as widely used by drug traffickers and gang members as commonly assumed? If not, what weapons do they rely on, and are they the same as the weapons acquired by other criminals? Do the types of weapons seized from criminals vary from city to city?

This chapter seeks to answer these questions through an analysis of data on firearms and other weapons recovered by US law enforcement authorities. It is the third instalment of the Small Arms Survey's multi-year study on illicit small arms and light weapons, which seeks to improve public understanding of illicit weapons by obtaining and analysing previously unreleased or under-utilized data from official (government) sources. To this end, the Survey obtained records on more than 140,000 small arms, light weapons, and rounds of light weapons ammunition taken into custody by police in eight US cities and towns. The records shed light on weapons seized from felons, drug traffickers, gang members, and other violent criminals.

The main findings of this chapter include the following:

- The majority of the firearms seized from felons, drug traffickers, and gang members in the eight US cities and towns studied were handguns, accounting for 77 per cent of firearms recovered from these groups.
- At least 70 per cent of the seized handguns were semi-automatic pistols of various makes and models—the most common type of firearm recovered from criminals in the municipalities studied.
- Seizure rates for handguns and long guns in the United States are the inverse of those in Mexico, where approximately 72 per cent of the seized weapons studied in the second phase of this project were long guns.
- Rifles accounted for only a small fraction of seized firearms: less than 12 per cent, with only about half of them semi-automatic models, including those commonly termed 'assault rifles'. This is noteworthy given widespread civilian ownership of rifles in the United States and their frequent seizure from criminals in Mexico.
- US-designed AR-15-pattern rifles—often called 'the most popular rifle in America' (Goode, 2012)—were seized at less than half the rate of Kalashnikov- and SKS-pattern rifles.
- Despite a ban on the importation of firearms from China, a large proportion of the seized semi-automatic rifles were Chinese-made.
- The number of machine guns seized in the eight cities and towns was negligible.

Box 8.1 Terms and definitions

For the purposes of this study, 'illicit small arms and light weapons' are weapons that are produced, transferred, held, or used in violation of national or international law. The chapter uses the term 'illicit' rather than 'illegal' to include cases of unclear or contested legality. The terms 'small arms' and 'firearms' are used interchangeably and refer to the following items:

- revolvers and self-loading pistols;
- rifles[3] and carbines;
- shotguns;
- sub-machine guns; and
- light and heavy machine guns.

The term 'light weapons' refers to:

- mortar systems of calibres of 120 mm or less;
- hand-held, under-barrel, and automatic grenade launchers;
- hand grenades;
- recoilless guns;
- portable rocket launchers, including rockets fired from single-shot, disposable launch tubes;
- portable missiles and launchers, namely anti-tank guided weapons (ATGWs) and man-portable air defence systems (MANPADS);
- landmines;
- improvised explosive devices (IEDs); and
- ammunition for light weapons.

Unless otherwise specified, data analysed and referenced in this chapter includes only these items.[4] 'Kalashnikov-pattern', 'SKS-pattern', and 'AR-15 pattern' rifles refer to the various automatic and semi-automatic rifles modelled on the Kalashnikov series and SKS rifles originally produced in the Soviet Union and its client states, and on the US-designed AR-15 rifle. Semi-automatic versions of these rifles are popular among civilian firearm owners in the United States.

For the purposes of this chapter, the term 'municipality' is defined as 'a city or town that has corporate status and local government' (Oxford Dictionaries, n.d.). The definition of 'crime of violence' is taken from the US Sentencing Commission's federal sentencing *Guidelines Manual* (USSC, 2012, pp. 262–63). The definition for the term 'drug trafficking' is based on the same manual and refers to the 'manufacture, import, export, distribution, or dispensing of, or offer to sell a controlled substance (or a counterfeit substance) or the possession of a controlled substance [. . .] with intent to manufacture, import, export, distribute or dispense' (p. 263).

A police officer holds a handgun seized from a suspected drug dealer, Los Angeles, September 2007. © Robert Nickelsberg/Getty Images

- Light weapons constitute a very small percentage of weapons taken into custody by police departments in the United States. Those that are recovered tend to be old, improvised, inert, or incomplete.

The chapter begins by providing a brief overview of the data used in the study and by defining key terms and concepts (see Box 8.1). It then offers an in-depth analysis of firearms seized from felons, drug traffickers, and gang members, along with firearms linked to certain violent crimes in Columbus, Ohio. The chapter then assesses the types and prevalence of light weapons recovered by US authorities. It concludes with additional observations about illicit small arms in the United States, including a comparison with illicit weapons in other countries.

ANALYSING THE DATA

The Small Arms Survey submitted requests for data on seized firearms, ammunition, and other weapons to police departments in 43 cities and towns,[5] with the aim of obtaining a geographically diverse sample of data on weapons seized by police forces in municipalities of different sizes. Police departments from 19 municipalities provided data in response to the requests.[6] Of these data sets, the records provided by the following eight municipalities were sufficiently comprehensive[7] and detailed to use in this study:

- Albuquerque, New Mexico;
- Boise, Idaho;
- Columbus, Ohio;
- Denham Springs, Louisiana;
- Houston, Texas;
- Los Angeles, California;

- Satellite Beach, Florida; and
- Washington, DC.

Combined, these cities and towns provided records on more than 140,000 small arms, light weapons, and rounds of light weapons ammunition taken into custody.

Nearly all of the data used in this study provides the date of the seizure; the quantity of weapons seized; and the type, make, model, and calibre of each seized weapon. The data also identifies the reason why the weapons were taken into custody, including any criminal charges linked to the weapons. Some of the data also identifies the location of the seizure, the serial number, the condition of the serial number, and/or the country of manufacture of the seized weapons. With the exception of the data from Columbus, the data sets reflect weapons taken into custody from 2007 to 2012 inclusive.

The Columbus Police Department (CPD) provided the most detailed data. In addition to the above-mentioned information, the CPD records—which cover weapons taken into custody from 2010 to 2012—identify the magazine capacity and barrel length of each seized firearm, and provide a complete accounting of the ammunition found in the weapon. The records from Columbus also include the date of birth, sex, and race of the individual from whom the weapon was seized or received, and a brief description of the events that led up to the seizure or receipt of the weapon (see Box 8.2).

Table 8.1 lists the municipalities studied, the number of small arms and light weapons identified in the records provided by their police departments, and the type of data the records contain.

Table 8.1 **Data on small arms and light weapons taken into custody by the eight municipalities studied**																	
City	Number of weapons*	Years	Items		Incident number	Quantity	Type	Make or manufacturer	Model	Calibre	Serial number	Serial condition	Country of manufacture	Seizure location	Seizure location description	Offence code	Seizure or crime date
			Small arms	Light weapons													
Albuquerque, New Mexico	10,035	2007-12	X	-	X	X	X	X	X	X	X	-	-	X	-	X	X
Boise, Idaho	1,601	2007-12	X	-	X	X	X	X	X	X	X	-	-	X	-	X	X
Columbus, Ohio	7,000**	2010-12	X	-	X	X	X	X	X	X	X	-	-	X	-	X	X
Denham Springs, Louisiana	27	2007-12	X	-	X	X	X	X	X	X	X	-	-	-	-	X	X
Houston, Texas	83,489	2002-12†	X	X	X	X	X	X	X	X	-	-	-	X	X	X	X
Los Angeles, California	30,672	2007-12	X	X	-	X	X	X	X	X	-	X	-	-	-	X	X
Satellite Beach, Florida	59	2007-12	X	-	X	X	X	X	X	X	X	-	X	X	-	X	X
Washington, DC	13,662	2007-12	X	-	-	X	X	X	X	X	X	X	X	X	-	X	X

Notes:

* The numbers in the weapons column reflect only seized small arms, light weapons, and rounds of light weapons ammunition.

** Figure rounded to minimize potential double-counting.

† The study uses data on small arms seized from 2007 to 2012 and on light weapons seized from 2002 to 2012.

As revealed by the data, police departments take custody of small arms and light weapons for a variety of reasons. For example, nearly 25 per cent of the 13,662 firearms recovered in Washington, DC, were 'found' weapons or weapons taken into custody for 'safekeeping' or for 'destruction'. The vast majority of the remaining weapons were linked to criminal charges ranging from 'carrying a firearm without a license' and 'hit & run' traffic accidents to carjacking, kidnapping, and homicide. Crimes linked to firearms in Los Angeles are similarly broad, including not only murder, kidnapping, assault, and other common violent crimes, but also more unusual criminal activity. Since 2009, officers from the Los Angeles Police Department (LAPD) have seized firearms from individuals suspected or accused of 'possess[ing a] game cock for fighting', 'challenging to [a] duel', and 'tamper[ing with a] railroad apparatus'.

While the data sets obtained for this study are notable for their size and detail, they have certain limitations. First, not all weapons taken into custody by police departments are crime guns. Although the data permits identification of some of the guns that were not used in crime or by criminals, the coding is often ambiguous. For example, a firearm categorized under the offence code 'murder' could be the weapon used to commit the murder or it could have been found on the victim or at the residence of a suspect. To minimize the effects of this ambiguity, the chapter focuses on 10,435 firearms that were linked to offence codes involving felons, drug traffickers, and gang members.[8] This approach allowed for the exclusion of firearms linked to offence codes for which a high percentage of seized firearms were probably not possessed or used illegally, or for which

Guns seized by the police in Washington, DC, are stored in the firearms examination section at police headquarters, March 2008. © Nicholas Kamm/AFP Photo

the legal status of the possession or use is difficult to assess. It also facilitated more in-depth evaluations of specific crimes and clearly defined categories of criminals, including felons, drug traffickers, and gang members—three groups of particular concern to US authorities.[9]

Another data limitation is the lack of information on court verdicts, given that it is possible that some suspects were acquitted of the charges mentioned in the data. The weapons taken from those suspects would not normally have been held or used illegally. The data also reveals little about how weapons enter and circulate in the black market. With some exceptions, the records do not identify the proximate or ultimate source of the weapons, or how the most recent end users acquired them. Annual summaries of data on weapons traced by the Bureau of Alcohol, Tobacco, Firearms and Explosives (ATF) identify the source states of traced weapons, but these summaries provide little information on how they are diverted or their movement after they enter the black market.

Nor is it clear whether the seized weapons are representative of the broader population of illicit small arms in the United States. The data only reflects weapons taken into custody by police, rather than a random sample of weapons that were held by illicit end users or used illegally. Furthermore, the data only covers seizures in eight municipalities. The number of records and the geographic and demographic diversity of the municipalities studied increase the likelihood that the data represents firearms taken into custody by police nationwide, but the extent to which these firearms are representative of the broader population of illicit small arms in the United States is uncertain.

This concern particularly applies to the data on seized light weapons, which is less complete than the firearm data. Only two of the eight municipalities studied—Houston and Los Angeles—provided light weapons data, and even this data may not fully account for all light weapons taken into custody. Interviews with officials from the sample municipalities reveal that at least some police departments do not take custody of live munitions (such as grenades, mortars, rockets, and missiles). Instead, these items are collected and stored by other government entities or departments and, as a result, they are not captured in police data.

Newly released data sheds important light on illicit small arms.

To compensate for these gaps, the research for this study included a review of media reports and other open-source accounts of seized light weapons in the states where the eight municipalities are located: California, Florida, Idaho, Louisiana, New Mexico, Ohio, and Texas, along with Washington, DC. Combined, these reports include information on nearly 400 light weapons and rounds of light weapons ammunition recovered by authorities from 2007 through 2012. When viewed alongside the records provided by the Houston Police Department (HPD) and the LAPD, the data offers some insight into the illicit acquisition, possession, and use of light weapons in the United States. The resulting data set is more robust than the limited data on the 123 light weapons and ammunition provided by the HPD and the LAPD, but the extent to which it is representative of light weapons seized in the United States as a whole is unknown.

Comparing data on the small arms and light weapons seized in the municipalities is complicated by differences in database coding and offence terminology. Some of the municipalities include very specific coding on criminal charges linked to seized weapons while coding in other data sets is more general or vague. In the data set from the HPD, for example, offences categorized as 'assault with a deadly weapon' are broken down by weapon type (such as 'aggravated assault (deadly weapon)/by firearms' or 'by cutting instrument'), while the Metropolitan Police Department of Washington, DC, aggregates all such assaults in a single category ('assault with a deadly weapon').

Local gun laws also affect the comparability of different data sets. Some weapons or activities that are illegal in one municipality are not illegal in others. For example, the state of California bans a sub-set of semi-automatic rifles defined as 'assault rifles' that are legally owned and sold in other states. Thus, a comparison of aggregated data on weapons seized by authorities in Los Angeles may include more 'assault rifles' than in Houston simply because there are more restrictions on the possession and sale of such rifles in Los Angeles than in Houston. These differences also highlight the difficulty of distinguishing 'illicit weapons' from 'legal weapons' in countries such as the United States, where laws on firearms vary from municipality to municipality and often change over time.

Despite these limitations, the newly released data sheds important light on illicit small arms and light weapons in the United States, including the type, make, model, and calibre of these weapons, and the crimes to which they are linked. Few publicly available data sets on illicit firearms are as large or detailed, and the release of this information underscores the immense, largely untapped analytic potential of the millions of unclassified records on seized weapons compiled and stored by local, state, and federal government agencies.

ARMED VIOLENCE IN THE UNITED STATES

Few countries have a larger or more diverse civilian market for firearms than the United States. The Small Arms Survey estimates that, as of 2007, there were 270 million firearms owned by US civilians (Karp, 2011), which range from palm-sized .22 calibre derringers to five-foot-long .50 calibre sniper rifles. In so large a civilian market even a very low rate of illegal acquisition and usage translates into substantial numbers of illicit weapons.

Firearms factor prominently in violent crime in the United States. In 2011, nearly 70 per cent of homicides were committed with firearms, according to the US Department of Justice. Firearms were also involved in roughly 26 per cent of robberies and 31 per cent of aggravated assaults (Planty and Truman, 2013; see Table 8.2).

The types of firearms used in violent crimes vary, but recent data suggests that most were committed with handguns. Data published by the US Federal Bureau of Investigation (FBI) indicates that at least 72 per cent of firearm murders in 2012 involved handguns. Shotguns and rifles accounted for just 3 per cent and 4 per cent of firearm murders, respectively. Handguns were also used in most of the gang- and drug-related murders identified in the FBI's data. At least 77 per cent of firearm murders that were linked to drug charges involved handguns, as were 75 and 83 per cent of 'gangland killings' and 'juvenile gang killings,' respectively (FBI, 2013, table 11). Data from 2011 on the use of firearms

Table 8.2 **Percentage of violence involving a firearm in the United States, by type of crime, 1993–2011**				
Year	Homicide	Non-fatal violence[a]	Robbery	Aggravated assault
1993	71.2	9.1	22.3	30.7
1994	71.4	9.2	27.1	31.9
1995	69.0	7.8	27.3	28.0
1996	68.0	7.8	24.6	25.7
1997	68.0	7.6	19.9	27.0
1998	65.9	7.0	20.1	26.5
1999	64.1	6.0	19.2	22.4
2000	64.4	7.2	21.1	26.6
2001[b]	55.9	7.5	29.5	26.0
2002	67.1	7.3	23.4	28.7
2003	67.2	6.1	22.4	22.2
2004	67.0	6.8	19.7	23.6
2005	68.2	7.2	21.8	25.7
2006	68.9	7.3	16.6	24.3
2007	68.8	8.1	20.0	32.6
2008	68.3	5.8	19.6	24.6
2009	68.4	7.2	27.0	23.2
2010	68.1	8.4	24.7	25.4
2011[c]	69.6	8.0	25.7	30.6

Notes:

For standard errors, see Planty and Truman (2013, appendix table 4).

a Non-fatal violence includes rape, sexual assault, robbery, and aggravated and simple assault. A small percentage of rape and sexual assaults involved firearms but is not shown in the table due to small sample sizes.

b The estimated number of homicides that occurred as a result of the events of 11 September 2001 is included in the total number of homicides.

c Figures for 2011 are based on preliminary homicide estimates.

Source: Planty and Truman (2013, p. 3)

in non-fatal criminal firearm violence[10] indicates that handguns were used in more than 88 per cent of these offences (Planty and Truman, 2013, p. 3).

While still high compared to other industrialized countries (UNODC, 2013), firearm violence in the United States has decreased significantly over the past 20 years. The number of firearm homicides fell by nearly 40 per cent from 1993 to 2011, and non-fatal firearm-related violent victimizations[11] fell by 70 per cent from 1993 to 2004 (Planty and Truman, 2013, p. 1). The percentage of violent crimes involving firearms has remained fairly consistent, however. Even as crime rates have fallen in the United States, criminal activity involving firearms has remained relatively common and continues to be a major concern for policy-makers and the public.

In 2013, after several high-profile incidents of firearms violence, US lawmakers put forward proposals to strengthen federal laws and regulations on the manufacture, ownership, and transfer of firearms. These included legislative proposals to establish a nationwide ban on the manufacture and import of 'assault weapons'[12] and detachable large-capacity ammunition magazines, expand the current system of background checks and record-keeping requirements,[13] and increase penalties for firearms trafficking. There was insufficient support to enact these proposals into law, however.[14]

> The Survey received records on more than 140,000 small arms and light weapons.

ILLICIT SMALL ARMS IN THE UNITED STATES

As noted above, the Survey received records on more than 140,000 small arms, light weapons, and rounds of light weapons ammunition taken into custody by police departments in the eight municipalities studied. The vast majority of these weapons were firearms. The records shed light on the type, calibre, make, and model of firearms recovered by authorities in the United States, including weapons seized from groups of particular concern for US policy-makers. This section assesses data on seizures from three of these groups: felons, drug traffickers, and gang members.

Possession of small arms by felons

US federal law prohibits the possession of firearms by several categories of individuals, including:

- convicted felons;[15]
- fugitives from justice;
- unlawful users of controlled substances;
- illegal aliens;
- individuals who have renounced their US citizenship;
- individuals 'adjudicated as mentally defective' or committed to a mental institution;
- individuals dishonourably discharged from the military; and
- individuals convicted of domestic violence-related offences, or subject to a court order restraining them for 'harassing, stalking, or threatening' intimate partners or their children (US, 2011, para. g).

With some exceptions,[16] it is illegal for anyone falling within one or more of these categories to receive, possess, ship, or transport firearms. It is also illegal to transfer firearms to them.[17] Firearms seized from these individuals are therefore considered illicit for the purposes of this study.

Of the eight cities and towns studied, law enforcement agencies in Albuquerque, Columbus, Denham Springs, Houston, Los Angeles, and Satellite Beach provided data that explicitly identifies firearms seized from felons or otherwise linked to charges associated with possession of a firearm by a felon.

The data reveals notable similarities across the municipalities studied in terms of the types of small arms recovered from felons and the ratios of the various types of small arms seized. In four of the major metropolitan areas,[18] most of the seized firearms were handguns, most of which were semi-automatic pistols.[19] Shotguns accounted for 8–9 per cent of firearms seized from felons in three of these cities, with the figure for Columbus slightly higher, at 16 per cent.

Seized rifles constituted 6–16 per cent of firearms recovered from felons in the four major metropolitan areas studied. Semi-automatic rifles, including rifles commonly categorized as 'assault weapons', accounted for just 3–8 per cent of seized firearms. A large proportion of seized semi-automatic rifles were identified as Chinese-made—this despite a US ban on the importation of most Chinese firearms since 1994. With some exceptions, the ban applies to all firearms and components, along with 'any unfinished forgings, castings, extrusions, and machined bodies for the component parts used in the assembly/manufacture of these firearms [that] may have originated in the People's Republic of China' (ATF, 2011). Exempt from the ban are sporting shotguns, along with older firearm models that qualify as 'curios or relics'[20] and 'have been stored for a five year period immediately prior to importation in a non-proscribed country or area' (US, 2012a).[21]

Of the 106 semi-automatic rifles[22] seized from felons in Houston, 23 were Chinese-made Kalashnikov- and SKS-pattern rifles. The data does not identify the date of manufacture of the seized firearms and thus it is unclear whether the rifles were imported before or after the import ban took effect in 1994. Given the large numbers of Chinese-made rifles imported prior to the ban (Nalder, 1993), it appears likely that many of the seized rifles were imported before 1994. Some of the rifles may also be 'curios or relics'. Any rifles of recent vintage and bearing markings indicating that they were manufactured or imported after 1994 would normally have arrived in the United States in violation of the import ban. Determining how many, if any, of the rifles fit this description would require more data than is currently (publicly) available.

Taxation and ownership controls limit the quantity of machine guns in the United States.

The seized semi-automatic rifles also reflect the popularity of Kalashnikov- and SKS-pattern rifles in the United States. In Houston, nearly half of the rifles identified by make or model were identified as Kalashnikov- or SKS-pattern rifles, as were approximately one-quarter of such rifles seized in Albuquerque and Columbus. In Los Angeles, other types of semi-automatic rifles were more common. While the LAPD recovered Kalashnikov- and SKS-pattern rifles, the majority of the rifles seized from felons in Los Angeles were other makes and models.

Few large-calibre rifles and machine guns were recovered. Only four .50 calibre rifles were seized from felons in the cities and towns studied, and the only firearm identified as a 'machine gun' is a .45 calibre weapon made by a US-based manufacturer that sells semi-automatic military-style pistols and rifles. The data also lists several 'machine pistols', most of which appear to be semi-automatic variants of fully automatic firearms. This is not surprising given the limited number of machine guns in the US civilian inventory and the comparatively strict controls to which such guns are subject. Starting in 1934, the US government began to require that machine guns be registered and imposed a tax of USD 200—the inflation-adjusted equivalent of approximately USD 3,400—on each transfer.[23] In 1986, the US Congress passed a law banning the private possession of machine guns except for those already legally owned and registered with the US government as of May 1986 (Krouse, 2013, pp. 6–7).

Decades of heavy taxation and strict controls on ownership have limited the quantity of machine guns available in the United States, among both criminals and the law-abiding population. Data published by the ATF indicates that, as of April 2013, it had records of 505,861 registered 'machine guns' and parts for machine guns (ATF, 2013a, p. 14). Since the data includes parts, the number of assembled, fully functional machine guns is significantly lower—approximately 182,000 units according to one estimate (E. Johnson, 2013). The combination of strict controls on the possession and transfer of machine guns and the small national civilian inventories helps explain the extremely low rate of illegal use and possession of these weapons in the United States. 'To the extent it can be known', observes analyst William Krouse, 'legally registered [National Firearms Act] machine guns are rarely, if ever, used in crime' (Krouse, 2013, p. 7). The data on firearms seized from felons in the six municipalities is consistent with this claim.

Small arms linked to drug trafficking offences

As noted above, the widespread depiction of machine-gun-toting gangs battling for control over street corners has shaped public perceptions of drugs and guns. These perceptions were reinforced by initial research on assault weapons (AWs), as Christopher Koper explains:

> *Early studies of AWs, though sometimes based on limited and potentially unrepresentative data, [. . .] suggested that AWs recovered by police were often associated with drug trafficking and organized crime [. . .], fueling a perception that AWs were guns of choice among drug dealers and other particularly violent groups* (Koper, 2004, p. 14).

Data on weapons seized from drug traffickers in the eight municipalities studied challenges these perceptions and provides new information on the firearms most frequently carried by drug traffickers.[24]

Media portrayals of drugs and guns are correct in that firearms are an integral part of the drug trade and the violence that accompanies it. Since 2008, the FBI has identified

A detective with the Los Angeles Police Department gang unit searches the apartment of an arrested drug dealer, April 2010. © Robert Nickelsberg/Getty

Table 8.3 Firearms recovered in drug trafficking cases, 2007–12

Weapon type*		Albuquerque No.	%	Boise No.	%	Columbus No.	%	Denham Springs No.	%	Houston No.	%	Los Angeles No.	%	Satellite Beach No.	%	Washington, DC No.	%
Handguns	Derringers	11	1	1	<1	4	4	-	-	15	<1	30	1	-	-	2	<1
	Pistols, semi-automatic	506	55	37	30	61	54	-	-	984	52	1,082	45	-	-	238	62
	Pistols, other	-	-	-	-	2	2	-	-	6	<1	17	<1	-	-	1	<1
	Pistols, unclear or unspecified	-	-	13	11	-	-	1	50	12	<1	-	-	-	-	-	-
	Revolvers	115	13	12	10	15	13	-	-	341	18	536	22	1	50	76	20
	Handguns, unclear or unspecified	-	-	5	4	1	<1	-	-	2	<1	-	-	1	50	-	-
	Total	632	69	68	55	83	74	1	50	1,360	72	1,665	69	2	100	317	83
Rifles	Bolt-action	25	3	10	8	-	-	-	-	35	2	107	4	-	-	3	<1
	Carbine	†	†	†	†	†	†	†	†	42	2	9	<1	†	†	-	-
	Semi-automatic	81	9	17	14	12	11	-	-	108	6	229	10	-	-	12	3
	Automatic	-	-	-	-	-	-	-	-	8	<1	4	<1	-	-	1	<1
	Other	18	2	2	2	1	<1	-	-	29	2	60	2	-	-	-	-
	Unclear or unspecified	66	7	11	9	-	-	-	-	7	<1	-	-	-	-	-	-
	Total	190	21	40	33	13	12	-	-	229	12	409	17	-	-	16	4
Shotguns	Semi-automatic	4	<1	1	<1	-	-	-	-	21	1	34	1	-	-	4	1
	Other	58	6	10	8	9	8	1	50	197	11	291	12	-	-	12	3
	Unclear or unspecified	30	3	3	2	5	4	-	-	12	<1	-	-	-	-	-	-
	Total	92	10	14	11	14	13	1	50	230	12	325	13	-	-	16	4

more than 2,200 murders linked to 'narcotics drug laws.' Firearms play a role in the vast majority of these murders. Of the 362 homicides in 2012 identified by the FBI, for example, more than 85 per cent involved firearms (FBI, 2013, table 11). Yet most of these murders were committed with handguns, not machine guns; indeed, at least 240 of the 311 homicides identified involved handguns. This affinity for handguns extends beyond the small number of drug traffickers who commit murder. Of the 5,824 seized firearms linked to drug trafficking offences in the eight municipalities studied, more than 70 per cent were handguns, most of which were conventional semi-automatic pistols (see Table 8.3).[25]

Machine guns accounted for only a small fraction of seizures from drug traffickers. Less than one per cent of the seized firearms linked to drug trafficking offences were identified as 'automatic rifles', 'machine guns', 'machine pistols', or 'submachine guns'. Furthermore, many of the firearms categorized as 'machine pistols' or 'submachine guns' appear to be semi-automatic models.[26] Semi-automatic rifles were seized at higher rates but still constituted only a small percentage of all seized firearms. Table 8.3 provides a detailed summary of the types of firearms seized in drug trafficking cases.

Another (often implicit) assumption about firearms wielded by drug traffickers is that they are equipped with high-capacity magazines. Only a small percentage of the records from the eight municipalities identify the magazine capacity of the seized weapons and therefore a definitive assessment of this assumption is not possible. Nevertheless, data provided by the CPD provides a snapshot of

Weapon type*		Albuquerque No.	%	Boise No.	%	Columbus No.	%	Denham Springs No.	%	Houston No.	%	Los Angeles No.	%	Satellite Beach No.	%	Washington, DC No.	%
Machine guns	'Machine guns'	–	–	–	–	1	<1	–	–	1	<1	8	<1	–	–	–	–
	'Machine pistols' and 'submachine guns'	–	–	–	–	–	–	–	–	17	<1	2	<1	–	–	1	<1
	Total	–	–	–	<1	1	<1	–	–	18	<1	10	<1	–	–	1	<1
Other firearms	Air guns, starter guns, stun guns	–	<1	1	<1	–	–	–	–	8	<1	–	–	–	–	29	8
	Other, unclear, or unspecified firearms	2	<1	–	–	1	<1	–	–	31	2	2	<1	–	–	3	<1
	Total	2	<1	1	<1	1	<1	–	–	39	2	2	<1	–	–	32	8
Total firearms linked to drug trafficking cases		916		123		112		2		1,876		2,411		2		382	

Notes:

Percentage totals may not add up to 100 per cent due to rounding of sub-totals.

* As identified by the HPD, the LAPD, and the Metropolitan Police Department of Washington, DC. The Small Arms Survey categorized some of the data on firearms provided by the police departments of Albuquerque, Boise, Columbus, Denham Springs, and Satellite Beach based on the model of the relevant firearms.

† Sub-category not used by the data source.

Table 8.4 Magazine capacity of firearms taken into custody by the Columbus Police Department, 2010-12						
Magazine capacity	**All weapons taken into custody**		**Violent crimes[†]**		**Drug trafficking cases**	
	Quantity	**%**	**Quantity**	**%**	**Quantity**	**%**
≤10 rounds	1,277	70	160	71	72	72
11-29 rounds	489	27	61	27	21	21
≥30 rounds	70	4	5	2	7	7
Total firearms identified by magazine capacity	**1,836**		**226**		**100**	

Notes:
The figures in this table only include firearms for which magazine capacity is identified. Percentage totals may not add up to 100 per cent due to rounding of sub-totals.
[†] These figures only include violent crimes in which it is clear from the record that the seized firearm was used in the crime or seized from the suspect.

magazine capacity in that city. For the purposes of this study, a large-capacity magazine is one that holds more than ten rounds of ammunition. Of the 100 firearms the CPD seized in drug trafficking cases and in which magazine capacity is identified, only 28 reportedly held more than ten rounds. This figure is roughly comparable to the percentage of large-capacity magazines in all weapons recovered by the CPD during the time period studied. The percentage of magazines holding 30 or more rounds was higher in cases of drug trafficking, but the difference is not great—7 per cent in drug trafficking cases vs. 4 per cent for all weapons taken into custody (see Table 8.4).

The data also reveals several important differences between the small arms linked to drug traffickers in the United States and those seized from their counterparts in neighbouring Mexico. These differences illustrate the diverse nature of illicit small arms worldwide, which vary not only by region, but also from country to country. Whereas pistols are the most frequently seized firearm in the United States, including from drug traffickers, data compiled by the Small Arms Survey suggests that rifles are the most common illicit firearms seized in Mexico, including from drug cartels. In fact, the seizure rates for handguns and long guns (machine guns, rifles, shotguns, and sub-machine guns) in the United States are the inverse of those in Mexico, where approximately 72 per cent of the roughly 4,200 seized weapons studied were long guns (Schroeder, 2013b, p. 290).

There are other differences between the types of firearms seized in the United States and in Mexico, although these differences are less significant than depictions of caches seized in Mexico might suggest.[27] As noted in the *Small Arms Survey 2013*, Mexican authorities have recovered .50 calibre anti-materiel rifles and machine guns, which are often prominently displayed in photos of weapons seized from drug traffickers. Yet, of the 4,200 weapons seized in Mexico that were analysed by the Survey, only 11 were identified as .50 calibre rifles or machine guns, suggesting that they constitute a very small percentage of cartel inventories. The same is true of 5.7 × 28 mm 'cop killer' pistols, often described as a 'weapon of choice' of the drug cartels.[28] Pistols of this calibre account for less than two per cent of the 996 handguns identified by model or calibre in Mexico (Schroeder, 2013b, pp. 291–93).

Even fewer large-calibre firearms and 5.7 mm pistols are identified in the data on weapons seized from drug traffickers in the United States. There are no records of seized .50 calibre machine guns in any of the eight cities and towns studied, and authorities only recovered five .50 calibre rifles, two of which were identified as muzzle-loading models. The only other .50 calibre firearms were handguns: four semi-automatic pistols and a revolver. Similarly, very few 5.7 × 28 mm pistols were seized. Of the more than 4,100 handguns recovered in drug trafficking cases, only 11 were identified as having or presumed to have a calibre of 5.7 mm, and nine of these were seized in Houston. No pistols of this calibre were identified in the drug trafficking cases studied in Albuquerque, Boise, Columbus, Denham Springs, Satellite Beach, or Washington, DC.[29]

Small arms linked to gangs and gang activities

Another subcategory of criminal activity that is of great concern to US policy-makers and the public is the illegal possession and use of firearms by street gangs.[30] FBI homicide data reveals that 'juvenile gang killings'[31] accounted for at least 720 homicides in 2012. Ninety-five per cent of these homicides involved firearms (FBI, 2013, table 11). These figures suggest the continuation of a trend in which firearms have played an increasingly important role in gang violence. As documented by the US Department of Justice, the percentage of gang-related homicides involving firearms jumped from 73 per cent in 1980 to 92 per cent in 2008 (Cooper and Smith, 2011, p. 26).

Data published by the FBI indicates that most gang-related killings are committed with handguns, but it reveals little about the type, make, model, or calibre of the handguns or other firearms used, or whether they factor as prominently in other gang-related crimes. The data obtained by the Survey sheds some light on these questions—at least in regard to gang activity in Houston and Los Angeles, as only the data provided by police in these cities consistently allows for identification of seized firearms linked to gang activity.

The data on firearms linked to gangs indicates that the vast majority are handguns, accounting for 79 per cent of weapons seized in Houston, and 92 per cent of the weapons taken into custody by the LAPD (see Table 8.5). Most of the seized handguns

Table 8.5	Firearms seized from gang members or during gang activities, 2007–12				
Weapon type		**Houston**		**Los Angeles**	
		Quantity	%	Quantity	%
Handguns	Derringers	8	1	3	<1
	Pistols, semi-automatic	464	59	262	57
	Pistols, other	3	<1	4	<1
	Pistols, unclear and unspecified	4	<1	-	-
	Revolvers	142	18	152	33
	Unspecified	-	-	-	-
	Total	621	79	421	92
Rifles	Bolt-action	16	2	2	<1
	Carbine	9	1	-	-
	Semi-automatic	43	6	10	2
	Automatic	5	<1	-	-
	Other	11	1	1	<1
	Unclear and unspecified	1	<1	-	-
	Total	85	11	13	3
Shotguns	Semi-automatic	5	<1	-	-
	Other	62	8	23	5
	Unclear and unspecified	2	<1	-	-
	Total	69	9	23	5
Machine guns	'Machine guns'	-	-	-	-
	'Machine pistols' and 'submachine guns'	2	<1	-	-
	Total	2	<1	-	-
Other firearms	Air guns, starter guns, stun guns	4	<1	-	-
	Other and unspecified firearms	1	<1	-	-
	Total	5	<1	-	-
Total firearms linked to gang members or gang-related activities		**782**		**457**	

Note: Percentage totals may not add up to 100 per cent due to rounding of sub-totals.

were conventional semi-automatic pistols. No single make (or manufacturer, in the case of Los Angeles) accounted for more than 12 per cent of seized pistols linked to gangs in these cities.

Rifles constituted a small percentage of seized weapons. Combined, less than 8 per cent of firearms recovered in gang-related seizures in Houston and Los Angeles were rifles. Of the 98 rifles that were seized, roughly 60 per cent were semi-automatic models.[32] Among the most frequently encountered types of semi-automatic rifle were 7.62 mm SKS- and Kalashnikov-pattern models, accounting for approximately half of the rifles identified by make and model in the two cities (combined).

Notably, no machine guns are identified in the data, and only two firearms categorized as 'machine pistols' and 'submachine guns' are listed. One is a semi-automatic model and the other is a model that is produced in both semi-automatic and fully automatic versions. Even if both of these weapons are indeed fully automatic firearms, the overwhelming majority of firearms seized from gang members in Houston and Los Angeles are still semi-automatic weapons—not the machine pistols and automatic Kalashnikov-pattern rifles wielded by gang members in the movies (see Table 8.5).

Combining the data

As demonstrated above, the data obtained for this study reveals much about illicit firearms in the United States. This includes records on 10,435 firearms seized from felons, drug traffickers, and gang members—groups of particular concern to US policy-makers and the public. These records reveal that the majority of the firearms recovered from these groups were handguns: 77 per cent of the firearms in the sample. At least 70 per cent of seized handguns were semi-automatic pistols, the actual 'weapon of choice' of US criminals. These figures are consistent with ATF reports on traced weapons, which provide aggregated data on the type and calibre of these weapons but reveal little about their make and models, or about the criminals who acquire them (ATF, 2013b). The records obtained by the Survey help to fill in some of these data gaps. They reveal a diverse assortment of makes and models. Dozens of makes are identified, none of which account for more than 11 per cent of the seized pistols.[33]

Rifles account for a small fraction of seized firearms: less than 12 per cent. Moreover, only

Firearms seized during Armed and Prohibited Persons System sweeps, a programme in California in which firearms are confiscated from 'prohibited persons', Los Angeles, May 2013.
© Kevork Djansezian/Getty Images

about half of the seized rifles were semi-automatic models, including those commonly categorized as 'assault rifles'.[34] This is noteworthy given widespread civilian ownership of rifles in the United States and the frequent seizure of rifles from criminals in neighbouring Mexico (Schroeder, 2013b, pp. 289–92). The data also highlights the popularity of Kalashnikov- and SKS-pattern rifles in the United States, including among felons, drug traffickers, and gang members. Kalashnikov- and SKS-pattern rifles accounted for approximately 32 per cent of all semi-automatic rifles that were identified by make or model. US-designed AR-15 pattern rifles—often called 'the most popular rifle[s] in America' (Goode, 2012)—were seized at less than half the rate of Kalashnikov- and SKS-pattern rifles.

An area requiring further research is the relatively large proportion of Chinese-made semi-automatic rifles recovered from felons, drug traffickers, and gang members in the eight municipalities studied—nearly 15 per cent of seized semi-automatic rifles. It is unclear what proportion of these rifles, if any, arrived in the United States after the introduction of a 1994 ban on imports since very few of the records list the date of manufacture or import of the seized weapons. More information about the rifles, including their date of manufacture and of last known retail sale, would allow for a better understanding of these rifles and their origins.

Box 8.2 Firearms recovered in Columbus, Ohio

Of the 19 municipalities from which data was received, Columbus provided the most detailed records. They include the type, make, model, magazine capacity, and serial number of the seized weapon, along with a brief summary of the circumstances surrounding the seizure (or receipt) of each weapon. These details allow for an analysis of the weapons seized in Columbus that is not possible with the data provided by the other municipalities, including an assessment of some weapons used in violent crime.[35]

Through a careful review of each record, the Survey was able to compile a sub-set of data on violent crimes committed in Columbus that includes only those records in which the identified firearm was used in–or seized from the perpetrators of–the crime to which it is linked. This allowed for a more precise analysis of crime guns. Of the weapons taken into custody by the CPD from 2010 to 2012, 290 explicitly indicate that the gun was used in a violent crime or seized from the suspected perpetrator of the crime.[36]

The type, model, and make of the 290 weapons are quite similar to those of firearms seized in other municipalities. The vast majority were handguns, with semi-automatic pistols alone accounting for at least 58 per cent of all seized weapons. Only 6 per cent of the seized weapons were rifles, most of which were semi-automatic. This is consistent with the other data sets assessed above, as is the prevalence of 7.62 mm Kalashnikov- and SKS-pattern rifles, which accounted for four of the 11 semi-automatic rifles. Three of the four rifles were Chinese-made. No machine guns or sub-machine guns were identified.

Narrative descriptions of the seizures highlight the diversity of violent criminal activity that occurs in cities such as Columbus–an aspect that statistics on crime guns cannot convey. The cases range from acts commonly associated with firearms violence, such as carjackings and robberies of gas stations, to random and irrational acts of violence. In June 2010, for example, Columbus police officers seized a .22 calibre rifle, a .380 calibre pistol, and a .223 calibre AR-15-pattern rifle after receiving reports that the owner, who was being evicted from his home, was pointing an empty gun at people walking past his residence.

The data also challenges many common notions about gun crime in the United States. Rather than the stranger-on-stranger violence commonly highlighted in the media, the case descriptions suggest that many violent firearms offences are unplanned, motivated by fear or anger, and directed at neighbours, family members, or other individuals with whom the perpetrator had a personal relationship. These cases include 'crimes of passion', such

as a 2011 incident during which a 21-year-old man used a 9 mm pistol with a 30-round magazine to shoot up the car of his ex-girlfriend's boyfriend. Police officers also seized firearms after disputes between neighbours turned (or threatened to turn) violent. In at least two cases, the disputes were over matters as mundane as access to parking spaces.

The data set also reveals more fully the diverse set of circumstances in which firearms are taken into custody. Many were voluntarily surrendered by legal owners, or by individuals who found the weapons and reported them to authorities. Firearms were found in every conceivable location, including mailboxes, gutter pipes, bushes, trash cans, and towed vehicles. In October 2010, a Columbus resident whose apartment had recently been burgled found a 9 mm semi-automatic pistol in her dryer. As underscored by the summaries, found (unsecured) firearms can be just as dangerous as crime guns. In August 2012, police received a call about a loaded .32 calibre pistol found on the ground by two 6-year-olds. The children were playing with the weapon when an adult noticed the gun and took it from them.

A surprisingly large number of guns were found in hotel rooms, apparently forgotten by guests and discovered by hotel staff in night stands, dresser drawers, and between mattresses. In at least one case, the guest was an off-duty police officer. While many firearms were found in plain view, some were well hidden, such as two pistols recovered by CPD officers during a homicide investigation in June 2010. One had been hidden in a laundry room ceiling and the other was found in a box of crackers inside a refrigerator.

The reports from Columbus also highlight the importance of routine, daily law enforcement activities involving firearms–activities that are rarely reported by the media but undoubtedly save lives. During the three years studied, police officers took custody of dozens of firearms for safekeeping, often during or immediately after a domestic dispute in which one or more of the disputants feared the firearm would be used by the other. Police officers in Columbus also seized firearms from individuals who were intoxicated, mentally ill, suicidal, or suffering from dementia. Descriptions of the events leading up to the seizures strongly suggest that many of the weapons were extremely vulnerable to misuse. In February 2011, police took possession of a 9 mm pistol for 'safekeeping' after the owner–a 25-year-old man who had recently been hospitalized for mental illness–tried to kick in his neighbour's door while naked and wielding a six-inch military-style knife.

Finally, the number of machine guns seized in the eight municipalities studied was negligible. Authorities recovered only 42 items categorized as 'submachine guns', 'machine guns', or 'machine pistols' from felons, drug traffickers, and gang members, and nearly half of these weapons were semi-automatic models. The remaining firearms were either not identified by model or were models that are made in both fully automatic and semi-automatic versions, making it difficult to determine which were indeed fully automatic weapons. Regardless, it is clear that machine guns are rarely seized by police in the eight municipalities studied, suggesting that few criminals or criminal organizations have incorporated them into their arsenals. The data offers no clue as to why so few machine guns were seized but it is probably due to a combination of supply-side factors—strict laws on imports, ownership, and domestic sales—and limited illicit demand for such weapons, most of which are expensive, tend to be more difficult to conceal than pistols, and offer few, if any, advantages over other firearms for most criminals.

ILLICIT LIGHT WEAPONS IN THE UNITED STATES

Data obtained from military and law enforcement agencies and compiled from media reports indicate that authorities recovered relatively few light weapons in the states studied, and that they seized even fewer from violent criminals. Furthermore, most of the recovered light weapons and ammunition were expended, improvised, inert, or less-lethal, and many of the items identified as operational were decades-old munitions reported by individuals with no apparent criminal intent. These seizures suggest that access to functioning, factory-built light weapons by criminals in the United States is minimal, even among drug traffickers and other criminal groups that have comparatively easy access to light weapons in other countries.

As noted above, data provided by the HPD and the LAPD included references to 123 light weapons and rounds of light weapons ammunition, the vast majority of which were grenades or grenade launchers. Many of the grenades were described as inert, practice, or less-lethal rounds. More than half of the 44 grenades recovered by the HPD were described as dummy, flash bang, hollow, inert, practice, or smoke grenades. Similarly, the two grenade launchers recovered by Houston police appear to be models designed primarily for less-lethal ammunition. The first, which was taken into custody in July 2007, is identified as a 40 mm 'multi-launcher' produced by a US-based manufacturer of less-lethal ammunition and launchers. The second grenade launcher, which was linked to the burglary of an apartment in June 2012, is identified as a 37 mm launcher. The make and model are not identified but accounts of 37 mm launchers seized elsewhere suggest that many are flare launchers, some of which are converted to fire lethal 40 mm rounds. As noted in the *Small Arms Survey 2013*, Mexican authorities have seized several dozen converted 37 mm flare launchers from drug traffickers (Schroeder, 2013b, p. 302). The Houston record does not indicate the type of ammunition fired by the launcher or whether the owner was affiliated with any organized criminal group.

The data indicates that the LAPD recovered 56 grenades in seven incidents from 2007 to 2009. It provides little specific information about the grenades or the events leading up to their acquisition by the police. Only two of the 56 grenades listed are identified by calibre, and none are identified by make or model. Among the largest seizures was a cache of weapons recovered in May 2009. While the data does not identify the location of the seizure, the cache appears to be the same one identified in a press release from the LA County District Attorney's Office. Police discovered the cache in the home of a Los Angeles resident after an explosion ignited a fire in his backyard. They found 14 grenades, 32 pistols, 19 shotguns, and a landmine, among other items. None of the light weapons are identified by

Authorities recovered only 42 items categorized as 'submachine guns', 'machine guns', or 'machine pistols'.

their make or model. At the time of the explosion, two children aged nine and 17 were living at the house with the owner of the weapons, who was charged with, among other crimes, possession of a destructive device and child endangerment (LADA, 2009). It is not clear why the cache was assembled or what the owner intended to do with it, but the incident does highlight the danger of stockpiling light weapons in residential areas.

Media accounts of other seizures—those not reflected in the police data—include additional references to seized grenades taken into custody by authorities. These range from a fragmentation grenade seized during a drug raid in Midlothian, Texas, to memorabilia from the Second World War found among the belongings of deceased veterans in California, Florida, and elsewhere (USAO Texas, 2012).[37] Many of the roughly 300 grenades documented in these accounts were decades-old relics found in backyards, attics, and parks. While unlikely to be used in violent crimes, some of the weapons still posed a threat to the communities in which they were found. A surprisingly large number of these munitions were reportedly operational, including a Second World War-era grenade found in a patch of grass by children playing with a metal detector, and three grenades found in a Florida park during a birthday party (UPI, 2008b; Grimes, 2008).[38]

Many of the grenades were decades-old relics found in backyards, attics, and parks. At least 61 of the grenades and grenade launchers studied were linked to violent crime, drug trafficking, or gun-running. Many were seized from drug traffickers, including some with apparent ties to the Mexican cartels. Other grenades were seized from a motorcycle gang, a survivalist, a right-wing militia group, a Houston bank robber, and a former FBI agent accused of plotting to kill his wife and the head of the Dallas FBI office (Trahan, 2011; *Dallas Morning News,* 2010). One of the most significant seizures occurred near Laredo, Texas. While executing a search warrant, US authorities found a large cache of components for constructing IEDs—in this case, craft-produced grenades. Among the items recovered were 5 grenade shells, 26 grenade triggers, 31 grenade spoons, and 40 grenade pins, along with 9 pipe bombs (Forman, 2006, p. 7). While summaries of the seizure do not explicitly identify Mexico as the intended destination of the grenades, it appears likely given the proximity of the assembly line to the US–Mexican border and the widespread use of these weapons in Mexico (Schroeder, 2013b, pp. 301–02). Despite the many and varied connections between criminal groups in the United States and Mexico, the number and severity of light weapons attacks are still low in the United States compared to Mexico.[39]

The data provided by the HPD and the LAPD includes references to just 21 light weapons other than grenades and grenade launchers. These items include 1 mortar tube and 3 rocket launchers seized in Houston, as well as 8 unidentified mortars, 3 'bombs', 1 mine, and 5 rockets[40] recovered in Los Angeles. The most intriguing of these items are the rockets, at least two of which are identified as AT-4 anti-armour systems (or components)—one in Houston and one in Los Angeles. The AT-4 is a modern single-shot rocket system that is widely deployed by the US military. Modern variants of the AT-4 can penetrate 500 mm of vehicle armour and can be fired from within confined spaces (SAAB, n.d.).

The seizure of one of the launchers by the HPD in 2009 attracted the attention of a local television station, which aired a brief segment on the incident. The station reported that the launcher was found with 'jihadist writings' and that, 'in the wrong hands, the launchers can be dangerous'. The station did, however, note that the launcher was 'unarmed' and that the HPD 'did not find any ties to terrorists or a terrorist network' (KPRC Local 2, 2009). The caveats were ignored or dismissed by bloggers eager to view the case as yet another example of 'the asymmetric war being waged against us by Islamic terrorists from within' (Hagmann, 2010). Additional documentation obtained by the Survey casts the seizure in a very different light. Not only do the documents confirm that the rocket launcher was 'inert' and that 'no other bomb squad related items were found at the scene' (HPD, 2010b), but they also reveal that media descriptions of the written material found with the launcher were incomplete and potentially misleading.

In addition to any 'jihadist writings', police found 'biblical scriptures', 'papers on the Houses of God for Christ', 'lyrics depicting homage to the Sun God', and 'notes on ingredients to developing any living faith' (HPD, 2009). The documents also cast doubt on implied links between the owner and any active terrorist networks. A year after the launcher was seized, HPD officers located the owner, who was homeless and living in a park (HPD, 2010a).

Little information was provided about the AT-4 recovered by authorities in Los Angeles, including whether it was operational. However, similar seizures of AT-4s by the Los Angeles authorities, documented elsewhere, were of expended AT-4 launch tubes or otherwise inoperable systems, not of complete, operational systems.[41]

Media reports document the recovery or destruction of an additional 97 light weapons other than grenades and grenade launchers in the eight states studied. Half of these weapons were IEDs, including 44 pipe bombs. The rest were landmines, mortar rounds, and rocket launchers, most of which reportedly date back to the First or Second World War. Some still contained explosives and therefore posed a threat to the neighbourhoods in which they were found, but few were complete, operational weapon systems.

Notably, no MANPADS or ATGWs were recovered. The absence of seized portable missiles is likely to be of particular interest to US policy-makers, many of whom have voiced concern about the terrorist threat from MANPADS. Publicly available reports on illicit MANPADS suggest that there are few, if any, complete systems outside of government control in the United States. There are no confirmed cases of MANPADS attacks against aircraft in the United States, and the only MANPADS-related items recovered by US authorities in recent years are empty launch tubes,[42] training aides, and inert systems used in undercover operations (Schroeder, 2013a, p. 9).

> There are no confirmed cases of MANPADS attacks in the United States.

The data also reveals striking differences in the quantities and types of light weapons seized in the United States and those seized in the five other countries studied as part of this project (Afghanistan, Iraq, Mexico, the Philippines, and Somalia). Even in Mexico, which shares a long border with the United States and a common struggle against the same regional trafficking networks, illicit light weapons are seized more frequently and in larger quantities. Indeed, grenades, grenade launchers, and rockets are routinely seized from criminal groups in Mexico whereas such weapons are infrequently encountered by law enforcement in the United States, where many recovered weapons have no apparent link to violent criminal activity.

Why are so few light weapons seized from violent criminals in the United States? There are several likely explanations. First, the US government has strong statutory and regulatory controls on private ownership and transfers of light weapons, comparatively robust border control and domestic law enforcement capacities, and intelligence and counter-trafficking agencies with significant resources and global reach. As evidenced by the arrest, extradition, and conviction of seemingly untouchable arms traffickers such as Monzer al-Kassar and Viktor Bout, the US government has the resources and juridical latitude necessary to thwart at least some of the transnational criminals who illicitly supply light weapons to groups that target US citizens, even when these criminals are located outside of the United States.

Yet these are, at best, partial explanations. Even the best-financed and most robust law enforcement and border control agencies cannot prevent every smuggling attempt, let alone every attempt along the border of a country the size of the United States. Thus, there are other factors that explain the differences in the type and quantities of illicit weapons in the United States as compared to other countries. These factors are apparent in the illicit acquisition and use of MANPADS. One key factor is political stability. Among the most significant contemporary sources of illicit light weapons, and particularly MANPADS, are arms stockpiles rendered insecure as a result of regime collapse. Thousands of MANPADS were looted from government depots in Iraq and Libya after the overthrow of their ruling regimes in 2003 and 2011, respectively (Schroeder, 2013a, pp. 13–14). Many of these missiles ended up on local black markets. Regime collapse is often followed by prolonged periods of intrastate conflict, which fuels demand for—and trafficking in—light weapons to one or more of the parties to the conflict. The net result is a significant increase in the supply of and demand for light weapons on local and regional black markets that can last for years.

The absence of extreme political instability in the Western Hemisphere helps to explain why there are far fewer illicit MANPADS in this region than in regions where heavily armed regimes have imploded. Credible reports of illicit MANPADS in North and South America are limited to three countries, and in one of these countries the reported diversion is disputed by the military. Of the handful of illicit MANPADS that have been documented, most were first-generation systems that are militarily obsolete. Publicly available information suggests that even the well-financed and globally connected Revolutionary Armed Forces of Colombia have only succeeded in acquiring a limited number of SA-7-pattern MANPADS—a system that was first fielded more than 40 years ago. Publicly available information suggests that the drug cartels in Mexico have had even less luck acquiring portable missiles (Schroeder, 2013b, p. 301). Given the difficulty in acquiring MANPADS experienced by these groups—which are among the largest and best-financed armed non-state actors in the hemisphere—it is doubtful that any of the small US-based groups that might use MANPADS against targets in the United States have the capacity to acquire them from abroad.

Diverting MANPADS from domestic sources would be equally difficult. The US military's stockpile security requirements for MANPADS are among the most robust in the world. These requirements include rigorous physical security measures;[43] regular audits of accountability and inventory procedures; and monthly, semi-annual, and annual

Table 8.6 **Light weapons destroyed, lost, missing, recovered, or stolen from the US Marine Corps, 2009–12**						
Weapon type	**Model**	**Status**				
		Destroyed	**Recovered**	**Lost**	**Missing**	**Stolen**
Grenade launchers	M203	-	48	6	3	-
	M32A1	-	-	-	1	-
	M79	-	2	-	-	-
	MK19 MOD 3	-	10	-	1	-
Mortar systems	M224 (60 mm)	-	4	1	-	-
	M252 (81 mm)	-	1	-	1	-
Portable rocket launchers	M72 (LAW) sub-calibre trainer	-	73	-	-	-
	SMAW MK 153 MOD0 launcher	-	9	-	1	-
	Tube assembly (unspecified model)	-	-	-	1	-
Portable missile systems	Javelin M98A2 command launch unit	-	2	-	-	-
Total		**-**	**149**	**7**	**8**	**0**

Source: USMC (2012)

physical inventories (or counts) of Stinger missiles in the US national inventory (USDOD, 2012, pp. 16, 47). Auditors have documented violations of these requirements at some facilities,[44] yet such violations appear to be isolated and there are no known, publicly reported cases of diversion of MANPADS from depots in the United States.

While less rigorously controlled than MANPADS, the US military's other light weapons are also subject to robust stockpile security requirements (USDOD, 2012). Data obtained by the Survey suggests that these controls are generally effective. Under the Freedom of Information Act, the Survey obtained data on small arms and light weapons reported by the US Marine Corps as destroyed, lost, missing, recovered, or stolen from 2009 to 2012. The data reveals that, of the thousands of light weapons in the Marine Corps inventory, only 164 were identified as lost, stolen, or missing in that three-year period. Of those weapons, only 15 were still unaccounted for as of mid-2012, and at least some of these weapons were listed as missing or lost due to 'incorrect demilitarization procedures, loss at sea, destruction due to an improvised explosive device (IED) detonation, or loss during Marine combat operations in Iraq or Afghanistan' (USMC, 2012). Thus, the number of light weapons actually diverted from the Marine Corps to unauthorized end users, if any, is even smaller. Table 8.6 summarizes the data obtained from the Marine Corps.

The Survey was unable to obtain comparable data from the Army, Navy, or Air Force, but, given that similar rules and regulations apply to their depots, it is likely that the other services have comparably low rates of diversion. Better data on lost and stolen weapons from the rest of the US military would permit a more definitive assessment of the effectiveness of its stockpile security procedures and of the role of these procedures in limiting the availability of illicit light weapons in the United States.

CONCLUSION

As summarized above, the thousands of records obtained for this study reveal much about illicit small arms and light weapons in the United States. The data indicates that the majority of firearms seized from felons, drug traffickers, and gang members in the eight cities studied were handguns, which accounted for 77 per cent of seized firearms. At least 70 per cent of seized handguns were semi-automatic pistols of various calibres, makes, and models—the actual 'weapons of choice' of US criminals.

These figures are consistent with ATF data on traced firearms and other government and non-governmental accounts of crime guns in the United States. Semi-automatic rifles account for just under 7 per cent of seizures, which is notable given their popularity among firearms collectors, hunters, and sports shooters. The data also contrasts sharply with records on weapons seized in other parts of the world, where rifles are the predominant type of firearms recovered by authorities. These differences highlight the heterogeneity of regional and national markets for illicit weapons, the contents of which are shaped by many different factors, including regional stability; the security of government arsenals; the civilian market; and the objectives, resources, and sophistication of armed groups and other consumers of illicit weapons in the different regions.

There are also several similarities between the criminals and armed groups in the countries studied—Afghanistan, Iraq, Mexico, the Philippines, Somalia, and the United States—including their affinity for Kalashnikov- and SKS-pattern rifles. These rifles account for approximately 32 per cent of semi-automatic rifles identified by make or model that were seized from felons, drug traffickers, and gang members in the United States. In Mexico, Kalashnikov-pattern rifles were seized even more frequently, accounting for at least one-third of all seized rifles (not just semi-automatic models)

(Schroeder, 2013b, pp. 291–92). In Afghanistan, Iraq, and Somalia, Kalashnikov- and SKS-pattern rifles accounted for the overwhelming majority of the seized rifles studied—from 70 per cent in Afghanistan to more than 90 per cent in Iraq and Somalia (Schroeder and King, 2012, pp. 320–21, 338). The prevalence of Kalashnikov- and SKS-pattern rifles is not surprising given that these rifles are inexpensive, plentiful, and reliable.

Another similarity is the prevalence of Chinese weapons. Nearly 15 per cent of semi-automatic rifles recovered in the US sample cities and towns were Chinese-made. The significant presence of Chinese weapons on the illicit US market is mirrored elsewhere in the world. Of the roughly 2,700 weapons seized in Iraq that were identified by country of origin, 13 per cent reportedly came from China, making it the third largest country of origin after Iran[45] and the Russian Federation (Schroeder and King, 2012, p. 317). Chinese weapons were even more prevalent in the caches seized in Afghanistan, accounting for nearly 70 per cent of the weapons studied that were identified by country of origin (Schroeder and King, 2012, p. 330; AMMUNITION PROFILING; WEAPONS TRACING).

Also significant is the extremely small number of large-calibre rifles, machine guns, and light weapons recovered by police in the United States. As noted above, only nine .50 calibre rifles were seized from felons, drug traffickers, or gang members, and some of them were antique-style muzzle-loading rifles. Given the destructive power of anti-materiel rifles and the ready availability in the United States of civilian variants, this is noteworthy. Few fully automatic pistols and rifles are identified in the data, and many of the firearms included in this category appear to be semi-automatic variants of automatic weapons. Few, if any, light machine guns, general-purpose machine guns, or heavy machine guns are identified in the data. The apparent absence of these weapons is attributable, at least in part, to rigorous stockpile security at US military depots, the effect of which is evident in data on lost, missing, and stolen weapons provided by the US Marine Corps.

While the data compiled for this study sheds important light on illicit weapons in the United States, significant gaps remain. Much of the data on firearms linked to violent crime is too vague or ambiguous to distinguish the firearm used by the perpetrators from other weapons taken into custody, precluding meaningful analysis of the data. The records also include little information on the proximate source of the weapons or the chain of custody leading up to their seizure by police. With the exception of the records provided by the Columbus Police Department, the data reveals little about the individuals from whom the weapons were seized. Access to more of this data, which is often included in police reports and other documentation compiled and archived by local authorities, would improve public understanding of illicit weapons, how they are diverted to the black market, and which end users are most likely to seek them out, with potentially significant implications for current and future efforts to combat arms trafficking and reduce the illicit use of small arms and light weapons in the United States. ◼

LIST OF ABBREVIATIONS

ATF	Bureau of Alcohol, Tobacco, Firearms and Explosives
ATGW	Anti-tank guided weapon
AW	Assault weapon
CPD	Columbus Police Department
FBI	Federal Bureau of Investigation
HPD	Houston Police Department

IED	Improvised explosive device
LAPD	Los Angeles Police Department
MANPADS	Man-portable air defence system

ENDNOTES

1   See, for example, *Boyz n the Hood* (1991), *Falling Down* (1993), and *Friday* (1995). Another notable example is the influential 1987 song 'Public Enemy No. 1' by the rap group Public Enemy. This song—and particularly the lyrics, 'I'll show you my gun—my Uzi weighs a ton'—has inspired songs, art exhibitions, and poetry (Public Enemy, 1987; SBG'z, 2007; NFG, 2010; Common, 2007). More recently, a US-based company introduced a cigar named 'My Uzi Weighs a Ton' (Drew Estate, n.d.).

2   See, for example, *End of Watch* (2012).

3   This category includes all military and civilian rifles.

4   Some of the data sets obtained for this study also include parts, accessories, and ammunition for small arms, along with casings, jackets, and wadding for ammunition, and bullet fragments and expended bullets. Accessories identified in the data include holsters, pistol grips, silencers, and weapon sights, among other items. All of these items were excluded from the data set compiled for this study.

5   These municipalities are Albuquerque, NM; Anchorage, AK; Atlanta, GA; Baltimore, MD; Baton Rouge, LA; Boise, ID; Bonham, TX; Boston, MA; Carroll, IA; Charlotte, NC; Chicago, IL; Cleveland, OH; Columbus, OH; Denham Springs, LA; Denver, CO; Emeryville, CA; Groton, CT; Honolulu, HI; Hope, AR; Houston, TX; Jacksonville, FL; Kansas City, MO; Las Vegas, NV; Los Angeles, CA; Louisville, KY; Memphis, TN; Merrill, WI; Milwaukee, WI; New York, NY; Oakland, CA; Philadelphia, PA; Phoenix, AZ; Pleasant Grove, AL; Portland, OR; Rutland, VT; San Antonio, TX; San Jose, CA; Satellite Beach, FL; Seattle, WA; Smyrna, DE; Tulsa, OK; Washington, DC; and Wichita, KS. These municipalities were selected based on their population size and their location. Seven of the municipalities had a population of more than 1 million, 15 had populations of between 500,000 and 1 million, 10 had populations of between 100,000 and 500,000, and 11 had populations of less than 100,000. Of these municipalities, eight are located in the Midwest, five in the north-east, 17 in the south, and 13 in the west (USCB, n.d.).

6   These municipalities are Albuquerque, Baltimore, Boise, Boston, Cleveland, Columbus, Denham Springs, Denver, Groton, Hope, Houston, Los Angeles, Merrill, Milwaukee, Phoenix, San Jose, Satellite Beach, Seattle, and Washington, DC.

7   Only data sets with three or more years of data were used in this study.

8   The term 'offence code' is used here to refer to the code assigned to individual weapons by police departments based on the circumstances surrounding the recovery of the weapons. It is possible that some of the weapons linked to the offence codes studied were recovered from individuals who were not known felons, drug traffickers, or gang members. Data limitations did not allow for a full assessment of every seized weapon.

9   See Krouse (2012, pp. 19–20).

10   These offences include aggravated and simple assault, rape, robbery, and sexual assault.

11   The data covers victimization of persons aged 12 and older (Planty and Truman, 2013, p. 1).

12   Definitions of 'assault weapons' vary, but in the United States the term is frequently used to refer to a sub-set of semi-automatic pistols, rifles, and shotguns that share certain features that are viewed as military in nature. These features include folding stocks, threaded barrels that allow for the attachment of silencers, bayonet mounts, and the ability to accept large-capacity magazines (Koper, 2004, p. 4; Krouse, 2013, pp. 36–37). For more information on the 1994–2004 federal assault weapons ban and the proposals presented in 2013 to reinstate such a ban, see Krouse (2013, pp. 35–37).

13   For more information on background checks and proposals to expand them, see Krouse (2013, pp. 12–23).

14   See Krouse (2013).

15   In this context, a felon is anyone convicted of a crime punishable by a prison term of one year or more (US, 2011, para. g).

16   See Braga et al. (2002, p. 322).

17   See US (2011, para. d).

18   These cities are Albuquerque, Columbus, Houston, and Los Angeles.

19   Handguns accounted for 79 per cent of firearms seized from felons in Albuquerque, 85 per cent of firearms seized in Houston, and 79 per cent of firearms seized in Los Angeles. While fewer firearms recovered in Columbus were handguns (67 per cent), they still accounted for a majority of the seized firearms.

20   For a definition of the term 'curios and relics' as it applies to firearms, see (US, 2012b) and ATF (2007).

21   The firearms must also have been 'manufactured in a proscribed country or area prior to the date, as established by the Department of State, the country or area became proscribed [or] manufactured in a non-proscribed country or area' (US, 2012a, para. e(1)).

22   This figure includes rifles categorized as 'carbines', most of which are semi-automatic.

23   Calculated with the US Bureau of Labor Statistics' consumer price index inflation calculator; see BLS (n.d.).

24   It is possible that not all of the weapons studied were seized from manufacturers or distributors of narcotics. The HPD indicated that narcotics distribution charges are sometimes filed against individuals found in possession of large quantities of drugs (quantities that exceed certain statutory thresholds), even if they had no intention of selling them (author phone interview with an HPD official, September 2013). The same may be true of other municipalities.

25   As reflected in Table 8.3, seizures in Houston and Los Angeles account for the bulk of the sample (74 per cent). As a result, the overall ratio of handguns to other firearms seized from drug traffickers is largely determined by the data from these two cities. That said, the percentage of seized weapons that are handguns is roughly the same in all of the municipalities under review (69–83 per cent), except for Boise, where handguns constituted 55 per cent of firearms linked to drug trafficking cases.

26   Based on the make and model of the seized firearms.

27   Photos of caches seized in Mexico often feature .50 calibre sniper rifles and machine guns. See, for example, *Telegraph* (2009) and T. Johnson (2013).

28   See, for example, Harris (2009) and Tucker (2011).

29   These figures are roughly consistent with data on traced guns published by the ATF. In 2012, 0.1 per cent of traced firearms had a calibre of 5.7 mm (ATF, 2013b).

30   With regard to firearms seized in Houston, there is significant overlap between the data in this section and the data on firearms seized from felons and from drug traffickers.

31   The FBI defines a 'juvenile gang' as 'a group of persons who go about together or act in concert, especially for antisocial or criminal purposes; typically adolescent members have common identifying signs and symbols, such as hand signals and distinctive colors; they are also known as street gangs' (author correspondence with an FBI official, December 2013).

32   These figures include carbines, most of which appear to be semi-automatic models (RCMP, 2013).

33   Six of the eight municipalities studied identify seized weapons by make, although some of the records do not provide this information. Data from the two remaining municipalities—Columbus and Los Angeles—identifies seized weapons by manufacturer rather than by make and therefore was not used in these calculations.

34   An additional 77 rifles were identified as 'carbines' in the data sources. Most of these rifles appear to be semi-automatic models.

35   The term 'violent crime' is used in this section to refer to the definition of 'crime of violence' referenced in Box 8.1.

36   Note that the 290 firearms are a small percentage of all the firearms linked to violent crimes. The remaining firearms were excluded because their relationship to the offences identified in the corresponding record is unclear. In other words, the weapon might have been used in the offence, taken from the victim, or perhaps found at the residence of the perpetrator but owned by a family member.

37   See UPI (2008a) and AP (2007; 2011; 2012).

38   See also AP (2011).

39   One notable exception is an attack in 2009 in which a member of a South Texas gang lobbed a fragmentation grenade into a bar in Pharr, Texas. The South Korean grenade used in the attack reportedly came from the same batch as grenades thrown at a US consulate building and a television station in Mexico. Fortunately for the bar's patrons, the assailant failed to arm the grenade and it bounced harmlessly onto a pool table (Bunker, 2013).

40   The data does not specify whether the seized items were rockets, rocket launchers, or complete systems (rockets and launchers).

41   A recent example is the June 2012 seizure of an 'inoperable' AT-4 launcher from gang members (LASD, 2012). See also CNN (2007) and Winton (2012).

42   The launch tube is for the FIM-43 Redeye system, which was fielded in the 1960s. It is not clear when the missile was fired (or removed), but the Redeye has been out of service long enough that—if the launch tube was diverted from US arsenals—it was not diverted recently.

43   Examples include intruder detection systems, back-up communications systems, perimeter fencing, and the use of high-security padlocks. See USDOD (2012).

44   See, for example, GAO (1994).

45   Iranian weapons were probably over-represented in the sample. See Schroeder and King (2012, p. 318).

BIBLIOGRAPHY

AP (Associated Press). 2007. 'Discovery of Grenade Prompts Evacuation.' 18 October.

—. 2011. 'Grenade in Family's Attic for Years Wasn't a Dud.' 19 November.

—. 2012. 'Grenade Found in Late Veteran's Rented Garage.' 17 September.

ATF (United States Bureau of Alcohol, Tobacco, Firearms and Explosives). 2007. 'Firearms Curios or Relics List.' Revised December.

—. 2011. 'Guide to Standard Restriction Stamps for ATF Import Permit Applications.' Revised 7 April.
    <http://www.atf.gov/firearms/guides/standard-restriction-stamps-for-import-permits.html#44>

—. 2013a. 'Firearms Commerce in the United States: Annual Statistical Update.'

—. 2013b. 'Firearms Trace Data: 2012.' <https://www.atf.gov/statistics/trace-data/2012-trace-data.html>

BLS (United States Bureau of Labor Statistics). n.d. 'CPI Inflation Calculator.' <http://www.bls.gov/data/inflation_calculator.htm>

Boyz n the Hood. 1991. John Singleton, dir. Columbia Pictures.

Braga, Anthony, et al. 2002. 'The Illegal Supply of Firearms.' *Crime and Justice*, Vol. 29.

Bunker, Robert. 2013. 'Mexican Cartel Tactical Note #16: Grenade Attack in Pharr, Texas Bar Containing Off-duty Law Enforcement Officers.' *Small Wars Journal.* 28 January. <http://smallwarsjournal.com/blog/mexican-cartel-tactical-note-16>

CNN. 2007. 'Rocket Launcher Tube Found on Lawn.' 20 July.

Common. 2007. 'A Letter to the Law.' <poetry.rapgenius.com/Common-a-letter-to-the-law-annotated#note-199512>

Cooper, Alexia and Erica Smith. 2011. 'Homicide Trends in the United States, 1980–2008.' Washington, DC: United States Department of Justice. November.

Dallas Morning News. 2010. 'Regional Roundup.' 24 September.

Drew Estate. n.d. 'My Uzi Weighs a Ton Cigars.' <http://drewestate.com/?portfolio=my-uzi-weighs-a-ton-cigars>

End of Watch. 2012. David Ayer, dir. Exclusive Media Group et al.

Falling Down. 1993. Joel Schumacher, dir. Warner Bros. et al.

FBI (Federal Bureau of Investigation). 2013. *Crime in the United States 2012.* September.
    <http://www.fbi.gov/about-us/cjis/ucr/crime-in-the-u.s/2012/crime-in-the-u.s.-2012>

Forman, Marcy. 2006. 'Statement of Marcy M. Forman, Director, Office of Investigations, U.S. Immigration and Customs Enforcement, Department of Homeland Security.' 1 March. <http://www.ice.gov/doclib/news/library/speeches/060301homeland.pdf>

Friday. 1995. F. Gary Gray, dir. New Line Cinema and Priority Films.

GAO (United States Government Accountability Office). 1994. 'Inventory Management: Handheld Missiles are Vulnerable to Theft and Undetected Losses.' GAO/NSIAD-94-100. Washington, DC: GAO. 16 September.

Goode, Erica. 2012. 'Popular AR-15 Style Rifle Used in Recent Mass Killings.' *Seattle Times.* 16 December.

Grimes, Elyce. 2008. 'Live Grenades Found at Local Park.' 10News (Tampa Bay). 1 November.
    <http://www.wtsp.com/news/article/93324/8/Live-grenades-found-at-local-park>

Hagmann, Douglas. 2010. 'Connecting the Terror Dots.' Northeast Intelligence Network. 2 January.

Harris, Byron. 2009. 'Texas Is Arming Mexican Drug Cartels.' WFAA-TV (Dallas/Ft. Worth). 13 March.

HPD (Houston Police Department). 2009. 'Current Information Report Incident No. 189457309: Supplement Narrative.' 29 December. Redacted copy obtained by the Small Arms Survey from the HPD in November 2013.

—. 2010a. 'Current Information Report Incident No. 189457309: Supplement Narrative.' 29 December. Redacted copy obtained by the Small Arms Survey from the HPD in November 2013.

—. 2010b. 'Current Information Report Incident No. 189457309: Supplement Narrative.' 4 January. Redacted copy obtained by the Small Arms Survey from the HPD in November 2013.

Johnson, Eliana. 2013. 'The NRA of Automatic Weapons.' *National Review Online.* 12 April.

Johnson, Tim. 2013. '253,000 U.S. Guns Smuggled to Mexico Annually, Study Finds.' *McClatchy Newspapers.* 18 March.
    <http://www.mcclatchydc.com/2013/03/18/186216/253000-us-guns-smuggled-to-mexico.html>

Karp, Aaron. 2011. 'Estimating Civilian-owned Firearms.' Research Note No. 9. Geneva: Small Arms Survey. September.

Koper, Christopher. 2004. *An Updated Assessment of the Federal Assault Weapons Ban: Impacts on Gun Markets and Gun Violence, 1994–2003.* Philadelphia: Jerry Lee Center of Criminology, University of Pennsylvania. June.

KPRC Local 2. 2009. 'Rocket Launcher Found in [. . .] Apartment.' YouTube. December. Uploaded 13 May 2010.
<http://www.youtube.com/watch?v=EMHUkIzLGzA>

Krouse, William. 2012. *Gun Control Legislation*. Washington, DC: Congressional Research Service. 14 November.

—. 2013. *Gun Control Proposals in the 113th Congress: Universal Background Checks, Gun Trafficking, and Military Style Firearms*. Washington, DC: Congressional Research Service. 7 June.

LADA (Los Angeles County District Attorney's Office). 2009. 'Man Charged in Reseda Explosion Faces Arraignment.' 2 July.
<http://da.lacounty.gov/mr/archive/2009/070209a.htm>

LASD (Los Angeles County Sheriff's Department). 2012. 'Rocket Launcher, More Weapons and Suspected Methamphetamine Seized, 4 Gang Members Arrested by LASD OSS.' 20 June. <http://local.nixle.com/alert/4843767/>

Nalder, Eric. 1993. 'Cheap Rifle Imports Flood U.S. Market.' *Seattle Times*. 1 September.
<http://community.seattletimes.nwsource.com/archive/?date=19930901&slug=1718860>

NFG (Neon Forrest Gallery). 2010. 'My Uzi Weighs a Ton.' Art exhibition, Orlando, FL.

Oxford Dictionaries. n.d. 'Municipality.' <http://www.oxforddictionaries.com/definition/american_english/municipality?q=municipality>

Planty, Michael and Jennifer Truman. 2013. 'Firearm Violence, 1993–2011.' Special Report. Washington, DC: Bureau of Justice Statistics, United States Department of Justice. May. <http://nssf.org/share/PDF/USDOJ_FirearmViolence1993-2011.pdf>

Public Enemy. 1987. 'Public Enemy No. 1.' *Yo! Bum Rush the Show*. Def Jam Recordings.
<http://www.publicenemy.com/album/5/14/public-enemy-no-1.html>

RCMP (Royal Canadian Mounted Police). 2013. 'Firearms Reference Table.' Version 4.4. February.

SAAB. n.d. 'AT4 CS Light Anti-armour Weapon.'
<http://www.saabgroup.com/en/Land/Weapon-Systems/support-weapons/AT4_Anti_Armour_Weapon/AT4_CS_Light_anti-armour_weapon/>

SBG'z (SilverBack Gorillaz). 2007. 'My Uzi Weighs a Ton.' *The Code*. Affluent Records.

Schroeder, Matt. 2013a. *The MANPADS Threat and International Efforts to Address It*. Washington, DC: Federation of American Scientists. August.

—. 2013b. 'Captured and Counted: Illicit Weapons in Mexico and the Philippines.' In Small Arms Survey. *Small Arms Survey 2013: Everyday Dangers*. Cambridge: Cambridge University Press.

— and Ben King. 2012. 'Surveying the Battlefield: Illicit Arms In Afghanistan, Iraq, and Somalia.' In Small Arms Survey. *Small Arms Survey 2012: Moving Targets*. Cambridge: Cambridge University Press.

Telegraph. 2009. 'Mexican Drugs War: Woman Arrested with Anti-aircraft Machine Gun.' 15 April. <http://www.telegraph.co.uk/news/worldnews/centralamericaandthecaribbean/mexico/5158184/Mexican-drugs-war-woman-arrested-with-anti-aircraft-machine-gun.html>

Trahan, Jason. 2011. 'Former Dallas FBI Agent Gets Two Years in Prison for Plan to Kill Boss.' *Dallas Morning News*. 25 March. <http://www.dallasnews.com/news/community-news/dallas/headlines/20110325-former-dallas-fbi-agent-gets-two-years-in-prison-for-plan-to-kill-boss.ece>

Tucker, Will. 2011. 'Photo Gallery: The Top Ten Favorite Guns of the Mexican Drug Cartels.' *Texas on the Potomac*. 15 July.

UNODC (United Nations Office on Drugs and Crime). 2013. 'UNODC Homicide Statistics.'
<http://www.unodc.org/unodc/en/data-and-analysis/homicide.html>

UPI (United Press International). 2008a. 'Possible Grenade in Veteran's Keepsakes.' 8 December.

— 2008b. 'Kids Uncover Live Grenade in Pace, Fla.' 17 February.
<http://www.upi.com/Odd_News/2008/02/17/Kids-uncover-live-grenade-in-Pace-Fla/UPI-92351203295692/>

US (United States). 2011. 18 USC s. 922: Unlawful Acts.
<http://www.gpo.gov/fdsys/granule/USCODE-2011-title18/USCODE-2011-title18-partI-chap44-sec922/content-detail.html>

—. 2012a. 27 CFR 447.52: Import Restrictions Applicable to Certain Countries.
<http://www.gpo.gov/fdsys/granule/CFR-2012-title27-vol3/CFR-2012-title27-vol3-sec447-52/content-detail.html>

—. 2012b. 27 CFR 478.11: Meaning of Terms.
<http://www.gpo.gov/fdsys/granule/CFR-2012-title27-vol3/CFR-2012-title27-vol3-sec478-11/content-detail.html>

USAO Texas (United States Attorney's Office Northern District of Texas). 2012. 'Ellis County Man Sentenced to 84 Months in Federal Prison on Firearms and Drug Convictions.' 16 August.

USCB (United States Census Bureau). n.d. 'Census Regions and Divisions of the United States.'
<http://www.census.gov/geo/maps-data/maps/pdfs/reference/us_regdiv.pdf>

USDOD (Department of Defense). 2012. *Physical Security of Sensitive Conventional Arms, Ammunition, and Explosives (AA&E)*. DOD Manual 5100.76. 17 April. <http://www.dtic.mil/whs/directives/corres/pdf/510076m.pdf>

USMC (United States Marine Corps). 2012. 'SA/LW CY2009–2012 MLRS.' Released in response to a request under the Freedom of Information Act submitted on 20 August 2012. 7 November.

USSC (United States Sentencing Commission). 2012. *Guidelines Manual*. Effective 1 November 2012.
<http://www.ussc.gov/Guidelines/2012_Guidelines/index.cfm>

Winton, Richard. 2012. 'Rocket Launchers Turned in to LAPD Apparently Were from Military.' *Los Angeles Times*. 29 December.
<http://latimesblogs.latimes.com/lanow/2012/12/rocket-launchers-turned-in-at-lapd-event-from-military-owners-say.html>

ACKNOWLEDGEMENTS

Principal author

Matt Schroeder

INDEX

Printed in the United States
By Bookmasters